QUEEN ELIZABETH I

J. E. Neale, who was recently knighted by Queen Elizabeth II, is Astor Professor of English History at the University of London. He is the author of *The Age of Catherine de Medici*, *The Elizabethan House of Commons*, and *Elizabeth I and Her Parliament*.

QUEEN ELIZABETH I was first published in 1934 and has been translated into Danish, French, German, Hungarian, Norwegian, Italian, Spanish, and Swedish. The book was awarded the James Tait Black Memorial Prize for Biography in 1934. A hardcover edition is published in Britain by Jonathan Cape.

QUEEN
ELIZABETH I

A Biography

J. E. NEALE

DOUBLEDAY ANCHOR BOOKS
DOUBLEDAY & COMPANY, INC.
GARDEN CITY, NEW YORK

Cover by Antonio Frasconi

Typography by Edward Gorey

Queen Elizabeth I was originally published in 1934 by Jonathan Cape Limited. The Anchor Books edition is published by arrangement with Jonathan Cape Limited.

Anchor Books edition: 1957

CONTENTS

QUEEN ELIZABETH I

CHAPTER I

BEGINNINGS

ON Sunday, September 7th, 1533, between the hours of three and four in the afternoon, Anne Boleyn gave birth to a child at the pleasant river-palace of Greenwich. Its destiny was bound up with accidents of State, which none could then foretell; but this at least might have been discerned, that the birth was a symbol of the most momentous revolution in the history of the country.

It was six years or more since Henry VIII's fancy had been stirred by the black eyes, vivacious personality, and easy French manners of one of Catherine of Aragon's ladies-in-waiting, and thoughts of divorce had taken final form in his mind. His was not a tale of light-of-love. He had opportunities enough of diversion, with no complicating problem of marriage; and if other overwhelming reasons had not suggested divorce and re-marriage, who can tell how long Anne Boleyn's virtue would have withstood his siege? For it was not dishonour—certainly not at the French Court where she had spent three years—to be a royal mistress. The fact was that Henry as a king, and the second of a new dynasty, had no duty more urgent than to secure the future of his house by providing an heir to the throne. While there was no Salic Law in England to exclude his only legitimate child, the girl Mary, from the succession, the most distinguished legal writer of the previous century had argued that a woman could not succeed to the English throne; and in the four and a half centuries since the Conquest there had only been one queen regnant, Matilda, whose singularity and fate were nearly as decisive against a female sovereign as any Salic Law. The dangers accompanying a woman ruler were grave and obvious. She must marry, either at home or abroad: if at home, the country faced the risk of being plunged into civil war through jealousy of her husband's power; if abroad, of being converted into a province of another realm. The law on the subject might leave room for argument, but prudence was certainly flat against a woman ruler.

This it was which set Henry forth in quest of a son. He had borne with Catherine of Aragon as long as there was any hope of a prince, and in all probability would have borne with her till death if she had produced his heir. But in 1527 she was forty-two years old, six years older than her husband; stout, without charm, and aged with disappointment. She had been tragically unfortunate in childbed. Five children—three of them boys—had been stillborn, or, in one instance, had died within a few weeks of birth. The last was born dead in November 1518. In an age accustomed to see the visitation of God in plague or dearth or in the collapse of a flimsy floor under a conventicle of heretics, it was neither hypocrisy nor undue sensitiveness in Henry to associate his wife's misfortunes with the wrath of God. Had He not spoken clearly in Leviticus? 'And if a man shall take his brother's wife, it is an unclean thing . . .; they shall be childless'. The divine hand, as emphatically as reasons of State, pointed to the King to put away Catherine of Aragon.

Thus the famous divorce began, bringing in its train the incalculable results of the breach with Rome. Deep as was Henry's infatuation for Anne Boleyn—she was his great folly—her place in the revolution was none other than prospective mother of the heir to the throne. In the autumn of 1532, after the divorce suit had dragged on for six years and Henry had drawn nearer and nearer to the last act of defiance against Rome, he and Anne began to live together. By January she was with child, and as the political object of the divorce now seemed assured, further delay was pointless. On January 25th Henry married her in secrecy and haste, and once Cranmer had obtained the Pope's recognition of his election to the see of Canterbury, the breach with Rome was completed. In May Cranmer declared Henry's marriage with Catherine null and void and recognized the legality of his marriage with Anne. The English Church had cast off the supremacy of Rome. And the proximate cause was the child that Anne was bearing. Whatever fame the future held in store, its birth at least ensured that it would be the child of the English Reformation.

'I pray Jesu, and it be his will, send us a prince': so a chronicler of the time prayed. Rarely has the sex of a child mattered so much. No one dared to contemplate a girl. The physicians and soothsayers assured the King of a boy. Its name—Edward or Henry—was decided in advance, and one of the richest beds in the royal treasury, a prince's ransom, was brought to Greenwich to grace the event. There were to be jousts and rejoicings.

Alas! for hopes and prophecies. The child was a girl. If it was a bitter disappointment for Henry, it was worse for Anne. She had failed the King; far more, she had failed herself. Her rise to power had made many enemies: those whose influence at Court she had diminished or eclipsed, those opposed to the new radical tendencies in religion, and those who resented the arrogance of her upstart relations and the sharpness of her own and her brother's tongues. It was an age in which political power created implacable opponents. Woe to the day on which the King's favour wavered, for courtiers who saw their own advancement in another's fall seldom missed an opportunity of poisoning the royal mind; and 'the wrath of the Prince was death'. To some extent Anne's position as Queen guarded her against malicious tongues; but much more than with Catherine her security depended upon being the mother of a prince. Only a week or two before the birth of her child—so it was said—when she was protesting against a flirtation of Henry's, she was told to close her eyes and put up with it as her betters had done. She must understand, said Henry, that in a moment he could debase her even further than he had raised her. For Anne, as for Catherine, God and a prince were a dangerous concatenation in the King's mind; and the girl she had borne was the edge of the cloud that ultimately blotted her out.

But for the time being the prospect was not desperate. Anne had given Henry a princess, and with God's favour would yet give him a prince. At the news of the birth bonfires were lit in the city and bells rung—for joy in the King's disappointment, said a malicious ambassador. The next day a solemn *Te Deum* was sung at St. Paul's, and on the Wednesday, with splendid ceremonial, the child was christened, London's mayor and aldermen, in bright gowns and gold chains, and accompanied by councillors and citizens, taking barge to Greenwich where with lords and ladies they joined in a procession that moved by arras-covered walls and along ways strewn with green rushes to the Franciscan church. Cranmer was godfather, the old Duchess of Norfolk and the Marchioness of Dorset godmothers. When the christening was over, Garter King-of-Arms, in a loud voice, proclaimed the child's style: 'God of his infinite goodness, send prosperous life and long to the high and mighty princess of England, Elizabeth!'

Seventeen and a half years before, the same proclamation had saluted Catherine of Aragon's daughter. At the time of her mother's disgrace Mary was adolescent and was swept by her emotion into a passionate resistance to the new order of things. Under the secret stimulus and guidance of the Imperial ambassador she flouted her father's wishes and commands with a tenacity that roused his wrath to dangerous levels. Anne Boleyn she persisted in regarding as a concubine, her child as a bastard, with the result that the relations between the two women became charged with venom. An excellent opportunity of curbing Mary's pride and reminding her that she was no longer princess, nor indeed anything more than Henry's illegitimate daughter, presented itself when Elizabeth was three months old, for following precedent a separate household was then set up for the baby princess at the royal manor of Hatfield. As the child was borne there, passing through London on its way and providing a diversion for the spectacle-loving people, part of the escort was detached to break up Mary's household and bring Mary to pay court to Anne's child and live as a member of the new household. It was in vain that she protested. All that she could do was to continue in her obstinacy, refusing to surrender the title of princess or to recognize Anne or her child. She spurned overtures from the Queen and the two became implacable enemies. Nor did relations with her father improve, and whenever he visited Elizabeth, he ordered Mary to be confined to her room, refusing to see her. This manner of life went on during the years 1534 and 1535. The Princess and her household were now at Hatfield, now at Eltham or Hunsdon or at some other royal manor, and occasionally at Court.

Meanwhile the sands were shifting under Anne Boleyn. God had not favoured her with a prince. In the summer of 1534 she was believed to be with child, but by September Henry knew that it was untrue. His affections, temporarily drawn back to her, reverted to a very beautiful damsel of the Court, and when Anne was resentful he again reminded her rudely of her origins. The Court watched these signs like vultures their prey. She still retained something of that power over Henry which had kept him in thrall as a lover; but her bursts of temper were irritating, his old ardour was gone, and, ominous sign! conscience was once more in the ascendant. He began to think of the possibility of release from her. Catherine, however, was a stumbling block, for during her life Henry might free himself from Anne only to revive the old trouble over her. He hesitated, and while he did so Anne became pregnant. The prince was coming.

At the opening of the year 1536 Anne Boleyn's position rested on two supports: the life of Catherine of Aragon and the prospect of a prince. Never was fortune more cruel. On January 7th Catherine died, and on the twenty-ninth, the day of the funeral, Anne gave premature birth to a male child. She had miscarried of her saviour. The tragedy must obviously move to a close; and it moved swiftly. On May 2nd she was arrested and sent to the Tower, accused of adultery with five men, one of whom was her brother. In the subsequent trials all were found guilty and the law took its course. Anne herself was executed on May 19th. Whether she was guilty or not, no human judgment can now determine, and contemporaries differed. In all probability she had been indiscreet. If she had gone further, if she had really committed adultery—and the possibility cannot be lightly dismissed—then it is likely that a desperate woman had taken a desperate course to give England its prince and save herself from ruin. Whatever the truth, she had played her game and lost.

Lost indeed! She was denied even the hope of triumphing through her child. In the four days between her trial and execution Cranmer had to find cause for nullifying her marriage, thus reducing Elizabeth to the status of a bastard. It mattered little that it was illogical to condemn and execute for adultery a woman who had never been a wife: Henry was not averse to having it both ways. What cause Cranmer found is unknown: it may be that he relied upon the fact that Anne's elder sister had been Henry's mistress, which in ecclesiastical law established a relationship between the two that prohibited marriage. In any case it was a sorry business although it achieved a rough sort of justice and was not unstatesmanlike. Elizabeth was reduced to the same status as Mary, who therefore took priority by age, while both gave place in sex to their base-born brother, the Duke of Richmond. The succession to the throne thus became clearer, for at worst people could now look to a prince, though an illegitimate one; at best they could trust in God to bless the King with an indisputable heir. Henry was only forty-five, and with Catherine and Anne dead, the past was liquidated. He could start again on his quest for a son.

Elizabeth was two years and eight months old when her mother was executed and even the wrench that a child of that age might feel was spared her through living in a household of her own. Her emotional life, in contrast with Mary's, was unaffected by her mother's misfortunes. Neither shame nor resentment ate like a canker at her pride. Not shame, for she grew up in a society with feelings differently tuned from ours. A royal father was parentage enough: it could glorify the bar sinister, remove the taint of an adulterous mother. Nor did the scaffold matter seriously: it was an instrument of state to which the great families of the age paid tribute in turn. A Mantuan, describing England in the middle of the century, remarked that 'many persons, members of whose families have been hanged and quartered, are accustomed to boast of it. Lately, a foreigner, having asked an English captain if anyone of his family had been hanged and quartered, was answered, "Not that he knew of". Another Englishman whispered to the foreigner, "Don't be surprised, for he is not a gentleman"'. It was enough for Elizabeth that she was Henry VIII's daughter. He was a father of whom she could be, and she was, justly proud and fond. Against her mother's shame there always stood a large interrogation mark; and if Catholic writers later remembered and embroidered her wickedness, Protestant writers extolled her virtues.

At the time of her mother's death, Elizabeth was at Hunsdon under the charge of Lady Bryan, who had been Lady Mistress, or Governess, to Mary when a baby. It was a household of troubles; or so Lady Bryan thought as she poured them out in a letter to Thomas Cromwell. Elizabeth, she wrote, was put from her rank of princess and she had no notion, except from hearsay, of her charge's new rank, or how she should order her, or order herself and the women and grooms under her authority. The child, too, was lamentably short of clothes; she had neither gown, nor kirtle, nor petticoat, nor any manner of linen for smocks, nor several other necessaries. It was impossible to make shift any longer. Moreover, the male head of the household, Mr. Shelton, had been lording it over Lady Bryan, interfering with her charge and insisting on my Lady Elizabeth dining and supping in state, publicly. 'Alas! my Lord,' wrote the harassed lady, 'it is not meet for a child of her age to keep such rule yet. I promise you, my Lord, I dare not take it upon me to keep her Grace in health, and she keep that rule; for there she shall see divers meats and fruits and wine, which would be hard for me to refrain her Grace from. Ye know, my Lord, there is no place of correction there. And she is yet too young to correct greatly. I know well, and

she be there, I shall neither bring her up to the King's
Grace's honour, nor hers; nor to her health, nor my poor
honesty.' 'God knoweth,' she went on, 'my Lady hath great
pain with her great teeth, and they come very slowly forth,
and causeth me to suffer her Grace to have her will more
than I would. I trust to God, and her teeth were well
grafted, to have her Grace after another fashion than she
is yet; so as I trust the King's Grace shall have great comfort in her Grace. For she is as toward a child, and as gentle
of conditions, as ever I knew any in my life. Jesu preserve
her Grace!' The lack of clothes, distressing as Lady Bryan
made it seem, was a misfortune that might have befallen
the household at any time. It was no sign that Anne
Boleyn's fate had weakened Henry's affection for his daughter. He was much too good a parent, and Elizabeth's precocious intelligence endeared her still more to him. At six
years old, it was said, she had as much gravity as if she
had been forty. 'If she be no worse educated,' Secretary
Wriothesley wrote, 'she will be an honour to womanhood.'

The love that a child needs was not lacking. Especially in
her stepmother Catherine Parr, Elizabeth found a second
mother; and even her sister Mary's attitude changed, for
the death of Catherine of Aragon followed closely by the
execution of Anne Boleyn, prepared the way for a general
reconciliation. Mary found it painful to submit to her father,
no half-measures being tolerated; but her cousin, the Emperor, needing Henry's political support, urged her to give
way, and in July, 1536, she did. Outwardly the submission
was complete, but she treasured her real thoughts in the
secret places of the heart. No longer was there any irksome
injunction to call her sister 'Princess', and instead of having
to pay court to Elizabeth, Mary was given a suite of attendants of her own, as became a king's daughter, and
shared a common household in which she was now the
senior partner. Her natural affection was able to find its
voice: 'My sister Elizabeth,' she wrote to her father, 'is such
a child toward as I doubt not but your Highness shall have
cause to rejoice of in time to come'.

The two sisters were frequently at Court. They were

present in October, 1537, at the christening of the prince, Edward, whom God, in His great goodness had sent to console Henry, a consolation the more important since his illegitimate son, the Duke of Richmond, had died. Mary was lady godmother, Elizabeth bore the richly garnished chrisom or baptismal robe, but on account of her tender age had to be borne herself by two lords. As Edward grew up, it was natural that a close affection should develop between him and Elizabeth, for they were near in age, and their tutors and guardians were of the same school of thought. She plied her needle to make him New Year presents in his early years, and when his education began exchanged Latin and French letters with him.

In these happy relations there was one flaw, Elizabeth's illegitimate status being left unaltered, as was Mary's. But it became less and less of a reality. Both were the King's 'dearest children' equally with Edward, taking their place as such at Court and in various public ceremonies; and when in 1544 an act of parliament established them in the succession to the throne, their nominal status appeared for what it was—no more than a formal survival of past events. They had the substance of legitimacy, and it would have been gratuitous folly on Henry's part to go farther, to traverse old judgments and question his own justice. It was best to let sleeping dogs lie.

In these years Elizabeth began her formal education. She was fortunate to be born in the full flush of Renaissance enthusiasm. In many of its ways the sixteenth century may seem infinitely remote from us, but in the education of women it touched the finest achievements of our day. No drastic change of thought was involved; rather, a development of medieval Christian tradition. Had not St. Paul taught that in Christ Jesus 'there can be no male and female'? Women were men's equals, at least in the possession of a soul, and from a spiritual point of view it was therefore desirable to train them in a school of Christian manners. Such training, given in the nunneries or in schools attached to gilds and chantries, had been fairly widely diffused in medieval England; and from this tradition Renaissance teachers could start. They kept the Christian purpose, while quickening the spirit and altering the type of education. Greek and Latin were to be taught to the perfection of Christian maidenhood, and the books pupils read were to be chosen with the same purpose. Learning, as the greatest theorist of the age wrote, was to lift one's mind into the knowledge of goodly matters and pluck it from the remembrance of such things as be foul. Critics were not wanting, morbidly impressed with the frailties of the sex—its love of novelty and innate tendency to vice—who thought women dangerous enough, without adding to their subtlety and forwardness by training them in the craft and eloquence of classical writers. In their eyes Eve as a blue-stocking was a terrifying prospect. They were unable to prevent her appearance.

Henry VII's mother, the Lady Margaret, was one of the first in England to indicate the trend in women's education. It was little Latin she had, but she knew French well enough to translate into English 'The Mirror of Gold for the Sinful Soul', and was the patron of Caxton and a liberal benefactor of the universities. In the generation following her death the new woman definitely made her appearance, thanks largely to two converging influences. The one was native and came from a group of Oxford humanists and Catholic reformers, with the sparkling, venturesome intelligence of Sir Thomas More for inspiration; a group which included Linacre, Grocyn, and Colet, and enjoyed the intimate friendship of the great Erasmus. More's three daughters, and their kinswoman, Margaret Giggs, brought up in this household where women were treated as men's peers in conversation and where knowledge and wit passed to and fro, were famous for their learning. A perfect mastery of Greek and Latin, some knowledge of philosophy, astronomy, physic, arithmetic, logic, rhetoric, and music—these were the accomplishments of Margaret More. Such women were the pattern of the age, and humanists boasted of them in their letters to foreign scholars.

The movement was strengthened by a foreign influence which came through Catherine of Aragon. In the Spain of her childhood ladies of rank were the friends of scholars and patrons of literature, and there were even women teachers in two of the universities. Catherine's mother took part in the education of her daughters and brought foreign scholars to Spain as their tutors. It was an example which, in the congenial court of Henry VIII, Catherine naturally followed in the education of her own daughter. More's friend Linacre was engaged to compile a Latin grammar, and the Spanish scholar Vives, one of the most refreshing figures in the history of education, was brought to England and wrote a 'Plan of Studies for Girls' to direct the lines of Mary's education. It is some measure of the point reached in the education of highly-born women since the days of Lady Margaret's French and smattering of Latin, that the princess Mary, though not an intellectual type of woman, became proficient in Latin, French, and Spanish, and moderately so in Italian.

This was the heritage into which the sharp-witted child Elizabeth entered. Her education fell into the second great generation when the centre of influence had shifted from the older Oxford scholars to a young Cambridge group. Several were to win fame and their names are well enough known, but the group as a whole was to play a significant part in Elizabeth's career. Its pattern of scholarship was John Cheke. He, his favourite pupil, Roger Ascham, Ascham's own favourite pupil William Grindall, together with William Cecil, James Pilkington and William Bill were all from one college, St. John's. Nicholas Bacon, Thomas Smith, Thomas Wilson, Walter Haddon, Mathew Parker, Ponet, Ridley, Richard Cox and John Aylmer were from other colleges. In the last years of Henry VIII's reign, except for the discordant possibilities associated with Mary Tudor, the youth and future of England seemed to be in their control. Cox and Cheke were the tutors of the heir to the throne, Grindall and Ascham were successively Elizabeth's tutors, and Aylmer was the tutor of Lady Jane Grey. Fashioning as they did, in accordance with the Christian purpose of education, the religious as well as the intellectual outlook of their pupils, they could look forward to intellectual leadership in Church and State. Their friends became their pupils' friends. Younger men, they were radical in their religious leanings, in contrast with the More circle whose liberalism was Catholic and conservative and whose sympathies were with the older order, with Catherine of Aragon and her daughter, against Henry VIII. Fate had conceived the lives of Mary and Elizabeth as an antithesis, and in linking them, each with one of these brilliant, contrasting groups of scholars, it was assured of a masterpiece.

Nothing is known of Elizabeth's education until the end of her tenth year. Her brother Edward, also a precocious child, began to learn Latin at the end of his sixth year and tackled a modern language, French, at the end of his tenth. Elizabeth was already learning Italian and French in her tenth year, and must by then have been fairly well grounded in Latin. The first of her surviving letters is one in Italian written to Queen Catherine Parr in July, 1544. By the end of that year she had finished a translation, bound in an elaborate needlework cover worked by herself, of Margaret of Navarre's poem, 'The Mirror of a Sinful Soul'. It was a New Year's gift for the Queen. Prefaced to it was a letter making liberal use of those books of *sententiae* or weighty sayings which made Tudor children appear in their writings, as in their pictures, little versions of maturity. Thus early she began a habit which was to grow into a curse, making her studied writings insufferably obscure and involved. 'Knowing', began the letter, 'that pusillanimity and idleness are most repugnant unto a reasonable creature, and that (as the philosopher sayeth) even as an instrument of iron or of other metal waxeth soon rusty unless it be continually occupied, even so shall the wit of a man or woman wax dull and unapt to do or understand anything perfectly unless it be always occupied upon some manner of study: which things considered, hath moved so small a portion as God has lent me, to prove what I could do.'

The proof of ability was an excessively dreary French poem in Elizabethan prose. Its title recalled the literary feat of Elizabeth's great grandmother Lady Margaret; its subject was but too painfully expressive of the belief that learning was intended to lift the mind to the knowledge of most goodly matters. 'Where is the hell full of travail, pain, mischief, and torment? Where is the pit of cursedness, out of the which doth spring all despair? Is there any hell so profound that is sufficient to punish the tenth part of my sins?'—and so on. Need we wonder at the preternatural gravity of clever children then? Nor has the worst been quoted, for the poem plunges into erotic mysticism: 'But thou which hast made separation of my bed and did put thy false lovers in my place and committed fornication with them; yet for all this thou mayest come unto me again . . . O poor soul! to be where thy sin hath put thee; even upon the highways, where thou didst wait and tarried for to beguile them that came by . . . Therefore, having fulfilled thy pleasure, thou hast infected with fornication all the earth which was about thee'.

It was in the year of this translation that Elizabeth's studies were linked with the Cambridge group of humanists. In July, John Cheke had been summoned from Cambridge to help Prince Edward's first tutor, Richard Cox; and on his advice, a couple of months or so later, Ascham's pupil, William Grindall was brought to Court and appointed tutor to Elizabeth. He was an excellent Greek scholar and a lovable man. Which to admire more, the ability of the pupil or the diligence of the teacher, Ascham did not know. For rather more than three years he directed Elizabeth's studies in Greek and Latin, but in January 1548 caught the plague and died, a young man of great promise.

At the time of Grindall's death Elizabeth's home was with Henry VIII's widow, Catherine Parr. Both Catherine and her new husband were anxious to have someone else to succeed Grindall, but Elizabeth wanted Ascham, whom she had come to know through Grindall, and with whom she had corresponded, writing in the language of scholars, Latin. It says much for her independence of spirit that, with the aid of Ascham's own wire-pulling, she got her way. The choice was a happy one, though Ascham did not long retain his post, resigning it at the end of 1549 or early in the new year owing to a quarrel with some members of the household. Tradition has made him Elizabeth's tutor *par excellence;* rightly so, for even before his appointment he had been counsellor to Grindall in his teaching, and after resigning the tutorship he remained connected with Elizabeth's studies until his death. He helped to form that beautiful, characteristic Italian hand which she wrote on all special occasions. In his book *The Schoolmaster* and in his letters, published shortly after his death, he left posterity many delightful eulogies of his mistress and nearly all the information that we possess about her education.

During the two years under Ascham, Elizabeth devoted her mornings to the study of Greek, beginning the day with the Greek Testament and then reading and translating classical authors such as Isocrates, Sophocles, and Demosthenes, turning them first into English and then back into the original, on the plan of double translation of which Ascham was a keen advocate. The afternoons were given over to Latin, and she read almost all Cicero and a great part of Livy. As a supplement to the Greek Testament there were Saint Cyprian, Melanchthon's *Loci Communes*—a celebrated commentary on Protestant theology and statecraft —and other writings of a similar character. In addition she kept up her French and Italian, and later—probably several years later—learnt Spanish.

'It is difficult to say,' Ascham told his friend Sturm, the celebrated Strasburg scholar and Protestant, 'whether the gifts of nature or of fortune are most to be admired in my distinguished mistress. The praise which Aristotle gives, wholly centres in her; beauty, stature, prudence, and industry. She has just passed her sixteenth birthday and shows such dignity and gentleness as are wonderful at her age and in her rank. Her study of true religion and learning is most eager. Her mind has no womanly weakness, her perseverance is equal to that of a man, and her memory long keeps what it quickly picks up. She talks French and Italian as well as she does English, and has often talked to me readily and well in Latin, moderately in Greek. When she writes Greek and Latin, nothing is more beautiful than her handwriting. She delights as much in music as she is skilful in it.

In adornment she is elegant rather than showy'. In her style of writing, he says, she likes one 'that grows out of the subject, chaste in its appropriateness, beautiful in its clarity. She admires, above all, modest metaphors and comparisons of contraries well put together and contrasting felicitously with one another'. If only, one murmurs, she had not admired them! Ascham closed his letter: 'I am inventing nothing, my dear Sturm; there is no need'.

It is easy to be cynical about the reputed accomplishments of the great: 'The rich man speaks folly and all praise him, the poor man is wise and they mock'. Ascham, of course, was enthusiastic over his pupil, and touched a little by her state. But Elizabeth lived in an age that schooled its children with cruel diligence. She was notoriously quick and intelligent, and she had a real love of learning. Even as a sovereign, with a perplexing round of duty and worry, she did not abandon her studies. In 1562 Ascham was reading Greek and Latin with her every day, and he said that she read more Greek in a day than some prebendary of the Church did Latin in a whole week.

CHAPTER II

THE SEYMOUR EPISODE

EVENTS revealed another Elizabeth than the girl poring over Saint Cyprian, Sophocles, and Cicero. Her father died in January, 1547, when she was thirteen and a half years old. She was spared the harrowing sight of a death-bed, and as she precociously indicated in her letters to her brother, she was able to take her loss with Christian and philosophic fortitude. The future seemed bright. She shared the religious and intellectual outlook of the new king. Protestantism was in the saddle and the uncertainties of the old reign at an end. It might mean, it did mean ill for her sister Mary, but that was calculated to throw into even greater relief the perfect harmony between Elizabeth and Edward.

Across this prospect, marring its happiness and mellowing the lessons of the schoolroom, there stole the restless ambition of a man. 'Woe to thee O land', cried the Preacher, 'when thy king is a child.' The century was to demonstrate only too clearly that the strength of monarchy lay in the god-like solitude of the king, which removed his person and power from the jealousy of aspiring noblemen. But during a minority the king, being a mere child, could not exercise power, while a regent could not command from fellow-subjects a loyalty that was offered, not to the State, but to the person of the king. Thus the divinity of kings hedged childish impotence, while power was left to become a plaything of ambition, for which great noblemen contended. Henry VIII had foreseen the danger and tried to avoid it by committing the government during Edward VI's minority, not to a regent but to a group of councillors, who were the executors of his will. His precaution availed nothing, for it was no solution of the problem, ignoring the natural tendency towards individual leadership, and being contrary to precedent, which favoured the claims of the King's uncle, Edward Seymour, to become the guardian of his nephew and head of the government. Henry's arrangements were immediately modified, and Edward Seymour became Protector Somerset.

Alas! for the harmony of the kingdom; Somerset had a younger brother, Thomas Seymour. He was a person with many attractive qualities; handsome, of manly build, strong-limbed, bold, skilful in war and the tournament. He was capable of warm and open-hearted friendship, but equally of gnawing jealousy, which he had not the prudence to conceal. He was ambitious, but also rash and obstinate. He talked too much and too openly. He was made for action, not statesmanship, and politics brought out the worst features of his character. Henry VIII—in this a shrewd judge of his man—had allotted a minor role to him in Edward's government, but the exaltation of his brother inevitably led to his. He was raised to the peerage, made a privy councillor, and given the office of Lord High Admiral. It was far from satisfying him, and his brother's pre-eminence remained a perpetual irritant.

At the time of Henry VIII's death, Seymour was about thirty-eight years old and unmarried. He was as good and attractive a match as any woman—even a king's daughter—could look for in England, and was resolved to make marriage serve his ambition. Failing Mary, whose religious ardour prevented any hope of success with her, the best match in the land was Elizabeth. If he had been able he would have had her, but his brother and other councillors headed him off with irresistible firmness. He therefore turned to the next best, and secretly wooed the late king's widow, Catherine Parr. His suit went easily, for Catherine had been ready to marry him in her former widowhood, before Henry VIII had stepped in and taken her. For her it was a love-match, and by playing on her affection Seymour induced her to marry him secretly and in indecent haste, within two or three months of Henry's death. It was imprudent, even dangerous, but they kept the marriage quiet while he went through the farce of persuading the young King and his brother, Somerset, to support him in wooing the woman who was already his wife. Fortunately, his fellow-councillors, satisfied at having scotched the marriage with Elizabeth, and as yet unaware of the deception practised upon them, raised no objection. But the marriage did not improve Seymour's relations with his brother, for Catherine, as a loving wife, came to share her husband's jealousy of the Protector, and in retaliation claimed precedence over the Protector's wife in virtue of her rank as Queen Dowager. Thus a brothers' quarrel was fed by a women's.

Seymour's marriage brought him into daily contact with the young princess on whom his ambitious hopes had been vainly centred, since after her father's death Elizabeth had gone to live with Catherine Parr, in this following the custom of the time which made use of ladies' households as finishing schools for girls. There was very close sympathy between Catherine and herself; but in any case, the Queen Dowager's household was the first in the land, and consequently the finest school of manners in which a girl could be.

The Seymour household, as may well be imagined with a man of his temperament at the head, was high-spirited, and life went along in a jolly and easy manner. They were unconventional in an age when conventions were not exactly prim. From the first weeks of his marriage Seymour frequently went into Elizabeth's chamber first thing in the morning. If she were up, 'he would bid her good morrow and ask how she did, and strike her upon the back or on the buttocks familiarly, and so go forth through his lodgings, and sometimes go through to the maidens and play with them, and so go forth'. If she were in bed, 'he would put open the curtains and bid her good morrow, and make as though he would come at her; and she would go further in the bed so that he could not come at her'.

Judged by Victorian standards, Seymour may well appear a lewd man, and Elizabeth a shameless hussy. But it was innocent enough fooling; innocent enough, so long as it did not give rise to comment and neither party was self-conscious. Unfortunately, it was liable to be misconstrued because it was an open secret that Seymour had wanted to marry Elizabeth, and would have preferred her to Catherine Parr. He himself had no idea that his conduct might cause scandal. 'God's precious soul!' he exclaimed, when Elizabeth's governess remonstrated with him. He swore that he would tell the Protector how people were slandering him, and as he meant no evil, vowed he would not alter his ways. The governess therefore spoke to his wife, but she laughed it away as a small matter, promising that in future she would accompany her husband. This she did, and if they found Elizabeth in bed when they entered the room, they would both tickle her. They romped together on other occasions. Once, in the garden, Catherine held Elizabeth while her husband cut the girl's gown into a hundred pieces.

But gossip, as was inevitable, robbed frolic of its innocence. It aroused unfortunate reactions in Elizabeth and in due course stirred up jealousy in Catherine. Elizabeth's governess, Kate Ashley, who was married to a kinsman and servant of her mistress, was a well-meaning, affectionate, but not very sensible woman. She was devoted to her charge, but fascinated by Seymour's charm and friendliness. She talked often of him, and was misguided enough to tell Elizabeth that it was she, and not the Queen, upon whom his affections had been set when he married. Probably this was said when the relations with Catherine were a little strained. The girl became self-conscious; her heart beat faster. People noticed that she took pleasure in Seymour's attentions, and that she was apt to blush when he was the subject of conversation.

There was only one prudent course to take; namely, to send her away. Perhaps the step was a dispassionate one;

more probably not, and Catherine was jealous, for she was with child. Whatever the motive, the week after Whitsun in 1548 Elizabeth left and re-established her own household at Cheshunt. Even if the parting was not altogether harmonious, Catherine and she became good friends again, and kept up a correspondence. In her first letter—her guest letter—Elizabeth closed an episode in admirable good sense. 'Although,' she wrote, 'I could not be plentiful in giving thanks for the manifold kindnesses received at your Highness' hands at my departure, yet I am something to be borne withal, for truly I was replete with sorrow to depart from your Highness . . . And albeit I answered little, I weighed it more deeper when you said you would warn me of all evils that you should hear of me. For if your Grace had not a good opinion of me, you would not have offered friendship to me that way, that all men judge the contrary. But what may I more say, than thank God for providing such friends to me?'

The following September, Catherine Parr died in childbed. There was no obstacle but caution, with which she was not well endowed, to prevent Kate Ashley from matchmaking. 'Your old husband that was appointed unto you at the death of the King,' she said to Elizabeth, 'now is free again. You may have him if you will.' 'Nay,' said the girl. 'Ywiss,' answered Mistress Ashley. 'You will not deny it if my Lord Protector and the Council were pleased therewith.' Much badinage of this sort passed between them. Elizabeth would draw a card in play, representing the Lord Admiral, laugh and blush, and Mistress Ashley would have the apposite remark ready. In the closing months of 1548, whatever her coquettish denials, her fancy seems to have been on Seymour, and her attendants, whether through devotion or for more mercenary reasons, were the Admiral's *aides de guerre*. Thomas Parry, her Cofferer, was in London before and after Christmas, having frequent and long conversations with Seymour. They talked of Elizabeth's financial position. Seymour wanted her to hasten the issue of her letters patent by which, under her father's will, she was to receive lands to the value of

£3,000 per annum. He had gathered from a talk with the Lord Privy Seal, the blunt and laconic Lord Russell, that the Council might jib at the grant; emphatically they would do so if he married her before the grant was through. He wanted her to take steps so that her lands would be in the west, in Gloucestershire and Wales, near to his own estates. The conversations went farther; how far, we do not know. Parry came back to have heart-to-heart talks with Mistress Ashley and to probe Elizabeth's mind. He found the woman a babbler, and the girl a cautious, clever person, moving with that circumspection which her elders ought to have been showing.

The situation was indeed dangerous. There had been transient reconciliations between Somerset and Seymour, but the younger brother could not forget what he fancied was a grievance, and his restless spirit led him into continuous intrigue. With his personal charm he had wormed his way into the King's childish affections, making him free of his pocket, and constantly alluding to his brother's meanness and rigour. 'Ye are but a very beggarly king now', he would say. 'Ye have not the means to play or give to your servants.' Time and again he urged the boy to draw on him for money, and through one of the attendants maintained a clandestine correspondence, forwarding Edward various sums—sometimes as much as forty pounds. He had persuaded himself that precedent entitled him to become the governor of the King's person, and in the autumn of 1547, had tried to prevail on the boy to write a letter asking Parliament to favour a suit of his, which was for a grant of this office in defiance of the Council. He failed, but he was now plotting to bring the King's minority to an end as soon as possible, and through the King's favour dispossess his rivals of power.

At the same time Seymour had been trying to build up a party among the nobility. By promising to marry Lady Jane Grey to the King—a plan which promised the additional satisfaction of preventing his brother from making a son-in-law of Edward—he had persuaded the girl's father to place her in his household, and so won the family to his cause. His actions all pointed to a *coup d'état*. He invariably asked his friends where their lands were situated and what power they had in their counties, urging them to cultivate the gentlemen in their neighbourhood, and not to stop short with the gentry, since, having more to lose, they were less reliable in a crisis: they must win over the chief yeomen and freemen, who were the ringleaders in the country and able to persuade the multitude, dining on occasions like good fellows in their houses, and taking them a flagon or two of wine and a pasty of venison. This, he explained, was what he did himself, and it had got him a following which he put at ten thousand. His lands being more or less concentrated in the west, he set about preparing the castle of Holt, on the borders of Denbighshire, as a possible centre of revolt. His wish to have Elizabeth's lands in the same area was extremely sinister. One of his followers was the corrupt official in charge of the mint at Bristol, and he arranged with him to strike a sum of £10,000 to pay his men in the event of rebellion. Even his office of Lord Admiral was turned to account. 'Why, marry!' he told a friend who thought it a poor position for him to hold, 'now I shall have the rule of a good sort of ships and men; and I tell you, it is a good thing to have the rule of men.' It should have been his business to put down piracy. Instead, he entered into collusion with offenders, shared their spoil, and looked for their aid in case of need. The Scilly Isles fell into his hands, and he came to regard the sea as a line of retreat.

It may conceivably be that there was more folly and bluster in it all than downright conspiracy. Naturally, Seymour did not regard himself as a traitor. How should he, when he was the King's dearest uncle and friend, receiving surreptitious little notes from Edward, hidden under a rug? The situation from his point of view was simple: he felt no loyalty and cherished no respect for a Protector and Council, who were his brother and his fellow-noblemen. All the same, his behaviour was exceedingly dangerous; and if in a moment of exacerbation he had blundered into insurrection, there is no knowing what discontents he might not have attracted to his banner, nor where his own feverish ambition would have stopped.

The intrigue to marry Elizabeth was the last straw. Knowing now how they had been duped over Catherine Parr, the Council could not ignore it. Tongues were wagging. Seymour's friends in vain told him of the reputation that he was earning; a covetous man, ambitious of honour, slothful in service. He was determined to brazen it out. And so the Council was forced to take action. On January 17th, 1549, the blow fell. He was arrested and sent to the Tower.

During the inquiries which followed, Elizabeth passed through distressing anxiety. On January 21st Kate Ashley and Thomas Parry were brought to London and committed to the Tower, while Sir Robert Tyrwhitt was sent down to Hatfield to extract the truth from their mistress. He found that he had embarked on a contest of wits and wills. On January 22nd he wrote to tell Somerset that Elizabeth would in no way confess to any practice between Mistress Ashley or the Cofferer and Seymour. 'And yet,' he added, 'I do see it in her face that she is guilty.' The next day's letter carried the same burden: 'I do assure your Grace she hath a very good wit, and nothing is gotten of her but by great policy.' Policy was tried; it had little effect. Two days later Tyrwhitt bethought himself of Lady Browne—Surrey's fair Geraldine—who had been introduced into Elizabeth's household by Seymour the previous year. She had a way with the girl that no one else possessed, and he therefore asked for her to be returned to Hatfield under orders to wean Elizabeth from her obstinate silence. A gentle letter from the Protector was tried next. It drew from Elizabeth a brief, quite innocent story, but her letter closed with a glimpse of the methods that were being used to break her spirit. 'Master Tyrwhitt and others have told me', she wrote, 'that there goeth rumours abroad which be greatly both against my honour and honesty (which above all other things I esteem) which be these: that I am in the Tower and with child by my Lord Admiral. My Lord, these are shameful slanders, for the which, besides the great desire I have to see the King's Majesty, I shall most heartily desire your Lordship that I may come to the Court after your first determination, that I may show myself there as I am.'

Tyrwhitt was baffled. 'I do verily believe,' he wrote, 'that there hath been some secret promise between my Lady, Mistress Ashley, and the Cofferer, never to confess to death.' He was not far wrong. A week later the most pliant of the three, the Cofferer, gave way and blurted out Kate Ashley's confidences. This lady, however, would say nothing herself until she was faced with Parry and heard him confirm his confession. Then, she called him 'false wretch', and reminded him of the promise that he had given not to confess to the death. The whole story—or all of it that we know—was now got from both. Elizabeth was in a fearful predicament when confronted with it. 'She was much abashed and half breathless ere she could read it to an end, and perused all their names perfectly and knew both Mrs. Ashley's hand and the Cofferer's with half a sight, so that fully she thinketh they have both confessed all they know.' She took a day or two to answer the questions that had been framed on her servants' confessions, and then—well, she carried the story no further. The Council wanted evidence of a definite plot, but she refused to confess that Mrs. Ashley or Parry, either by message or writing, had urged her to any practice with Seymour. 'They all sing one song,' Tyrwhitt lamented; 'and so I think they would not do unless they had set the note before.' The days passed; the outlook for Seymour grew black. When she understood this, Elizabeth began to droop. At the same time, if anyone spoke ill of Seymour she would defend him with vehemence, showing a concern for him that she had hitherto reserved for Mistress Ashley.

A new trouble arose over Tyrwhitt's wife, who had been sent to Hatfield to take Kate Ashley's place and found herself in the unpleasant position of being reprimanded by the Council for not doing her duty, while at the same time she was passionately repudiated by her charge. Elizabeth wept all one night and loured all the next day. She insisted that Mistress Ashley was her mistress. She had not so demeaned herself, she asserted, that the Council should now need to set any more mistresses over her. She preferred to have none. Tyrwhitt drily added that in his opinion she needed two! She sat down and herself wrote to the Protector, not allowing Tyrwhitt to make any suggestions as to what she ought to say. Somerset in reply administered a sharp reproof, telling her that she seemed to stand in her own wit in being so well assured of herself. Unabashed she wrote once more with increased vigour, reminding him that she was the King's sister and that it was his and the Council's duty to let the people see that they had regard for her honour.

A month later Seymour paid the penalty of his follies. He had treated the Council with disdain, refusing at first to answer the thirty-three articles against him, and then standing mute after answering three. On February 25th a bill of attainder was brought before Parliament, and on March 20th he was executed. He had put his trust in the King's goodwill, little thinking with what sang-froid the boy would sacrifice him. On the eve of death, his spirit still defiant, he wrote notes to Mary and Elizabeth with an aglet of a point plucked from his hose, in which he inveighed against his brother and urged them to conspire against him. His last words were to bid his servant, who had the notes sewn between the soles of a velvet shoe, deliver them speedily. The manner of his condemnation—he was attainted without being heard in his own defence; his brave and unrepentant death—'the man died very boldly', people said; 'he would not have done so had he not been in a just quarrel': these caused murmurs and misgivings, which Latimer set himself to allay in the Court sermons that he preached during the following weeks. 'He shall be Lot's wife to me as long as I live,' he declared. 'He was, I heard say, a covetous man, a covetous man indeed: I would there were no more in England! He was, I heard say, an ambitious man: I would there were no more in England! He was, I heard say, a seditious man, a contemner of common prayer: I would there were no more in England! Well! he is gone.'

The rest of this unhappy reign, the fall of Somerset, the rise of Northumberland, left Elizabeth unscathed. She applied herself to her studies and carried herself prudently and modestly. Aylmer, Lady Jane Grey's tutor, wrote to Bullinger in 1551, begging him to admonish his pupil 'as to what embellishment and adornment of person is becoming in young women professing godliness', and suggesting that he make mention for her emulation of the Princess Elizabeth, 'who goes clad in every respect as becomes a young maiden'. 'And yet,' he added, 'no one is induced by the example of so illustrious a lady, and in so much gospel light, to lay aside, much less look down upon, gold, jewels, and braidings of the hair.' For the most part, Elizabeth passed her time at Hatfield or Ashridge. In 1551, if not earlier, she recommenced her visits to Court. She wrote regularly to her brother; sententious, dutiful, sisterly letters, now sending him her portrait—'For the face, I grant I may well blush to offer, but the mind I shall never be ashamed to present'—now congratulating the consumptive, precocious boy on his recovery from illness. There was talk of marriages for her: nothing came of it.

In May, 1553, when Edward lay in his last illness, there was a rumour that Elizabeth was coming to London, and that Northumberland's eldest son intended to repudiate his wife and marry her. Fortunately it proved false, and along with her sister she was made a victim of Northumberland's ambitious attempt to divert the crown from its proper descent and place his daughter-in-law, Lady Jane Grey, on the throne. Elizabeth stood aloof from this rash conspiracy, despite its religious appeal. She wrote congratulating Mary on its collapse, and on July 29th came to London accompanied by an army. Two days later she rode out to meet her sister, with a train of a thousand horse and a hundred velvet coats, and at the ceremonial entry into London on August 3rd, had her place in the procession, next after the Queen.

The two half-sisters were a striking contrast. Mary was

in her thirty-eighth year; short, very thin, with a round face, reddish hair, large light eyes, and broad, rather low nose. She had once been attractive, but worry had marred her looks and made her prematurely grave; ill-health, too, the result perhaps of her sufferings, had helped to steal her youth away. Elizabeth was just on twenty, in the full bloom of life. Some thought her very handsome, others rather comely than handsome. She was moderately tall, with a fine figure to which her dignified carriage lent impressive majesty. Her hair was golden, but more red than yellow; her skin very fine, though of an olive complexion. She had striking eyes, and above all, beautiful hands which she knew how to display. The old world and the new; such were these two daughters of Henry VIII.

CHAPTER III

THE EXPERIMENT OF A WOMAN RULER

ENGLAND was now faced with the very situation from which Henry VIII had wanted to save her. She was to make the experiment of a woman ruler. Thanks to Northumberland, it began in abundant goodwill: such was the disgust with his selfish conspiracy that even the great divide of religion was temporarily levelled. The bells and thanksgivings, the feastings and pageants with which London welcomed the Queen, gave expression to the loyalty and favour of the people.

The Queen had no easy task. She was a devout Catholic, about to rule a country where the Reformation was twenty years old and a generation had reached manhood to whom papal authority was strange and alien; a country which rejoiced in its insularity and hated foreigners and foreign jurisdiction. An observant Venetian—a Catholic—after nearly three years' residence in Mary's Court, thought that genuine Catholics were very few, and none under thirty-five. For the most part, he believed that Englishmen were ready in outward show to follow their Prince's example and order, even were he a Mohammedan or a Jew. His impression was probably derived from a limited area but was not without justification, for the Council of Trent had not yet defined Catholic doctrine nor the Counter-Reformation reawakened enthusiasm, and for the time being Protestantism was the live and attacking force. What is more, it held the strategic parts of the country—the towns and the home counties, and was strongest and keenest in London, which in the late reign had been a refuge for religious exiles from abroad. From many points of view, London was the kingdom. Finance, trade, government were centred there; the monarchy was attached to it with indissoluble bonds; and if later in the century Paris was worth a Mass, London was equally worth a Sermon. It was no accident that the ultimate religious character of both France and England was that of the capital.

Nor was this all. The sale of monastic and chantry lands had converted the Reformation into a colossal business interest in which everyone, yeoman, merchant, gentleman, and nobleman, with any free capital, had invested. Lands had changed hands like shares in a modern company, involving a range of speculators far greater than the actual number of holders, many as these were. For most people of any importance, when doctors and laymen in divinity had argued themselves hoarse, this remained the ruling consideration; and if Catholics offered truth, why so also did Protestants, and along with it a reliable guarantee, free from all scruples of conscience, of a nation-wide investment. The issue was not simple even for the clergy, since a large number of them had married in the last reign, and if Catholic practice were restored would have to quit either their calling or their wives. The Reformation had become a great vested interest.

It might have been practical politics to go back on the doctrinal changes of Edward VI's reign, though even then there would have been trouble, especially in London. It was crass folly, politically speaking, to think of restoring papal supremacy. Yet nothing was more characteristic of Mary than her determination to commit this folly. For well over twenty years, from adolescence to mature womanhood, religion had been everything to her—her rights, her pride, her courage, her consolation in adversity. She had surrendered to her father, but only after an obstinate struggle, and while openly compliant had secretly executed a deed repudiating her action. In the late reign she had set her brother and his Council at defiance, vowing that she would lay her head on the block and suffer death, rather than give way. Experience had bred in her the single-mindedness of the martyr, and she longed with intense passion to bring her country back to the papal fold.

Within a month of Mary's entry into London Mass began to be said in some of the City churches. It was greeted with riots. A royal chaplain, preaching at St. Paul's Cross on August 13th was interrupted with cries of 'Papist, Papist! Tear him down!' Someone hurled a dagger at him and he barely escaped with his life. Loyalty looked like wearing thin with astonishing rapidity; and though the first of the Protestant *émigrés* began to fly from the wrath to come, their departure left no lack of leaders for the resistance to Mary's religious policy.

As if troubles were not to come singly, there was another question in which emotion and not policy directed Mary's mind. This was her marriage. She recognized, as did most people, that she must marry, for a virgin Queen was unthinkable. The country needed a king, both to help in ruling and to beget a prince. Among her advisers and in Parliament, as well as throughout the country, there was singular unanimity about the person whom she ought to choose. He must be a subject, not a foreigner; and by common consent the right person was the young Edward Courtenay, great grandson of Edward IV. His father had been executed for treason by Henry VIII and he himself had been a prisoner in the Tower for nearly fifteen years, when Mary released him. He may not have been the beau ideal of a husband. Though tall and handsome and attractive physically, his life after his release was not altogether edifying, nor was his character strong. All the same, she would have been well advised to marry him.

Yet once more Mary showed herself ridden by the past and incapable of ordering her life afresh as a Queen. In all her former troubles she had leant for advice upon her cousin, the Emperor Charles V, and this relationship continued as unalterable as her faith. She made the Imperial ambassador, Simon Renard, her close confidant, her English councillors in comparison being almost strangers. Already she had promised Charles to follow his advice about a husband; he grasped eagerly at the opportunity thus offered him. His son Philip was then a widower, and marriage with Mary, bringing England into the orbit of Spain and keeping it from alliance with France, was an irresistible diplomatic attraction.

To Mary the match opened a flattering and peculiarly congenial prospect. Philip was the son of her protector and friend; she herself was half Spanish. Duty, not concupiscence, she modestly said, led her to marry; but once her mind was made up, desire for Philip rushed like a flood over her, and she became as a headstrong, lovesick girl. Nothing —not her councillors' advice, not the frank words of Parliament, not the growing murmurs of the people—could stop her. She preferred death, she said, to any other husband. Her marriage was the most personal act of the reign, and it was fatal. It struck harshly upon insular prejudice and aroused the Englishry of everyone. In the fear it bred of secular foreign dominance, it emphasized all the more the alien character of papal supremacy; and two oppositions— Politique and Protestant—were wedded. To be mere English and to be Protestant began to seem one and the same thing.

What wonder if, when men turned from Mary in disappointment, their hopes rested on her sister! Elizabeth was Protestant and in her Englishry was no foreign strain. If Mary died childless she would be their ruler, and the more rash were tempted to make such a future certain and speed its coming. It was a position of infinite difficulty. Let Elizabeth's prudence be divine, she could not keep her name from every hot-head's lips; and sisterly affection could not live in such an atmosphere.

Affection was in fact ebbing away. Anxious as she was to restore the old faith as rapidly as possible, Mary had re-established Mass at Court, and councillors and courtiers had quickly adapted themselves to the changed order. Elizabeth held aloof, conspicuous, along with Anne of Cleves, by her absence from every Catholic service. With

London seething over religion, it hardly needed the Imperial ambassador, Renard, to point out the danger of her example. He was alarmed at Mary's headstrong and precipitous ways, and in the first months of the reign was gloomily expecting a successful rising in favour of Elizabeth and Courtenay. Inevitably, his oft-repeated fear communicated itself to Mary and helped to turn her goodwill into suspicion and resentment.

By the first week in September the Queen was so cold and the peril so clear that Elizabeth determined to give way. She went to her sister and with tears begged for books or teachers to correct the errors in which she had been bred. On the Nativity of the Virgin Mary she attended her first Mass, and the Queen's heart was full of joy. Renard was sceptical; as well he might be, for by erratic attendance at Mass Elizabeth took care to let her friends see the perfunctory nature of her conversion. Within a fortnight, the more trustful Mary was doubting whether her convert was not wandering off the path of truth again, and begged Elizabeth to tell her frankly whether she fully believed the Catholic doctrine, or whether her conversion, as people thought, was mere pretence. Elizabeth assured her that it was the dictate of conscience, without fear or dissimulation; she was thinking, she said, of making a public declaration to this effect. Mary did not know whether to believe her or not. Renard for his part remained sceptical. He was seeing French plots and intrigues on every hand. He noticed Elizabeth's friendly relations with the French ambassador at the coronation, and overheard her complain of the weight of her crown, to which the ambassador replied, 'Have patience; it will soon produce a better.' His master, Charles V, and he kept urging Mary, on some pretext or other, to send Elizabeth to the Tower.

The tension was not improved when the first Parliament of the reign met in October. To a point business ran smoothly. The religious innovations of the late reign were swept away, not, however, without opposition, nor without the generality of members making it clear that they had no desire to go farther and re-establish papal supremacy. In addition, there was an eloquent act to declare the divorce of Catherine of Aragon erroneous and void, and to nullify all statutory pronouncements against Mary's legitimacy while leaving unrepealed the clauses declaring Elizabeth illegitimate. So far, progress was satisfactory. But Mary desired to go farther, for though Elizabeth was illegitimate by law, she was by statute next in the succession to the throne. Mary wanted this statute repealed, and therefore consulted one of her most influential councillors, Paget. Parliament, Paget told her, would certainly refuse, and it was vain to think of transferring the succession to another. Better settle it publicly on Elizabeth and marry her to Courtenay, thus offering a sop to nobility and people, and relieving them of their fear lest Philip should seize the crown at her death or England be handed in perpetuity to a foreigner. By doing this, she would reconcile them to her marriage.

Paget's advice was gall and wormwood. Mary turned to Renard, and as she spoke to him, the past lived again and Catherine of Aragon and Anne Boleyn were resurrected in herself and Elizabeth. Her conscience, she told him, would not permit her sister's succession. Elizabeth was a bastard, her mother had been the cause of all the troubles and alterations in the realm, and she in turn would ruin things once more; her attendance at Mass was hypocrisy, there was not a single servant or lady in her service who was not a heretic, she was always talking with heretics, she lent an ear to every evil practice, she was French in her sympathies. There were other claimants to the succession, Mary went on to say; there were the Queen of Scots, the Duchess of Suffolk, and the Countess of Lennox. For herself, she preferred the last.

By the end of November Elizabeth was in such disfavour that courtiers were afraid to visit or speak to her. Sometimes she found herself displaced from her precedence and made to follow after the Countess of Lennox and the Duchess of Suffolk. Retreat seemed best, and she asked and was granted leave to withdraw from Court. On December 6th she started out for Ashridge, escorted by nearly five hundred gentlemen on horseback. The parting of the sisters was outwardly friendly. Elizabeth begged Mary not to listen to tale-tellers, but to give her an opportunity of justifying herself if evil were spoken of her. Ten miles on the way, she sent back for a litter, at the same time asking her sister for copes, chasubles, and the other accompaniments of Catholic ritual. A characteristic trick! But Mary was no longer in the mood to be fooled. She was soured, anxious, and unhappy.

The barometer was moving to storm. The day that Elizabeth left for Ashridge, which was the day that Parliament was dissolved, a dog was thrown into the Presence Chamber at Court with shaved head, cropped ears, a halter about its neck and a label saying that all priests and bishops should be hanged. About Christmas Eve there appeared in London copies of a tract against the papal supremacy written in Henry VIII's reign by Gardiner, now Lord Chancellor, which had been published by the Protestant *émigrés*, along with a scurrilous preface. Reports were coming in of unrest and of speeches and writings against the Spaniards and the marriage. Mary's ladies were afraid; she herself fell ill of melancholy, and began to reconsider Paget's suggestion of marrying Elizabeth to Courtenay. Down in a Cornish parish on Christmas Eve, one, Sampson Jackman, announced that before New Year's day 'outlandish men will come upon our heads, for there be some at Plymouth already'. 'We ought not to have a woman bear the sword,' a companion declared. 'If a woman bear the sword,' said Jackman, 'my Lady Elizabeth ought to bear it first.' The ambassadors sent by Charles V to conclude the marriage treaty entered London on January 2nd, 1554. The day before, their retinue had been pelted with snowballs by London boys, and now as they themselves went through the City 'the people, nothing rejoicing, held down their heads sorrowfully'.

Behind the unrest, conspiracy was at work, and on January 25th it declared itself in Kent in Wyatt's rebellion. The outbreak was premature, for Courtenay, who was connected with the plot, had, like the weak man he was,

played his fellows false. As a result, sectional risings in
Devon, the Midlands, and Wales went wrong, and Wyatt
alone made headway. But for a fortnight it was touch and
go with Mary's throne, and had it not been for her splendid courage, the rebellion would probably have succeeded.
It collapsed in the defeat and capture of Wyatt on February 7th.

As Charles V and his ambassador saw the situation, the
imperative need was to rid the world of the young woman
whose mere existence was at once a challenge to Mary's
policy and an incentive to rebellion. Mary had been keeping
careful watch on Elizabeth. Two or three days before
Wyatt's rising she had written to her, and received a grateful reply: ill-health, Elizabeth said, had kept her from
writing before. The answer breathed an air of innocence,
but this was rapidly dissipated, for the Government discovered that Wyatt was wanting her to move from Ashridge to Donnington Hall in Berkshire, where she would
be further from London and could defend herself, if need
be, until the rebellion succeeded. An order was promptly
sent for her to come to London. As Mary waited for the
reply, fate played Elizabeth a cruel trick. Anxious to probe
Wyatt's plot, the Government had decided to turn high-
wayman and waylay the French ambassador's courier. Enclosed in his dispatch was found a copy of Elizabeth's
letter to the Queen! Though, in fact, the girl was not responsible, Mary's officials could not know this, and they
naturally jumped to the conclusion that she was in regular
communication with the ambassador. The Chancellor,
Gardiner, as he opened the courier's packet and found its
tell-tale enclosure, felt the thrill of a gambler whose throw
had been marvellously successful. To make matters worse,
Elizabeth wrote to say that she was too unwell to obey the
Queen's order and travel to London. This seemed damning
confirmation of the Government's suspicions.

As soon as Wyatt's defeat left her free, Mary acted with
vigour. She sent three councillors accompanied by her
physicians and a strong escort, who were to bring Elizabeth
to London if she could possibly be moved. Her illness was

not make-believe; her body was all swollen—a recurrent malady of hers at this time—and she was prostrate with anxiety. But she could be moved. By slow stages she came to Court, rumour flying ahead, now whispering that she was poisoned, now that she was *enceinte*. On February 22nd she passed through the City to Westminster. Her litter was uncovered that she might show herself to the people, clothed all in white, her face sickly pale, but with a proud and prince-like bearing, masking her fears. It was a city of horror and desolation, where traitors' heads and quarters spoke their obscene warning from the City gates and twenty gallows stood to recall a day of awful butchery just past. The pathetic Queen of twelve days, Lady Jane Grey, had perished on the scaffold; the slaughter was not yet ended. 'So much noble blood shed for foreigners!' men murmured. Was another and a nobler life on its way to sacrifice for this Spanish marriage? If Simon Renard could have his way, it was.

Mary, like Renard, had no doubts about Elizabeth's complicity in the plot, and if this could only be proved, there was small hope of mercy. Wyatt and others were examined and re-examined for evidence to convict her. It was discovered that Wyatt had twice written to her and received answers, but they were verbal only and amounted to nothing. They may not even have been hers, for some of her servants had been involved in the conspiracy, and there is no saying what use they had made of her name. Anyhow, verbal answers could always be repudiated. Elizabeth did not stop at this: 'As for the traitor Wyatt,' she said, 'he might peradventure write me a letter, but on my faith I never received any from him.' Whether she was speaking the truth, or whether, as is possible, it was a clever half-truth, there is no means of saying. It is difficult to believe that she was ignorant of the conspiracy. She may not have approved of it, for it was not in her nature to rejoice at the prospect of receiving a crown at the hands of rebels and at the expense of her sister's life. But supposing—as hints in later life suggest—that she both knew and disapproved, she could neither resist nor betray men who were

devoted to her cause. Her only possible line of conduct was
to keep clear of anything that might fatally compromise
her. It called for skill, but skill of a kind that was su-
premely hers. The Government could say no more, nor can
posterity say more, than the words which she was said to
have scratched on a window pane:

> Much suspected by me,
> Nothing proved can be.

However, there was sufficient of a case to keep Elizabeth
under restraint. It was decided—though some of the Council
objected—to send her to the Tower, and as Wyatt was to
be tried on March 15th, when the people would learn how
Elizabeth was compromised, the following day was selected
for her removal. She was aghast when told to make ready.
Not crediting that it was her sister's doing, she begged for
an interview, and when this was refused, asked that she
might at least be allowed to write her a letter. The kind
heart of the Earl of Sussex yielded, and she sat down to
plead with her sister that she might not be sent to the
Tower, 'a place more wonted for a false traitor than a true
subject'. 'I protest before God, who shall judge my truth
whatsoever malice shall devise, that I never practised, concealed, nor consented to anything that might be prejudicial
to your person any way, or dangerous to the state by any
mean . . . Let conscience move your Highness to take some
better way with me than to make me be condemned in all
men's sight, afore my desert known.' She prayed to be allowed to answer the accusations before her sister. 'I have
heard in my time,' she added, 'of many cast away for want
of coming to the presence of their Prince.'

As the distraught young woman wrote, the tide of the
Thames turned, and London Bridge could no longer be shot
with safety that day. She had got what she desired—time
for her appeal to move Mary. Moved she was; not with
pity, but with indignation against her councillors for their
indulgence to Elizabeth. They dared not have done such
a thing in her father's time, she cried: would he were alive
again but for a month! The next day, Palm Sunday, about

ten in the morning when all were at church bearing their palms, a barge slipped downstream from Whitehall and landed Elizabeth at the Traitors' Stairs. It was raining and dejection claimed everything. Death seemed very near. As she entered—people heard—she said to the warders and soldiers, looking up to heaven, 'Oh Lord! I never thought to have come in here as prisoner; and I pray you all, good friends and fellows, bear me witness that I come in no traitor but as true a woman to the Queen's Majesty as any is now living: and thereon will I take my death.'

The Government kept at its search for proof. Wyatt was not executed until April 11th, in the hope of new discoveries; Sir James Croft, one of the principal conspirators and a person in Elizabeth's service, was 'marvellously tossed and examined'; every possible witness was questioned. Elizabeth herself was put through a fresh catechism. Simon Renard kept urging Mary on. He dwelt upon the need of security before Philip set foot in England, in this touching her in the quick, for she was pathetically anxious to consummate the marriage as soon as possible. She was thirty-eight and felt creeping time at her gate.

Proof there was not, and at last it was recognized that Elizabeth could not be put to death. The judges declared the evidence insufficient for a conviction. True, there was an extraordinary weapon for use in such a predicament—an act of attainder; but there was no hope of turning it against Elizabeth. Parliaments might be pliant, but pliant only within limits. In a rough way they reflected public opinion, and this was not in the humour to tolerate abnormal proceedings against the heiress to the throne. The Council itself was divided: some members, including the Admiral, Lord William Howard, Elizabeth's great uncle, were ready to express themselves with fierce heat. As for London, it was Mary's despair. On March 5th some three hundred children had gathered in a meadow, ranged themselves in two companies, and played at the Queen against Wyatt, not ending until they had captured the Prince of Spain and hanged him on a gibbet from which he was cut down in the nick of time. Nine days later people were flocking in thousands to hear the spirit in the wall, the latest wonder, which when people cried 'God save Queen Mary!' answered nothing, but when the cry changed to 'God save the Lady Elizabeth!' replied 'So be it!' and when asked 'What is the Mass?' retorted 'Idolatry!' The day Parliament met—April 2nd—the streets were strewn with a highly seditious letter in Elizabeth's favour, and with a paper bearing these words: 'Hold fast, keep together, and we shall prevent the Prince of Spain from entering this realm!' The following Sunday a dead cat was hung on the gallows in Cheapside, arrayed in a garment like a priest's vestment with cross back and front, the crown of its head shorn, and a piece of paper like a singing cake or wafer placed between its forefeet. Three days later Wyatt was executed. He told the people from the scaffold that neither Elizabeth nor Courtenay had any previous knowledge of his rising, a statement, which despite its limitations, was embarrassing to the Government, as was shown by the setting of two men in the pillory for spreading the news that Wyatt had cleared my Lady Elizabeth. On April 17th came another blow when a respectable London jury acquitted Sir Nicholas Throckmorton of treason, for doing which they were imprisoned and heavily fined. The same day Wyatt's head was stolen from the gallows on which it stood, and a few days later a paper was thrown on the Queen's kitchen table, threatening Mary, Gardiner, and others, slandering Philip, and declaring that he must take his chance when he landed in England. Renard was looking for another rebellion in May.

The position between Mary and Elizabeth was not unlike stalemate. Paget was convinced that they could neither put her to death, nor oust her from the succession. She could not be kept in the Tower, for that would be dangerous; nor set at liberty, for that would be inconvenient; nor lodged at Court, for that would offend Mary's dignity. The one expedient left was a period of more or less honourable but close captivity in a country house. The royal manor of Woodstock in Oxfordshire was chosen as the place, and a member of the Privy Council, Sir Henry Bedingfield, as custodian.

On Saturday, May 19th, after two months in the Tower, Elizabeth was taken by barge to Richmond, the first stage on her journey. Thinking that she was being set at liberty, Londoners rejoiced, and as her barge passed the Steelyard its merchants fired off three salvoes of artillery. In daily moves she went from Richmond to Windsor, then to Sir William Dormer's house at West Wycombe, and so to Ricote, the home of Lord Williams of Thame, where she was marvellously well entertained. From Ricote she reached Woodstock on May 23rd. In the villages and fields by the way the simple folk, coming to gaze upon her, gave many a token of sympathy. The wives of Wycombe passed cake and wafers to her until her litter became so burdened that she had to beg them to stop. Four men of Aston hurried to the church and rang the bells, and were afterwards clapped in ward for their pains. At Wheatley and Stanton St. John the whole village turned out and cried 'God save your Grace!'

At Woodstock stringent precautions were taken to prevent a rescue or any secret communication with the outside world. Every night a troop of soldiers watched on a hill outside, while nothing could be received, nor anyone enter the house, without Bedingfield's permission. The ladies and servants were limited in number and carefully chosen. Mary herself gave order that one of them should be removed, an order which made Elizabeth sulk. The 'Mother of the Maids' was recruited from the Queen's own ladies, and Kate Ashley—we may be sure—was kept at a safe distance. As Cofferer, Thomas Parry had to arrange for the feeding and paying of the household, but was not allowed to stay in the house. The Council intended that he should retire altogether from the neighbourhood, but he established himself at the sign of the Bull in Woodstock and added a new terror to Bedingfield's life with the daily coming and going of men, some of them in his own livery, and others servants of his mistress, in number out of all proportion to the conduct of his business. The sign of the Bull, in fact, became a barely disguised headquarters for Elizabeth's friends. Young Francis Verney was there, of whom Bedingfield wrote, 'If there be any practice of ill within all England, this Verney is privy to it'. Elizabeth and her servants were altogether too effervescent a company for the slow wit of her custodian.

Sir Henry was excessively honest, excessively unimaginative, excessively mistrustful of himself. 'This great lady'—for so he found himself writing of her—with her hundred moods and subtle incessant attempts to wring some new concession from him, just left him bewildered. Instinctively he held to his instructions with bull-dog tenacity, refusing to dot an 'i' of them without writing first to the Council. Parry sent in a volume of Cicero and a Latin version of the Psalms for his mistress: the Council had to be asked if she might have them. She herself wanted an English Bible: Bedingfield offered her Cicero and the Psalms to be going on with, while he wrote to London about the Bible. Life for Elizabeth became an odd tussle with this bucolic obstinacy, and through it—for, as she no doubt guessed, Bedingfield was painfully faithful in his reports to the Council—with the authorities at Court. She wheedled permission to write to Mary, but her letter, with its air of misunderstood innocence, so annoyed the Queen that order was given for no more of her 'disguised and colourable letters' to be sent. Wishing to reply, Elizabeth asked Bedingfield to listen to her and then convey her words as a message to the Council. He refused. She thereupon complained that she was worse treated than a prisoner in the Tower—indeed, as another day's rumination convinced her, worse treated than the worst prisoner in Newgate. All this went to the Council, and as a result she got her way. She merely reiterated her declarations of innocence. Next, she began an agitation for leave to write to the Council herself. When permission came she let a week slip by before asking for pens and paper, and then, declaring that she never wrote to councillors except through a secretary, made Bedingfield act as her secretary. She fell ill with the old swelling in her face and body, and asked for the Queen's physicians to be sent. She was told that they were unavailable, and the services of other physicians were offered. These she refused: 'I am not minded,' she exclaimed, 'to make any stranger privy to the state of my body, but commit it to God.' In the end she got her way. And so the comedy went on.

Meanwhile, in the world without, Mary's policy moved forward to its fulfilment. Philip landed at Southampton in July, 1554, and was married at Winchester five days later. The people behaved themselves and the impressive ceremonies passed without a hitch. London made itself gay. Its twenty gallows, which had been standing since Wyatt's rising, were taken down and the citizens primed with good liquor. When the King and Queen made their public entry into the City on August 19th they were greeted with a magnificent display of pageantry. There was only one slight mischance, and this was the fault of a painter who, portraying the nine worthies on the winding turret of the conduit in Gracechurch Street, thoughtlessly showed Henry VIII, not with mace or sword or pole-axe in his hand like the other worthies, but with a Bible on which was written 'Verbum Dei'. Gardiner's quick eye caught this as he rode in the procession. He was furious and rated the painter, who, expressing surprise at the fuss, went back, blotted out the Bible, and put a pair of gloves in Henry's hands!

For all Philip's studied affability and the care taken to keep his proud retinue in hand, close acquaintance did not make Englishmen love Spaniards the more, nor Spaniards Englishmen. 'At this time,' notes a diarist, 'there was so many Spaniards in London that a man should have met in the streets for one Englishman above four Spaniards, to the great discomfort of the English nation.' His remark may be interpreted to mean that a quarter of the number was as much as the average Londoner could stand. On September 5th there was 'a talk of twelve thousand Spaniards coming more into the realm, they said to fetch the crown'. Then followed a rumour that the archbishopric of Canterbury was given to a Spanish friar. Swords were apt to leap from scabbards when the two nations met, and many were the affrays between them. Too true it was that Mary had given her critics and enemies a powerful weapon in bringing the

Spaniards to England. But to a lovesick, passionate woman
what did that count?

The other heart's desire of the Queen now lay open to
her. For a whole year Cardinal Pole, as the Pope's legate,
had fretted on the threshold of the kingdom; Peter seeking
admission to the house of Mary. For various reasons he had
been denied entry until the marriage was over, but at length
the door opened to him. On November 30th, 1554, amidst
scenes of infectious emotion—the Queen quietly sobbing,
Members answering 'Amen, amen!' and weeping in one another's arms—Parliament bowed itself in humble penitence
and supplication before the Pope's representative and listened to his solemn absolution of the nation. England had
returned to the bosom and unity of Christ's Church. But
neither their emotion that day, nor Pole's anguish of soul
at the spectacle of a barter over spiritual redemption, could
prevent them as practical and now sober men from devising
a pope-proof guarantee to safeguard their possession of
monastic and chantry property.

As a result of this Parliament, faggot and stake were able
to add their terrible argument towards conformity. The
dreadful holocaust which began in February, 1555, and
has attached the epithet 'bloody' to the names of Mary and
Bonner, was a horror that most of those who voted the
heresy laws could not have anticipated. The Imperial,
Venetian, and French ambassadors, Catholics and foreigners though they were, were shocked by it; and well
might Englishmen be. It did not make better Catholics; it
only filled people with admiration at the courage of the
martyrs. The first to suffer, John Rogers, was so acclaimed
by the spectators that, according to the French ambassador,
it seemed as though he were being taken to his wedding.
The burnings opened an old sore, for Englishmen were not
fond of ecclesiastical jurisdiction, and though they were
hardened to the spectacle of executions, and even to the
horrible death of traitors, these heresy trials appeared to
them in abhorrent form as an alien, priests' business. Fur-
thermore, a Queen with sympathies that seemed more foreign than English was ridding herself by their means of

subjects who were obnoxious, not only in religion, but also in politics.

No doubts entered Mary's devout mind. Exalted in spirit by her marriage and by the reconciliation with Rome, she awaited the last manifestation of God's overflowing bounty —a child, to inherit and preserve her work. It was in the ecstasy of her meeting with Pole in November, 1554, that she announced her pregnancy, and orders were given for *Te Deum* to be sung in all the churches. 'Fear not, Mary!' chanted the preacher at St. Paul's, 'for thou hast found favour with God. And behold, thou shalt conceive in thy womb, and bring forth a son'. The other section of the people had their opinion expressed in a paper attached to the Palace door at Hampton Court: 'Shall we be such fools, good Englishmen, to believe that our Queen is with child?'

As the signs of pregnancy developed, Mary's mind began to run on what might happen if she died in childbed. In this way the problem of Elizabeth arose again. For some time Mary had been uncertain what to do with her. If she kept her captive she ran the risk of alienating powerful lords, whereas if free Elizabeth might become the object of fresh plots. Renard was no longer the devil's advocate, having executed a complete *volte-face*. Instead of pressing for Elizabeth's death, he was supporting Paget's policy of recognizing her claim to the succession. There was a simple explanation. If Mary died, Spanish interests had more to gain from Elizabeth than from the alternative successor, Mary Queen of Scots, who was the affianced wife of the French Dauphin. Elizabeth in consequence found a powerful friend at Court in Philip.

Mary was slow, very slow to respond. Thoughts of death ultimately made her act, for if she died it was more than likely that the people would give rein to their hatred of Philip and his Spaniards; and as a guarantee of their lives it became expedient to bring Elizabeth to Court. At the end of April, 1555, Bedingfield escorted his charge from Woodstock to Hampton Court. To the end, he showed himself the same timorous, rigorous custodian.

For a time Elizabeth was kept in strict seclusion. She

saw the Queen in private, and the story goes that on her knees she begged her sister to believe that she was, and had been, as true a subject as anyone. 'You will not confess your offence,' answered Mary, 'but stand stoutly in your truth: I pray God it may so fall out.' 'If it doth not,' Elizabeth replied, 'I request neither favour nor pardon at your Majesty's hands.' 'Well,' said Mary, 'you stiffly still persevere in your truth. Belike you will not confess but that you have been wrongfully punished.' 'I must not say so, if it please your Majesty, to you.' 'Why then,' answered the Queen, 'belike you will to others.' 'No, if it please your Majesty, I have borne the burden and must bear it. I humbly beseech your Majesty to have a good opinion of me, and to think me to be your true subject, not only from the beginning hitherto, but for ever, as long as life lasteth.' They parted, the Queen with her misgivings, Elizabeth with her conscience. The signs of captivity were gradually removed. Soon courtiers were allowed access to her—a permission used with discreet reserve.

Mary's time was drawing near. Tidings spread in London on April 30th that she had been delivered of a prince, and *Te Deum* was sung, bells set ringing. The next day there was disillusionment. 'But it shall be when it please God,' noted a devout diarist; 'for I trust God that He will remember His true servants that put their trust in Him, when they call on Him.' Letters announcing the birth to foreign princes were made ready in May and arrangements completed for delivering them. To sustain Mary's courage three fine babies were shown her, borne at a birth without ill effect by a woman 'of low stature and great age' like herself. June came and she took to her bed.

Then the weeks passed and nothing happened. Tongues wagged: some made broad jokes; the Protestants swore that it was all a conspiracy to pass off a supposititious child on the country. A Polish ambassador arrived, with a well-conned Latin oration into which had been woven congratulations on the birth of the child; and the wretched man spoke the whole speech to the King! The business was fast becoming a Court farce. Philip had been chafing for months to get away from a country that he hated and a wife who was too old and worn to heat his blood; but he was compelled to wait while the tragi-comedy of false pregnancy was played to its limits.

On August 3rd, in order to be rid of the crowds at Hampton Court, stop the constant religious processions, and allow Mary to re-emerge into public life with least embarrassment, the Court moved for ten days or so to Oatlands. Philip had but a single thought—to leave the country. On August 26th, 1555, Mary and he passed through London *en route* for Greenwich, whence three days later he took his leave for Dover and Flanders.

Mary remained at Greenwich, a place she loved, where she had re-established the Observant Friars in their monastery, and where in the midst of her duties she could live a nun-like round of religious offices. She would sit far into the night, sorrowful, lonely, writing to Philip about English affairs. She fondly thought that he would be returning in a few weeks, but as month after month dragged by, deep melancholy would at times possess her. She had been prone to tears since childhood, and now the weakness was aggravated by her sense of frustration in public and private affairs. Her marriage had been fruitless and the tragic farce of her childbed made people believe that it could not be otherwise. As openly as they might they were beginning to court her successor in Elizabeth, the rock upon which Catholic England was drifting. She cherished no illusions about the danger. So far from opposition lagging, scarcely a week passed without some incident or arrest. Were she to die childless, Elizabeth and Protestantism were bound to succeed her. Childless, however, she would not be, she must not be. She would not despair of issue. If only Philip would not stay away while she aged!

Elizabeth too was at Greenwich. Her position was more secure than it had been when at Court in the autumn of 1553, two years before. Her enemies knew her popularity; they knew also the limits of their power. Philip was her friend, and she had used every art to ingratiate herself with him and his Spanish followers. Let her be prudent, time was her ally. She had to guard against a marriage dictated by Spanish interests. In addition, there was the danger that she might be treated like Courtenay, who had been sent abroad, out of the way. The suggestion was repeatedly made, and she could only trust that her friends at Court and fear of popular anger would save her from such a fate.

Prudence was able to do much, but there was one incalculable factor in Elizabeth's fortune, and that was the indiscretion of friends. The opposition to Mary's policy was constantly expressing itself in ballads and pamphlets, seditious speeches and plots; and Elizabeth's household was a plague spot in the contagion. In July, 1554, one of her servants had been imprisoned for seditious words; the following March another was sent for by the Council; in April a third was imprisoned; in May her Italian tutor, Baptista Castiglione, who apparently had been in prison before, was sent to the Tower on suspicion of being concerned with a seditious dialogue, of which a thousand copies were said to have been seized by the Mayor of London. In June, John Dee the astrologer and three others, one or two being her servants, were arrested for casting her horoscope along with the King's and Queen's.

So long as Elizabeth lived under the watchful eye of the Court she was in no real danger, but in October, 1555, when Mary moved to St. James's to be in London for the meeting of Parliament, Elizabeth left her sister, and, with the immoderate plaudits of the people to speed her, passed through the City to Hatfield. She had last made such a journey in the winter of 1553–54, and it had led to the Tower and well nigh to death. As she moved once more into the same dangerous isolation her reflections must have been disquieting.

With uncanny promptitude events began to repeat themselves. Parliament was meeting as in 1553, and as in 1553 was troublesome. There was a party of young hot-heads in the Commons who gathered at an eating-house, known as Arundel's, and formed a Protestant opposition to resist all Catholic measures. They came near to defeating the Government bill which Mary had most at heart, and then, when another bill was read, directed against Protestant refugees abroad, they obtained the keys of the House, locked the doors, forced a division, and rejected the bill. It was not long before some of these men and other young Protestants were drawn into a more dangerous game. This was a plot, in being in the new year, the aims of which were to collect an invading force of *émigrés* in France, raid the English exchequer, and start a rebellion to place Elizabeth and Courtenay on the throne. Its ramifications were too extensive for secrecy and the Government struck before anything came of it.

As the Council, with the aid of rack and dungeon, threaded its way into the details of the plot, the names of members of Elizabeth's household began to emerge. Somerset House, her London residence, was searched, and there in a secret place a great coffer was discovered full of seditious, anti-Catholic books and papers, ballads and caricatures. Kate Ashley—back with her mistress in her old place —the Italian tutor, Castiglione, Francis Verney, and a fourth person were brought from Hatfield and sent to the Tower; a few days later two more dependents were arrested. Kate Ashley, disclaiming any knowledge of the plot, asserted that her mistress's feelings were such, that it was as much as her place was worth to harbour any evil thoughts of the Queen. But the coffer of books and papers was apparently hers, and she was kept in prison for three months, being forbidden to see Elizabeth again. Francis Verney was tried for treason and found guilty, but he was pardoned.

Again Elizabeth stood out as the danger spot in the State, but how different was her position from that two years before! Mary did not trust her councillors, and was half afraid that they might desert her as they had deserted Northumberland. She feared the people. A barren, prematurely aged woman, she had no lien on the future, which belonged to Elizabeth by the irresistible right of popular expectation. The angry comments that arose when Kate Ashley and her fellows were arrested, warned the Queen that times had changed; and she was constrained to send a kindly, apologetic message to her sister, along with a costly ring. As in

Wyatt's time she wished to bring Elizabeth to Court, but on this occasion was compelled to accept the lame excuses with which the invitation was declined. Angry thoughts of sending her to the Tower might pass through her mind, but she was powerless. Officially, Elizabeth had to be regarded as the victim of irresponsible knaves who had taken her name in vain; a person 'of too much wisdom, honour, truth, and respect to duty and honesty' to be a party to conspiracy.

True, Elizabeth was submitted to a three months' wardship, but it was of an honourable and most pleasant nature. Sir Thomas Pope—the founder of Trinity College, Oxford—was sent as major-domo to Hatfield, and Elizabeth gladly accepted his congenial guardianship, for she was eased of responsibility by his presence. The advantage of this was made clear when in July a man appeared in Essex in the role of Courtenay, proclaiming 'the lady Elizabeth Queen, and her beloved bedfellow, Lord Courtenay, King'. Pope was instructed to pass on the news to Elizabeth as a homily, whereupon his charge, thinking the occasion too good to be missed, sat down to write a loyal letter to Mary in her most impressive style and most exquisite handwriting. 'When I revolve in mind, most noble Queen,' she began, 'the old love of Paynims to their Prince, and the reverent fear of the Romans to their Senate, I can but muse for my part, and blush for theirs, to see the rebellious hearts and devilish intents of Christians in name, but Jews in deed, toward their anointed King.' She ended the letter by wishing that there were as good surgeons for making anatomies of hearts as there were expert physicians for the body, since then 'the more such misty clouds obfuscate the clear light of my truth, the more my tried thoughts should glister, to the dimming of their hid malice'.

The misty clouds of Elizabeth's style reflected a more or less tranquil mind. There was no longer any doubt that with caution she could ride the storms caused by political and religious discontents. One pitfall still remained. That was marriage. And perhaps the death of Courtenay, which took place at Padua in September of this year, 1556, by removing the husband whom the popular voice had chosen for her, exposed her to greater risk. Philip, with a view to maintaining the English alliance after Mary's death, was impatiently desirous of marrying her to his ally, the Duke of Savoy, and was putting all the pressure he could upon his wife. Mary, however, was stubborn, for the marriage would involve recognizing her sister as the successor to her throne. Elizabeth, she told Philip's confessor, was neither her sister, nor the daughter of Henry VIII, but the child of an infamous woman who had greatly outraged her mother, Catherine of Aragon, and herself. But with Mary so intoxicated with love that, as the French ambassador expressed it, she would not stick at offending God or man to please Philip, the tussle between husband and wife could have only one end. In November she was apparently prepared to do as he wished, and Elizabeth was summoned to Court and pressed to marry the Duke of Savoy. She refused, and after a painful scene was sent back to Hatfield in disgrace. In her anger Mary once more nursed the impossible idea of getting Parliament to strike Elizabeth out of the succession. The danger was not yet over. The following April the French ambassador warned Elizabeth of a design to marry her and take her to Flanders. She told him that she would die rather than submit. But in fact, every month, as it made the future of the realm clearer and brought its steady growth of supporters, even including councillors, saw her more and more mistress of her fate.

Mary's years were running out. After nineteen months' absence Philip returned to England in March 1557. For Mary they had been months of agonizing grief and suspense. In November it had been remarked that 'Nothing is thought of, nothing expected, save this blessed return of the King'. And now, Philip remained with the Queen only three and a half months; long enough to embroil England in his war with France. It was what all the enemies of the marriage had foretold, what its supporters had tried to guard against—love's crowning folly. It brought the disaster of Calais to tinge Mary's tragedy with still deeper gloom. Nothing had prospered. English blood had been spilled;

spilled in a frenzy of religious and marital devotion that awakened little or no response in the feelings of the people, and achieved nothing but the certain overthrow of all that Mary held most dear. At the beginning of 1558, such was her longing for an heir to preserve her work, she thought herself pregnant. But it was an illusion again. She had to drink her cup of sorrows to the dregs. On November 6th, under pressure from her councillors, she was brought to recognize Elizabeth as her successor, coupling the recognition with a request that she would retain the Catholic religion. On November 17th, about seven in the morning, she died, and as though to close an unhappy chapter with overwhelming finality, Cardinal Pole died twelve hours later.

CHAPTER IV

THE THRONE

WHILE Mary lay dying at St. James's the nation had been quietly transferring its support to her sister at Hatfield. Before the end of October she was acknowledging offers of help; soon she had received the adherence of the whole nobility. Men flocked to her: 'There is not a heretic or traitor in the country,' a Spaniard wrote, 'who has not started as if from the grave to seek her with expressions of great pleasure'. The old order was passing, passing with that inexorable certainty with which death was coming to the Queen. Even among those whose fortunes were most intimately linked with it, there were many caught by the prevailing mood to let the dead bury the dead; and Mary's councillors received an envoy of Philip's as though he came with the bulls of a defunct pope.

This envoy was the Count de Feria. He was among Elizabeth's visitors in the busy days before Mary died. He was no stranger to England; in fact was about to marry one of the ladies of Mary's Court. Philip fully expected him to be *persona grata* with the new sovereign. But he was a typical grandee of Spain, devoid of humour, proud and patronizing. With another envoy, a more tactful man, Elizabeth had been gracious, acknowledging Philip's services in the past, and promising her goodwill in the future. Her tone changed when Feria started boasting that she owed her throne solely to his master. She was not inclined to be anyone's puppet, certainly not Philip's. It was not Philip, she retorted, nor yet the nobility who had placed her where she was; it was the people. 'She is much attached to the people,' Feria wrote, 'and is very confident that they are all on her side; which is indeed true.' He went from the interview full of forebodings, as well he might.

No gift of prophecy was needed to forecast the broad lines of Elizabeth's future policy. Her birth and training, her role during Mary's reign, the religious leanings both of her household and of the group of intimates now around her, left room for little doubt. All the same, she was moving with extreme caution, and did not lack advice. Sir Nicholas Throckmorton, the man who had been acquitted by a London jury after Wyatt's rebellion, was sending her elaborate suggestions as to her initial actions when the crown should be hers, the gist of which was to succeed happily by making a discreet beginning. Others were to add their memoranda during the next weeks; they too advocated caution.

The effective core of the new government was ready to hand in those brilliant sons of Cambridge with whom Elizabeth's education and life had been so intimately linked. In this she was fortunate, and most fortunate in one of them, Sir William Cecil, now with her, planning and managing everything. He was a man of thirty-eight, sprung from that middle class from which the Tudors drew their best servants. He had been personal secretary to Protector Somerset, and had managed not only to survive his fall but to obtain the office of Secretary in Northumberland's Government. It says still more for his prudence that he came through the perilous days of Lady Jane Grey's usurpation with no graver penalty than the loss of his office. Though a convinced Protestant, like the rest of his Cambridge friends, he had conformed under Mary. He was a person in whom intellect and not emotion ruled; and he sought intelligence even in marriage. His first wife was Cheke's sister, his second one of the brilliant daughters of Sir Anthony Cooke, whom Ascham named with Lady Jane Grey as the most learned women in England. His capacity for work, his care for detail, his grasp of difficulties, amounted to genius; and if ever there was a perfect minister, it was he. No step was more propitious at the opening of Elizabeth's reign than his appointment as Principal Secretary.

On November 20th, the first day of public business after the conventional paralysis of mourning had relaxed a little, Elizabeth had Cecil sworn as a member of her Council. 'This judgment I have of you,' she said to him, 'that you will not be corrupted with any manner of gift, and that you will be faithful to the State, and that without respect of my private will you will give me that counsel that you think best.' The same day she addressed what in effect was her first public utterance, to a group of Mary's councillors who had come to Hatfield. 'The law of nature,' she said, 'moves me to sorrow for my sister; the burthen that is fallen upon me maketh me amazed; and yet, considering that I am God's creature ordained to obey His appointment, I will yield thereto, desiring from the bottom of my heart that I may have assistance of His grace to be the minister of His heavenly will in this office now committed to me.'

In the listeners' minds one question was uppermost: the composition of the new Council. It was a delicate and important problem. Elizabeth desired to be neither weak nor rash; not to have an unwieldy Council, nor one whose complexion was old-fashioned, nor yet to alienate those who must find themselves in retirement. She begged any whose services she might forego not to think that her decision proceeded from any disability in them, but rather from her conviction that a multitude made discord and confusion, instead of good counsel. Who the unfortunates were to be she did not reveal. She made her first appointments to office and the Council that day, including her faithful and now corpulent Cofferer, Thomas Parry, whom she knighted and made Controller of the Household. But the appointments for the moment were few. It was prudent to let hopes linger as long as possible.

The same circumspection was shown in regard to religion. In the first public document of the reign an '&c.' was put at the end of the Queen's titles, where in her father's and brother's reigns the title of Supreme Head of the Church had been. It was both a bold and a cautious step;

bold, because implicitly it maintained the theory of the English Reformation that the supremacy of the Papacy was a usurpation of the Crown's ancient authority, and that no parliamentary statute was needed to confer the headship of the Church on the monarch; cautious, because, after all, no more appeared than the words 'et cetera', which left the Catholic world guessing and hoping about the future—hopes which Elizabeth in her talks with Feria did her brilliant but shameless best to sustain. Her hand would be shown in time, perhaps before some of the more cautious of her advisers believed it possible; but for the moment what mattered most was to prevent Catholic bishops and clergy from attempting to stir up trouble before the country became accustomed to her authority.

At the same time it was necessary to paralyse hostility at Rome. The Pope, Paul IV, was an irascible old man, from whom the last quality to be expected was moderation; and he had at hand a possible Catholic candidate for the English throne in the person of Mary Queen of Scots, the great granddaughter of Henry VII. If the succession to the throne had gone by mere heredity, then strictly speaking Mary was the nearest heir, for not only was Elizabeth illegitimate by Catholic Canon Law, but, until Parliament could meet, she was also illegitimate by English law. The danger was no airy, merely speculative one. Mary's father-in-law, the King of France, might quite well induce the Pope to declare against Elizabeth in favour of Mary, or even depose her and commit the fulfilment of his sentence to French arms. Provided, however, that Elizabeth made no open move against Catholicism, then she could count on Philip II exerting his powerful influence in her favour at Rome. Good Catholic though he was, the last thing that Philip could tolerate was a French conquest of England.

These were the considerations governing Elizabeth's policy, and she pursued her way with consummate skill. She beguiled the Pope by retaining the former English ambassador at Rome as her agent, promising to send a proper embassy in the not-distant future. At home she kept Mass going in her private Chapel, and in the opening proclamation of her reign forbade any religious alteration or change. She was playing for time—time to establish her throne on popular support. On November 23rd she set out from Hatfield to London, her purpose to court the people, to whom, as she well knew 'no music is so sweet as the affability of their Prince'.

Accompanied by a thousand or more lords, gentry, and ladies, Elizabeth came to the Charterhouse, where she remained for five days. On the twenty-eighth, clad in purple velvet and with a scarf about her neck, she rode in public procession through the crowded streets to the Tower. At certain places on the route children welcomed her with speeches, at others there was singing and playing with regals, and 'such shooting of guns as never was heard afore'. On December 5th she proceeded from the Tower by water to Somerset House, 'with trumpets playing, and melody and joy and comfort to all true English men and women'. There she stayed until December 23rd when she moved to Whitehall for Christmas.

In these few weeks Elizabeth captured the devotion of the City. 'If ever any person,' wrote an annalist, 'had either the gift or the style to win the hearts of people, it was this Queen, and if ever she did express the same it was at that present, in coupling mildness with majesty as she did, and in stately stooping to the meanest sort. All her faculties were in motion, and every motion seemed a well-guided action: her eye was set upon one, her ear listened to another, her judgment ran upon a third, to a fourth she addressed her speech; her spirit seemed to be everywhere, and yet so entire in herself as it seemed to be nowhere else. Some she pitied, some she commended, some she thanked, at others she pleasantly and wittily jested, contemning no person, neglecting no office, and distributing her smiles, looks, and graces so artificially that thereupon the people again redoubled the testimony of their joys, and afterwards, raising everything to the highest strain, filled the ears of all men with immoderate extolling their Prince.' That she could be delightfully unconventional was not the least of her charms. On one of these processional occasions, spying at a window the Marquis of Northampton, Catherine Parr's brother, who was ill of a quartan ague, she stopped her palfrey and was for a long while asking him about his health in the most cordial way in the world. The only true reason for this, so the querulous Feria told Philip, was that he had been a great traitor to her sister.

As Elizabeth felt her hold on the throne becoming firmer each week so she let her religious policy gradually unfold itself. Her eye was on the leaders of the Catholic Church, the bishops especially. White, Bishop of Winchester, speaking the funeral oration over Mary's corpse on December 14th, called on all bishops and ministers, and lay magistrates too, to resist the wolf of heresy if they saw it entering the fold. Trajan, he reminded them, had charged his chief officer to use the sword of justice in his favour if he ruled justly, but against him if he ruled unjustly. A whole bench of such bishops would have been a formidable obstacle to the new order. Fortune, however, had done its best for Elizabeth. Five bishoprics had been vacant at the time of Mary's death. Pole's death added a sixth, and before the year was out four more died. They were so many potential leaders of resistance the less. 'That accursed Cardinal,' complained Feria, 'left twelve bishoprics to be filled, which will now be given to as many ministers of Lucifer.' His figure was wrong, his prophecy correct.

The 'ministers of Lucifer', in the persons of the Marian exiles, were hastening to England as fast as they could free themselves from their continental ties. 'The wolves,' Bishop White exclaimed, 'be coming out of Geneva and other places of Germany, and hath sent their books before, full of pestilent doctrines, blasphemy, and heresy, to infect the people.' The first of the eminent divines, who were to be in the van of the new Protestant advance, arrived in England before the close of the year. The news of Mary's death and Elizabeth's accession had moved them and their continental hosts to rapture and exultation: 'The Lord has caused a new star to arise'; 'Now is the time for the walls of Jerusalem to be built again in that kingdom, that the blood of so many martyrs, so largely shed, may not be in vain.' Peter Martyr and Bullinger were among the famous Reformers who wrote to salute the new Queen, and as she read their letters she wept. The remnants of the Marian persecution, still in prison, were gradually released, and heretic congregations in London emerged into the open. On January 9th, 1559, an image of St. Thomas which had had its neck broken twice in a single month in 1555, was once more beheaded and cast into the street. The religious complexion of London was beyond doubt, and early in January the City fathers were planning wonderful pageants for the Coronation, as outspoken as they well could make them.

But Elizabeth was for making haste slowly. She gave the world a sign on Christmas Day when she ordered the bishop who was to celebrate Mass in her chapel not to elevate the host. When he refused, she walked out from the service immediately after the Gospel was finished. Two days later she issued a proclamation which permitted certain parts of the service to be in English, but forbade all preaching and teaching. The prohibition seemed to be aimed at restraining Protestant hot-heads, but it equally achieved the purpose of silencing Catholic preachers and crippling their power for making mischief. She was moving slowly towards the day—January 25th—when she was to go to the opening of another Reformation Parliament, dramatically bidding the abbot and monks of Westminster, as they met her in broad daylight with tapers burning, 'Away with those torches! we can see well enough.'

Before that day arrived Elizabeth had brought her wooing of the people to its climax in the Coronation procession through London; and the character, as well as the dazzling success, of that occasion must have encouraged her in the plan of overthrowing the Catholic Church at once.

The actual ceremony of the Coronation took place on Sunday, January 15th, 1559. The previous Thursday Elizabeth moved from Whitehall to the Tower, making the journey by water; a spectacle which an Italian observer likened

to Ascension Day at Venice, when the Signory go out to
wed the sea. On Saturday came the great Coronation procession, the City's day of days. In the morning the whole
Court gathered at the Tower, and although it snowed a
little, their sparkling jewels and gold collars seemed to clear
the air. In the afternoon the procession, which numbered
a thousand people on horseback, set out on its slow progress
through the streets to Westminster. Dressed in a royal robe
of rich cloth of gold and wearing the crown of a princess,
as yet without the emblems of sovereignty, the Queen was
carried in an open litter, trimmed to the ground with gold
brocade, and borne by two fine mules, covered with the
same material. On either side of her walked the gentlemen
pensioners in crimson damask, bearing their gilt battle-axes,
while all round was a multitude of footmen in crimson velvet jerkins studded with massive gilt silver and ornamented
back and front with a white and red rose and the letters
E. R. As a contemporary remarked, 'In pompous ceremonies a secret of government doth much consist.'

From Fenchurch Street to Cheapside the streets were
lined with wooden rails draped in cloth and hung with
tapestries, velvet, damask, satin and silks, behind which
stood the members of the City Companies in their livery
and costly furs. Rich banners and streamers waved from
windows, and everywhere people crowded, some of whom,
their patience inexhaustible, had been waiting for hours in
their places. Well were they rewarded; and not by a spectacle only, but by a hundred little touches that stirred their
loyalty and set them talking afterwards in tavern and home,
reconstructing the day's epic and inflaming their hearers
with their own affection. At one place an old man turned
his back and wept. 'I warrant you it is for gladness', exclaimed Elizabeth; and so in very deed it was. Another
time she was seen to smile, and being asked the reason,
answered that she had heard someone say, 'Remember old
King Henry VIII'. Many a simple body moved forward to
speak to her, for whom she stayed her litter. She accepted
untold nosegays at poor women's hands, and it was noticed
that a branch of rosemary, given with a supplication by a

poor woman near Fleet Bridge, was in her litter when she reached Westminster.

At intervals in the journey the City authorities had prepared pageants, each equipped with its 'noises of loud instruments', making a heavenly melody, and each with its Latin expository verses and a platform from which a boy delivered a doggerel translation. They expressed London's religious inclinations and the faith in the new Queen. The first show was at Gracechurch; a stage of three tiers, displaying Unity and Concord. In the lowest were Henry VII and his Queen; in the next—happy sight after twenty-two years!—Henry VIII and Anne Boleyn; in the highest, Elizabeth. The second was placed in Cornhill by the conduit. A child representing Elizabeth sat on the seat of worthy governance, the seat being supported by four persons representing virtues treading their contrary vices under foot. Pure religion was one of the virtues: it trod upon superstition and ignorance. Very gay was Cheapside, with a 'noise of trumpets' at one place, the noise of the waits further on, and its Cross fair and well trimmed. Here the City Recorder presented the Queen with a thousand marks in gold, in a richly wrought purse of crimson satin. 'I thank my Lord Mayor, his brethren, and you all', said Elizabeth in acknowledgement. 'And whereas your request is that I should continue your good Lady and Queen, be ye assured that I will be as good unto you as ever queen was to her people. No will in me can lack, neither do I trust that there lack any power. And persuade yourselves that for the safety and quietness of you all, I will not spare, if need be, to spend my blood. God thank you all'. 'If it moved a marvellous shout and rejoicing', says the narrator, 'it is nothing to be marvelled at, since both the heartiness thereof was so wonderful and the words so jointly knit.'

The fourth pageant was now reached at the Little Conduit, its centrepiece Time. 'Time!' exclaimed Elizabeth; 'and Time hath brought me hither.' It was set in the form of two hills. One was green and fruitful, and on its summit was a handsome youth, gay in dress and spirits, standing under a green laurel tree: this represented a flourishing commonwealth. The other was all withered and dead, and a youth in rude apparel sat mournfully under an arid tree: this was the decayed commonwealth. Between was a cave from which Time emerged, leading his daughter Truth who carried an English Bible in her hand. A child told the meaning:

This old man with the scythe, Old Father Time they call,
And her his daughter Truth which holdeth yonder book,
Whom he out of his rock hath brought forth to us all,
From whence these many years she durst not once out look.

The Bible it was, continued the expounder, that taught the way to bring a commonwealth from a decayed to a flourishing state; to bring it—who could doubt the implication? —from what it had been in the reign just ended. Truth presented her book to the Queen, who received and kissed it and with both hands held it up and then laid it on her breast, giving great thanks to the City for it.

At St. Paul's one of the boys of Colet's School spoke a Latin oration, commending Elizabeth's virtues and her knowledge in a pleasing comparison with Plato's eulogy of the philosopher-king. Then, passing through Ludgate where the gate was bedizened and music saluted her, she came to Fleet Street and to the fifth and last pageant. This was a delicate tribute to her sex and her task. It showed Deborah, 'the judge and restorer of the House of Israel', sitting enthroned in parliament robes, consulting with her three estates for the good government of Israel! Temple Bar was 'dressed finely with the two images of Gogmagog the Albion, and Corineus the Briton, two giants big in stature, furnished accordingly'. Here it was that the City took leave of its Queen, with one set of verses summing up the lessons of the pageants, and another, spoken by a child richly attired as a poet, bidding her farewell:

Farewell, O worthy Queen! and as our hope is sure
That into error's place thou wilt now truth restore,
So trust we that thou wilt our Sovereign Queen endure,
And loving Lady stand, from henceforth evermore.

'Be ye well assured I will stand your good Queen', exclaimed Elizabeth. Ten days later there was a pamphlet on sale commemorating these events. 'Thus', it boasts, 'the Queen's Highness passed through the City, which without any foreign person, of itself beautified itself'.

The following day Elizabeth was crowned at Westminster Abbey with all the elaborate and symbolic ceremonies. As she was presented to the people for their acceptance, such was the shout and the noise of organs, fifes, trumpets, drums, and bells, that it seemed, said an observer, as though the world had come to an end. The procession afterwards returned to Westminster Hall for the usual lengthy and stately feast, Elizabeth being now in full regalia, carrying sceptre and orb, and very cheerful, with a most smiling countenance for everyone, giving them all a thousand greetings. 'In my opinion,' said a Mantuan envoy, disapproving, like the proud Feria, of the informalities with which Elizabeth loved to temper pomp and ceremony, 'she exceeded the bounds of gravity and decorum.'

Majesty had spoken with the captivating modulations of a woman's voice, and employed an attractive young woman's every art. But it was one thing to charm, quite another to rule. And in this, sex was an almost desperate impediment. The country had already made its first experiment of a woman ruler; it was anything but a happy augury for the second. 'I am assured' wrote John Knox in his notorious *First Blast of the Trumpet against the Monstrous Regiment of Women,* 'that God hath revealed to some in this our age that it is more than a monster in nature that a woman should reign and bear empire above man.' Women, he declared, were painted forth by nature to be weak, frail, impatient, feeble, and foolish; they were the port and gate of the Devil; their covetousness, like the gulf of Hell, was insatiable. For the weak to nourish the strong, the foolish to govern the discreet, in brief, for women to rule men, was contumely to God and the subversion of good order and justice. The Bible, the Fathers, Aristotle, the Classical world, were at one on the subject; and men, Knox thought,

were less than the beasts to permit such an inversion of
God's order.

Knox had meant 'thrice to blow the trumpet in the same
matter if God so permit'; but He did not permit, for Elizabeth came to the throne a few months after the first blast.
Naturally, most of Knox's fellow-Protestants, disconcerted
by such a *contretemps*, disapproved of his book. Yet it was
not from any fundamental difference in their view of
women. John Aylmer, who published a courtly answer to
Knox in 1559, expressed his feelings rather tamely by saying that 'the Blast was blown out of season'. Calvin's
apology, which he made in a letter to Cecil, was also odd.
'Two years ago,' he wrote, 'John Knox asked of me in a
private conversation, what I thought about the government
of women. I candidly replied that, as it was a deviation
from the original and proper order of nature, it was to be
ranked no less than slavery among the punishments conse-
quent upon the fall of man.' Yet, 'there were occasionally
women so endowed that the singular good qualities which
shone forth in them, made it evident that they were raised
up by divine authority; either that God designed by such
examples to condemn the inactivity of men, or for the better
setting forth of His own glory'.

The Protestant fraternity, Knox included, were only too
ready, now that a Deborah was on the English throne, to
cease blowing this trumpet; and as the Catholics, if they
were to favour an alternative ruler, must likewise look to a
woman. Elizabeth was not likely to be disturbed by theo-
ries about the legitimacy of feminine rule. Her problem was
not the theory, but the mentality behind it and the practical difficulties that faced a Queen.

Government was a masculine business, with its world a
Court constructed for a King, the complexion of which
could not be appreciably altered. It was possible to reduce
the number of gentlemen ushers, and dispense with some
grooms, replacing them with a feminine element—a score or
so of ladies, including the maids of honour, girls of good
birth finishing their education at Court; but the royal
household still remained a great masculine community of

about fifteen hundred persons, ranging from high and noble officials down to kitchen menials. To a large extent, it was a resident community. The chief officials lodged at Court, while the lesser at least fed there, dining at one or other of the great functionaries' tables. Whether in gentle, or noble, or royal household, the profession of service in sixteenth century society played much the same part as the services *par excellence*, the navy and army, have played in modern society; and the royal household offered to men of birth the finest splendour, the finest society, the finest career, and unrivalled patronage. Anyone aspiring to become a professional courtier had to find a place on its establishment, the result being that offices which had once been menial had become honourable, and their holders crowded the Court with retinues of personal servants.

The Sovereign—the sun round which this world revolved—was the source of the Court's well-being, and had to live a life balanced between the privacy of the Withdrawing Chambers, the semi-publicity of the Privy Chamber, access to which was strictly limited, and the greater publicity of the Presence Chamber, where access was easy. For a woman, and a young unmarried woman at that, it created a serious problem of conduct; a problem virtually without precedent. She had to win and retain the loyalty and devotion of her Court, on which the success or failure of her reign depended. She had also to maintain its splendour and high spirits in order to attract men to it, for a Sovereign without a 'Presence' to dazzle and impress visitors was but a beggarly, down-at-heel ruler. Again, the internal peace of the country turned on keeping the nobility, like butterflies chasing round a candle, spending their wealth on the relatively harmless but prodigal ways of Court life.

Courtiers themselves proffered the solution of the problem, for the adulation which they would have given to a king, quite naturally became tinged with the admiration, flattery, and coquetry which they used towards an attractive young woman. Thus, by a paradox, sex, having created a problem, itself solved it, and the reign was turned into an idyll, a fine but artificial comedy of young men—

and old men—in love. Being without precedent, it was a little shocking to the unimaginative—it still is; but it secured service, which it was a monarch's function to do, and charged service with emotion, which it was Elizabeth's desire to do. Her genius rose to the game. Her royal sense, her intellectual temperament, her quick mind and gift of repartee, kept it artificial enough for safety; her humanity saved it from fatuity.

Discipline was another problem. It was a factious age, and the quarrels that set family against family in the county were often reflected at Court. But the Court created its own rivalries in the struggle for royal favour, office, place, and patronage. High and low, statesmen and clerks, courtiers and outsiders, were involved. It was a Monte Carlo where men experienced the elations and depressions of Fortune's suitors:

> Full little knowest thou that hast not tried
> What Hell it is in suing long to bide;
> To lose good days that might be better spent;
> To waste long nights in pensive discontent;
> To speed to-day, to be put back to-morrow;
> To feed on hope, to pine with fear and sorrow;
> To have thy Prince's grace, yet want her Peer's;
> To have thy asking, yet wait many years;
> To fret thy soul with crosses and with cares;
> To eat thy heart through comfortless despairs;
> To fawn, to crouch, to wait, to ride, to run,
> To spend, to give, to want, to be undone.

There was a perpetual clash of interests and ambitions, and if one were satisfied, several might be offended. Faction was rarely or never absent, and quarrels might be so serious as to threaten the peace of the country. Altogether, it was a feverish community. Officials' salaries were low, having remained stationary for decades or even centuries, and were supplemented by fees, perquisites, gifts, hopes and debts. Power in unscrupulous hands could bring incalculable profits. A correspondent, attempting to estimate for a friend the value of the great offices of state—all with fixed salaries—

made a triple calculation for each, according as the holder hoped for Heaven, would be content with Purgatory, or cared nothing for his soul. Under the last category his remark in one instance was, 'No man can tell!'

For a woman to stop corruption from passing all bounds of decency, or prevent her proud, child-like nobility from turning the Court into a bear-garden, was exceedingly difficult. In any case she could not inspire the fear of a king; nor would crude fear have been compatible with Elizabeth's love-tricks, or her womanly compassion. She was dependent on her remarkable qualities of character and intelligence. She had always been wilful; she knew how to be imperious. She had need to be both.

However they disguised their belief, statesmen held government to be a mystery revealed only to men. They had less faith in Deborah than John Knox, and were more dangerous for being more reasonable. Even after two years in Elizabeth's service, Cecil reprimanded an ambassador's messenger for discussing a particular subject with the Queen; 'a matter', he said, 'of such weight, being too much for a woman's knowledge'. Confronted by this mentality, circumspection, as well as an indomitable will, was needed to prevent the monarchy from being put into commission. If Elizabeth had adopted the practice of referring her problems regularly to the Council, in formal sittings, she would have found it hard to resist the withering assumption of masculine superiority; while, if she had rejected their corporate advice, as she was constitutionally entitled to do, she would simply have centred responsibility for any misfortune on herself. And a woman's blunders are twice cursed; as blunders, and as a woman's.

Elizabeth had no intention of surrendering her powers, or acquiescing in men's views of women. She had a great longing, she said, 'to do some act that would make her fame spread abroad in her lifetime, and, after, occasion memorial for ever'. 'She seems to me', wrote Feria, 'incomparably more feared than her sister, and gives her orders and has her way as absolutely as her father did.' She kept matters of state very largely in her own hands, and generally consulted her councillors individually, on the principle of 'divide and rule'. Here the happy accident of being a Renaissance woman stood her in good stead. Had she not been a fine linguist, she would have been compelled to refer an extensive branch of statecraft—diplomatic relations—to her Council, for no foreign ambassador spoke English. It was not a language of diplomacy. Latin, Italian, French, Spanish, German; the manuals of the age included these as languages that the perfect ambassador should know, and one Italian writer included Turkish: none thought of English. Elizabeth could carry on conversations with perfect ease in Latin, French, and Italian. It pleased her vanity to do so. She was a good talker, and could beat the subtlest diplomat at his game of deception—perhaps because she was a woman. She had real genius for this work, and no sovereign of her day maintained so close a monopoly of it.

No one, however, at this time was giving serious thought to the phenomenon of 'the modern woman' as a ruler, for the simple reason that everyone expected Elizabeth to marry. Had not Mary, though thirty-eight, instantly acquiesced in its inevitability on coming to the throne? As Philip wrote, Elizabeth must marry, if only that her husband might 'relieve her of those labours which are only fit for men'. Feria echoed his thought: 'After all, everything depends on the husband she chooses, for the King's wish is paramount here in all things.' The woman-ruler's way lay through political impotence to marriage—itself a state of impotence.

CHAPTER V

THE MARRIAGE PROBLEM

ELIZABETH was far and away the best marriage to be had in Europe, a fact of which every eligible bachelor and widower was aware. Philip II realized it, and among the duties which brought Feria to England on the eve of Elizabeth's accession, was the management of this market. Philip had not yet made up his mind whether he wanted to marry her himself, but Feria was to see that whoever obtained the titbit received it at his master's hands. The ambassador imagined himself playing much the same role as Simon Renard at the accession of Mary; and there was good reason for his expectations. In her sister's reign, as my Lady Elizabeth, the focus of discontent, Elizabeth had naturally been friendly with France, but times had changed, and unless she was to repeat Mary's blunder, she would have to live in the present, not the past. The present meant hostility to France, where a rival claimant to the English throne was the Dauphin's wife. It meant also friendship with Spain; nay, possibly dependence on Spain, for England was in a dangerous state. Its finances were in disorder, its fortresses defenceless, its military forces negligible, while to emerge honourably from the peace negotiations, closing Mary's unfortunate war with France, it must have Philip's support.

No wonder Feria was patronizing! He was surprised that Elizabeth did not see the situation as clearly as he did; but then, he remarked, 'what can be expected from a country governed by a Queen, and she a young lass who, although sharp, is without prudence?' He was exasperated at the cool

manner in which he was treated. Instead of being given a
room at Court and taken into counsel on every question,
as he expected, he found himself in embarrassing ignorance
of what was going on. 'They run away from me as if I were
the devil,' he wrote; and their glib, irresponsible talk nearly
drove him crazy. At first there was an arrogant confidence
in his reports. On November 21st he thought that his master had merely to ask for Elizabeth in order to have her:
'If she decides to marry out of the country she will at once
fix her eyes on your Majesty.' A month later his assurance
had evaporated: 'I am afraid that one fine day we shall find
this woman married, and I shall be the last man in the place
to know anything about it.'

The warning made Philip apply the spur to his slow-
moving mind. On January 10th he wrote to Feria that his
doubts on the subject of marriage with Elizabeth were
many: he could not be much in England owing to the
claims of his other dominions; then Elizabeth had been un-
sound in religion, and marrying her would seem like entering upon a perpetual war with France, owing to Mary
Queen of Scots' claim to the throne; again, he would find
himself involved in costly entertainments in England, which
his treasury was not in a state to afford; there were other
difficulties, equally grave. However, it was important that
England should not relapse into its old religious errors, and
for this reason he was prepared to put aside all doubts and
marry her, as a service to God. But it could only be on
conditions: she must profess his religion and maintain it in
her country; she must obtain secret absolution from the
Pope. In this way it would be evident to the world that he
was serving the Lord in marrying her and that she had been
converted by his act.

Pathetic illusion! It would be hard to imagine rumina-
tions more remote from reality. If Englishmen in 1553 had
loathed the prospect of a Spanish marriage, how much
more did the tragic experience of Mary's reign make them
loathe it now? The mere suspicion that Elizabeth was hesitating, brought a torrent of dissuasions from her councillors.
They were needless. The lessons of yesterday were as clear

in her mind as in anyone's. Did she not boast that she was 'descended by father and mother of mere English blood, and not of Spain, as her late sister was'? But it was inexpedient to refuse Philip's offer at once, for the peace negotiations with France were still proceeding, and she was in an appreciably stronger position to bargain, with Philip as her suitor; moreover, Parliament was about to meet in order to reverse the religious settlement of Mary's reign, and there was a double service that Philip could perform. He could keep the Pope quiet, and avoid giving the English Catholic opposition a lead.

Feria was therefore well received when he broached the subject. She must consult her Parliament, Elizabeth said, but Philip could be certain that if she married at all she would prefer him. The lie earned a month's breathing space, at the end of which she again managed to evade an answer. Early in March, unable to prevaricate longer, she announced that she had no desire to marry. The advantages of the marriage to both sovereigns, she urged, could be attained by a continuance of their good friendship. With malicious humour, she asked Feria how she could possibly marry her sister's husband without dishonouring the memory of her father, he having repudiated his brother's wife. Some of her remarks looked so much like an echo of Philip's complacent letter of January 10th that the ambassador was left wondering whether his correspondence was tapped, and he was even more uneasy when at his next interview she turned the tables on Philip by declaring that she would not marry him as she was a heretic. That ended the wooing. Philip married the French king's daughter—a diplomatic setback for Elizabeth, but unavoidable. She accepted the news with an easy air, now and again giving little sighs that bordered on laughter. Philip, she remarked, had a fortunate name. Feria tried to impress upon her a proper sense of her blunder; she retorted that it was all Philip's fault, for she had given no answer, and he could not have been much in love, since he had not had the patience to wait four months for her.

As a matter of fact, Elizabeth was far from blind to her

interests, as Feria thought. She knew as well as he that she needed Philip's support, but she knew also that Philip was not a free agent, and that as the rival of France and the ruler of the Netherlands, commercially dependent upon England, he could not afford to desert her. She might exploit Philip just as much as he exploit her, and which should be the victim depended on their temper, wit, and acumen. Philip told his ambassador to frighten Elizabeth and make her thoroughly understand that she was ruined unless he succoured and defended her; but this done, she was to be assured that he would never fail to help her, both on account of his great love and affection, which his marriage alliance with France would not weaken, and also for his own interests, which would be greatly injured if—as God forbid!—her kingdom were to fall into other hands. Could naïveté go farther? Neither master nor servant was a match for the young woman at the diplomatic game of bluff. 'I try all I can to keep her pleasant and in good humour,' Feria wrote, 'and although sometimes I speak to her very freely, as I ought to do, having right and truth on my side, yet I think that for this very reason she does not get tired of me, but likes to discuss matters with me.' Like to discuss matters with him! there is no doubt that she did. She poured out nonsense and wit, shifted her ground and her sentiments, until, sometimes convinced of his great influence, at other times he was bewildered and angry. 'In short,' he wrote on one of the latter occasions, 'what can be said here to your Majesty is only that this country, after thirty years of a government such as your Majesty knows, has fallen into the hands of a woman who is a daughter of the Devil, and the greatest scoundrels and heretics in the land.'

Philip was only one, the most transient and so the most fortunate, of Elizabeth's suitors. The King of Sweden's ambassador was in England offering his master's eldest son, Eric, as he had done a year before, and bestowing lavish presents on the ladies and gentlemen of the Court, who took his gifts but laughed at his outlandish ways. The Emperor, also, was bidding on behalf of his two younger sons, the

Archdukes Ferdinand and Charles; and with Philip out of the market, the Imperial and Spanish ambassadors joined forces to bring off yet another fortunate marriage for the House of Hapsburg. Feria was confident of success; confident, if only the Emperor and his sons would understand, which apparently they would not, that the marriage was virtually in Philip's gift! At first, both sons were mentioned, but Ferdinand the elder was soon withdrawn, for his Catholicism was unassailable and his father had learnt that Elizabeth was not sound in religion. It was distressing enough to offer Charles, whose youthful judgment was less firmly based; and the Emperor confessed to his ambassador that without weighty political reasons he would not have thought of subjecting his son to the danger of forfeiting the eternal salvation of his soul.

At home, among Englishmen, two names were being canvassed, the Earl of Arundel and Sir William Pickering. Arundel had nothing but rank and family to commend him. He was about forty-seven, not handsome, and rather silly and loutish; he had been married twice and had two married daughters. They were disabilities, which in that age of mercenary marriage customs and moving love lyrics would have mattered little if the disparity of rank had been reversed. Pickering was about forty-two, tall, handsome, very much a ladies' man, and said to have enjoyed the intimacy of many. These qualities, not rank or fortune, gave him hope; and perhaps there was an old friendly attachment between the Queen and him. Londoners rather favoured his chances and took bets on them, while he himself, courted by councillors and others with their eyes on the future, lost his head and plunged into an extravagant life, giving himself airs by dining apart, with music playing. One day the talk went that he was sending a challenge to the Earl of Bedford for speaking ill of him. Six or seven weeks later he was quarrelling with Arundel who had stopped him as he went through to the Chapel inside the Queen's apartments, saying that he knew quite well that a man of his rank had no right to be there; his place was in the Presence Chamber. Pickering answered that of course he knew, as he also knew that Arundel was an impudent, discourteous knave.

Suitors, statesmen, everyone, talked of marriage. They assumed, as a matter of course, that Elizabeth would marry. All women did, who could; and the political reasons in Elizabeth's case seemed overwhelming. When Parliament met at the end of January, 1559, the House of Commons urged this step on her. She answered that since reaching years of understanding she had chosen the virgin life, and if ambition, or danger, or the peril of death could have led her into marriage, she would not now be in that trade of life with which she was so thoroughly acquainted and in which God had preserved her. They could assure themselves, she went on, that whenever it might please God to incline her heart to marry, her choice would light upon one who would be as careful for the preservation of the realm as she herself; or if it pleased Him to continue her still in this mind to live unmarried, provision would be made for the succession to the throne. 'And in the end,' she concluded, 'this shall be for me sufficient, that a marble stone shall declare that a Queen, having reigned such a time, lived and died a virgin.'

Being men of the world, the Commons did not think that there was anything alarming in this prating about virginity. Let political considerations or passion single out some man, and another protesting spinster would go the way of most flesh. Her virgin state, which Elizabeth ascribed to a godly vocation, might with more conviction be ascribed to politics, for she had been forced to eschew marriage in the past to avoid being a pawn for either Northumberland or Philip. Experience, no doubt, had left its effect. The Seymour affair, at the age of fifteen, had been her first cautionary tale: and as her many perils had grafted a wary mind upon an impulsive nature, so in regard to marriage she found herself thinking twice, and thinking yet again. Among the legion of her remarks on the subject, some false, some true, and some betwixt and between—and which were which no one really knew—she said that marriage was a matter of earnest with her and that she could not marry as others did. On the other hand, she confessed that 'she was but human and not insensible to human emotions and impulses, and when it became a question of the weal of her kingdom, or it might be for other reasons, her heart and mind might change'.

The weal of the kingdom or *other reasons*: the latter had to wait on fancy and the emotions, the former did not. In abstract the public good required marriage, but in practice everything depended upon the person, and principally whether he was to be a subject or a foreigner. Naturally, Elizabeth had the lessons of Mary's reign in mind when she faced the problem. The country had then wanted Courtenay for king, a person, thanks to his Yorkist descent, whom Mary could have married without serious risk of arousing the jealousy of her nobles. By the irony of fate England had then had a Queen out of tune with her people, while now that the situation was reversed, there was no Courtenay. Perhaps the fevers of Padua, which took his life, were to give England a virgin Queen. At any rate, there seemed to be some risk of this, for what Englishman was there to replace Courtenay? Pickering, whom, for lack of a better, many would have liked, was at daggers drawn with some of the nobility; and there was no other whom Elizabeth could have married without a fair certainty of setting her nobility by the ears. Celibacy might be the better of the two evils.

A foreigner offered no better prospect. Elizabeth was prejudiced by the knowledge that Mary's major blunder had been her marriage, and by the feeling that a foreign match would be unpopular. Her doubts might have disappeared if Court and Council had given a unanimous lead; but some were for one candidate, some for another. The result was that she kept on hesitating, ever ready to dilate on the attractions of a maiden life, baffling everyone with her art and wit and coquetry. She had never purposed never to marry, she told them; but they must believe her when she said that she had never had a mind to marry.

Ambassadors kept up their siege. In October, 1559, there were ten or twelve competing for Elizabeth's favour and eyeing one another in far from friendly manner. Cecil was just as perplexed as they were: 'How he shall speed,' he said of one envoy, 'God knoweth and not I.' Feria's successor, Bishop Quadra, rang every change of mood: one day he did not understand her; another day he was confident that the Archduke would get her; another day he qualified his hopes; and then he was in despair and angry. 'Your Lordship,' he told Feria, 'will see what a pretty business it is to have to treat with this woman, who I think must have a hundred thousand devils in her body, notwithstanding that she is for ever telling me that she yearns to be a nun and to pass her time in a cell praying.' In another blue mood, he lost all hope in the affairs of this woman. 'With her all is falsehood and vanity.'

Elizabeth was not entirely to blame for all protracted wooings. She was a great prize, and hope is tenacious. It was incredibly tenacious in Eric of Sweden. After being formally turned down in May, 1559, he announced in July that as soon as she gave the word he would hasten to her through seas, dangers, and enemies, confident that she would not chide his faith and zeal. A second, a third, a fourth rejection—and more; he nevertheless remained buoyant. His brother was in England from the autumn of 1559 till the following spring, a munificent, but unsuccessful envoy. The following August he set out himself, and though turned back by the winds, started again, only desisting in the face of a storm that scattered and damaged his fleet. Fortune, he wrote to Elizabeth, had been harder than steel and more cruel than Mars; but as he had attempted to come to her through the stormy seas, so would he at her first summons rush through armies of foes.

Even Elizabeth found courtship wearing at times. But it had compensations, for during the year 1559, when the weak, poverty-stricken England of Feria's imagination was pursuing a policy that annoyed the Papacy, troubled Philip, and threatened to lead to hostilities with France, it was no little advantage to have a number of princely suitors. Their hopes became a safeguard for her throne, and since of all the suitors, the Archduke Charles was politically the best match, she took care to retain him as a kind of insurance. Whenever the Imperial ambassador's hopes ran low, she set herself to revive them. One evening in June, having met him rowing on the Thames, she offered him a seat in the Treasurer's boat, laid her own alongside, talked at great length, and played for him on the lute. She invited him to Court the next day, then to breakfast the following morning, and in the evening had him on the river in her boat, made him take the helm, and was altogether very talkative and merry.

There were two obstacles to marriage with Charles. Religion was the first. Although Elizabeth herself might be tolerant enough to allow the Archduke and his suite to hold the Catholic form of worship at her Court, 'One king, one faith' was the essence of political stability, and she could risk neither the anger of her Protestant subjects at the spectacle of the Mass, nor the danger of taking a husband who might become the focus of Catholic discontent. The second obstacle was personal. Time and again Elizabeth declared that she would marry no one whom she had not seen. She knew very well, she said, how Philip had cursed the painters and envoys when he first beheld Queen Mary, and, as she politely put it, she would not give the Archduke Charles cause to curse. The Imperial and Spanish ambassadors were eager to bring Charles to England *incognito*, but the Emperor would not hear of it. It was undignified; it was not the way princes wooed; it would make a laughing stock of them in case of failure; and Elizabeth's whims were notorious. She would not sacrifice a fraction of her freedom of decision to induce him to come. Equally, she would not marry him without seeing him. And this repugnance towards the unknown was becoming deeper because her fancy had been caught by one of her courtiers, Lord Robert Dudley. Until the problem of Dudley was settled, *other reasons* looked like being in the ascendant, and the *weal of the kingdom* in eclipse.

Dudley was a name of ill omen. Lord Robert's father was the Duke of Northumberland, his grandfather the notorious Edmund Dudley of Henry VII's reign; both had perished on the scaffold. His enemies gibed at his tainted blood, but with Elizabeth it was the man that mattered. In the gorgeous clothes of the time he was a magnificent, princely-looking person, tall and dignified, finely built, with clear-cut features, and long slender fingers such as the Queen admired. He was an accomplished courtier, a good talker, and not uncultured, though to the regret of Ascham, who warned him that languages opened the way to politics, he had neglected Cicero for Euclid's pricks and lines. Like Somerset's unfortunate brother, Thomas Seymour, he was an expert jouster; the sort of man whom Elizabeth wanted for a husband, not, she said, one who would sit at home all day among the cinders. The Queen and he were much about the same age and must have met frequently in their youth. During Mary's reign he had been one of her supporters and had sold some of his land to aid her in her troubles. On her accession he was one of the first to be appointed to office, becoming Master of the Horse, an honourable and valuable post which gave him a lodging at Court.

It is not strange that a lively young woman of twenty-five, unmarried, and living, so to speak, as the hostess of an exclusive men's club—the Court—should delight in the company of one of its most fascinating members. Nor is it strange that she felt an emotional response to his manhood. On the other hand, it was not discreet. 'A young princess,' wrote one of her ambassadors, 'cannot be too ware what countenance or familiar demonstration she maketh, more to one than another.' And when that one was a married man, tongues were bound to wag. Dudley had married Amy Robsart as long ago as 1550. Probably he was not a bad husband, but his affection for her was dead and there were no children to act as a bond between them or as a solace to the wife. Like other courtiers' wives, Amy Robsart had to live apart from her husband in the country for much of her time, while he attended on the Queen at Court; and she must have brooded on the gossip and foul rumours that gathered about her husband's name and the Queen's.

The intimacy was first noticed in April, 1559. 'During

the last few days,' Feria wrote, 'Lord Robert has come so much into favour that he does whatever he likes with affairs and it is even said that her Majesty visits him in his chamber day and night. People talk of this so freely that they go so far as to say that his wife has a malady in one of her breasts and the Queen is only waiting for her to die to marry Lord Robert.' By August things looked so bad that Kate Ashley implored her mistress on her knees and in God's name, to marry and put an end to disreputable rumours, as her affection for Dudley threatened to sully her honour and rouse discontent in her subjects. Elizabeth took the rebuke well. If she showed herself gracious to Dudley, she answered, it was because his honourable nature and dealings deserved it. She did not see how anyone could think evil of her conduct: she was always surrounded by her ladies of the bedchamber and maids-of-honour, though indeed—she added with a flash of spirit—'if she had ever had the will or had found pleasure in such a dishonourable life—from which may God preserve her!—she did not know of anyone who could forbid her'.

Such was the scandal that the Imperial ambassador, to reassure his master, found it necessary to make inquiries about Elizabeth's virtue among those who had brought her up since childhood. They swore by all that was holy that she had most certainly never been forgetful of her honour. But gossip took no heed of truth. In December the English ambassador at Brussels felt compelled to write to his mistress and Cecil about the rumours current there, which were so bad that he did not dare to say all, even in a covering note for Cecil's own eyes. Some of the nobles and councillors, such as Cecil, were overwhelmed with anxiety, others lusted for Dudley's blood. Quadra told of a plot to murder him, and someone was said to have asked whether England was so poor that none could be found to stab him with a poniard. It was the Imperial ambassador's opinion that if the Queen married Dudley, she might one evening lay herself down as Queen of England and rise the next morning as plain Mistress Elizabeth. Quadra heard people say that they wanted no more women rulers. It mattered little if a

King's passions ran away with him, but a Queen, like Cæsar's wife, had to be above suspicion. In the summer of 1560, old mother Dowe of Brentford was telling her acquaintances that Dudley and the Queen had played at legerdemain and that he had given her a child. There was a similar rumour current in Hertfordshire. But far more sinister, in the light of what was about to happen, was a persistent report that Dudley intended to get rid of his wife —to poison her was the usual story.

On September 11th the Spanish ambassador, Quadra, had a very remarkable budget of news. Probably three days before, after a futile interview with Elizabeth on the subject of marriage, he had met Cecil, in the gloomiest of moods. Cecil had been away from Court that summer, negotiating a treaty in Scotland, and on his return had found Dudley in high favour and the Queen difficult. He was still inclined to treat Elizabeth as a young woman whose proper business was marriage and babies, not politics, and her refusal to follow his advice was the last straw to a jealous, disgruntled, and overwrought statesman. He went the astounding length of making a confidant of Quadra, telling him that he thought of retiring, although he expected to be cast into the Tower if he did. It was a bad sailor, he added, who did not put into port when he saw a storm brewing, and he clearly foresaw that Dudley's intimacy with the Queen would be the ruin of the country. He was convinced that she meant to marry him. She was abandoning the government to him and spending her days hunting, to the great danger of her life and health. Twice he repeated that Lord Robert would be better in paradise than here, and begged Quadra, in God's name, to point out to Elizabeth the effect of her misconduct and persuade her to give some attention to business. In conclusion he remarked that Dudley was thinking of killing his wife, who was said to be ill, although she was quite well and would take very good care that they did not poison her.

The conversation probably took place on September 8th, 1560. That very day Amy Robsart was found dead at the foot of the stairs in Cumnor Place, near Oxford. Cecil, however, was ignorant of the tragedy that was to lend such terrible significance to his petulant outpourings, nor was it until the following day that Dudley himself received the news at Court. Returning from hunting, Elizabeth told Quadra in confidence that Dudley's wife was dead, or nearly so; but the tragedy was not made public until further particulars had been obtained. On the eleventh the Queen informed the Court: 'She has broken her neck,' she said in Italian; and Quadra added the news in a postscript to his letter.

A coroner's jury which investigated the facts brought in a verdict of accidental death. At our distance of time, it is difficult to be certain, but so far as one can judge, it was a case of suicide. Several times Amy Robsart had been heard praying to God to deliver her from desperation, and on the fatal day, although it was Sunday and some objected, she had insisted on her household going to the fair at Abingdon. Apparently, neglect and the scandalous stories current about her husband and the Queen had preyed upon her mind until at last, for all her prayers, desperation had mastered her.

Rumour had been prophesying murder too long for contemporaries to think anything else. Thomas Lever, the Rector of Coventry, wrote to two councillors on September 17th of the mutterings in his neighbourhood, urging that the truth should be earnestly searched out. To Elizabeth's ambassadors the news came as a thunderbolt. They had been ill enough at ease already in the face of unrestrained gossip; and their mistress seemed now to be on the edge of the abyss. The tragedy 'so passioneth my heart', wrote Randolph from Scotland, 'that no grief ever I felt was like unto it'. Throckmorton in France wished himself dead. People, he declared, were saying things 'which every hair of my head stareth at and my ears glow to hear'. 'One laugheth at us, another threateneth, another revileth the Queen. Some let not to say "What religion is this, that a subject shall kill his wife, and the Prince not only bear withal but marry with him?"' All he could do was to pray God that this cruel hap might not be the messenger of a further disaster, namely, the marriage of Elizabeth and Dudley.

As for Elizabeth, discretion was her last thought. She believed completely in Dudley's innocence. Even if she had not been so fond of him, it is probable that pride, courage, and loyalty would have revolted at the idea of letting his enemies drive him from Court and favour, as a result of the tragedy. Actually she wanted to marry him, imagining that she could best satisfy English humour by marrying a subject; and it was hard to bring herself to recognize that the scandal attaching to the death of Amy Robsart, coupled with the jealousy of her councillors and nobility, made the one marriage that appealed to her impossible. There were few as wise and tolerant as the Earl of Sussex who wrote to Cecil in October suggesting that it would be best to let her follow her affections, since if she chose a man at sight of whom her whole being was suffused with desire, it would be the readiest way of getting an heir to the throne. Elizabeth herself blew now hot now cold, to the perplexity of everyone. She was inclined to defy all opposition and have her way, and yet there was a fundamental caution in her. While in her defiant mood, the opponents of her marriage, Cecil among them, were in eclipse, business was apt to come to a standstill, and it looked as though all was going to the dogs.

In November it was rumoured that Elizabeth and Dudley had been secretly married at the Earl of Pembroke's, for the Queen's ladies, seeing them both return together from Pembroke's house, had momentarily jumped to this conclusion. But Elizabeth's mood changed, and when a patent, raising Dudley to the peerage, was ready for signature, she took a knife and cut it in two. Then her mood changed again. In January Kate Ashley's husband was in trouble for being too outspoken on the subject, while Cecil and a friend wrote to Throckmorton begging him to restrain his blunt expressions of opinion as they were doing more harm than good with his mistress. 'What the Queen will determine to do, God only knows,' Cecil added.

Thus the affair drifted on, with its ups and downs, and

gossip ever busy. In February, Drunken Burley of Totnes was regaling his neighbours with the story 'that the Lord Robert did swive the Queen'. In March, the Earl of Bedford wrote to Throckmorton the welcome news that 'the great matters whereof the world was wont to talk are now asleep', and Cecil again in control of everything; but it is typical of the situation that ere he sealed his letter the great matter was alive again and flourishing. The peerage proposal once more cropped up, only to be rejected as before, Elizabeth remarking that she would not confer the title on those who had been traitors three descents. Dudley sulked, and her mood changed; Robin was clapped on the cheek, with 'No, no, the bear and the ragged staff is not so soon overthrown'; he was in as great favour as ever. Some of her courtiers, who favoured Dudley, took courage to urge his suit; she would only 'pup with her mouth' and say that she would not be fellow with the Duchess of Norfolk, for when they were married folk would be coming and ask for her husband as 'My Lord's Grace'. In vain did the courtiers reply that the remedy was simple; she should give Dudley the title of King. She would never agree to the suggestion.

By the summer of 1561, although the romance was by no means at an end and continued spasmodically to trouble Cecil and others for years, the crisis was past, and Elizabeth was proving that her intelligence could control her emotions. This was the significance of the episode. At one time it had looked as though the second woman ruler, like the first, would take the bit between her teeth and let passion have its ruinous way. But while not unfeminine or sexless, Elizabeth was a less emotional type than her sister. Experience had added caution to a quick and active mind, and she was consumed with ambition to be a great popular ruler like her father. Momentarily she had sacrificed her good name and popularity; that is a measure of her infatuation for Dudley. But in the long run it was *the weal of the kingdom* and the limits of practical politics that directed her judgment.

If ever she married, she remarked a few years later, it would be as a Queen and not as Elizabeth. She had not yet, in 1561, abandoned all hope of marrying as both—that is, of marrying Dudley with the approval of her nobles and people. But even if Dudley had been less envied and hated by his fellows, the tragedy of Amy Robsart was too black a cloud over his reputation with Englishmen to permit marrying him. And so, having decided not to marry simply as Elizabeth, it was certain that, unless another man appeared to stir her emotions, she would never marry except as Queen —as Queen alone. And that, she said, she would only do from stern necessity.

CHAPTER VI

FIRST ESSAYS IN FOREIGN POLICY

ELIZABETH, at her accession, had found herself involved in peace negotiations with France and faced with the formal surrender of Calais. In his dispassionate way Cecil might cast a balance-sheet and doubt whether the town was worth the cost of its upkeep. With his mistress it was different. National pride burnt its fiery way through such arguments. She felt acutely the humiliation of parting with the last remnant of what once had been an extensive English domain; did she not, as her predecessors before her for generations, call herself Queen of France? She knew that there was not the least likelihood of recovering the town, and yet she haggled with extraordinary effrontery, exploiting Philip II's friendship and his distrust of France, and driving the negotiations as near a breach as she dared before she at last accepted the utmost that could be exacted—a face-saving compromise. By the peace of Cateau-Cambrésis, concluded on April 2nd, 1559, Calais was nominally left an English possession in the temporary custody of France; in reality, it was sold for the price of half a million crowns, to be paid in eight years' time unless France could find a way of wriggling out of the payment or Elizabeth wanted an excuse for another war.

It was peace neither with honour nor dishonour, satisfactory only in this neutral way. It left the foreign situation as an Englishman described it: 'The French king bestriding the realm, having one foot in Calais and the other in Scotland. Steadfast enmity, but no steadfast friendship abroad.'

France was the enemy *par excellence;* 'When the Ethiopian is white,' ran a proverb, 'the French will love the English.' It was with France that Englishmen were wont to make their fond and complacent comparisons of England and English customs, and there was no Englishman but felt himself equal to two Frenchmen. And now, to sharpen an agelong rivalry, there was the smart of Calais, and more serious still were the pretensions of the Dauphin's wife, Mary Queen of Scots, to the English throne. Mary's claim had been mooted as a debating point during the peace negotiations. If we surrender Calais, the French said to the Spaniards, to whom shall we surrender it, for the Dauphin's wife is the rightful Queen of England? After the peace, Mary openly quartered the arms of England on her coat of arms, and English ambassadors were invited to feast off plate that flaunted her claim.

The claim might have been harmless—little more than a reminder that Mary would have a right to the succession should Elizabeth die childless—if religion had not cut athwart politics. Sooner or later, the Pope was bound to excommunicate Elizabeth and look for some Catholic prince to depose her; she was the principal Protestant prince in Europe, and there could be no finer move with which to inaugurate a victorious counter-Reformation. Do what she would: use the courtship of the Archduke Charles as a shield; stimulate Philip's protective interventions at Rome; bring out her crucifix, candles, and vestments in the royal Chapel, to the infinite grief of godly Englishmen returning home from exile, who sorrowed over the New Jerusalem with its dumb remnants of idolatry; try by timely comments, when the heavens looked black, to create the impression in ambassadors' minds that she was not half as Protestant as her radical young councillors and had been their reluctant tool in the religious changes; for all her art, Elizabeth could hardly expect the blow to be delayed long.

It seemed as though the history of the late reign would be repeated, and as Elizabeth had then been the focus of Protestant hopes against her sister's Catholicism, so Mary Queen of Scots would now become the focus of Catholic hopes. Repeated, however, with this difference, that while, compared with her sister's, Elizabeth's resources had been negligible, Mary could hope for the blessing and support of the Pope, and would certainly have the might and ambition of France behind her. Scotland would be her base, and only the ill-fortified town of Berwick stood between her and the Catholic north of England.

The situation was grave, but worse was to come. On July 10th, 1559, the French king, Henry II, died from a wound received in a tournament, and Mary's husband, Francis II, a weakling of fifteen and a half, became king. The government of France passed to Mary's ambitious uncles, the Cardinal of Lorraine and the Duke of Guise. It was they who had been mainly responsible for her marriage, and there was every reason to fear that with the help of their sister, Mary of Guise, who was Mary's mother and Regent of Scotland, they would turn the combined resources of France and Scotland against Elizabeth.

Fortunately, the Guise family did not hold all the trump cards. In Scotland, Protestantism and national feeling had joined forces against a Catholic, alien government, much as they had done against Philip and his Spaniards in England in Mary's reign. The Church was corrupt, Reformist preachers active and eloquent, while the nobility both coveted the Church lands and resented the intrusion of Frenchmen into office and influence. Elizabeth's accession in England, coinciding with a more vigorous Catholic and French policy in Scotland, had given a great fillip to the opposition, so that when the intrepid Reformer, John Knox, came back from his continental exile in May, 1559, he found Scotland on the edge of rebellion. Preaching at Perth, his eloquence stirred an insolent boy to cheek a bishop and fling a stone at the tabernacle on the altar of the church. The crowd immediately ran amuck, wrecking and burning. The revolt had begun.

'The Congregation,' as the rebel Protestant nobility and preachers called themselves, naturally turned for help to Elizabeth. The quarrel, as they saw, was as much in her interests as theirs, for France was certain to send a strong army to the Regent's help, and if the rebels were over-thrown, what was to stop the French army from advancing into England and realizing the ambition of the Guise family by turning Elizabeth off her throne? If on the other hand they were successful, if they could oust all Frenchmen from Scotland, overthrow the Catholic Church and themselves govern the country in Mary's name, Elizabeth would be relatively secure and her worst fears at an end. England and Scotland would then be united in policy. They might even, if Elizabeth would only marry the young Earl of Ar-ran, be united in name; for Mary might die childless—which many people expected—or the rebels might be com-pelled to depose her; and Arran's family, the Hamiltons, were next in the succession. Let Elizabeth not be hasty in choosing a husband, they urged; a request that she found as little difficulty in granting as in adding to her list another suitor with political assets. When told that Francis II was about to be proclaimed King of Scotland, England, and Ire-land, she remarked with grim satisfaction that he little knew what a buffet she could give him; she would take a hus-band who would make his head ache. Arran was on the Continent at the time, and the French were doing their best to lay hands on him; but by a fine piece of secret-service work Elizabeth spirited him safely over to England, took a look at him, and sent him on to Scotland to lend authority and respectability to the revolt. He was full of gratitude: 'When I call to mind,' he wrote to Cecil some months later, 'the private cause that oft moves me to have her Grace in remembrance, I find myself in such perplexity that I know not where my wits are become.' Alas! a prophetic remark, for the poor man did actually lose his wits. But before that happened he had served his turn, like other suitors, as a pawn in Elizabeth's policy.

It was a risky business helping the Scots, and a violation of the treaty of Cateau-Cambrésis; but Elizabeth was never pusillanimous and could not afford to be more scrupulous than her enemies. She and Cecil saw clearly that they must seize the opportunity fortune offered. At the same time Elizabeth wished to preserve an appearance of correct behaviour, in order to make it difficult for France or any other power to take open action against her. Cecil therefore kept her name out of his correspondence, and replied to the first overture from the rebels with a letter that was shown but not given to his correspondent. English policy, however, was not in doubt. Assure the Scots, Cecil told Sir James Croft at Berwick, that England will not see them ruined; kindle the fire in any way you can, for if it be quenched such an opportunity will not recur in our lifetime.

It was a situation after Elizabeth's own heart, demanding caution, secrecy, and valiant lying. Clerks were dispensed with, Cecil wrote the dispatches himself, and ciphered and deciphered all of any consequence. The Queen, Sir Thomas Parry, and he formed an inner secret council with the result that older and more conservative councillors, who were kept in the dark, went about fulminating against young upstarts. Everyone was vaguely aware of what was happening. It could not be otherwise, with negotiations constantly going on, representatives crossing the Border, and money being sent to Scotland. The Regent, Mary of Guise, had her spies, and the Scots blabbed, and John Knox was not the sort of person who could hide a visit to England. It became still harder to maintain appearances when the Congregation started paying their troops in English and Flemish coin, and when a thousand pounds was intercepted on its way to them.

The harder it was, the harder Elizabeth lied. Early in August the Regent protested against these activities on the Border. Elizabeth merely expressed her surprise that persons who were her subjects and public officials and knew perfectly well how displeasing their action would be to her, had of their own device consorted with such people as the Scottish rebels. She knew nothing herself; let the Regent furnish details and she would punish the offenders. At the end of the month came more complaints. Of course, said Elizabeth to the French ambassador, it was possible that some of her servants had behaved unwisely; there were fools among them. She had sent a person to make inquiries; but this she could tell him, that the members of the Congregation would be grievously deceived if they hoped for any favour from her in their foolish enterprise. She had neither written nor promised anything to them, a statement that could easily be proved or disproved, for her signature was unmistakable: let him produce it. The audience took place at Hampton Court, and at the end she invited the ambassador into the gallery to see the Regent's portrait hanging there, talking of her kindness, honesty, and uprightness, and sending most affectionate greetings to her. 'If one can judge from outward show,' he reported to the Regent, 'it seems, Madam, by her words and other demonstrations, that she has none but good intentions to keep the peace and friendship between your Majesties.' Little did he know that Arran had just arrived in England, and that a councillor going to the Border to settle various questions with the Regent's commissioners, had secret instructions to negotiate with the Congregation and hand over to them a sum of three thousand pounds!

Towards the end of September, a further complaint brought the same confident denial, but by this time protestations were wearing thin and during the audience Elizabeth smiled as though she was thoroughly enjoying the joke. She assured the ambassador that what the Regent heard was nothing but malicious rumour, while she held her honour too dear to say one thing and do another. She laughingly charged him to report her very words, repeating them at the end of the audience so that he would get them right. The ambassador's opinion of her had changed: 'There is more dissimulation in her than honesty and goodwill; she is the best hand at the game living.'

Cecil was pleased with his mistress: 'God send her as good health as she hath a heart,' he wrote. True, she had to be carefully managed; she was touchy on some subjects. One was John Knox. Never were two such incompatibles. Pity it was that they did not meet! In view of the need for Elizabeth's help, Knox had written to her in July to make his peace over his tract, *The First Blast of the Trumpet*, and to convey his unfeigned love and reverence. The letter was typical of the man: 'I cannot deny the writing of a book against the usurped authority and unjust regiment of women; neither yet am I minded to retreat or call back any principal point or proposition of the same till truth and verity do further appear.' This was his considered judgment on his tract! Why Elizabeth should be annoyed with him he did not understand. It was not as though the tract had been directed against her specially, or, as a matter of fact, was in any way prejudicial to her rule. She reigned, he told her, by a peculiar dispensation of God's mercy, permitting in her what law and nature denied to all other women. And if she humbled herself in God's presence, he, John Knox, was ready to justify her authority and regiment with tongue and pen, as the Holy Ghost had justified the same in Deborah, another peculiar dispensation. 'Forget your birth,' he adjured her, 'and all title which thereupon doth hang; and consider deeply how, for fear of your life, you did decline from God and bow in idolatry. Let it not appear a small offence in your eyes'. 'Such as refuse the counsel of the faithful, appear it never so sharp, are compelled to follow the deceit of flatterers, to their own perdition.' No wonder that Cecil warned his colleagues at the Border not to mention Knox's name in their letters: of all others it was the most odious at Court. They were to send on any communications they received from him, but it was Cecil's custom to suppress them: 'they do no good here.' 'God keep us from such a visitation as Knox has attempted in Scotland,' prayed Archbishop Parker; 'the people to be orderers of things.' To which Elizabeth would have given a decided 'Amen!'

Fortune proved a sorry jade to the Congregation. Their men were beaten in almost every fight with the Regent's troops, and towards the end of 1559 it became clear that they lacked the means and the resolution to dislodge the French forces already in Scotland; much less would they be able to face the fleet and army then preparing in France. More vigorous and open help would have to come from England. This, however, was the point at which Elizabeth was likely to stick. For anything short of open hostilities she was quite ready. William Winter, for example, was given charge of a fleet, told to sail to Berwick, and thence to the Firth of Forth where he was to prevent any succour in the form of victuals or men reaching the Regent and to do all the damage he could to any French ships at sea or in the Firth. But his actions were to be unauthorized, and he was to make what excuses he could to save the Queen from all responsibility. At the same time an army of four thousand foot and two thousand horse was levied, to be quartered at Berwick under the command of the Duke of Norfolk. Cecil wanted this army to advance into Scotland and besiege the French in their fortress of Leith; in other words, he wanted to take a step that must surely mean open war with France.

Such a decisive move could not be made without first consulting the whole Council. It is said that the discussion went on for eight days. At first Sir Nicholas Bacon, the Lord Keeper of the Great Seal and Cecil's brother-in-law, was against the proposal. England, he said, lacked the money, the men, and the friends that such an enterprise required. The revenue was insufficient to maintain even a peace establishment and pay off the internal and external debts—amounting in November, 1559, to more than a year's ordinary revenue—without prolonging part of the debt at excessive interest. Most of the nobility were bare and needy, the bishops and clergy squeezed dry, and the gentlemen and commons quite unable to bear the burden. Plague and famine had not left enough men to till the fields, much less supply an army; and there was no money to employ foreign mercenaries, even if it were safe to bring foreigners into the country. As for friends, there were none with the exception of the Scottish rebels, and they had shown that they could not expel three thousand Frenchmen, while their soldiers were able to keep the field no longer than thirty days, unless hired as mercenaries. It must not be forgotten, he added, that England had its own discontents; those who disliked the religious complexion of the Government—not few, nor stupid; and those displaced from the Council or office. It would be found that most people were against a war of invasion. Looking abroad, there was the appearance of injustice in helping subjects against their sovereign and in being the first to break a treaty. France was four times the size of England, had four times the revenue and four times the men, possessed expert captains and tried soldiers and the friendship of most of the princes of Europe. In all likelihood, considering his religion and how little reason Spaniards had to like Englishmen after their experience here in Mary's reign, Philip II would join France. Supposing he did not, the Pope certainly would.

Bacon concluded his speech with positive advice, which was to aid the Scots secretly by all the ways and means possible during the coming summer, thus weakening the French while conserving England's strength. In the following summer the Scots and they together could drive the French out of the country for ever. Scotland could not be conquered in a year, and there was no knowing what might not happen in the meanwhile. Mary Queen of Scots, being a very sick woman, might die, the House of Guise might lose control of France, or Elizabeth might make a marriage that would go far to solve the whole problem. Bacon was not alone in his views; and Granvelle and Feria in the Netherlands, speaking to the English ambassador, were even more insistent on the folly of Elizabeth pitting herself against France. To them and to others it seemed as though she was rushing to certain and utter disaster.

Cecil thought otherwise. His friend, Throckmorton, a master of intrigue and something of a fire-eater, was over from his embassy in France. He had come, it was said, to visit a sick wife—who was perfectly well; in all probability it was to tell Elizabeth of a conspiracy against the Guise party in France, in which he himself had had a hand. He was all for action. Now was the time to strike. His presence strengthened Cecil's case. In the end, Bacon and four others were talked round, and the Council, with one dissentient, gave advice to the Queen contemplating intervention, with its probable consequence of open war. The advice was given on December 24th. Four days later it was turned down.

Being accountable to no one, Elizabeth did not, like her

councillors, have to explain herself on paper, and therefore the reasons for her decisions are as a rule matters of inference. Apart from temperamental differences between herself and Cecil—and differences there were—her position inevitably made her more hesitant. She was in the position of a judge whose business was to listen to both sides of an argument, whereas Cecil, though he might, and usually did, draw up the pros and cons of a situation, played the part of an advocate. Further, it was her word that was final. She made decisions, her councillors merely gave advice; and however keen the sense of responsibility in a man like Cecil, there was a subtle psychological difference in the two roles. Elizabeth must have known of the initial clash of opinion in the Council, and in such a grave emergency it was not enough that Cecil had talked his opponents round. It was certainly not enough if, as is probable, she shared Bacon's early views. She had a lively sense of the cost of war in men and money, and having to gamble, preferred to gamble on the success of secret and underhand ways, in which she was expert to the point of genius and from which she expected more than Cecil did. There was not unanimity for war; there were doubts. Where there were doubts, she preferred indecision.

Thus Cecil's victory in the Council did not avail, and he resorted to the only means that he had of coercing his mistress—resignation. What happened we do not know; nor can we be certain that the resignation got beyond the draft which is all that survives. Probably Elizabeth conceded the principle of open intervention. There was nothing very decisive in doing so, for action had to wait on her will and she could let events determine that.

Events were moving steadily in favour of Cecil's policy. On December 27th, 1559, Winter set sail for the Forth. Wind and storm interrupted the passage, but if he lost his ships' boats, he kept the fleet intact, and on January 23rd sailed into the Firth with the tide. There he found two ships of war, a hoy full of munitions, and several barques; and learning that they were supporting the French army which was advancing through Fife on St. Andrews, he captured all but some of the barques, which he drove ashore to be destroyed by the Scots. When the Regent sent a herald and trumpet to demand an explanation, he told a cock-and-bull story, and according to instructions asserted that he acted without his Queen's orders. 'The disguise is too transparent,' wrote the Regent; 'as if a simple subject and officer should have the inclination, and still more the power, to make war without the will and express orders of the Queen!' She was right. It was too transparent. But unless the French cared to make a *casus belli* of Winter's action—and at the moment they did not—it had the supreme merit of maintaining a nominal state of peace. Elizabeth was as unblushing as Winter when she in turn was asked for an explanation: The Duke of Norfolk, she said, had commission to inquire into the matter and to send the offender as a prisoner to London; but she could not do to Winter, a man of credit and a principal officer, that which she would not do to a Jew, namely condemn him without answer. Needless to say, the young Admiral was left in the Forth to carry on his blockade.

The Elizabethan navy had done its task in its first enterprise with complete efficiency and no fuss, under the command of a young man. The French fared differently. At the beginning of December they had lost four ships and a thousand men, and now the same storm that caught and delayed Winter's ships smashed up their main fleet with the long-awaited army aboard. Four vessels and two thousand men, it was said, were lost and the rest driven back to port.

It was as good as a battle won, and gave Elizabeth another welcome breathing space. Cecil fretted at the slowness of the pace: 'We seek peace so long as it may be endured.' But every time his mistress put the question whether the Scots could drive the French out by themselves, the answer came with convincing certainty; they could not. Early in February, 1560, the country was alive with preparations for war, and each day the Queen was to be seen—a fine sight—exercising with the train bands, mounted on a Neapolitan courser. Gresham, her financial agent, was in the Netherlands raising a great loan and se-

cretly buying up and despatching huge quantities of pow-
der and munitions, described in his letters as velvets and
crimson satins. He even managed to get hold of two thousand corselets from the royal armoury at Mechlin, which
caused no little ado when they were missed. On February
27th the situation advanced another stage with the Treaty
of Berwick. Elizabeth took Scotland under her protection
in order to save its freedom and liberties, and agreed to open
intervention; the rebel Scots for their part undertook to
send help should the French invade England. A month later the English army advanced into Scotland.

Philip II now intervened. Poor man! he was in a quandary. He did not want Elizabeth to annex Scotland, and
much less France to annex England. Nor did he want the
Scots to get away with their revolt and impose their heresy
on Scotland. If they did, that woman would set all Europe
by the ears with her encouragement of heretics, and his
own dominions, the Netherlands, would soon be in turmoil.
If it came to war between England and France he was convinced that he would be drawn in, for the French could
not help but be victorious and in his own interests he would
have to challenge their victory. He saw one way out of his
difficulty; that was to prevail on Elizabeth to withdraw her
help, while he sent a Spanish army from the Netherlands
to punish the rebels in conjunction with a limited number
of French troops. Then, if the French attempted to invade
England after crushing the Scots, his army would aid Elizabeth. Her safety would thus be assured at the cost of deserting the Congregation.

The situation required the most careful handling, for
Philip might easily be stung into action by a false move.
Here the gradualness of Elizabeth's policy and her baffling
powers as a talker justified themselves. Cecil wanted to go
ahead and damn the consequences; her instinct was to blur
the line so thoroughly that it would be hard to say when she
overstepped it. The combination worked admirably, though
Cecil, contending with his mistress's private doubts and depressions, knew little peace. Fortunately, Philip's advisers
were not smitten with his bright idea. Far from expecting

the French to fall in with it, they anticipated an agreement with Elizabeth at Philip's expense. Some were so anti-French as to be pro-English.

The envoy sent by Philip in April to convey his proposition to Elizabeth and let her understand that she had the alternative of retreat or war with France and Spain, was a Flemish nobleman; and in the Netherlands people were loud in their praise of Elizabeth. A friar who had preached against her could not stir out of doors for fear of being lynched, while it was said that the Spanish soldiers would refuse to march. In his sympathy with England the envoy effectively blunted the edge of his commission, by telling Cecil and the Lord Admiral in strict secrecy to get on with the war. The Spanish ambassador at Paris, in private conversation with Throckmorton, was equally reassuring. In May—though it would be June before the ambassador's dispatch reached Elizabeth—the Duke of Alva told the English ambassador a Spanish proverb: 'If the enemy be in the water to the girdlestede, lend him thy hand to help him out; if he be in to the shoulders, set hold on him and keep him down'. In other words, if Elizabeth could drive the French out of Scotland without peril to herself, then let her go ahead and do it without further talk.

The army was in fact going ahead, but not with the quiet efficiency of the navy. An assault made on Leith on May 7th was repulsed with the loss of about a thousand killed and wounded. Outwardly Elizabeth did not quail; more men were hastily levied, the army was reassured and promised support and reinforcements. But in private all her old misgivings burst forth again, swollen by stories of military corruption, indiscipline, and inefficiency, and even of action little short of treason; swollen too by anticipation of war with Spain if victory were not swift. She renewed the opinion of Cassandra and prophesied disaster, while the weak-hearted and flatterers at Court spread the gloom. 'God trieth us with many difficulties', Cecil wrote to Throckmorton. 'The Queen's Majesty never liketh this matter of Scotland.' 'I have had such a torment herein . . . as an ague hath not in five fits so much abated.'

But the French were in no condition to hope for victory. The conspiracy of Amboise, which Throckmorton had talked about when home in December, had been crushed in March but had left the Guise party with its hands full of trouble, and it would be the end of August before succour could be sent to Leith, by which time the besieged would probably be starved out. Again, Mary of Guise was ill, indeed she was dying. They must snatch peace while they could, and so, notwithstanding the good news from Scotland, the French sent to treat. Elizabeth insisted upon entering into negotiations, and with the help of the Council prevailed upon Cecil to be one of the English commissioners and go north to Edinburgh. He and his friends exchanged the most dismal forebodings of what would happen through his being away from Court. 'Who can or will stand fast against the Queen's arguments and doubtful devices?' they asked. 'Who will speedily resolve the doubtful delays? Who will make despatch of anything?' 'I know none can love their country better: I would the Queen's Majesty could love it so well.'

Cecil went reluctantly, with no faith in the negotiations. Once engaged in them, however, using his powers with masterly skill and subtlety, and seeing for himself the strength of Leith, he became keener on peace than his mistress. During the discussions the political situation veered round still further in England's favour; Mary of Guise died, news arrived of a terrible disaster to Spanish arms in Tripoli, removing every vestige of fear of Philip, and the troubles in France increased. Elizabeth's spirits soared. She was now in a position, as Gresham ecstatically declared, to 'make the proudest prince in all Christendom to stoop and yield unto that noble carcass of hers'; and she was ready to insist, not only on the restoration of Calais, but on the payment of half a million crowns as compensation for the use of her arms and title. The Scots had got what they wanted; she too would have her pound of flesh. She viewed the breakdown of negotiations with complacency, and was ready for any madcap scheme. Strange irony! Cecil was now preaching restraint, and trying to uproot from his mistress's mind the seeds that he himself had sown. That he was right there can be no doubt. Nor can there be any doubt that if he had had his own way earlier there would have been no peace negotiations. The fact was that both minds and temperaments, in happy if sometimes discordant combination, had been needed to bring this business through. At the last minute—fortunately the letter arrived too late—Elizabeth wrote in her own hand in cipher to Cecil, as a secret which they two alone were to share, about invading France in aid of the rebels there and getting hold of a French town as pledge for Calais. It was evidently a scheme with which Cecil had once toyed; but since then the roles of Cecil and his mistress had changed.

On July 6th, 1560, the Treaty of Edinburgh was concluded. It was a triumph for English prestige and honour, recognizing Elizabeth's right to the throne and binding Francis and Mary to abstain from her arms and title. There were other concessions as well; but even from the English standpoint the essence of the peace lay in the withdrawal of all but a negligible handful of French troops from Scotland, the destruction of the fortress of Leith, and the transference of the government to a Council of Scottish nobles. Whatever the fate of the treaty, whether Francis and Mary ratified it or not, the essentials were secure, for the troops were to be removed immediately—'We to carry them and the Scots to curse them hence'—the fortresses destroyed, and in a week or two no one would be left to take charge of the country but the rebel Lords. Elizabeth was pleased, as well she might be. Her prestige abroad, among Catholics no less than Protestants, rose phenomenally. So much she had accomplished, despite the gloomy forebodings of patronizing Spaniards; and accomplished in the beginning of her reign, and, as Cecil put it, while yet in her maidenhood.

In Scotland it was bliss to be alive during the next few weeks; or so Elizabeth's agent, Thomas Randolph, thought. All the nobles stood in love and friendship one with another and in common gratitude to the paragon of their time, whose goodness to their realm had been such as they could never recompense. They longed to come to England to see Elizabeth and kiss her hand. In the Parliament which they assembled in August, they proceeded, unchecked by any authority, to remould the State to their heart's desire. The Pope's authority was abolished, the saying of Mass prohibited under a penalty of death for a third offence, and a Protestant confession of faith adopted; the Treaty of Berwick was confirmed, and to bind the two lands in indissoluble union they resolved to petition Elizabeth to marry the Earl of Arran, whose place in the succession they settled by statute. No one withstood the proposal; the very Papists, it was said, could be content to renounce their God the Pope for it, and all were resolved 'with tooth and nail' to set the marriage forward. It became their daily, their nightly, their hourly talk, and anxiously they canvassed Arran's chances against Elizabeth's other suitors. They spoke of the King of Sweden's son, admitting much force in his great wealth, but more in the goodliness of person, religious rectitude, and other qualifications of the Duke of Holstein. 'This is he', wrote Randolph, 'this is the man that hath given us many a sharp alarm in our camp. This is he that breaketh our sleep and tieth oft our tongues.' But what with Arran's virtue and other commodities they hoped to countervail. Nothing was impossible to a willing, bold heart. And Arran was certainly willing.

Meanwhile Cecil returned home, feeling deservedly virtuous and ready to distribute largesses all round to conclude a happy stroke of business. He found Dudley in the ascendant at Court—it was just before Amy Robsart's death—and the Queen in an economical mood; and probably attributing much to Dudley's evil influence that was Elizabeth's own stubborn determination, he brooded on his wrongs and fed on the sympathy of friends till in less than a month he was once more thinking of retiring. What was to be expected, he asked, when the Duke of Norfolk, a rare nobleman and a kinsman of the Queen, was merely thanked for his services and sent home without allowance in credit or promise? He himself would feel the pinch of his own expenditure, he said, for seven years to come; yet he had saved Elizabeth £15,000 in one day by his prompt discharge of her forces. He wanted her for policy's sake, as a sound investment, to take pity on the poverty of the Scottish Lords: with one thousand pounds he would undertake to save twenty in five years, with two thousand, forty. The Earl of Glencairn was poor, honest, constant and wise; Maxwell very wise and religious; Hume would be caught with a hook of a few ducats; Maitland was a rare man for all good qualities; the Lord James would be gratified; Kircaldy had need and reason to be remembered.

An old, old, story! Easy to yield, difficult to resist! Broad is the way to insolvency; a way that England's great neighbours, France and Spain, were both treading. Elizabeth had fought her war on credit, as was inevitable, and on short credit which it would be hard to prolong at reasonable rates. The army alone had cost £132,000, armour and munitions bought by Gresham £109,000, and the money borrowed abroad totalled £247,000. She was faced with the task of liquidating a debt equalling more than a year's ordinary revenue, and Gresham and she during the next year were desperately put to it, trying by one device and another to save her credit, on which depended her ability to borrow for any future emergency. If the past had any lesson to teach, then neither gifts nor pensions were the foundation of loyalty. Common interest, not a fleeting mood like gratitude, was of lasting value; and Elizabeth had forged the strongest bond of union imaginable in expelling the French and placing the Scottish nobility in charge of their own country against their Sovereign's will. To do more would be to do charity, which is the prerogative of affluence and begins at home. As for Cecil himself, he may have been momentarily out of pocket, but in the long run his reward was ample enough. Had he but known, it was in that financial sense of Elizabeth's, her resolute, irritating parsimony that the secret of greatness lay.

CHAPTER VII

MARY QUEEN OF SCOTS

To Francis II the Treaty of Edinburgh seemed hard and intolerable. That a great prince should be reduced to the extremity of receiving law from his own subjects was, he declared, unendurable; and although he and Mary had given their royal word to ratify its terms, on one pretence and another they refused. Worse, they continued to bear the English arms. It was an impasse. But before anything could be done, Francis died, on December 5th, 1560. His brother, Charles IX, a minor, succeeded him, and the government of France passed into the hands of the Queen-mother, Catherine de Medici. The House of Guise went into eclipse, and, dear as France was to her, Mary had no alternative but to return to her strange, dour and inhospitable kingdom of Scotland, which she had left as a child twelve years before.

The crowding drama of Elizabeth's reign changed, and interest began to centre on the personal relations between herself and Mary, two young Queens, cousins and neighbours. What was to be expected but relentless enmity? Elizabeth had as good as robbed Mary of the allegiance of her subjects, and set up a religious and political rule in Scotland that was obnoxious to her. Mary on her side had refused to ratify the Treaty of Edinburgh, and, given the will and power, could take a leaf out of her rival's book, stir up Catholic discontent in England, perhaps make a bid for the English throne. There was provocation and danger in her very widowhood, for she could challenge her cousin's attraction as the best marriage in Europe. Suitors who had spent money, time and temper on Elizabeth, were turning to woo a woman less virginal and elusive, and it was not many weeks before the names of Don Carlos of Spain, the Archduke Charles, the King of Sweden, and the King of Denmark were on people's lips. With Elizabeth it was political necessity—perhaps also it was instinct—to begrudge another her half or wholly rejected suitors. Any one of these princes, if married to Mary, was likely to regard the English throne as a tempting morsel, and behind Don Carlos and the Archduke Charles there was powerful Catholic backing. The national boundary between England and Scotland might disappear, the two people be embroiled in religious war, and the greater part of the Continent be drawn in, setting Catholic against Protestant throughout Christendom. A nightmare these fears might be; but not an idle one. Europe was ripe for such folly. Knox and his like were Protestants first and Scotsmen, Frenchmen, or Germans afterwards, and it was the same with the growing number of ardent Catholics. Let the future, by happy fortune, escape the peril; still, the well-being of Christendom was linked with the relations of these two Queens.

The start was unpromising. Elizabeth once more demanded the ratification of the Treaty of Edinburgh, Mary once more refused. The result was that when Mary asked for a safe-conduct in order to pass through England on her way to Scotland, Elizabeth replied with:—No ratification, no safe-conduct. She told her ambassador, Throckmorton, to explain her refusal. When he came to his audience, Mary bade her courtiers draw back lest her passion got the better of her; she had no desire, she said, to make a public show of her wrath as Elizabeth had done. Nothing grieved her more, she told Throckmorton, than the fact that she had so far forgotten herself as to beg a favour which she had no need to ask. She could return to Scotland as she had come, by sea and despite England; and if the winds cast her upon English coasts, why then Elizabeth might do her pleasure and make sacrifice of her. Peradventure, she added, that casualty might be better for her than to live;

but God's will be done. Elizabeth had said that she was young and lacked experience: at any rate, she had a heart not inferior to hers.

They were bitter words, but Mary's anger was not really deep. Like Elizabeth, she was reconsidering her policy in the light of the new situation, and like her, searching for a *modus vivendi*. Each had something to ask and something to concede. Elizabeth wished to keep Scotland from returning to the old league with France; and Heaven alone knew what might happen in that country as a result of Mary's sympathies and religion. 'Here will be a mad world,' wrote Randolph; 'our exactness and singularity in religion will never concur with her judgment.' The Protestant, Anglophil party in Scotland seemed strong, but who could tell what a clever, attractive monarch might not do in time to undermine it? Already, people less far-seeing than the capable Secretary, Maitland of Lethington, or less single-minded than John Knox, were being lulled asleep by a new sense of security and were entering into some devotion to their Queen. 'Many simple men,' wrote Maitland, 'shall be carried away with vain hope, and brought abed with fair words.' In such a situation it would have been extremely shortsighted for Elizabeth to brave Mary, relying on the support of the Congregation. Better, if possible, reach a friendly agreement with her.

Mary, on her side, though in moments of anger she talked of turning every Englishman out of Scotland, was not averse to agreement. The French alliance had lost much of its appeal for her, now that her Guise relatives had fallen from power. Moreover, without a strong and organized party in Scotland, she could not hope to pursue a policy diametrically opposed to that of the Congregation. What she had to recognize was that her fortunes henceforward were linked with the British Isles. And recognize it she did. It was because the clause in the Treaty of Edinburgh, binding her to renounce the title and arms of England, was obscurely worded and might be held to nullify her future claim to the English throne, that she was now refusing to ratify the Treaty. Surely a compromise was possible? Maitland, and Mary's illegitimate brother, Murray, both of whom were friends of England, suggested that she should surrender any claim or pretension to the English throne in favour of Elizabeth and her offspring, on condition that Elizabeth recognized her as heir presumptive, to succeed if she left no children. The suggestion was brought to Elizabeth's notice before Mary left France. Cecil told Throckmorton of it as a matter secretly thought of, 'too big for weak folks, and too deep for simple'. Still brooding on the well-nigh catastrophic folly of Elizabeth over Dudley, he added that he did not intend to be an author of the compromise. He wanted no more women rulers in England. 'Well,' he ended, 'God send our mistress a husband, and by time a son, that we may hope our posterity shall have a masculine succession.'

At the eleventh hour, as she thought, Elizabeth relented towards Mary, and sent her a safe-conduct. It could only mean that she was prepared to see her on her way through England and discuss the terms of an agreement; action rich with promise of mutual understanding and friendship. Alas! Mary had already taken ship for Scotland. Thus the first opportunity of a meeting was lost. The Fates had proved implacable.

On the morning of August 19th, 1561, Mary arrived at Leith. The weather was depressing: it was wet and there was a thick, dark mist. The sun was not seen to shine two days before, nor two days after, and to John Knox it seemed as though 'the very face of Heaven did manifestly speak what comfort was brought into this country with her—to wit, sorrow, dolour, darkness and all impiety'. Her arrival was unexpected, but the sound of the cannon shot off by her galleys soon brought the multitude running to see her. The Palace of Holyrood was got ready in haste, and all was joy and enthusiasm. That night, a company of the most honest citizens with instruments of music gave their salutations at her chamber window. So says John Knox; but to the refined ears of one of her train, that notorious raconteur of French amours, Brantôme, they were five or six hundred knaves who murdered sleep with their wretched fiddles and rebecks and their psalms sung all out of tune.

Mary had come intending to please. She was not quite nineteen years of age, though much older in experience and the ways of the world. Tall, like her mother, of pale complexion, with dark brown eyes and dark chestnut hair, she may not have been strikingly beautiful in feature, but her vivacious personality was well-nigh irresistible. To men she presented the strongest appeal, and Queen though she was, more than one tried to take liberties with her. She was clever, and as might be expected of Renaissance France, had been well educated. But it was in music, dancing and horsemanship that she excelled, not in learning; being brought up, as Knox said, in 'joyousity', for so she termed her dancing, which he for his part termed 'skipping—not very comely for honest women'. She was another type than her cousin of England. She learnt languages, but did not become really expert in them; she could read Latin and continued to read it under George Buchanan's guidance, but could not speak it readily. Whereas nothing delighted Elizabeth so much as long theological arguments, Mary, in contrast, would cut such discussions short, saying that 'she could not reason, but she knew what she ought to believe'; or as she told Knox, 'Ye are over sair for me, but and if they were here that I have heard, they would answer you'. She would sit patiently in her Council sewing, while her advisers talked; Elizabeth as a rule kept away from hers to avoid being dominated, and on the rare occasions that she attended, was quite capable of arguing her ministers into silence. Maitland told Randolph that he found no such maturity of judgment and ripeness of experience in high matters in her as in Elizabeth, in whom both nature and time had wrought much more than in many of greater years. Tears came easily, very easily. She was in fact a woman in whom emotion, not intellect, was the stronger force, one who could be patient to bear and indeed bore much, but whom a crisis of passion, like Elizabeth's with Dudley, might easily ruin.

From the Tuesday of Mary's arrival until the following

Sunday all was mirth and peace, but on that day the first careless rapture vanished, when preparation was made to say Mass in her chapel. The godly then rose up: 'Shall that idol,' they cried, 'be suffered again to take place within this realm? It shall not!' They clamoured for the idolater priest to die the death according to God's law, so that, as Randolph put it, when the wretched man had his God at the highest he 'had almost for fear——I say no more for reverence'. Fortunately, Murray was there. He placed himself at the chapel door, and no graver outrage was done than seizing and destroying the candles. Nine days later it was Edinburgh's turn to show its godly zeal, the occasion being Mary's ceremonial entry into the city, when pageants greeted her as they had greeted Elizabeth three years before in London. One was a bonny bairn coming as it were from Heaven out of a round globe, to present her with a Bible, a psalter, and the keys of the city. Another pageant showed Korah, Dathan and Abiram being burnt in the time of their sacrifice, as a terrible signification of the vengeance of God upon idolaters. The citizens had intended to burn a wooden effigy of a priest, arrayed in robes at the altar and in the act of elevating the Host. The Earl of Huntly stayed that pageant.

Meanwhile John Knox was thundering out of his pulpit, and Randolph feared nothing so much as that one day he would mar all. 'He ruleth the roost, and of him all men stand in fear—would God you knew how much.' One Mass declared Knox, on the second Sunday after Mary's arrival, was more fearful to him than if ten thousand armed enemies were landed in the realm to suppress their religion. Mary resolved to see the intrepid preacher. It was vain: her arts and fascination, even her authority, were lost on him. He 'knocked so hastily upon her heart' that he made her weep, as much in anger as grief. The opinion he formed of her at the interview was as clear and confident as the words he then spoke: 'If there be not in her a proud mind, a crafty wit, and an indurate heart against God and his truth, my judgment faileth me'.

Sorrow, humiliation, and anger, paved the way that

Mary was forced to tread. She, however, had this advantage, that time and patience were on her side. Knox noticed
how each Protestant lord bristled at the spectacle of the
Mass when first he came to Court, yet after a while quiet-
ened down as others had done before him. A godly man
said to a new arrival: 'My lord, now ye are come, and almost the last of all the rest; and I perceive by your anger
that the fire-edge is not off you yet. But I fear that after
the holy water of the Court be sprinkled upon you, ye shall
become as temperate as the rest; for I have been here now
five days, and at the first I heard every man say, "Let us
hang the priest", but after that they had been twice or
thrice in the Abbey, all that fervency was past. I think
there be some enchantment whereby men are bewitched'.

In truth, Mary was showing herself as moderate as she
was attractive. She kept her Mass, but in political questions placed herself in the hands of Murray and Maitland
and took up the project of friendship with Elizabeth at the
point it had reached with the arrival of the belated safe-
conduct. Within a fortnight Maitland, who was 'the flower
of the wits in Scotland', 'an honest man somewhat more
given to policy than to Mr. Knox's preaching', was on his
way to England with friendly greetings from Mary.

Elizabeth received the envoy with pleasure. She pretended surprise when he made his proposal that she should
recognize Mary as heir presumptive to her throne. 'I looked
for another message from the Queen, your sovereign', she
retorted, reminding him that Mary was bound in honour
to ratify the Treaty of Edinburgh. Let her do that first, and
then would be the time to make concessions. 'I have long
enough been fed with fair words.' Maitland soon let her see
that, unimpeachable as her attitude no doubt was, it would
make no appeal to Scotsmen, whose interests were no longer
what they had been, but were now bound up with those of
their Queen, and therefore with her claim to the English
succession. Elizabeth answered that the succession was a
matter in which she would not meddle; like pitch, dangerous to touch for fear of being fouled, or—changing the
simile—like the doctrine of the sacrament on which some

think one thing, some another, and God only knows whose judgment is best.

Elizabeth spoke feelingly. Only the previous month the matter had cropped up when she had discovered that the Lady Catherine Grey, the next person in the succession under Henry VIII's will, was with child. Inquiry revealed that she had secretly married the Earl of Hertford, Protector Somerset's eldest son. It was not the first time that Catherine had been an anxiety. At the beginning of the reign, there had been a plot to spirit her over to Flanders and use her in Catholic interests, and although she was no longer connected with the Catholics, Elizabeth felt sure that some of the nobility must have been behind her clandestine and all-but-treasonable marriage. If the unreliable Quadra is to be trusted, the marriage was in fact a plot, promoted by Dudley's enemies when it was thought that he was going to marry the Queen. As neither the officiating priest nor responsible witnesses dared show themselves, Elizabeth had the marriage declared void, and sent Hertford and the Lady Catherine to the Tower. There, in due course, to her indescribable disgust and anger, they proceeded to have a second surreptitious baby.

The succession was a thorny subject, and Elizabeth told Maitland that it was quite enough to know that while she herself lived she would be Queen of England. 'When I am dead,' she went on, 'they shall succeed that have most right. If the Queen your sovereign be that person, I shall never hurt her; if another have better right, it were not reasonable to require me to do a manifest injury.' She was prepared to go a little farther and reveal her own opinion, admitting that she knew of no better right than Mary's, nor of any that she would prefer to hers, nor indeed of any claimant who was strong enough to keep Mary from the throne: 'You know them all,' she said; 'Alas! what power or force has any of them, poor souls?' True, some of them, she caustically added, by showing that they were not barren but were able to have children, had made a declaration to the world that they were more worthy of the throne than either herself or Mary. Wretched Lady Catherine!

When Maitland argued that his project would promote friendship; 'Think you,' Elizabeth retorted, 'that I could love my winding-sheet, when as examples show, princes cannot even love their children who are to succeed them?' However, it was the peril that weighed most with her. She knew the inconstancy of her people, that they preferred the rising to the setting sun. 'I have good experience of myself in my sister's time, how desirous men were that I should be in place, and earnest to set me up. And if I would have consented, I know what enterprises would have been attempted to bring it to pass.' Now, she continued, the affections of some were perhaps altered. As children dream in their sleep of apples, and weep when they awake in the morning and do not find them, so every man who bore her goodwill when she was Lady Elizabeth, imagined that immediately she came to the throne he would be rewarded according to his own fancy; and finding now that the event had not answered his expectation could perhaps be content with a new change on the chance of faring better. 'No prince's revenues be so great'—how wise the reflection!— 'that they are able to satisfy the insatiable cupidity of men.' Moreover, there was the religious problem—the likeliest line of fracture in the kingdom; and if she recognized a Catholic Mary as her successor, a puissant princess and her near neighbour, she might be creating a wedge to split her realm in two. Promises, she declared, could not be relied upon; witness Mary's refusal to ratify the Treaty of Edinburgh. 'It is hard to bind princes by any security where hope is offered of a kingdom.' 'If it were certainly known in the world who should succeed her, she would never think herself in sufficient security.'

And so, as Maitland reported, 'the matter was left *re integra*'; nothing accomplished. Yet Elizabeth had been more than friendly, she had been helpful. What she was prepared to offer was benevolent neutrality, which would serve her as a political insurance, guaranteeing Mary's friendship. The future of that neutrality—whether it became anything more or anything less—would depend upon Mary's

behaviour. Elizabeth's intentions were as genuine as her
statesmanship was masterly.

For form's sake, to retain the advantage of her position
in the diplomatic game, Elizabeth sent once more to demand the ratification of the Treaty of Edinburgh, but she
had told Maitland that she was prepared to review the
Treaty and qualify it, and by a letter to Mary she led up
to what she really wanted, a proposal that Mary and she
should meet. It was impossible for her to commit her intentions to representatives, whereas at a personal interview
the two Queens would be able to reach an understanding
that would pass beyond the formal words of a treaty. There
is no resisting the conclusion that Elizabeth was prepared
virtually to assure Mary of the succession; assure her of it
on conditions that are easy to guess: no league with France,
friendship with England, an acceptable marriage, and
probably ultimate conversion to Protestantism. The way
was set with difficulties, but there is no reason to think that,
provided the two met and could inspire one another with
confidence, the difficulties were insurmountable. Maitland
did not think his mistress irretrievably wedded to her Mass:
'Surely, I see in her a good towardness', he told Cecil, 'and
think that the Queen, your sovereign, shall be able to do
much with her in religion if they once enter in a good
familiarity'.

Elizabeth told Maitland and Cecil to correspond freely
and confidentially, each with the knowledge of his mistress,
in order that the way to an agreement might be explored
before uttering it to the world. The correspondence went
on. It was freer on Maitland's side, for all his cards were
on the table, and it was he who controlled Mary, not Mary
him. On one occasion he delayed Mary's answer to a letter
of Elizabeth's in order that Cecil might tell him what she
ought to write! Cecil ignored his request.

Cecil at this time was in a queer way. He had lost his
poise and initiative, the Dudley episode having shattered
the old understanding between him and Elizabeth. He was
like a ship without headway. In December, 1561, he told
his gossip, Throckmorton, 'I might lament my place that I

hold, being to outward appearance, because of frequenta-
tion with her Majesty, of much credit; and indeed, of none
at all. But my remedy is only to leave the place; wherein
my only grief is to see likelihood of such successors as I am
sure shall or will destroy all my good purpose'. 'I see so little
proof of my travails, by reason her Majesty alloweth not
of them, that I have left all to the wide world.' He kept
on, he said, for a show, but inwardly he meddled not, 'leaving things in a course, as the clock is left when the barrel is
wound up'. Over this Scottish business he was afraid to take
responsibility. Perhaps his heart was not in it, and another
woman ruler still an insupportable prospect to him. Maitland was constantly expostulating. 'Many things may pass
between us two,' he wrote, which neither Mary nor Elizabeth 'will for the first face write to one another.' 'I pray
you, let us not weary to push forward till they have met,
when I doubt not one of them shall so govern the other
that they shall thereafter need no mediators; and then will
I say, *Nunc dimittis servum tuum domine.*' 'We shoot both
at one scope—the union of this isle.' Cecil, he complained,
always wrote parables to him, brief and dark sentences; to
which Cecil answered that being a minister he could not
in his sovereign's causes write otherwise than she pleased.

But for all these fears, or even the dark phrases, which
had a perfectly reasonable explanation, the momentum behind the interview was steadily increasing. Mary's uncles in
France, no longer identified with French policy, were keen
on it, and remarkable to relate, something like cordiality
grew up between their House and Elizabeth. Throckmorton
was for it. Mary was enthusiastic; so was Elizabeth.

Then came the rumblings of a storm from France. The
strange and uncertain religious peace which had descended
on that country with the accession of Charles IX was
broken through the massacre, by the followers of the Duke
of Guise, of a Protestant congregation at Vassy on March
1st, 1562. Catholics and Huguenots both armed, and the
next month were at war with one another. Immediately,
Throckmorton urged Elizabeth to abandon the meeting
with Mary. She must help the Prince of Condé and his

Huguenot followers; and seeing that Spain, Savoy and others were likely to intervene on the Catholic side, turning the war into a great scramble for spoil, she must be in at the game as well. She could get the Huguenots, Throckmorton said, to give her possession of Calais, Dieppe, or Havre, or even all three.

It was a poor look-out for the interview! Well Mary knew this, torn as she was between anxiety for her uncle of Guise and grief at the likely result of his actions upon her relations with Elizabeth. She cried over her misfortune—'Before God, it is true!' wrote Randolph. But the situation was not yet desperate. Elizabeth had little desire to go speculating in France, and although she noted what Throckmorton said and was prepared to take action if forced to do so, she preferred to try and bring about peace by mediation. Her mind was still set resolutely on the interview with Mary. Early in June her Council met to consider the question: they could find nothing but difficulties in the way. Nevertheless, Elizabeth said that she would go, and gave orders for the necessary preparations to be made.

Maitland now arrived in London, with an earnest letter from Mary. The Council was ordered to discuss the question over again, and as Elizabeth realized that there was little hope of a more favourable conclusion, she attended the meeting herself. It was a full Council. Each member spoke in turn, and Sir Nicholas Bacon's speech happens to have come down to us. He first insisted upon identifying Mary with the House of Guise, and then proceeded to review their past hostility to England. Mary herself, he showed, had ample reason to dislike Elizabeth, and if a sure indication were needed that there had been no change of heart, it could be found in her continued refusal to ratify the Treaty of Edinburgh. Words were one thing, acts another; and dulcet and pleasant speeches accompanied by promises were not materials on which wisdom could rely. Meetings of princes were rare; they were manifestations of great amity; and this meeting could not fail to strengthen the House of Guise, at a moment when they were fighting for Catholicism against Protestantism. Let the Guise party

recover control of France; the result might well be a league
of Catholic princes who would stick at nothing to overthrow
Protestantism in England. In such an event Elizabeth must
not hope for the help of other Protestant princes, supposing
she abandoned the French Protestants in their present need.
Moreover, who could doubt that if the Guise got control of
France they would help Mary to destroy the existing government and religion of Scotland? The interview with
Mary, he concluded, offered no hope of good but great fear
of ill, and therefore for his part he could not allow of it.

There was not a councillor who did not take the same
view. Elizabeth listened as speech after speech built up the
case against the interview with devastating unanimity.
Then, with a 'fineness of wit and excellence of utterance'
that won their praise, she answered them all. She would
allow no reply. Unless, she defiantly announced, she received news from Throckmorton in France justly causing
her to stay, go to the meeting she would. 'It is both groaned
at and lamented of the most and the wisest', wrote Sir
Henry Sidney to Throckmorton. He told Throckmorton that
no one but he could hope to influence Elizabeth, and
begged him to do as much and as cunningly as he could
to stop the meeting; incidentally, he would save the nobles
and gentlemen of England above forty thousand pounds.

The very stars in their courses appeared to be fighting
against the interview. The weather had been incredibly
bad, making the roads impassable for a long train of wag-
ons and horses. 'Neither sun nor moon, nor winter, nor
spring, nor summer, nor autumn have performed their appropriate offices', wrote Bishop Jewel in August, 1562—taking stylistic licence to put autumn in his list. 'It has rained
so abundantly, and almost without intermission, as if the
heavens could hardly do anything else.' A contagion of
monstrous births confirmed the omen: infants with hide-
ously deformed bodies—a man child, born at Chichester on
May 24th, whose head, arms, and legs were 'like an
anatomy', 'the breast and belly monstrous big from the
navel, as it were a long string hanging; about the neck a
great collar of flesh and skin growing like to a ruff of a shirt

or neckerchief, coming up above the ears, plaiting and fold-ing'. Similar births in abundance from swine, mares, and so on: a two-headed foal with a long tail growing out be-tween the heads; a pig with human arms, hands and fin-gers; another with two bodies, eight legs, and but one head.

Signs, portents, difficulties, did not worry Elizabeth. She left monstrous births to divines, chroniclers, and newsven-dors, the condition of the roads to her officials, and the wherewithal for their finery to the nobles and gentlemen themselves. It was the state of France with which she was concerned. There, peace was agreed to on June 25th; and on July 6th Elizabeth settled with Maitland the conditions for her meeting with Mary. Among the articles of agree-ment was one which maintained her right to demand the ratification of the Treaty of Edinburgh; a propitious clause, the reward of pertinacity. The two Queens were to meet at York or some other convenient place between August 20th and September 20th.

It was not to be. On July 12th the French peace col-lapsed and war was renewed. No longer could Elizabeth remain a spectator and let Condé be overthrown. As she told Mary some months later: 'When I saw that all my councillors and subjects thought me of sight too dim, of hearing too deaf, of spirit too improvident, I roused myself from such slumber and deemed myself unworthy to govern such a kingdom as I possess, if I were not also skilled in my own affairs'. On July 15th she sent Sir Henry Sidney to Scotland to put off the meeting till the following summer, 1563. Mary was heartbroken and kept her bed all day; but when she saw Sidney and learnt of Elizabeth's friendliness, her spirits revived. After all, the interview was only post-poned, and for no more, indeed for less, than a year. Pa-thetic optimism! The Fates are implacable.

CHAPTER VIII

THE SUCCESSION QUESTION

ELIZABETH was moving towards her second military adventure. Outwardly, all was commendable promptitude: orders were immediately given to levy troops and prepare a fleet and transports, while Gresham was sent off to the money-market of Antwerp to prolong old debts and enter into new. But behind the scenes Cecil and others were anxiously wrestling with their mistress's doubts, trying to wean her from peace and adjust her mind and temper to the wasteful repugnant business of war. They had the arguments for it set forth in cogent memoranda, and Throckmorton in France was given a hint to harp on the peril of a Guise victory.

It was a very natural situation. Both her instincts and her experience made Elizabeth reluctant to hasten into danger: she preferred to await its coming, knowing that chance so often makes fools of prophets. She had no crusading fervour. Something of a sceptic in politics, still more of a realist, she believed exclusively in English interests, and after her heavy expenditure on Scotland two years before, would have preferred to give military adventures a rest and husband her resources. Little wonder that in this mood she drove a hard bargain with the Prince of Condé and the Huguenots, forcing them to surrender Havre and allow her to keep it until France should restore Calais. In return, she was to pay them a subsidy, and send an army to occupy Havre. It was doubtful policy to compel her allies to become infamous as Frenchmen, and was almost certain to bring its own Nemesis in the event of peace returning to France.

Peace however seemed remote. Religious passion was running to incredible barbarity, neither sex nor age being spared in the orgies of torture, outrage, and slaughter. In Paris it was enough for a boy to cry out 'Voilà un Huguenot!" Straightway idle vagabonds and porters set upon the unfortunate victim with stones, out came the handicraftsmen and apprentices and thrust him through with a thousand wounds, while the boys, after spoiling the body of its clothes, trailed it down to the river and cast it in. The people's sympathy, like their rage, was at the service of any impostor. A resourceful murderer, when he was on the ladder and about to be hanged, called out, 'Ah! my masters, I must die now for killing a Huguenot who despised our Lady, but as I have served our Lady always truly and have put my trust in her, so I trust now she will show some miracle for me'. The people murmured, ran to the gallows, beat the hangman, and set the felon free. As may be imagined, Protestant opinion in England was profoundly stirred by the innumerable stories that were told of Catholic outrage.

By early October, 1562, the treaty with Condé was concluded and the English troops were ready. They occupied Havre. Except for a small company of men who played a valiant part in the defence of Rouen, the war hardly touched them. It was with peace that danger came. On March 25th, 1563, after Condé had been captured and the Duke of Guise assassinated, Catherine de Medici managed to end the war, and as was to be expected, Catholic and Huguenot united in a common front against the English. Terms were offered to Elizabeth, but she was determined, providing her army could defend Havre, to have Calais back; and so there was nothing to do save fight it out. Probably she would have won if a new and dreadful enemy —the plague—had not appeared. With this decimating her army, she hastily tried to make terms, but too late. Soon there were five hundred of the garrison dying per week, then a hundred a day with twice as many sick; the walls could not be manned properly nor the dead buried; reinforcements were hurried over, but were outpaced by death, and the supply of skilled men failed. Endeavour at home, high courage in the army, neither was lacking, but both were unavailing, and on July 29th Havre had to be surrendered. After much haggling peace was made. Honour was saved, as it had been at Cateau-Cambrésis in 1559, but by a still more desperate expedient. Calais, in fact, was irretrievably gone, and so was the compensation promised in the treaty of 1559.

It had been a luckless, costly adventure; and the slumbering prejudice against a woman ruler awoke again. 'God help England and send it a king', wrote someone to the ambassador in Spain, 'for in time of women it has got but a little.' The comment was unfair. Elizabeth had shown at her best in the face of adversity; stout of heart and anxious to blame no one except the Huguenot leaders. She would not let her people cry out upon her soldiers for the loss of Havre; on the contrary, if she had been allowed she would have gone to Portsmouth, at the risk of infection, to meet them on their return and thank them for their bravery.

The misfortune was not over when Havre fell, the disease-stricken garrison bringing the plague back to their homes, where it ravaged the country until the wet and colder weather of October to November arrived. In London alone the deaths mounted rapidly from one hundred to three thousand in a week; and here and in the outlying parishes some twenty thousand people perished. Among the victims was the Spanish ambassador, Quadra. He died in harness, intriguing to the end. 'I can do no more' were his last words. With his malicious reports and his encouragement of religious and political discontent, he had done his best to alienate Spain and England and undermine Elizabeth's authority; an ill service for which he had latterly been sharply treated by the English Council. But according to his own light he had been a faithful servant, and his monetary reward, like that of most ambassadors then, was hopelessly inadequate. He died so heavily in debt—to tradesmen and his own household, some of whom had been paid nothing for years—that his executors, during more than eighteen months, did not dare to send his body out of the country for burial, lest creditors, who were on the watch, should seize it to extract payment.

The French adventure over, interest centred again on the relations between Elizabeth and Mary. During the war Mary had steered an entirely praiseworthy course between sympathy for her 'dear sister, so tender a cousin and friend', and her equally dear uncles; lamenting her lot that victory must bring grief to her whoever won it, and refusing to be drawn from her neutrality into the old league with France. She shed bitter tears over the death of three of her uncles and was pathetically grateful for the tender letters of Elizabeth. All the same, the war was a tragic hiatus in the progress towards a common understanding and lasting friendship. For one reason, the House of Guise had renewed its hostility to Elizabeth, and was doing its best to convince Mary that her cousin was playing her false. Graver still, time and its events had complicated the issues between them.

In the spring of 1562, when both Queens had been intent on meeting one another, English people had not been bothering their heads over much about the succession to the throne. But their apathy vanished in October of that year when they were sharply reminded of 'the blind Fury with the abhorred shears'. Elizabeth had fallen dangerously ill of smallpox. The disease had vexed the country for two or three years and been particularly rife among ladies of rank. The Countess of Bedford and many others had died of it. Elizabeth had felt unwell, taken a bath to revive herself, and with an active person's impatience of ailments ventured out and caught a chill. She went down with a violent fever. For a time the eruption would not appear, and on the day of the crisis she was unconscious for a few hours. Death, as she said, possessed every joint of her; the Court mourned her as dying. The previous midnight Cecil had been hastily summoned from London to Hampton Court, and there the Council, faced as they imagined with Elizabeth's impending death, anxiously discussed who should succeed her. All that emerged was a conflict of opinion. Some were for Lady Catherine Grey, some for the Earl of Huntingdon, apparently none—or none openly—for Mary Queen of Scots.

As Elizabeth regained consciousness, her thoughts, according to a probable story, were on England and Dudley. In her confused, uncritical state of mind her instinctive desire was to commit her beloved and all-too-unfortunate country to the care of the one man in whom she had perfect trust. She begged the Council to make Dudley Protector of England, giving him a title and an income of twenty thousand pounds. She loved and had always loved him dearly, she said, but as God was her witness, nothing improper had ever passed between them. The story may or may not be true, but Dudley was certainly in her mind just then, for three days later, when she was on the road to recovery, she made him a Privy Councillor. She had, however, recovered her sagacity by then, and therefore at the same time made the Duke of Norfolk a Councillor, in order to quiet jealousy.

Naturally, the succession question flared into prominence as a result of this illness, and the rifts that had been evident in the Council began to show themselves outside. Henceforward, Englishmen could not fail to realize upon what a slender thread—a woman's life—depended the tranquillity of their land; and ambition, self-interest, religious leanings, or simple anxiety for a known and assured future, drove them to side with this claimant or with that.

In January, 1563, under the shadow of this fear the second parliament of the reign met. It was called to help in financing the French war, but the talk was common and widespread that an attempt would be made to settle the succession to the throne; and no sooner was business begun than a burgess rose in the House of Commons to speak at length on the subject. A committee was appointed to draw up a petition to the Queen, and the Lords were approached. Only too ready to lend support, the Upper House set to work on a petition of its own. In fact, it is hard to discern a single discordant mind. Cecil was in favour of the suit, although, being a prudent man and knowing the Queen's views, seeing, moreover, that it might some day be fatal to his fortunes to back an unsuccessful claimant, he kept silence. 'The matter is so deep, I cannot reach into it. God send it a good issue!' he wrote to a friend.

The Commons' petition, when ready, was full to overflowing with terms of loving affection; it contained in addition a request to Elizabeth to marry. But these were the trimmings to their real suit, which concerned the succession. Referring to the great terror and dreadful warning of Elizabeth's recent illness, they drew a harrowing picture of miseries unspeakable, of civil war and foreign invasion, waste of noble houses and slaughter of people, daily interchange of attainders and treasons during which lives and estates would be uncertain—of these and infinite other mischiefs if England were left to be disputed among rival claimants at her death. It was enough to recall the empire of Alexander the Great, or England's own Wars of the Roses; these and many other precedents proved that their prophecy was not foolish. The Protestant faith was at stake: 'We fear a faction of heretics in your realm', they said; 'contentious and malicious Papists'.

Elizabeth answered the petition in a brief, choice, and relatively simple speech, urging them not to think that she, who in other matters had such care of them all, would be careless in this, which concerned both her own and their safety. It touched her nearer than them; they at worst could lose their bodies, whereas she hazarded to lose both body and soul if her policy proved disastrous. She had read a philosopher whose custom it was, when faced with a knotty academic problem, to rehearse his alphabet before answering: she similarly would defer an answer to their petition till some other time, since she would not, in so deep a matter, wade with so shallow a wit. 'I assure you all,' she ended, 'that though after my death you may have many stepdames, yet shall you never have a more natural mother than I mean to be unto you all.'

A few days later the Lords came with their petition. They were more discreet, giving greater attention to the more palatable request for marriage; but Elizabeth was annoyed with them. She could understand the House of Commons, where, as she put it, there were 'restless heads in whose brains the needless hammers beat with vain judgment'. From the Lords she expected less impetuous and shortsighted action than to join the Commons, leaving their Queen isolated. If she declared a successor, she warned them, it would cost much blood to England. With some bitterness, she added that the marks which they saw on her face were not wrinkles but the pits of smallpox; she might be old, but God could send her children as He had done to Saint Elizabeth.

Fretfully the Commons waited for the answer that Elizabeth had promised them. Someone had suggested that they should hold up supplies until the succession was settled; but the temper and courage of the majority did not rise so high. Perhaps it would have been different if they had only realized that Elizabeth was determined to put off her reply until the money bill was safely through, and then dismiss Parliament with one of her 'answers-answerless'.

At last, when Lords and Commons were assembled for the closing ceremonies of the Parliament, Elizabeth gave Sir Nicholas Bacon her answer to read. She had written and revised it herself, going carefully over it, improving a word here and a phrase there until it emerged as a model of her more artificial and involved style. She made ironical use of the fervent wish that they had one time expressed to live only under her and her progeny, remarking that she thought it had been so desired as 'none other tree's blossom' should have been considered before hope had been lost of fruit from her. If any imagined, she declared, that she was determined not to marry, let them put out that kind of heresy; their belief was awry. She might think a spinster's life best for a private woman, but was striving to think it not meet for a prince. And so she brought a speech full of goodwill, uncertainty, and dark phrases to a close: 'I hope I shall die in quiet with *Nunc dimittis*, which cannot be without I see some glimpse of your following surety after my graved bones'.

Parliament was prorogued, and until financial or other pressing needs compelled her to summon it again, Elizabeth could breathe more freely. Its agitation, though unsuccessful, had helped to mobilize opinion in favour of certain claimants; and a year later Elizabeth discovered that during its meeting a tract had been written confuting Mary's claim and advancing Lady Catherine Grey's. The author was a member named John Hales, one of Ascham's Protestant friends and a Chancery official. He had not acted alone; inquiries implicated the Lord Keeper, Sir Nicholas Bacon, and for a time placed Cecil under suspicion. Despising Lady Catherine as she did and having Mary in mind as her successor, Elizabeth was extremely angry. She banished Bacon from Court and cast Hales into prison.

It was all very disturbing to the dispassionate pursuit of an agreement between Elizabeth and Mary. The succession, indeed, was not a gift which Elizabeth could lightly make and later withdraw if Mary embarked on a hostile policy. It was a right. Once declared, it could never be rescinded with any show of justice or hope of real effect. Even if she had wished—which she did not—Elizabeth could not have got Mary's claim recognized by any of her parliaments without clear proof that she was effectively tied to the interests of England and its Protestant establishment.

The crux of this problem was Mary's marriage. She must not marry a foreign, Catholic prince, such as Don Carlos of Spain, the Archduke Charles, or the King of France. The ideal husband from England's point of view would be an English nobleman in whose loyalty to herself and her country Elizabeth had perfect trust. It was a situation not unlike that in October when Elizabeth had thought herself dying of smallpox; and her mind now ran upon the same solution that she is said to have thought of then. There was only one person in whom, foolishly or wisely, she had such trust—Dudley; and being convinced that she

could not marry him herself, she decided to offer him to
Mary. In this way her affections would be vicariously satisfied, and she herself reconciled to celibacy and a career;
a reconciliation not excessively disturbing to a woman of
her temperament. As a Scottish ambassador said to her:
'Madam, I know your stately stomach: ye think if ye were
married, ye would be but Queen of England, and now ye
are King and Queen both; ye may not suffer a commander'.

Elizabeth enriched the comedy of history by her proposal, but, if only one could share her belief in her none-
too-admirable Dudley, it was neither unstatesmanlike nor
unfriendly to Mary. Naturally, others could hardly be expected to see with the same glamoured eyes. When she
broached her startling idea to Maitland, who was in London during the 1563 parliament, he extricated himself from
an embarrassing conversation with ready wit, suggesting
that Elizabeth herself should first of all marry Dudley, and
then when she died leave Mary heiress to both husband
and kingdom. Thus she would ensure that Dudley had
children by one or the other of them, who in due course
would succeed to her throne. And how happy that thought
would make her!

Whether Maitland told his mistress of the conversation or
not, gossip carried the news to France and thence to Scotland. Elizabeth, however, was not so foolish as to make the
proposal before putting out feelers. When the end of the
Havre adventure left her free, she gave instructions to her
ambassador, Randolph, to say to Mary, as from himself
and not from her, that he thought no one could better
content Elizabeth as her husband than some Englishman
of noble birth and of conditions and qualities meet for the
rank; 'Yea, perchance such as she would hardly think we
could agree unto'—so ran an insertion which Elizabeth
added in her own hand to Randolph's instructions! It was
not until March, 1564, that the name of the paragon was
divulged. Mary's official astonishment left her dumb.

Mary, indeed, was no longer as compliant as she had
been. She was older, more settled in her kingdom, and
ready to pursue a policy of her own; inclined, and not with-

out some justification from her point of view, to distrust Elizabeth. 'This, of all her faults, is the greatest,' wrote Randolph, 'that she conceives oft much evil where none is thought.' A woman of spirit, she was tiring of tutelage. Though she was not necessarily wanting to adopt a Catholic policy, being 'not so affectioned to her Mass that she will leave a kingdom for it', her Protestant zealots were getting on her nerves. Far the worst was John Knox, who was still full of mistrust of all her doings and sayings, as though, Randolph wittily said, he were of God's privy council and knew how the Almighty had determined of her from the beginning. He infuriated her in the spring of 1563 by preaching a sermon to the nobility in which he dilated on her marriage. 'And now, my Lords,' he exclaimed, 'I hear of the Queen's marriage: dukes, brethren to emperors, and kings strive all for the best gain. But this, my Lords, will I say: whensoever the nobility of Scotland, professing the Lord Jesus, consents that an infidel—and all Papists are infidels—shall be head to your sovereign, ye do so far as in ye lieth to banish Christ Jesus from this realm.'

Knox was summoned to Court, where the Queen in a vehement rage began to cry out that never prince was handled as she. 'I have borne with you,' she exclaimed, 'in all your rigorous manner of speaking, both against myself and against my uncles; yea, I have sought your favours by all possible means. I offered unto you presence and audience whensoever it pleased you to admonish me; and yet I cannot be quit of you. I vow to God, I shall be once revenged.' And with these words, says Knox, scarcely could Marnock, her secret-chamber boy, get napkins to hold her eyes dry for the tears; and the 'owling', besides womanly tears, stayed her speech.

Knox patiently abided all the first fume, and at opportunity answered: 'True it is, Madam, your Grace and I have been at divers controversies, in the which I never perceived your Grace to be offended at me. But when it shall please God to deliver you from that bondage of darkness and error in the which ye have been nourished, for the lack of true doctrine, your Majesty will find the liberty of my tongue nothing offensive'.

'What have ye to do with my marriage?' cried Mary. 'Or what are ye within this Commonwealth?'

'A subject born within the same, Madam', he answered. 'And albeit I neither be earl, lord, nor baron within it, yet has God made me, how abject that ever I be in your eyes, a profitable member within the same.'

From all Mary's troubles, whether at the hands of this dour preacher and his fellows, or of her provoking, elder cousin of England, marriage seemed the escape; a magnificent marriage, for her heart was great, remembering what she had been—a King's wife; and what she still was—a Queen. An eagle does not prey on flies, nor such as she match with such as Dudley, who came not of an old House and whose blood was spotted with treason. When Maitland was in London at the beginning of 1563 the Spanish ambassador talked to him about a marriage with Philip II's son, Don Carlos; Maitland reported the conversation to Mary. If she had been as particular about the personal qualities of a suitor as Elizabeth, she might have discovered that Don Carlos was a sickly, gluttonous, vile-tempered epileptic. But it was enough for her that it was a great match, and would assure her of the English succession, with or without the goodwill of Elizabeth. Indeed, what rival claimant at Elizabeth's death could hope to withstand the combined power of Spain and Scotland? She set her heart on the marriage. To the Spanish ambassador it opened a still more splendid prospect—of Elizabeth deposed, Catholicism restored, and the British Isles joined to the wide domains of Spain. He wrote with enthusiasm to his master, urging him to consent. In his quiet way Philip also saw the prospect, and approved; but time lost its urgency in his distant, sunny land, and caution for ever whispered: 'To-morrow, and to-morrow, and to-morrow'.

That Mary aimed at ousting Elizabeth from her throne, there is no reason to think. Yet her negotiations, coming to Elizabeth's ears, were certainly open to the sinister interpretation. This was especially true while the Treaty of

Edinburgh, with its repudiation of her pretensions to the
English throne, remained unratified. No marriage could
have been more alarming. All the same, the two maintained
the old show of friendship. There were continual messages,
'letters written in whole sheets of paper with their own
hands, the one to the other'; and Randolph continued in
high favour at Mary's court, more than once talking gaily
to the Queen while she indulged herself with a day in bed
—a foible to which Elizabeth was not given. All this was
on the surface. The deeper clash of interests appeared
when in the spring of 1564 Elizabeth proposed that the
long-delayed interview between her and Mary should take
place that summer. While secretly pursuing her Spanish
project and hoping to do much better for herself than she
could by an agreement with Elizabeth, there was nothing
Mary desired less. She declined the invitation.

Thus a third time was the opportunity of a meeting lost.
Yet between these two Queens, with distrust the bane of
everything, it was the only hope of mutual understanding.
Was tragedy inevitable?

Relations cooled; but in September Mary sent an adroit
young courtier, James Melville, a person Elizabeth knew
and liked, to breathe new warmth into them. He found
Elizabeth very sore about some malapert phrases in a letter
of Mary's, and she took out of her pouch a tart reply which
she said that she only held back because it was not vehement enough. She was easily placated, and finished by
tearing up both letters.

For the remainder of his nine days' stay, Melville was in
demand every day, and sometimes thrice in a day. He had
spent many years in foreign courts and Elizabeth could
therefore air her knowledge of French, Italian, and German—the last bad—and discuss the customs of other lands
with him. Women's fashions being compared, each day she
put on a different dress, one day English, another French,
and a third Italian. She was delighted when Melville announced that the Italian style suited her best, as it showed
her golden hair to advantage. She wanted to know what
coloured hair was considered best, and how hers compared

with Mary's. Then followed a whole series of comparisons. Who, she asked, was the fairer, Mary or she? a question Melville tried to dodge by declaring that she was the fairest Queen in England and theirs the fairest Queen in Scotland. As Elizabeth was not to be put off, he replied that they were both the fairest ladies of their courts, but the Queen of England was whiter, their Queen 'very lusome'. Next she wanted to know who was the higher. Mary was, answered Melville. Then is she over high, retorted Elizabeth; she herself being neither over high nor over low. What, she asked, were Mary's amusements, and did she play well on the lute and the virginals? 'Reasonably for a Queen', answered Melville. Here was a comparison that lent itself to demonstration. Accordingly that night the Queen's cousin, Lord Hunsdon, took Melville along to surprise Elizabeth, alone in her chamber, playing 'exceedingly well' on the virginals. When she caught sight of him and chid him for being there without permission, he had his answer pat: 'I heard such melody, which ravished and drew me within the chamber, I wist not how'. His departure was delayed a night so that he could watch her dance and draw a final comparison. Mary, he announced, 'danced not so high and disposedly as she did'.

During his stay Melville had witnessed the creation of Dudley as Baron of Denbigh and Earl of Leicester, dignities which were meant to fit him to wed Mary. The ceremony was performed with great solemnity, but as the new earl knelt gravely before Elizabeth, her sense of fun got the better of her and she tickled his neck.

Melville had played Elizabeth's court game admirably, but the humour of it rather eluded him. He thought her envious of Mary and took an unfortunate report back to feed his mistress's suspicions, telling her that in his judgment there was neither plain dealing nor upright meaning in Elizabeth, but great dissimulation. The fact was that he had given too sympathetic an ear and too much time to Elizabeth's critics and enemies.

One of Melville's secret tasks in London had been to make a last—but, as it turned out, a futile—attempt to liven up the Spanish marriage project, which had proved abortive. Mary wanted to make sure that hope was dead before turning to an alternative plan. This was a marriage with her cousin, the young Lord Darnley, whose mother, the Countess of Lennox, was the daughter of Margaret Tudor by her second husband, and therefore grand-daughter of Henry VII. Mary herself was descended from Margaret Tudor by the first marriage, and while her claim to the English succession was therefore stronger on the ground of descent, it was weaker in the fact that she was alien born. Both Darnley and his mother had been born in England, where the Earl of Lennox had lived since Henry VIII's reign as an attainted Scottish exile. The marriage offered a treble advantage; it would merge the two claims, obviate rivalry, and bring over to Mary's side the Lennox and Catholic faction in England. So glowing were the illusory accounts of the numbers and strength of this party that Mary was led to think that with Darnley as with Don Carlos she could afford to snap her fingers at the dilly-dallying Elizabeth. He might not be as great a match as Don Carlos, but at any rate he was of royal blood and infinitely preferable to the upstart Earl of Leicester, whose marriage portion was dependence on Elizabeth.

Darnley's mother, a masterful, ambitious woman, with more than a dash of Tudor spirit, had been angling for the match ever since Francis II's death, and in the spring of 1562, she and her husband had both been in trouble over their intrigue. They were restored to favour at the beginning of 1563, and induced Elizabeth to write to Mary, supporting their suit for the repeal of their attainder and restoration to their titles and lands in Scotland. Elizabeth's letter was a simple act of goodwill, of no importance and no danger at the time it was written—June, 1563. But a year later, Mary's thoughts had turned to the Darnley marriage, and the year-old letter became a godsend, offering the solution of her most difficult problem—how to get Darnley to Scotland. She could first bring Lennox to Scotland, ostensibly at Elizabeth's request, in order to rehabilitate him. It would then be easy to rig up an excuse for Darnley to follow.

It was very clever. Unless Elizabeth was ready to be churlish and give open offence to Mary and the Lennox family the plan could not be scotched. Elizabeth knew of course what was in the wind. When Dudley was made Earl of Leicester she turned to Melville and asked how he liked him. 'Yet ye like better of yonder long lad', she said, pointing to Darnley; to which the resourceful Melville replied that 'no woman of spirit would make choice of such a man, that was liker a woman than a man'.

Probably, Elizabeth nursed no fundamental objection to the marriage. If Mary definitely rejected Leicester, Darnley might not be a bad *pis aller;* anyhow, he would be better than a foreign Catholic prince. In November, 1564, Cecil told a confidant that he thought no marriage was more likely to succeed than this, if only it were suggested honourably by Mary. The condition he named was crucial. It was essential to Elizabeth's policy that Mary's marriage should be accompanied by an agreement, with adequate safeguards for England's present and future.

Anticipating the outcome of his journey, Elizabeth was uneasy at the idea of Lennox going to Scotland in the summer of 1564. But though she tried to prevent it by writing secretly to Mary, she was unable to do so without giving offence, for which she was not prepared. He arrived in Scotland in September, 1564, and in due course came the request for Darnley to join him.

At first Elizabeth gave a blank refusal. Her commissioners were about to meet Murray and Maitland to discuss the terms she would offer with Leicester, and she would on no account jeopardize her pet scheme. These negotiations failed. Randolph, like blind Bayard, 'whose heart served him well but his sight failed him to guide him the way', continued to write optimistic letters; but Cecil, and Leicester himself, knew that there was no hope left for Elizabeth's scheme. Perhaps they realized that personally they had much to gain by making the fortunes of one who would probably be their future king; anyhow, they urged Eliza-

beth to let Darnley go to Scotland. In the end they got their
way. As likely as not, Elizabeth knew in her heart that in
acquiescing she was surrendering her cherished dream.
Darnley arrived in Edinburgh on February 13th, 1565,
where people were anxiously discussing a recent and terrifying omen. At midnight on three successive nights before,
the cries and clash of arms of ghostly warriors had been
heard, fighting in the empty streets. But this presage of
misfortune did not trouble the Queen and Court. They
made merry, with banqueting upon banqueting.

It may be—who can tell?—that Mary was still hesitating.
Just before and just after Darnley's arrival she again asked
Elizabeth to recognize her claim to the succession, to which
Murray and Maitland added their earnest persuasions.
These two were in a cruel predicament. They preferred
Leicester to Darnley, but did not dare to put pressure on
Mary, without a previous assurance of the succession. It
would be hopeless; that they knew, and they would only
turn Mary and the person she married into bitter enemies.

On March 5th Elizabeth sent her reply, which Randolph
told to Mary on the 16th. If Mary would marry Leicester,
it ran, Elizabeth would advance him to all the honour she
could; she would also favour Mary's title to the succession
in every way possible, except that she would not hold a
formal inquiry into her claim and publish it, until she herself was married or had notified her determination never to
marry, one of which she meant to do shortly. From Elizabeth's point of view it was eminently reasonable; from
Mary's, whose mind had fed on suspicion and distrust, it
was provoking and impossible. There lay the tragedy of the
three lost opportunities of meeting. Mary exclaimed bitterly
and angrily that Elizabeth only abused her and frittered
away her time.

Pique drove Mary into Darnley's arms. But there was
another factor—desire for this boy who had all the freshness
and attraction of youth. He was nineteen years of age, exactly three years younger than Mary, tall like her, with long
slender legs, and open boyish face, set off by close-cropped
yellow hair; 'beardless and lady-faced'. He seemed to Mary

'the lustiest and best-proportioned long man that she had seen'. He had been carefully brought up by his ambitious mother, played admirably upon the lute, and was expert at manly, athletic pastimes. If his intelligence was contemptible, and if, as time was to show, his character was worse, there were graces to hide these defects from a woman's early, fascinated gaze. To Mary's indulgent mind his insupportable, stupid arrogance was merely spirit; like called to like. She was ready to abandon herself and her policy to him—ready, until the glamour wore off and her wretched misadventure was fully revealed.

If Mary had let Darnley return to England and had then negotiated the marriage through Elizabeth—a fit and proper procedure seeing that Darnley was an English subject—all would probably have gone well with the relations between the two Queens. She did send Maitland to ask for Elizabeth's approval, but the answer could have been none other than a refusal while Darnley remained in Scotland. Elizabeth had reason to believe that Mary would marry him whatever answer she gave; rumour had it that they were married already. Perhaps Maitland played his mistress false and secretly advised Elizabeth to oppose the marriage; while refusing to think of Leicester as a husband for Mary, he proposed the Duke of Norfolk, who, however, modestly declined the honour. Elizabeth summoned her Council. With one accord they advised opposition, and, as the crisis developed and Elizabeth's friendliness waned, revealed a hostility to Mary gravely significant for the future.

Elizabeth sent Throckmorton to Scotland to oppose the match. He was to offer her consent to a marriage with the Prince of Condé or any English subject except Darnley: she would, however, be prepared to face the risk of declaring her successor only in the event of marriage with Leicester. It was a hopeless mission. Free from the wise restraint of Maitland, during his absence in England, Mary was being led by a precious pair of irresponsibles, Darnley and a favourite secretary of hers, the musician David Riccio, who had become bosom friends and bedfellows. Maitland was only sorry that Throckmorton did not carry with him a threat of war to bring her to her senses. The day that the English envoy reached the Court at Stirling, Darnley was created Earl of Ross, a title that he accepted without Elizabeth's consent, swearing fealty with no reservation of his English allegiance. It was intolerable insolence, an act of defiance. Lady Lennox was sent to the Tower, Lennox and Darnley commanded on their allegiance to return to England. In vain. On July 29th, 1565, Darnley married the Queen of Scots.

Mary had defied England. More, she had committed the very blunder that Elizabeth had come so near committing over Robert Dudley: she had conjured up the evil spirit of faction. Though an English subject, Darnley's family was Scottish, and was embedded in the feuds of that clan-ridden country. His father's restoration to his old title and estates had revived slumbering quarrels, and the Hamiltons saw their utter ruin in his and his son's good fortune. Nor was their fear assuaged by hearing that Darnley had boasted he would knock the Duke's pate for him! Murray, too, believed that his influence and wealth were jeopardized, and again Darnley was a fool, blurting out, when shown a map on which Murray's lands were marked, that they were too many. As for Knox and his fellows; it was enough for them that the Lennox family was the hope of the Catholic party in England. They stood four square to resist an attack upon their godly edifice, and were not beguiled by Darnley's diplomatic attendance at their sermons. Odd as it may seem, it would have been better if Mary had married Leicester, for he would have brought no such damning heritage with him.

And so Mary found that the price of the Darnley marriage was the rebellion of Murray and other Scottish lords. They were encouraged by promises of support from England, and for the moment it looked as though war was bound to break out between the two Queens. But Mary was courageous and prompt; Elizabeth, while sending the rebels money, hesitated to break the peace. In the face of their sovereign's resolute action, the rebel forces melted away, and the leaders were compelled to fly for safety across the Border. The English Council, meeting to discuss the situation, could not agree over the issue of war or peace, and, following her own bent, Elizabeth decided for peace.

Mary had triumphed. She had successfully outwitted and defied her cousin, broken the opponents of her marriage, and secured for the marriage the approval—and therefore the countenance—of France, Spain, and the Pope. Yet, at what a price! Already by the autumn of 1565, when her victory was complete, she had more than an inkling of her misfortune in the arrogant ways and drunken, vicious habits of her despicable husband. 'Woe worth the time,' Randolph had written, 'that ever the Lord Darnley set his foot in this country!' 'What shall become of her, or what life with him she shall lead. . . . I leave it to others to think!'

CHAPTER IX

THE MARRIAGE PROBLEM AGAIN

ONE day during the crisis over the Darnley marriage the French ambassador found Elizabeth playing chess in her Privy Chamber. The game was like human affairs, he remarked; one lost a pawn and it seemed not to matter, but frequently the game was lost in consequence. Yes, answered Elizabeth, catching his meaning, Darnley is only a pawn but it may be checkmate if I am not careful.

It certainly looked as though it would be. Elizabeth's first impetuous impulse had been to back Murray and his fellows in their resistance to Mary's marriage. But when it became evident that this called for an army and war, she drew back. The risks were too many. She would merely drive Mary into the arms of France, the very danger she had always tried to avoid. She might even bring the Catholic powers down on England, and give substance to that spectre of a Catholic league that was haunting Protestant dreams. France told her in plain terms to keep her hands off Scotland; and this in spite of the fact that Catherine de Medici was angling for her as a wife for her son, Charles IX, and was therefore friendly. Philip II showed his goodwill to Mary by sending her a small subsidy: the money was lost with its bearer in a shipwreck off the Northumbrian coast, but the goodwill remained. Finally, the Pope sent a nuncio and funds to France, to wait there for the signal to cross to Scotland. What could Elizabeth do in such a situation, but play her rebel friends false? When Murray, against her command, hurried south to beg her aid, she staged one of those preposterous face-savings which the diplomacy of the day permitted. Dressed in black and kneeling before her in the presence of two French ambassadors, he speaking Scots, she French, he was taken to task for his rebellion, like a schoolboy. Probably the farce had been rehearsed in private the night before.

Mary knew her advantage. As the price of her friendship she made demands in regard to the English succession which in tone, if not in terms, surpassed all previous ones. She nearly succeeded. Elizabeth actually thought of sending ambassadors to offer what a few months before she had been ready to concede only if Mary married Leicester. She cancelled the embassy, on second thoughts, as damaging to her honour and likely to raise Mary's stomach and terms; but the fact remains that for a few days she was ready to concede so much. Would it prove to be checkmate?

But in throwing off the tutelage of the Protestant party and wedding a wretched misfit like Darnley, Mary had given scope for the defects in her character to ruin her. A passionate courage was all very well; indeed, she touched even Knox's imagination, riding with her troops in the face of the raging storm, through a little brook turned into a great river by the tempestuous rain, riding ever with the foremost, when the most part of her force waxed weary. Her manlike courage had won the initial victory: it was no substitute for the statesmanship that was needed to consolidate and perpetuate it. Her old advisers were in eclipse, with the breakdown of their policy. Murray was in exile and Mary hotly bent on his ruin; Maitland continued as Secretary, but was too compromised to be trusted and was finding ample leisure to make love to a sweetheart. It was unfortunate; it was perhaps unavoidable; but nothing could mitigate the utter folly of replacing a man like Maitland by the upstart Italian musician, David Riccio—Seigneur Davie as he was mockingly called.

This man, the son of a musician, had come to Scotland in 1561, at the age of twenty-eight, in the train of the Duke of Savoy's ambassador. Mary happened to be wanting a bass singer to complete a quartette and therefore prevailed upon him to stay in the country. Later he was promoted from the humble position of musician to the post of French secretary, to write her French correspondence, a post literary in character, not political, although the extent and importance of Mary's French correspondence gave its holder a chance of acquiring political influence. When Darnley came to Scotland he and Riccio became bosom friends, and Riccio advanced in favour and power as Murray and Lethington retreated. The tale was repeated as Darnley in turn lost his hold on Mary: Riccio stepped into his place. Wealth followed power; he was the way to the Queen's favour, and suitors had to pay their toll to him.

For a base-born person, a foreigner, and worse still, an Italian, a race of whom a contemporary Englishman complained that they 'serve all princes at once, and with their perfumed gloves and wanton presents, and gold enough to boot if need be, work what they list and lick the fat even from our beards'—for such a man to usurp such a position in the State was as gross a violation of the aristocratic decencies of the age as could well be imagined. Gentility might be, as Cecil told his son, nothing else than ancient riches, but the entry to rule and government in those days called for some degree of ancientry. Mary once wrote a democratic note in defence of a prince favouring a man of mean birth, poor in wealth, but generous in spirit; a strange utterance from a monarch whose great heart had spurned the Earl of Leicester as a parvenu! Probably the note was written at this time and in regard to Riccio; if so, it was surely suggestive of a blind, indulgent affection.

Certainly, it would be hard to exaggerate the folly of Mary's behaviour. Not only did it outrage opinion, it was a magnet to draw together a formidable opposition. The exiled lords and their unexiled friends—the whole Protestant party in fact—were ready to compass Riccio's fall as the symbol of Mary's new policy; while men like Maitland, whom he had robbed of influence, hated him with a personal hatred. So did Darnley. Mary had given her husband the title of King, but he was dissatisfied. He wanted the independent position that came with the crown matrimonial, granted by Parliament with assured power both during her lifetime and after. A courtesy title such as he had, together with his impotence as Mary's early passionate prostration to his will changed after a period of bickerings to contemptuous neglect, were galling. Riccio now had the Queen's ear, not he; early and late this upstart was attendant on her; and as the inevitable scandal formed about the relations of the two, it found easy lodging in Darnley's petulant, jaundiced mind. A powerless king and a cuckold to boot; such were his thoughts of himself. Mary was pregnant, and the talk went that it was David's child. 'Woe is me for you,' wrote Randolph, 'when David's son shall be a king of England!' And in later days Henry IV of France is said to have remarked that James I's title to be called the Modern Solomon was that he was the son of David, who played upon the harp.

So there came into being a conspiracy between Darnley and the Protestant lords to slay Riccio. Darnley was to have the crown matrimonial, Murray and his fellow-exiles pardon and restoration. Randolph, the Earl of Bedford at Berwick, Cecil, Leicester, and Elizabeth were let into the secret, with its bright prospects for English interests; though Elizabeth herself probably did not hear of it until the deed was done.

On Saturday evening, March 9th, 1566, as Riccio sat, cap on head, at supper with Mary and the Lady Argyll, Darnley entered the room, followed by the gaunt, disease-stricken Ruthven clad in full armour. The terrified victim clung to the Queen's dress crying on her to save him, but was dragged from the room and in an outer chamber struck down with fifty-six wounds. 'My Lord,' cried Mary to Darnley, 'why have you caused to do this wicked deed to me, considering that I took you from low estate, and made you my husband?' 'I have good reason for me,' answered Darnley, 'for since yonder fellow David came in credit and familiarity with your Majesty, you have neither regarded me, entertained me, nor trusted me after your wonted fashion; for every day before dinner you were wont to come to my chamber, and passed the time with me, and this long time you have not done so; and when I came to your Majesty's chamber, you bare me little company except David had been the third person; and after supper your Majesty used to sit up at the cards with the said David till one or two after midnight.' It may be, as Bedford heard, that in his jealous rage, he told her 'that David had more company of her body than he, for the space of two months'.

Distressing as the experience was, and dangerous to a woman six months gone in pregnancy, Mary did not lose her wits. 'No more tears,' she is said to have remarked, when told that Riccio was dead; 'I will think upon a revenge.' She persuaded her weak and cowardly husband to desert his fellow-conspirators, an incredibly foolish and mean thing for him to do; and with one of her astonishing displays of courage, energy, and endurance made her escape with Darnley from Holyrood and captivity. Then she brought Murray to her side, thus separating him from the conspirators, and soon was in control of her kingdom again, while another batch of exiles crossed the Border into England. In the anguish of her shattered emotions she did one or two foolish things; she had Riccio's body taken from its mean grave and buried in the Royal Chapel, and gave his office to his brother, a youth of eighteen who arrived in the country a month or so after the murder. But with Murray at her side a new era of moderation and sanity was dawning, and when on June 19th, 1566, she gave birth to a son, the clouds of the past year seemed to be dispersing and a bright future to await her. In those days when a childless sovereign, involving a succession problem, seemed a symbol of the wrath to come, much could be forgiven a Queen who produced a son before whose baby eyes ranged a prospect stretching beyond the throne of Scotland to that of England.

When in old age James Melville sat down to write his *Memoirs* and let an errant memory play its tricks, he told how Cecil came and whispered the news of this birth to Elizabeth as she was dancing one evening after supper. All merriness, he says, was laid aside for that night; the Queen sat down with her hand upon her cheek, and burst out to some of her ladies, 'The Queen of Scotland is lighter of a fair son, and I am but a barren stock!' It is a good story; probably nothing more.

Elizabeth's mind at that time was running on marriage, and had been since the Parliament of 1563. Marry where you please, whom you please, and as soon as you please— but marry: that had been the request of the nobility in Parliament, and it expressed the impatient urgency of national sentiment. The Queen could not ignore it. Nor was this all. In 1563 Elizabeth was thirty, she had looked Death in the face, and time no longer seemed lost in infinity. The malaise of a spinster of thirty was there. She protested still that she preferred a virgin life; but she protested altogether too much. In short, the time was propitious for marriage. Only the man was lacking.

The wooings of previous years had sorted out the Archduke Charles as the most eligible party. He brought dignity but not a kingdom, a useful alliance without the danger of merging England into another realm. The problem, however, was how to start the suit again without losing the advantage of being sought instead of seeking. For marriage in royal ranks involved a treaty which called for as much alert haggling over terms as a peace treaty; and coyness and procrastination, which Elizabeth carried to a baffling, preposterous length, were state diplomacy, directed to securing her terms instead of conceding the Archduke his.

Cecil started the negotiations in the autumn of 1563 by writing to Elizabeth's German agent. He wrote to the Duke of Würtemberg, who in turn communicated with the Emperor and sent an envoy to Elizabeth, ostensibly with a gift of books. When the envoy arrived, Cecil told him to proceed cautiously, as the Queen had dedicated herself to celibacy; Elizabeth, for her part, remarked, 'If I am to disclose to you what I should prefer if I follow the inclination of my nature, it is this: Beggarwoman and single, far rather than Queen and married.' A strange, but diplomatic opening! Stranger, but still diplomacy, was the rest of the negotiation. She blamed the Emperor for ruining the match on the previous occasion; she boasted of her many and great suitors; she provoked hope, dashed it, hedged, was inconsequent, sought compliments by dispraising her Latin and French; said everything—and nothing. The envoy told Cecil that it was quite useless to make a longer stay. 'But,' he answered in surprise, 'the Queen praised your French conversation highly, and said that she had much enjoyed it!' She did in fact send a letter to the Duke saying that she was ready to marry.

The death of the Emperor in the summer of 1564 caused a halt in the proceedings, but in the following spring the new Emperor, Charles' brother, sent an envoy who was to revive the old marriage negotiations if after careful inquiry he was convinced that Elizabeth's virtue was untouched and unimpaired. The envoy came to the conclusion that all the aspersions against her were the spawn of envy, malice, and hatred; he therefore proceeded with his mission. At first he fared no differently than the Duke's envoy and interpreted her prolix talk as a refusal; but after two negative, bewildering audiences, probably calculated to damp his confidence and render him more amenable over terms, the affair began to prosper. He thought that Elizabeth might send someone secretly to report on the personal appearance of the Archduke, and wrote to the Emperor to see that Charles had well-made and dainty costumes. 'From now on great attention must be paid to the dress of His Princely Highness, and he should no longer make use of hacks or palfreys, but of fiery steeds. . . . He should also show himself in public and be accessible to all, so that should anyone come unawares from the Queen—and this might happen very soon—he would be able to see all this. His Princely Highness should be the more willing to do this, as he could find no such second Queen in the world.'

After a good deal of argument about terms, the parties came to issue over a few questions. Elizabeth, as before, insisted that she must see the Archduke before deciding to marry him. She would trust no one else's eyes; *tot capita, tot sensus*. She was the more insistent because she apparently had an uneasy suspicion that her suitor was misshapen; which is not surprising if she saw a letter from her German agent to Cecil. 'Alexander the Great,' he wrote, 'is

said to have had his neck bent towards the left side; would
that our man—the Archduke—may be his imitator in magnanimity and bravery'. A year later Cecil's brother-in-law,
who had been sent to Vienna, reported that 'a man would
think him a very little round-shouldered', a passage which
Cecil noted in the margin as important; a postscript, however, gave later information—'he was as straight in the body
as any man alive'. Of medium height, sanguine complexion,
'for a man beautiful, and well faced, well shaped, small in
the waist, and well and broad breasted', looking in his
clothes to be 'well thighed and well legged, the same being
a little embowed'; this was the rest of the physical description sent to Elizabeth. As for his qualities, he was 'courte-
ous, affable, just, wise, and of great memory'. None the less,
she wanted to judge for herself.

Though at first unwilling, the Emperor soon agreed to
let Charles come and be inspected, provided that the terms
of the marriage could be satisfactorily settled beforehand.
One of the disputed points was the upkeep of the Archduke's household. Elizabeth wanted him to pay for it out
of his Austrian revenues; the Emperor contended that it
should be England's obligation. The point was argued with
tenacity, but at length was recognized as not a vital issue.
What really mattered was another, an old question—religion. Elizabeth appealed to the Emperor's own judgment
to show him the thousand inconveniences incident to a difference of faith between husband and wife. What worse lot
could befall a realm, she asked, thinking probably of Darnley and Mary in Scotland, than division into two parties,
one side championing the husband, the other the wife? It
would be like two beasts yoked together, but varying in
their paces; they would never draw evenly. What should be
a single will would be changed to mutual hate. The Emperor, however, insisted on a public place of Catholic worship being provided for Charles and his foreign courtiers.
The negotiations turned upon the issue.

The opponents of the marriage were thus given their
chance. Among them were the French. In her alarm at the
prospect of another English alliance with the Hapsburgs,

Catherine de Medici had come forward with rival bait in the person of the French king, Charles IX. He was a mere boy of fourteen, born in June, 1550, and therefore seventeen years younger than Elizabeth. The English ambassador in France, a friend of Cecil's and of the Austrian match, wrote an ambiguous appreciation of him; he was likely to be tall, for he had great knees and ankles, and legs not proportioned to them; he spoke somewhat fast and thick, but this was a token that he was hot of nature, a greater doer than speaker; he neither lisped nor stammered, he spoke no other tongue than his own. Elizabeth's jester in the presence of the Imperial envoy, for whom the Queen translated his remark into Italian, advised her not to marry him; he was 'but a boy and a babe'; she should take the Archduke, and then 'she would have a baby-boy.' 'Babes and fools speak the truth,' said the envoy; and Elizabeth laughed. She had no intention of marrying Charles IX, but she kept Catherine's negotiations in suspense as long as she could, both to hinder any rapprochement between France and Scotland, and to improve her bargaining powers in the Austrian match.

As for the Earl of Leicester, with a solatium awaiting him in the person of the Queen of Scots, he had at first lent genuine support to the Archduke; but when the Scottish plan miscarried and the Austrian hung fire, he began to aspire once more to marriage with Elizabeth, egged on by his cronies with their vision of a world delectable and bounties untold. They drew encouragement from Mary's marriage with Darnley, which might encourage Elizabeth also to venture where fancy prompted. But for many reasons, not least because ruin was the nemesis of unsuccessful rivalry with the future King of England, Leicester had to move cautiously and disguise his object for a time, exerting his influence in favour of the impossible French match in order to thwart the Austrian. The French, in their turn, when their own suit lapsed, disseminated damaging tales in Germany and England to wreck the negotiations between Elizabeth and the Emperor, and did all they could to forward Leicester's interests. In the eyes of the Spanish ambassador matters appeared to reach such a nice balance that he found himself in a pitiful quandary, anxious to promote the Archduke's suit and yet afraid to alienate Leicester, who might after all become Elizabeth's husband.

Leicester was having his ups and downs. In the summer of 1565, perhaps to lend variety to Court gossip, Elizabeth began to smile upon a handsome, witty, but married courtier, Thomas Heneage. Leicester quarrelled with him, started flirting with a beautiful lady to test Elizabeth's affections, and landed himself into momentary disgrace. The Queen's Majesty 'wrote an obscure sentence in a book at Windsor', Cecil noted in his diary. Openly she said that she was sorry for the time she had lost on him; upon which Cecil commented to a friend, 'And so is every good subject'. Heneage was chosen as King of the Bean for the Twelfth Night festivities the following January, and in a game of questions and answers compelled Leicester to ask Elizabeth which was the more difficult to erase from the mind, jealousy or an evil opinion implanted by a wicked informer. The jest seemed to have venom in it, and Leicester afterwards sent a friend to Heneage to say that he would beat him for his impertinence. He replied that if Leicester came to insult him he would discover whether his sword could cut and thrust. When Elizabeth heard of the incident she swore that if Leicester had become insolent through her favour, he would soon reform, for she would debase him as she had raised him. For four days he remained in his rooms, melancholic, until the Queen took pity on him.

The cracks of faction began to gape, as they were gaping in Scotland over the Darnley marriage. The Duke of Norfolk and his brother-in-law, the Earl of Sussex, were the leaders of the anti-Leicester party. Fortune and influence, possibly life itself in addition to the sweets of it, might be endangered if Leicester became King; their opposition was therefore sleepless and bitter. In June, 1565, and again a year later, Sussex and Leicester were at open feud, each walking about with a large company of armed men for protection. On each occasion Elizabeth had to intervene and compel them to be reconciled. At New Year's tide, 1566, Leicester got all his

followers to appear in blue laces or stripes in order to discover who were his friends and make a show of his strength.
Promptly the Duke of Norfolk put his men in yellow laces.
Elizabeth, apparently, trounced them both. In the following months, partly at the persuasion of friends but probably mainly through the forceful representations of his
enemies, Leicester twice went away from the Court for brief
intervals. It seems as though a determined attempt was being made to ruin him, for about this time someone approached Amy Robsart's half-brother, who, angry at not
getting all he wanted from Leicester, had been saying that
'he had for the Earl's sake covered the murder of his sister'.
He was offered a very heavy bribe if he would denounce
Leicester as a murderer; or, as it was put to him, if he
would join with those—Norfolk, Sussex, Heneage, and others
—'who do mind to charge him with certain things.'

The cautious Cecil kept aloof from these party squabbles
and remained on good surface terms with Leicester, for he
had suffered once as too warm a meddler in the business.
But in the quiet of his study in April, 1566, just at the time
that this attack seems to have been preparing, he drew up
tables of damning contrasts between the Archduke and
Leicester. Alongside of the entry 'birth'—'Born son of a
knight,' he wrote of Leicester, 'his grandfather but a squire'.
As for wealth—'All of the Queen, and in debt'. Likelihood
to bear children—'A childless marriage. No brother had
children, and yet their wives have. . . . Himself married,
and no children'. Likelihood to love his wife—'A carnal marriage begins in pleasure and ends in sorrow'. While as for
reputation—the Archduke was 'honoured of all men', Leicester 'hated of many' and 'infamed by the death of his wife'.
'It will be thought', runs another entry, 'that the slanderous
speeches of the Queen with the Earl have been true'—
speeches such as Drunken Burley's or Mother Dowe's, or
the more recent words of a Suffolk man that the Queen was
a naughty woman who could not rule her realm and was
'kept' by Lord Robert, or the recent remark of the French
ambassador that Leicester had slept with Elizabeth on New
Year's night. 'He shall study nothing,' continues Cecil's en-

try, 'but to enhance his own particular friends to wealth, to office, to lands, and to offend others.'

It was a difficult situation, but Elizabeth apparently managed it with skill, if to the contentment of few. Perhaps she recalled Leicester to Court to balk the attack upon him. At any rate, her behaviour, Cecil told a confidant, was blameless. She was serious over the Archduke's suit, he continued, although progress was hindered by many obstacles. God direct her to marriage in some place, was his prayer, for otherwise her reign will prove very troublesome and unquiet.

The negotiations with the Emperor were still in being when Parliament met once more in October, 1566; met to face the same situation as in 1563—an unmarried Queen and an unsettled succession. Elizabeth had merely prorogued the last Parliament, not dissolved it; an unwise action, as things turned out, for the Commons of 1563 came back with the sense that they had been thwarted and fooled three years before. There was no need for the 'restless heads' to waste time discovering what support they could count on; they knew the temper of the House. Nor were their tactics in doubt. Rumour beforehand had been prophesying that there would be no supplies of money if the Queen would not marry or proclaim a successor; and sure enough, when the committee for supplies was appointed, a debate followed on the succession. For two mornings they talked, coming to blows on the first day when the less venturesome element tried to stop the debate and go home, while the others were for locking the door and compelling them to continue. Councillor followed Councillor on Elizabeth's instruction, in a vain attempt to persuade the House that the Queen really intended to marry. Nothing could stop them from appointing a committee to draft a petition, or from approaching the Lords, who after some hesitation, finally agreed to join them.

Elizabeth was so angry with her nobles that she railed at them. The storm burst first on the Duke of Norfolk. Pembroke intervened to defend him, only to be told that he talked like a swaggering soldier. Then, turning to Leicester, she said that if all the world abandoned her, yet she had thought he would not have done so. He swore that he would die at her feet. What has that to do with the matter? she retorted. Rounding on Northampton, she told him that before he came mincing words with her about marriage, he had better talk of the arguments which got him his scandalous divorce and a new wife. She swept from the room. Certain of the Lords—Leicester and Pembroke among them—were excluded from the Presence Chamber. As for the Commons, she told the Spanish ambassador that she did not know what these devils wanted.

It was a lively beginning for the session! A joint committee of the two Houses started work on a petition, but Elizabeth had no intention of letting them state their case, with its cogent arguments. They should listen to hers. And so she interrupted, to summon a deputation of Lords and Commons before her. In her address to them, she turned her shafts first against those unbridled persons, whose mouths had never been snaffled by the rider who rashly rode into the subject in the House of Commons, where Mr. Bell and his accomplices alleged that they were natural Englishmen and bound to their country, which, she ironically remarked, they saw must needs perish if the succession were not limited. In the Lords, the bishops with their long orations had told members what they did not know before, that when her breath failed her she would be dead, and that would be a danger to the State! It was easy to perceive their object, namely to 'agree the cause against her'.

'Was I not born in this realm?' she exclaimed. And were not her parents? 'Is not my kingdom here? Whom have I oppressed? Whom have I enriched to other's harm? What turmoil have I made in this commonwealth that I should be suspected to have no regard to the same? How have I governed since my reign? I will be tried by envy itself. I need not to use many words, for my deeds do try me.'

Their petition, she was informed, was to consist of two points, marriage and the succession, wherein her marriage was placed first for manner's sake. As for that, she had sent word she would marry, and she would never break the word of a prince, said in a public place. She hoped to have children; otherwise she would never marry. She had a shrewd suspicion that the ringleaders would be as ready to mislike her husband as they now were to urge her marriage; 'and then it will appear that they never meant it.' 'Well', she added, 'there never was so great a treason but might be covered under as fair a pretence'.

As for the succession, she continued; none of them had been a second person in the realm as she had, and tasted of the practices against her sister, who she would to God were alive again! When friends fall out, ran the old proverb, the truth doth appear, and there were some now in the Commons who in her sister's reign had tried to involve her in conspiracies. Were it not for her honour, their knavery should be known. She would never place her successor in that position. The succession question, she said, was a baffling one, full of peril to the realm and herself; though in their simplicity, her hearers imagined that 'the matter must needs go very trimly and pleasantly when the bowl runneth all on the one side'. Kings were wont to honour philosophers, but she would honour as angels any with such piety that when they were second in the realm would not seek to be first, and when third to be second.

She hoped, she went on, that before their deaths the ringleaders in this agitation would repent and show some open confession of their fault, whereby the scabbed sheep might be known from the whole. 'As for my own part, I care not for death; for all men are mortal, and though I be a woman, yet I have as good a courage answerable to my place as ever my father had. I am your anointed Queen. I will never be by violence constrained to do anything. I thank God I am endued with such qualities that if I were turned out of the realm in my petticoat, I were able to live in any place in Christendom.'

Cecil was charged with reporting the speech to the House, and wrote three drafts before he got the acerbities properly moderated for delivery. But an ominous silence followed when he resumed his seat. Two days later, a member suggested that they should go on with their petition, despite the Queen's speech. Promptly, Elizabeth forbade further discussion of the question. Thereupon, Paul Wentworth, one of a pair of troublesome brothers, launched the House on a discussion of its privileges, and from 9 a.m. till 2 p.m.—the House in those days meeting at eight and rising nominally at eleven, usually at noon—they talked, finally adjourning the debate to the next day. The councillors in the House urged Elizabeth to give way and allow the Commons free discussion, but she would not. Instead, she sent for the Speaker before they met again and conveyed through him a peremptory and threatening veto. No business was done that day, and soon the House had another committee at work drawing up an address to the Queen on the three great questions, her marriage, the succession, and their privilege.

Tempers were on edge, and tongues inclined to be loose. A member saw in another member's hands a copy of a recent poem, written by a Scot in France on the occasion of the birth of Mary Queen of Scots' son. 'How say you,' he asked the House, 'to a libel lately set forth in print, calling the Infant of Scotland "Prince of Scotland, England, and Ireland"? . . . "Prince of England", and the Scottish Queen's child? "Prince of Scotland and England", and Scotland before England? . . . What true English heart may sustain to hear of the villainy?' 'With the indignity of this matter being as it were set afire', he confessed to the Council, 'I was carried with the flame thereof, well I know not whither, but I suspect something escaped me unawares'. No doubt it did—a denunciation of Mary's title to the succession; and it was probably popular.

All this while, the money bill lay asleep. Elizabeth and the Commons were at deadlock, and it threatened to be an Addled Parliament. But the Queen had a supple mind and knew both when and how to give way. She sent a message lifting her former vetoes on free discussion and followed it up three days later with an announcement that she remitted a third of the money they intended to grant her, preferring to hear of their faithful minds and dutiful actions, and esteeming them, in respect of their hearty good wills, her best treasurers. She had stooped to conquer. In their joy, they agreed among themselves to drop the obnoxious subject of the succession, and revived the money bill.

But some clever member hit on the idea of incorporating in the preamble to the money bill, thus disseminating it in print throughout the country, the promise that she had given in her speech to marry and to name a successor as soon as she safely could. The fat was once more in the fire. On the foot of the draft preamble which a councillor showed her, Elizabeth scribbled her flaming comment: 'Let not others regard themselves so holy as I have no corner left for me. Let them—the Commons—know that I knew, though I followed not, that some of them would my pure conscience better served me than their lewd practices could avail with me. I know no reason why any my private answers to the realm should serve for prologue to a subsidy book; neither yet do I understand why such audacity should be used to make, without my licence, an act of my words. Are my words like lawyers' books which nowadays go to the wire-drawers to make subtle doings more plain? Is there no hold of my speech without an act compel me to confirm? . . . I say no more at this time, but if these fellows were well answered and paid with lawful coin, there would be fewer counterfeits among them.'

The session closed with another drubbing for the Commons, administered, however, with a loving hand: 'Let this my discipline stand you in stead of sorer strokes never to tempt too far a prince's patience, and let my comfort pluck up your dismayed spirits and cause you think that . . . you return with your prince's grace, whose care for you, doubt you not to be such as she shall not need a remembrancer for your weal'.

When Elizabeth told Parliament that she intended to marry, she was not fooling them. Sending an envoy to Vienna the previous May she had said to him that if the Archduke would come to England, no matter of small importance—supposing always that he had no great deformity of person—would be allowed to hinder her marriage. But the Emperor on that occasion had demanded impossible terms, and so, possibly with the object of making him amenable through anxiety, she delayed sending the Order of the Garter to him, the dispatch of which was to be the excuse for the next bout of bargaining. For this mission the Earl of Sussex was chosen—a propitious choice. He got himself ready, but month followed month without the command to start. At last, in June, 1567, he went, taking a portrait of the Queen with him. His report on the Archduke's person left nothing to be desired. No deformity or blemish was there; his hands and feet even were praiseworthy. Elizabeth could be easy on that score. But the religious difficulty could not be smoothed out completely. If Elizabeth would concede him the practice of his religion, secretly in his own room, while publicly he would accompany her to the Anglican service, then he would come to England at once and the marriage might be arranged.

The demand was as accommodating, short of complete abandonment of faith, as the Archduke could make it. Should Elizabeth agree and bring him to England, or not? In November she summoned her Council to give their advice on the question, and a last tremendous struggle began. The issue was not the simple one of the Queen's marriage. Bound up with it was the fate of Leicester. For if anything seemed certain, in the event of the Archduke becoming King, it was the triumph of Leicester's enemies and his own overthrow. He and his party worked desperately—'the like hath not been'. They stirred up religious passion, helped by the fact that another religious war was raging in France, Alva busy suppressing heresy and revolt in the Netherlands, and religious refugees fleeing to England. At St. Paul's Cross Jewel preached on the text, 'Cursed be he that goeth about to build again the walls of Jericho'—in other words, to bring the Catholic faith into England. And at Vienna someone—perhaps an accomplice—sent exaggerated reports to England of the Archduke's Catholicism, at the same time misrepresenting at Vienna the position in England. Unfortunately the Duke of Norfolk, a powerful advocate of the marriage, was away from Court, ill; but the

Queen wrote to him for his advice, and he gave it. He urged her to make the concession to the Archduke and marry him. So did Cecil and others. But Leicester and his party were equally firm in opposition. The Council was divided, and could give the Queen no lead.

Left to her own judgment, Elizabeth decided that she could not concede what was asked. She was anxious to bring the Archduke to England if possible, in the hope that the difficulty would then dissolve away, but come he would not. Sussex, Norfolk, Cecil were heartbroken. They cursed Leicester and his followers for buttressing their selfish aims with the pretence of conscience: 'If Protestants be but only Protestants!' wrote Sussex; 'but if some have a second intent which they cloak with religion, and place be given to their counsel, God defend the Queen with His mighty hand'.

In fact, Elizabeth never revealed her gift of statesmanship more clearly; and if proof were needed, she had only to point to Scotland, where not many months before, Mary's tragic mistake in marriage had culminated in horror and in ruin. The supreme need of the country was not, as Cecil and others thought, a royal child to settle the vexed and threatening question of the succession, but salvation from civil and religious war; and the predisposing conditions to this were faction among the nobility and diversity of faith among the people. Even if he came as a Protestant King, the Archduke would probably have deepened party spirit; as a Catholic, how could trouble have been avoided? The godly were bound to arise, as in Scotland, with their cry, 'Shall that idol be suffered again within the realm?' Indeed, only a month or so back, a man had gone up to the altar in the Queen's Chapel while the service was in progress and cast down the cross and candlesticks, stamping upon them and denouncing them. He may have been mad—for that reason he was pardoned, only to repeat the offence—but there were hundreds similarly mad. On the other hand, the Catholics were certain to resort to the Archduke, seeking first to make him discontented with the restrictions on himself, and afterwards with those on his fellow-believers. And so by degrees the throne, the Court, and the country would be rent in two, and England follow its neighbours—France, the Netherlands, and Scotland—those 'present examples round about her' which, as Elizabeth told the Emperor, led her to refuse the Archduke's request.

No doubt, during these last four years of negotiation, the woman in Elizabeth had often been unsettled by the constant presence of Leicester. But it was as a Queen that she had decided to marry, and it was as a Queen that she now rejected the terms of marriage. Marriage, Cecil told his son, is an action of life like unto a stratagem of war, wherein a man can err but once. He expressed his mistress's sentiments. It must have been a question with Elizabeth whether a woman ruler could ever do otherwise than err in marriage; whether, in fact, to be a success as a Queen she might not have to be a Virgin Queen. Her sister's marriage had been a blunder; and at that moment Europe was agog with the tragic, passionate story of Mary Queen of Scots, who, in the words of a Venetian ambassador, had made manifest to all the world 'that statecraft is no business for ladies'.

CHAPTER X

THE DARNLEY MURDER

AFTER the murder of Riccio a sweet reasonableness had re-entered into the relations of Elizabeth and Mary. In April, 1566, the Spanish ambassador found Elizabeth with a portrait of Mary hanging from her waist by a gold chain. Apropos Riccio's murder she told him that if she had been in Mary's place she would have taken her husband's dagger and stabbed him with it. However, she hastily added, Philip II must not think that she would do this to the Archduke Charles if he came to England! The friendly correspondence of the two Queens was renewed, and Elizabeth resumed the role of elder sister, dispensing her habitual admonitory wisdom: 'remove bushes, lest a thorn prick your heel'; 'the stone often falls on the head of the thrower'; 'if your subjects see your words so honeyed while your acts are envenomed, what can they think?' She prayed God to send Mary as brief pain in her childbed and as happy a time as she could wish, and pronounced herself great with desire to hear the good news. In return Mary asked her to be godmother to her child, and when the christening took place in December, 1566, the Earl of Bedford went north with a massive font of gold, curiously wrought and enamelled, by good fortune escaping an ambush of thieves who laid wait for it near Doncaster.

The wheels were running very smoothly. Mary thanked her 'dearest sister' for the benevolent attitude that she had readopted towards her claim to the English succession. She approved of Elizabeth marrying the Archduke. She even declared that she was ready to ratify the Treaty of Edinburgh. This last was an astounding offer; no less than the surrender of the trump card of her diplomacy! Was it guile? It is at any rate significant that the envoy who took the message left Edinburgh on the eighth or ninth of February, 1567, and in less than forty-eight hours a tragedy was to be enacted that would make incalculable drafts on Elizabeth's charity.

All was not well in Scotland: the trouble was Darnley. So far from being more of a king after the murder of Riccio, as he had planned, this poor, witless youth was little short of an outcast, despised by all, hated by many. He had betrayed his fellows; he had cringed before his wife, a woman of spirit whose feelings he had outraged; he lacked the manly qualities to redeem a desperate situation. Mary's scorn and detestation gradually burnt through all pretence. 'The Queen and her husband', Bedford reported in August, 1566, 'agree after the old manner, or rather worse. She eateth but very seldom with him, but lieth not nor keepeth no company with him, nor loveth any such as love him. . . . It cannot for modesty nor with the honour of a Queen be reported what she said of him.' She 'fell marvelously out' with Melville for giving the King a water-spaniel which had taken his fancy, calling him dissembler and flatterer and saying that she could not trust a person who would give anything to one whom she did not love.

In this pathetic position, Darnley began to think of taking ship and leaving the country. Mary tried to reason with him in private, but failed. The Council did no better. 'Adieu, Madam,' he cried, 'you shall not see my face for a long space'. The foolish man continued to threaten bringing this scandal upon the country. He was impossible. It is a heartbreak for the Queen, wrote Maitland in October, 1566, to think that he should be her husband, and how to be free of him she sees no way. The following month some of her advisers discussed this question with her. Divorce was ruled out because it would bastardize her child. Another way was suggested—probably to arrest Darnley on a charge of treason and kill him if he resisted. But the christening of her child was at hand and such an outrage in the presence of foreign ambassadors could not be faced.

What would have happened if no further disturbing factor had been present, it is hard to say. Many of the leading councillors and noblemen would gladly have got rid of Darnley in any way that Mary was ready to approve; and to add to the number of the King's enemies, at the end of the year the Riccio exiles were pardoned.

But the Darnley drama had begun with passion and was to end with it. Mary had found the masterly lover for whom her nature craved, in the Earl of Bothwell, 'a glorious, rash and hazardous young man' of about thirty, with a veneer of French culture acquired in a chequered career. Probably she had been raped by him before falling in love: at any rate, the French 'sonnets' among the Casket Letters suggest this:

> Pour luy je jete mainte larme
> Premier quand il se fit de ce corps possesseur,
> De quel alors il n'avoyt pas le coeur.

Bothwell was insatiate with women, it was said. His morals certainly were loose; his tongue also. The previous year he had spoken of Mary as the Cardinal's—her uncle's—whore; she and Elizabeth together, he said, could not make one honest woman. Though a Protestant, he had been the foe of Murray and the Protestant party, and loyal to Mary's mother. Thus the change of policy after the Darnley marriage had naturally brought him back into favour, in which he remained. 'Bothwell continueth the most hated man of this realm,' reported Bedford in August, 1566, 'and it is said that his insolence is such as David was never more abhorred than he is now.' An unlucky choice for the Queen's grand passion! Moreover, he was but recently married to a woman whom he preferred to Mary, though not to the Queen of Scotland.

A husband whom Mary loathed, who as King was so utterly impossible that her councillors were ready to wink at, or even aid, any desperate device for being rid of him, a mad infatuation for the most reckless nobleman in the realm—was there ever a more dangerous amalgam of facts? Bothwell planned the King's murder; Mary's part was to lure the victim where he could be killed.

In January, 1567, Darnley lay at Glasgow recovering from smallpox. Mary visited him there, seemingly to effect a reconciliation, but really to fulfil her part in the plot. On the night of her arrival, after she had talked with Darnley, she sat up scribbling page after page to her beloved, opening news and heart. It is a remarkable letter; impulsive, with little discipline of thought, catching varied, fleeting moods. Now there is a touch of remorse: 'Had I not proof that his heart is of wax, and were not mine of diamond, which no shaft can pierce save that which comes from your hand, I would almost have had pity.' Then her jealousy of Bothwell's wife surges up and she is scornful. Later, Darnley and Lady Bothwell are together in her thoughts—the obstacles to her happiness: 'We are tied to two false races; the Devil sunder us, and God knit us together for ever, for the most faithful couple that ever were united. This is my faith. I will die in it'. She is ill at ease, she says, yet glad to write while others sleep, since she cannot sleep as she would desire, 'that is, in your arms, my dear love'. 'Cursed be this pocky fellow that troubleth me so much'. The next night she finished the letter, her mood again changeable: 'You make me almost play the part of a traitor. Remember that if it were not to obey you I had rather be dead than do it. My heart bleeds at it.' 'Alas! and I never deceived anybody; but I remit myself wholly to your will.' 'Now, since to obey you, my dear love, I spare neither honour, conscience, hazard, nor greatness, take it in good part.' 'See not her (Lady Bothwell) whose feigned tears should not be so much praised or esteemed as the true and faithful travails which I sustain in order to merit her place.' 'It is late; I desire never to cease writing to you; yet now, after kissing your hands, I will end my letter.'

At the close of the month, after lulling his fears and promising when he was well to be at bed and board with him again, Mary brought Darnley to Edinburgh, to lodge in a mean house at Kirk o' Field, just outside the city walls. There she had a bed for herself in the room below his, and spent much time with him. Sunday evening, February 9th, came; she was to have slept at Kirk o' Field, but suddenly remembered a promise to be at Holyrood for a wedding mask; and after giving Darnley a ring in pledge of her love, she departed by torchlight. About two that morning a violent explosion startled the city. Darnley's house had been blown up; he himself was found dead in an adjoining garden—strangled, it was said.

Catherine de Medici, on first hearing the news, declared that Mary was fortunate to be rid of the young fool. It was what many would have thought, if everything had been above board; but despite Mary's pretence that the mask at Holyrood had alone saved her from sharing Darnley's fate, many—including ambassadors—had either knowledge or suspicions, and it was Elizabeth who gave proper expression to public opinion: 'O Madam!' she wrote, 'I would not do the duty of a faithful cousin and affectionate friend if I thought more of pleasing your ears than saving your honour. I will not conceal from you what most people are saying: that you will look through your fingers at revenge for this deed, and that you have no desire to touch those who have done you such pleasure; as though the deed had not been committed without the murderers knowing they were safe.' 'I exhort you, I counsel you, I beg you to take this event so to heart that you will not fear to proceed even against your nearest.' A fortnight later Mary's own ambassador in France, a faithful subject, wrote even more plainly. The talk went, he told her, that she herself was 'the motive principal', and all done by her command; better she had lost life and all than not take a rigorous vengeance.

In Scotland the common people cried out on the murder as a shame to their nation, ministers urged prayer and repentance. Bills appeared in Edinburgh naming Bothwell as the murderer, and voices in the night took up the accusation. Early in April a man went nightly through the streets crying lamentably, 'Vengeance on those who caused me to shed innocent blood! O Lord, open the heavens and pour down vengeance on me and those that have destroyed the innocent!' The evil that Darnley did was evidently to be interred with his bones.

Though Bothwell's guilt was bruited openly, Mary took no steps against him: on the contrary, she showered favours on him. It was left for Darnley's father, Lennox, to bring forward an accusation, but the trial was so ordered that it was mere prudence for the accuser to stay away, and the judgment went by default. 'Bothwell was not cleansed of the crime, but, as it were, washed with cobbler's blacking'. A week later he gave a supper and 'induced' some of the lords to sign a bond declaring their belief in his innocence and readiness to support his marriage with the Queen. Mary herself was reported as saying that she cared not to lose France, England, and her own country for him, and would go with him to the world's end in a white petticoat ere she left him. On April 24th, as she rode with a small escort from Stirling to Edinburgh, Bothwell waylaid her and carried her off to Dunbar: 'Judge ye if it be with her will or no!' Divorce proceedings were now taken to free him from his wife, and after twelve days, Mary returned with her ravisher to Edinburgh, where they were married on May 15th, 1567, according to Protestant rites. The same Church, a few days previously, had pronounced Bothwell an adulterer and granted his wife a divorce on that ground.

Their married life—brief it was to be—was bitter-sweet. Bothwell was inordinately suspicious, resented any favour shown to other men, and frowned on her love of pleasure. Mary was probably jealous of Lady Bothwell. The French ambassador found her, two days after her marriage, sad and wishing for death; she called aloud for a knife to kill herself. Tears and lamentations, however, did not quench her passion.

Prudence had gone to the winds. Many of the nobility had been ready to condone Darnley's murder, and some of them doubtless expected his death; though whether any outside Bothwell's circle were parties to it, is uncertain. But they were not prepared to lie quiet while one of themselves, and above all the insolent Bothwell, enemy to many and friend of few, took the Queen and the Kingdom for his reward. They revolted, having a superb, if undeserved ally in the popular and righteous purpose of purging the realm of the King's murder. A month to the day from their marriage, Bothwell was a fugitive and Mary brought captive to Edinburgh. 'Burn the whore!' called out the soldiers with one voice. 'Burn her, burn her, she is not worthy to live, kill her, drown her!' cried the citizens. 'The women,' it was reported, 'be most furious and impudent against the Queen, and yet the men be mad enough.'

It was difficult, as the past had shown, to keep a person of Mary's courage and resource captive, and she was therefore immured in an island-castle at Loch Leven. Had she been repentant and willing to allow a divorce, or had the Lords been able to capture Bothwell, bring him to trial for Darnley's murder and dissolve the marriage by executing him, the way back to freedom and her throne would have been open. Popular feeling might have been difficult to handle, and her power would have been curtailed: that is all. But though her body was restrained, her heart was not dismayed; she gave very bitter words to many, and utterly refused to hear of divorce. She was with child—apparently she miscarried of twins in the following July—and scorned to bear a bastard. Also, her devotion to Bothwell was unshaken; she asked no more than to be put on a boat with him and let go where fortune would take them. It was obvious that if free she would take the first chance of recalling him, and as he ultimately escaped his pursuers and got to Norway, the Lords were left in a quandary. Depose her was the least they could do; kill her the only safe policy, for 'stone dead hath no fellow'. By persuasions and threats—they threatened to charge her with the murder of Darnley, using as evidence incriminating letters of hers to Bothwell found in a casket that came into their possession on June 20th—they induced her on July 24th to renounce the throne in her baby son's favour and appoint as regent Murray, who like a prudent man had gone on a visit to the Continent, when he perceived trouble blowing up.

Elizabeth watched these events with increasing misgiving and anger. Her policy at first had been simple; to press for justice against the murderers, and prevent Mary marrying Bothwell, who, the murder apart, had always been an enemy to English interests. Any of the Scottish nobles who were 'disposed to stand fast for the maintenance of God's honour' were to be comforted. But a month later, when this edifying purpose involved rebellion and the prosecution of Mary's husband, she began to wonder whether interference might not be more hurtful than profitable. Her aims were clear. She wanted Mary rid of Bothwell but still Queen; the Protestant Lords directing policy; no intervention from outside, especially the French must be kept from fishing in troubled waters. At the first hint that the Lords might crown the baby prince, James, if Mary married Bothwell, she sent a warning that it was a matter hard to be digested by her or any other monarch. As a matter of fact, French digestion was better than hers. The French offered, and continued to offer support to the Lords if they would send James to France. Mary countered by herself offering James—who was not in her custody—if she, not the Lords was given French support. Elizabeth invited the Lords to send the Prince to England, offering as an inducement, not support, but half-hearted promises and full-hearted doubts! She was not the least honest, nor the least shrewd.

The Earl of Bedford, at Berwick, through whom Elizabeth's note went to the Lords, glossed her doubts with a little private encouragement of his own. Cecil knew of this, perhaps suggested it. Elizabeth certainly knew the nature of her ministers and knew that she could roar like a lion, while they would echo her as like a sucking dove or any nightingale as they dared. Roar she did, when the Lords imprisoned Mary and talked of deposing her and even killing her. It shocked Elizabeth's political philosophy, her regal dignity, and her prudence, as well as her genuine friendliness to Mary. 'They have no warrant nor authority by the law of God or man,' she wrote, 'to be as superiors, judges or vindicators over their prince and sovereign, howsoever they do gather or conceive matter of disorder against her.'

From political theory, Elizabeth turned to political sense. It were well done, she warned the Lords, if before they proceeded any further, they considered how to stay where they were. An understanding with Mary was their only safe path. Though captive, she was bound to attract men to her side, some drawn by hope of gain, some by pity; the inevitable divisions and jealousies among the nobles would be to her profit; and the French were as ready to back her as them. She was a Queen; her offences would fade in time under a charitable coat of doubt and forgetfulness. How could they hope—for Mary was not yet twenty-five— to keep her prisoner all her life? A sound, but double-edged argument! It was also the case for killing Mary. And to make the case stronger, the Lords knew that if they put her to death they could bring the Hamiltons over from her side to theirs.

Cecil, Leicester, Bedford, Throckmorton, and others were in despair over their mistress. Their private letters would make a book of lamentations. They wanted full-blooded support for the Lords and were in deadly fear of driving them into the arms of France. 'If the Lords speak not English, which they would fain do, they will speak French'. But Elizabeth stormed along her own way. She sent Throckmorton, the most rampant of her critics, to Scotland to console Mary and to open her mind to the Lords. He did his duty sorrowfully. Yet he was as superb a piece in an inimitable game as John Knox, who was threatening 'the great plague of God' to the whole nation if Mary were spared from her condign punishment; though at the same time he was praying daily for the continuance of the old amity with England, thundering out cannon shot against the French alliance and admonishing his hearers to eschew it 'as they would fly from the pots of Egypt which brought them nothing but sugared poison.'

If Elizabeth had promised the Lords her support to put Mary on her trial and execute her for Darnley's murder, or if she had merely been indifferent, there is hardly a doubt that Mary would have died. On the contrary, she kept exploding in a crescendo of wrath. On August 11th about five in the afternoon, she sent for Cecil hastily and entered into a great offensive speech that nothing was thought of for her to do to revenge the Queen of Scots' imprisonment and deliver her. Cecil answered as warily as he could, but she increased so in anger that in good earnest she began to devise revenge by war. Nothing Cecil said satisfied her, but he must in all haste write a letter to Throckmorton with a message to the Lords, that if they continued to keep Mary in prison or touched her life or person, as Elizabeth was a prince she would not fail to revenge it to the uttermost; and he was to declare the message as roundly and sharply as he could, for sure she was that he could not express it with more vehemency than she meant and intended. Cecil ventured to point out that her action might drive the Lords to desperation, and if they killed Mary in consequence, malicious people would say that this had been Elizabeth's real object. Fortunately, even as Cecil entered with the letter ready for her signature, a packet of letters came opportunely from Throckmorton, with this very argument stated in them. She paused. Nine days later Cecil was moaning over the likelihood of losing the fruits of seven or eight years' negotiation with Scotland through Elizabeth's wrath, which try as he would he could not mitigate. The two chief motives that determined her attitude were, he thought, a wish that the world should not think her prejudiced against Mary, and a desire not to encourage her own subjects by the example.

On May 2nd, 1568, after ten and a half months' captivity, the inevitable happened; Mary escaped. Elizabeth's policy met the emergency. She wrote to Mary in her own hand; a nice distinction, for since the Bothwell marriage she had used Cecil as amanuensis, her perplexity being such, as she put it, 'that we cannot find the old way which we were accustomed to walk in by writing to you with our own hand'. Having now found it, she congratulated Mary on the joyful news of her escape; with a little moral aside on her prodigal past. The bearer was to offer Elizabeth's mediation to compound the difference between her and her subjects. If she agreed, Elizabeth would use all her means to persuade or compel Mary's subjects to do the same. If on the other hand she called in the aid of France—well, war was covertly hinted. 'Those who have two strings to their bow,' she reminded Mary, 'may shoot stronger, but they rarely shoot straight.'

The bearer never delivered his letter. On May 13th—before he started—Mary's army was routed, and three days later, in panic fear—for capture meant death, her supporters, the Hamiltons, were unsure, and to wait for a boat for France involved perilous delay—she crossed the Solway into England in miserable plight, having nothing in the world but her person.

What was Elizabeth to do? For a year she had been contending strenuously for Mary's life, liberty, and throne, and now Mary was a fugitive and suppliant in her realm. 'I fear,' Archbishop Parker wrote, 'that our good Queen has the wolf by the ears.' 'Nothing hath chanced externally to her Majesty wherein her prudence shall be more marked and spied; which God rule to His glory and to her own safeguard.' Her first generous impulse was to bring Mary to Court and treat her with all honour. But her councillors were at hand to check that folly of heart and after a tussle they made her see the peril. As though personal feelings can have any place in the government of great principalities! It was the French ambassador's pertinent remark. And if they had, he went on, the two women would be at loggerheads in eight days, and their friendship turned to envy and jealousy.

Sentiment checked, policy took its place; and the essence of Elizabeth's policy still was to compound the differences between Mary and her subjects. For success, both sides must be amenable to terms, and if Mary came to Court any hope of this would disappear. A few days' safety had banished her fear. While her first letter to Elizabeth dwelt on her pitiable state, her second declared that she had come to England to complain of her subjects to Elizabeth, who really was responsible—true, without ill-intention—for her misfortunes: she was annoyed at having forgotten to say this in her first letter! If Elizabeth would not repair the damage she had done, then Mary asked permission to seek aid of her other allies, of whom, thank God, she was not destitute. Her fiery stomach showed itself in bitter invectives against her rebels. Her custodian wrote that she was dedicated to revenge, saying she would rather see all her followers hanged than submit themselves to Murray, while, for herself, sooner than not be revenged, she would go to the great Turk for help. 'The thing that most she thirsteth after is victory, and it seemeth to be indifferent to her to have her enemies diminished either by the sword of her friends, or by the liberal promises and rewards of her purse, or by division and quarrels raised among themselves; so that for victory's sake, pain and peril seemeth pleasant unto her, and in respect of victory, wealth and all things seemeth to her contemptible and vile.' 'Now what is to be done with such a lady and princess?'

There was another consideration. For years Mary had been nourishing a party in England, and in the Catholic north there was spontaneous joy at her arrival in the country. Before Elizabeth could take control of the situation, many squires from the surrounding counties hastened to pay court to her, listening to her daily defence of her conduct, her protestations of innocence, and her diatribes against her enemies. With her alluring grace, pretty Scottish accent, and searching wit, clouded with mildness, she stole their hearts away. She had sugared speech in store, a disposition to speak much, to be bold, pleasant, and very familiar. No plain speech, said her Puritan custodian, seemed to offend her if she thought the speaker honest, and though she could not forbear 'to utter her stomach', yet she was soon pacified again and would seek reconciliation in pleasant sort. A rare and notable woman, and a sweet bait, what with her possible claim to Elizabeth's throne and her more reasonable claim to the succession.

To bring this woman to Court would, as Cecil said, merely increase the boldness of all evil subjects. It would give the countenance of England, which swayed the realm of Scotland, to her and her party, and probably drive Murray and the Lords in desperation to send James to France and make what terms they could with that country. Supposing she came, and, as was likely, proved intractable; Elizabeth would be compelled to restore her, if only to avoid nursing a serpent in her bosom and to 'stop the mouths of factious, murmuring subjects'. And an intractable Mary could return to her throne only over the ruins of the Protestant, Anglophil party in Scotland. That way lay madness. Equally mad would it be to let her go to France.

Consequently, Mary was kept in honourable custody, every effort being made to preserve the distinction between this and captivity, and even to indulge her insatiable love of hunting and hawking. Until mid-July she was at Carlisle, an insecure place, being near the Border, whence a body of her agility and spirit, 'with devices of towels or toys at her chamber window', could easily escape in the night; she rarely went to bed before one in the morning, outstaying her custodian. She was transferred to Bolton Castle in Wensleydale. 'Surely, if I should declare the difficulties that we have passed before we could get her to remove', her custodian wrote, 'instead of a letter I should write a story, and that somewhat tragical!' It was Elizabeth's cousin, Sir Francis Knollys, who had the harassing task of playing host to an unwilling, tempestuous, and tearful guest. He wrote copiously of his troubles.

A formula was needed to excuse this treatment of Mary, and was readily found. It would be very prejudicial to Elizabeth's honour—it ran—especially as an unmarried Queen and the near kinsman and former sovereign of Darnley, to receive Mary while she lay under the imputation of complicity in her husband's murder. It had the merit of leading by a natural step to the all-important plan of mediation. Mary having asked to justify herself before Elizabeth, she answered, 'O Madam! there is no creature living who wishes to hear such a declaration more than I, or will more readily lend her ears to any answer that will acquit your honour'. She announced that she would act as judge between her and her subjects—a request Mary was far from making—and once honourably acquitted, would receive her. It was in the interests of her own cause, she assured Mary, not to come to her presence, since otherwise her enemies would say that the Queen of England was no competent or meet judge for them. To signalize her impartiality she sent an order to Murray to cease harrying Mary's supporters, now that she was to judge between them. The messenger made a detour to call on Mary, while Cecil and others despatched a hasty warning, bidding Murray get his job done!

It was not without great passion and weeping and complaints of evil usage that Mary was brought to agree to the plan. She was an absolute prince, she declared, and had no other judge but God, whereas my Lord of Murray and his followers were but subjects, yea and traitors. How could they be a party against her, when there was no equality between her and them? In a different mood, she wrote, 'Good sister, be of another mind; win the heart, and all shall be yours and at your commandment. I thought to satisfy you wholly, if I might have seen you. Alas! do not as the serpent, that stoppeth his hearing, for I am no enchanter but your sister and natural cousin.'

In discussion with Mary's ambassador, Elizabeth did her best to meet his objections. It was not to be a trial, she said, but an inquiry into the conduct of Murray and his party towards Mary, carried out by English commissioners, and there would therefore be no judgment unless it were against them. If they were unable to justify themselves, as she expected, or said she expected, then she would restore Mary to her throne with full power. 'And what, Madam', asked the ambassador, 'if appearances are otherwise, which God forbid?' Then, she answered, she would make the best compromise that she could between Mary and her subjects. Elizabeth's fee as judge was to be the safeguarding of England's interests: the Treaty of Edinburgh was to be ratified, a treaty with England replace the treaty with France, and Mary was to give up the Mass, substituting the moderate service of the English Book of Common Prayer.

Mary had little choice but to yield, for her foreign friends had their own troubles. France had recently ended another religious war and was passing through six months of nominal peace and widespread violence before the chronic fit took her again. Spain was engrossed in the revolt of the Netherlands. The French ambassador gave her poor comfort; he thought her safer and better treated in England than she would be even in the Castle of Edinburgh, surrounded by the whole of her so-called supporters; she must have patience, he told her, till the troubles of Christendom were appeased.

And so Mary did the best she could for herself. She took to the Book of Common Prayer, listened with attentive and —so Knollys said—contented ears to the preacher inveighing against all sorts of papistry, and inclined towards 'the chief article of the religion of the Gospel', justification by faith. But if she tried to appear to Elizabeth like a hopeful convert, in her secret letters to the Spanish ambassador, Philip II, and the Pope, she was a good Catholic. She told them that she had been refused a priest; which was likely enough. She assured them that she would die sooner than change her faith. Towards the end of September, hearing of a rumour current in her neighbourhood that she had turned Protestant, with which her Catholic supporters were displeased, she publicly professed herself a Catholic, speaking in her Great Chamber. Knollys was upset. 'Why!' she said to him, 'would you have me to lose France and Spain and all my friends in other places by seeming to change my religion, and yet I am not assured that the Queen my good sister will be my assured friend?' She wrote to the Queen of Spain telling her that the whole of the country in her neighbourhood was given to Catholicism, and that since coming to England she had made the acquaintance of these people; what with this, she declared, and her right to the English throne, if she had ever so little hope of outside succour she would overthrow religion in England or die in the attempt. 'I have made great wars in Scotland', she said to Knollys in an explosive mood, 'and I pray God I make no troubles in other realms also'.

Mary can hardly be blamed. A sovereign, like an ambassador, was entitled to lie abroad, lie and scheme shamelessly, for her own good. Yet the wages of duplicity is distrust; and she ought to have borne in mind a favourite tag of contemporary statesmen—*littera scripta manet*, which had a subsidiary translation, 'Your correspondence may fall into other hands'. In those days corruption penetrated even into the Council Chamber, and authorities who were clever enough to intercept the correspondence of a prisoner, partly written with onions and conveyed to and fro in the stoppers of bottles and the codpieces of the prisoner's hose, were quite capable, with the help of Murray, of tapping Mary's correspondence and discovering her insincerity. The result showed itself at a full meeting of the Privy Council on June 20th when those present unanimously advised Elizabeth against restoring Mary to her throne, even with limited powers; for she could not be trusted to observe any restrictions, and it passed the wit of man to devise guarantees. But Elizabeth still clung to her plan, leaving Cecil and others to shake their heads in the name of wise men at her folly, and be perturbed at her tendency to relent and show too much affection for Mary. She had promised, and still intended, no actual verdict against Mary at the inquiry; she had promised, and still hoped to restore her to her throne.

The inquiry opened at York at the beginning of October, 1568. Elizabeth's commissioners, Norfolk, Sussex, and Sir Ralph Sadler, were instructed to work for a settlement which was a scheme of limited monarchy, to emerge in the form of a tri-partite treaty between Elizabeth, Mary, and James, containing safeguards against its breach, and giving Elizabeth specific functions as guarantor. But nothing came of it. The proceedings all went wrong. This was largely because Murray, while ready and anxious to accuse Mary of complicity in the murder of Darnley, insisted upon Elizabeth pledging herself, in the event of his case being proved, to recognize and support his government, with James as

King, either handing Mary back to him or keeping her in England and preventing her from ever becoming a danger. Elizabeth refused. Probably she hoped that there would be no need to go to extremes, but that the mere threat of doing so would force Mary to terms. Whether the murder charge was made or not, she wanted Mary returned to her throne under the conditions set out in her instructions.

If unable to secure the policy that suited his interests best, which was the murder charge and no composition with Mary, Murray was prepared to make his own reconciliation with his Queen. In consequence, the York inquiry degenerated into a series of intrigues. Sussex wrote that the two factions—Mary's and Murray's—were tossing the crown and public affairs of Scotland between them, neither caring either for Mary or James, save as they served their turn. If the rival Scottish parties could reconcile their private interests, there was no saying what they might not do; they might leave Elizabeth stranded, go off home, and, as suited them best, either let Mary stay, dumped in England, or proclaim her innocent and demand her return, which Elizabeth would be unable to refuse to a guiltless Queen. Worse still, Norfolk was not playing straight. Someone—Maitland probably—suggested reviving Elizabeth's former scheme of marrying Mary to an Englishman. Norfolk, now a widower, was mentioned, and Norfolk proved willing, although he and his fellow-commissioners had taken a private view of the Casket Letters and expressed to their mistress the abhorrence that they must induce in every good and godly man. Even the upright and unquestionably godly Knollys, hearing of the idea but not of the candidate, thought his cousin a good match for Mary. So much were they really affected by her share in Darnley's murder! Her little hand had but to clutch a crown, not seek the perfumes of Arabia, to sweeten it.

In imminent danger of being overreached by one or other of these intrigues, Elizabeth broke up the inquiry at York, and transferred it to Westminster, where she could be close at hand, residing at Hampton Court, while Cecil and the rest of the Council could be added to the tribunal. Her more indulgent plans had failed, and under pressure from the Council she now gave Murray the pledge he had demanded. The extreme charge against Mary was to be made, and among the proofs to be brought forward were the famous letters from Mary to Bothwell in their silver casket, which had been taken from one of Bothwell's servants on June 20th, 1567. It was a serious decision. 'God hold the Queen's Majesty in the mind you write she is in', said Sussex. In order to avoid any appearance of a prejudiced judgment, and to show what manner of Queen this was that some Englishmen preferred to her, Elizabeth summoned six earls to London to hear the charges and examine the proofs after her councillors had dealt with them.

The Westminster sittings began at the end of November. Day after day was spent listening to Murray's charges and scrutinizing closely his proofs. Mary's commissioners took no part in the inquiry, having repudiated it and withdrawn, after demanding and being refused permission for their mistress to answer the charges personally before Elizabeth. Mary kept on demanding this permission—the more earnestly, said Cecil, because she knew that it would be refused. She asserted vigorously that the Casket Letters were forgeries. This, of course, was only to be expected. As Sussex pointed out, by denying her letters she made it difficult to establish *judicial* proof of them.

There was a grotesque unreality about the situation. It was not her complicity in Darnley's murder but her loyalty to Bothwell that had brought misfortune on Mary. Yet after a fitful flare in the elation of escape from Loch Leven her passion was spent. The great illusion of romantic love was dispelled, and Bothwell, for whom she would once have joyfully given the whole world were it hers, could now languish in his Danish prison. As for her accusers, those who had not been ready to lay violent hands on Darnley, had been ready to look the other way. In death as in life this pitiful king was the pawn of political faction, and few but the common people were genuinely horrified at his murder. To complete the cynical picture, Mary's own commissioners, though it was their game to say otherwise, seem to have believed in her guilt. Three years later, one of them, the Bishop of Ross, then her ambassador, told a servant of Elizabeth's that Mary was not fit for any husband; 'for first he saith, she poisoned her husband the French King, as he hath credibly understood; again, she hath consented to the murder of her late husband, the Lord Darnley; thirdly, she matched with the murderer, and brought him to the field to be murdered!' 'Lord, what a people are these; what a Queen, and what an ambassador!' the Englishman exclaimed.

Though they had withdrawn from the inquiry, Mary's commissioners were secretly trying to bring about a settlement—'for covering of her honour', Cecil said. Three plans were under discussion: Mary to confirm the resignation of her throne and live in England; or she and her son to have a joint title while Murray remained regent; or thirdly, she to remain in title Queen but live secluded in England, while Murray continued as regent. They were the terms of defeat; very harsh compared with those Elizabeth had hoped for at York. Murray pressed for the first, refused the third; and just before Christmas Elizabeth told Knollys to persuade Mary, if he could, to agree to the first. With stout and round support from Court, Knollys thought that he could succeed; but stout support he did not get. The Council, while unanimous in believing Murray's evidence, was divided over the treatment of Mary. The Earl of Arundel wrote to Elizabeth: 'One that has a crown can hardly persuade another to leave her crown because her subjects will not obey. It may be a new doctrine in Scotland, but is not good to be taught in England'. Elizabeth imprudently dropped a hint of sympathy to the Bishop of Ross, which, told to Mary, dashed Knollys's hope. 'To be plain with your Majesty', Knollys wrote, 'it seems that this Queen is half persuaded that God hath given you such temperation of affections, that your Majesty will not openly disgrace her, nor forcibly maintain my Lord of Murray against her'.

The inquiry had to be ended, for Murray's presence was urgently needed in Scotland. And so, on January 10th, 1569, Elizabeth made an interim pronouncement. Nothing as yet, she said, had been produced against Murray and his adherents to impair their honour and allegiance: a vital statement, seeing that the *form* of the inquiry was a charge by Mary against her rebellious subjects. Secondly, nothing as yet had been sufficiently produced or shown against Mary for Elizabeth to conceive or take any evil opinion of her good sister: a prudent statement, seeing that Mary had made no answer to the charges and Elizabeth was still trying to secure one. Prudent also, because it left the way open for a settlement.

But Mary's mood had changed. On January 9th, she wrote that she would rather die than resign her crown; the last word in her life would be that of a Queen of Scotland. The fact was, her prospects had brightened. A fortnight or three weeks previously Elizabeth had seized a mass of bullion on its way to Alva in the Netherlands, the galleys conveying it having put into English ports to escape the Channel pirates. Alva retorted by seizing English men, ships, and goods in the Netherlands, to which Elizabeth answered by doing the same to Spaniards in England. Mary's spirits soared. There must surely be war between England and Spain. Ere March, she expected the aid of at least ten thousand men from France and Spain. And crowning joy! Englishmen were plotting a rising in her favour. 'Tell the ambassador,' she said to the Spanish ambassador's servant, 'that if his master will help me, I shall be Queen of England in three months, and Mass shall be said all over the country.' 'She hath courage enough,' wrote Knollys of her, 'to hold out as long as any foot of hope may be left unto her.' Hope! That will-o'-the-wisp!

CHAPTER XI

THE NORTHERN REBELLION

THREE months passed. April came. Instead of being Queen of England, Mary was in the custody of the Earl of Shrewsbury some hundred miles south of Bolton Castle, away from her Catholic friends of the north. Black news arrived of her party's fortunes in Scotland, and the heart went out of her. She lamented exceedingly, would eat nothing at supper, but sat weeping, her lips and whole face swollen.

Elizabeth seized the opportunity to try again for a settlement. She wanted Mary out of the country, without delay. She might, indeed, have handed her over to Murray without more ado, but conscience would not let her do this without guarantees for her life, and she was not prepared to risk another escape from Loch Leven, with the possibility of a different ending and the utter ruin of English interests in Scotland. There was no feasible solution of the problem —death apart—except one to which Mary could be brought to agree. Consequently, in spite of Cecil, and in spite of promises to Murray, she was still anxious to restore Mary to her throne—restore her under conditions as favourable to Murray's and English interests, and as proof against illfaith, as human foresight could devise. She sent the proposals to Murray in April, 1569. He delayed an answer, and then his party decided that they would negotiate on no other basis than the confirmation of Mary's abdication. Elizabeth was really angry. She threatened to proceed, when Murray would find the settlement go less in his favour. But before anything could be done, the intrigues that had long been gathering about Mary in England and had raised her spirits so high in January, began to come to light. Trouble was at last descending on Elizabeth.

Ten full years had gone by since Elizabeth came to the throne, and while her neighbours, one after another, had been caught in the maelstrom of civil and religious strife, England had enjoyed peace. Not the peace of Germany and Italy, which lay more or less supine after long suffering from war and troubles. For Elizabeth had reigned dangerously, and strode the world with her fame as Philip II did with his territories. To Protestants throughout Europe she was the bulwark of their faith, a triumphant Judith, a faithful and active Deborah; to Catholics, 'that wicked woman', 'the servant of infamy', 'the refuge of wicked men'. It was as though there were something uncanny or providential in her rule: 'In this country how wonderfully and beyond all expectation the God of all goodness and the Lord of Glory has preserved everything safe and sound'. She was 'indeed a child of God'. Even Cecil, as he analysed the situation about this time, and drew up a truly alarming catalogue of perils, invoked accident to explain past felicity and warned his mistress that it could not continue. When fortune failed, policy must provide. God could not always be looking after his Englishman.

To some extent Elizabeth had certainly been fortunate. The Channel cut England off from direct contact with the turmoil of western Europe; but it was policy that had made her political insularity complete by expelling the French from Scotland and nursing the Reformation there, without which the prevalent disease of religious war would certainly have been caught. Again, it was a mixture of fortune and policy that had given England, compared with her neighbours, an efficient, unified, and centralized constitution. There were no princes of the blood as in France to vie with the Crown and lend respectability to revolt; feudal liberties had all but vanished into the voracious maw of the monarchy; and family ties, which in Scotland led to chronic faction, were satisfied in a hundred forms of jobbery, relatively harmless to the State, even if acrimonious. Instead of spending their substance in private war, Englishmen indulged in pleasures as if they were to die to-morrow, and built as if they were to live for ever. The principal noblemen and others had their London houses, and came to Court to display their wit, or if they had none, their splendid, exotic fashions. They lived on the edge of bankruptcy and in pursuit of heiresses, so that in Elizabethan society a rich widow could marry and marry again to the margin of satiety or the brink of the grave.

It was a relatively stable society. But it was shot through with rancours, both public and private; and just as in France Condé had been a Huguenot because Guise was a Catholic, or in Scotland the Hamiltons were for Mary because Lennox and Murray were against her, so in England it was not beyond the range of probability that all manner of rivalries and discontents would one day merge in some major issue. The process of sophistication, with its unifying effects, had made little or no way in places. This was especially true of the north, with its wild moors and remote valleys, where time stood still, or resented southern efforts to jerk it forward, where old manners and the old faith and old loyalties persisted, where men were reluctant to know any prince but a Percy or a Neville, and private war went on in the form of Border affrays with the Scots.

When she came to the throne, Elizabeth had prayed God to give her grace to govern with clemency and without bloodshed. To keep her people united was her great aim. 'If I should say the sweetest speech with the eloquentest tongue that ever was in man', she told one of her parliaments, 'I were not able to express that restless care which I have ever bent to govern for the greatest wealth'. She was apt to rejoice more over one Catholic who was loyal than over ninety and nine hot-gospellers whose loyalty needed no demonstration. 'This good man is a clergyman of the old religion,' she proudly told the Spanish ambassador, when on a progress through the country a subject approached her open carriage and cried, 'Vivat Regina! Honi soit qui mal y pense'. No doubt her kingdom was to be Protestant, and in times of danger Cecil and her keener councillors

were allowed to harry disobedient Catholics. But she
wanted no inquisitorial practices, opening windows into
men's souls. Outward conformity was enough; a man's conscience should be his own, not the State's concern. And under the steady pressure of a broad church establishment
she hoped in time to wean her Catholic subjects from their
old mentality.

Elizabeth's Court contained crypto-Catholics and ardent
Puritans, men abreast of the time and men lagging behind.
To keep them all loyal she had to be above party and pursue a policy which, however much it owed to the suggestion
of others, was in fact nobody's but her own. 'Our part',
wrote Cecil, 'is to counsel, and also to obey the commander';
and his constant laments, in memoranda and in letters to
friends, are cogent proof of the far from passive mind with
which Elizabeth listened to her ablest and most trusted
councillor. Her obstinacy and wilfulness were indeed notorious. Sir Francis Knollys, who exercised the privilege of a
kinsman and councillor with the fearless frankness of a godly
man, told her that if she discouraged her faithful councillors
—by whom he meant Cecil and the militant Protestants—
through withholding her assent to their advice till all the
passions of her mind were satisfied, then how she could
expect them to stand by her in her hour of need, it was
fearful for him to consider. To Cecil he wrote disparagingly
of her desire to be 'the ruler or half-ruler' herself, instead
of winning her decayed credit, heartening her subjects, and
escaping peril, by meekly doing what her faithful councillors told her to do. To the men about her, as the tone of
Knollys's admonition shows, her sex was a stumbling block.
On her side there was a touch of feminism in the way she
protected her rights. An ambassador from France once
asked for an audience at which her Council should be present. She answered that he forgot himself in thinking her
incapable of conceiving an answer to his message without
the aid of her Council: it might be appropriate in France
where the King was a youth, but she was governing her
realm better than they were theirs.

A comprehensive policy inevitably pleased few. The

keenest and most vociferous element in the Church was denied what its members called 'a true ministry and regiment of the Church, according to the word'. Elizabeth would not let them reform the Church on the Genevan or Presbyterian model: purge the Prayer Book, an 'unperfect book, culled and picked out of that Popish dunghill, the Mass-book, full of abominations'; abolish Archbishops, Archdeacons, Lord Bishops, etc., whose names and offices were drawn out of the Pope's shop; be rid of their courts, especially that 'petty little stinking ditch—the Commissary's Court—that floweth out of that former great puddle'. Quite apart from her strong, personal dislike for Genevan views—a result of her Lutheran upbringing as well as temperament—if she had given way to the Puritan party she would have ruined her policy of comprehension, and perhaps goaded her Catholic subjects into revolt. Thus in the eyes of these godly men she sometimes seemed more favourable to Catholics than to themselves, and loud were their protests against the caps, copes, surplices, and ceremonies that she insisted upon, and the ritual she maintained in her own Chapel. Her temperament was much the same in secular policy. She generally preferred less clear-cut decisions and less open action than Cecil and his group advised, content perhaps that militant Protestantism should be the spirit of Elizabethan England, but exercising a wise and firm restraint both for financial reasons and because of the need of a tolerable life for old-fashioned folk.

Yet this government was no more pleasing to conservative councillors and their friends of the old nobility. They were irritated by the way Cecil, with the support of Sir Nicholas Bacon and other upstarts, controlled the Council, resented the influence which his unrivalled knowledge gave him, and were jealous of his constant access to the Queen. Since she herself was doubly irresponsible, as a sovereign and a woman, it was he whom they held to blame when things went wrong.

At this particular juncture everything seemed to them to be going seriously wrong. First there was a breach in the old friendship with Spain. It was implicit in the new age, but recent events, of an accidental character, had hastened it on. They began with the sending of Dr. John Man, Dean of Gloucester and Warden of Merton College, as ambassador to Spain in the spring of 1566. Formality located an embassy in that country, where there was little to do, instead of in the Netherlands, with which English relations were chiefly concerned; and in consequence, the ambassador groaned out his years of distant, uncongenial exile, neglected by the Government at home. It was hard to find any fitting person who could be coerced into going. Hence Dr. Man. He outraged the Spaniards and the diplomatic corps at Madrid. He was a dean and married, and he was no gentleman—he lived within his income. To crown all, he lacked discretion. After two years of scorn, he was dispatched home by Philip in disgrace; an insult of which Elizabeth made the most. She sent no more resident ambassadors to Spain, a blessing to those who might have gone, and an economy for her.

At this same time Philip changed his resident ambassador in England, thereby, though unintentionally, doing grave harm to his relations with the country, for while the old ambassador belied the haughty traditions of his race, the new was arrogant, humourless, and stupid. Also, he was an inveterate schemer who could not be happy without his finger in a plot—a fatal person to come to England at this particular time, and a malign attraction for such a passionate and sanguine fellow-schemer as Mary. The dispatches to Spain completely changed their character. When, for example, Cecil angrily expostulated with the retiring ambassador over the treatment of Dr. Man, 'I let him talk on', the ambassador wrote, 'and when he had done, I waited a little for him to recover somewhat from his rage, and then went up to him laughing and embraced him, saying that I was amused to see him fly into such a passion.' The temper of the new man, in contrast, can be judged from his descriptions of Elizabeth's councillors: Cecil, a man of mean sort, but very astute, false, lying, and full of all artifice, a great heretic and a clownish Englishman; Leicester, a light and greedy man; Bacon, an obstinate and most malignant heretic; the Lord Admiral, a very shameless thief without any religion at all; the Earl of Bedford, in person and manners a monstrosity and a great heretic; and so on. He wrote to Philip suggesting that when the troubles in the Netherlands were over, Spain and France might join in an economic blockade of England, and all Catholic princes send ambassadors to make a *démarche* and frighten Elizabeth into Catholicism. With his letter he enclosed a draft of the solemn admonition that he might himself speak on that occasion. It was consigned to the archives, and in the course of three to four centuries has acquired a fine, mature humour.

The seizure of the Spanish treasure in December, 1568, set every nerve in the ambassador's body tingling. As a matter of fact, it was nothing like so outrageous an act as it seems in modern eyes, nor so outrageous as Elizabeth's officials at the Channel ports were tempted to make it. Being blunt Englishmen and stout Protestants, and many of them the friends of privateers, these men thought the opportunity God-given. One offered to seize the treasure on his own responsibility, if, after the storms of Elizabeth's displeasure, shown at the beginning to colour the fact, he might find the calm of her favour. He was of mind that anything taken from that wicked nation was profitable to the common weal. Cecil was of like mind. As for Elizabeth, she wanted the bullion, for the money market at Antwerp was drying up owing to the troubles there, and she was experiencing the common perplexity of rulers to find ready cash, on which everything depended. But the crude ways of her port officials could not be hers.

Though the Spaniards and the captains of the vessels pretended otherwise, the bullion, which was a loan by Genoese merchant-bankers for Alva in the Netherlands, did not in fact become Spanish property until it arrived at its destination, and the owners bore the risks of the voyage. Their agent in London, to the intense anger of the Spanish ambassador, revealed this to the English government, and it is not at all unlikely that he made a secret deal with Elizabeth by which she agreed to take up the loan, to the gain of the owners who otherwise would have had to pay for a naval escort, or for transportation and reshipment at other ports to escape the privateers and pirates, swarming like sharks outside the harbours in which the treasure lay. At any rate, she took the money as a loan, and the custom of the time apparently permitted this.

It was not a friendly gesture towards Spain. But Elizabeth was in the mood to snap her fingers at Philip and take the offering of a beneficent Providence, moved to this defiance by Spain's intolerable arrogance—the treatment of Dr. Man, the hundred high-handed acts against English ships in Spanish ports, and the attack made upon Hawkins and Drake during their slave-trading expedition to the Spanish New World, news of which had just reached England. Her people sympathized with the Netherlands in their revolt, and she herself, mindful of the prevalent belief in a great Catholic combination to root out Protestantism in Europe, feared that Alva's troops, after subduing the rebels, might invade England on their way home. Spain and England were drifting apart, the vital link between them, the Netherlands, having now become a sentimental obstacle. Philip received and supported English Catholic exiles and rebels, their busy minds for ever planning invasion; while Elizabeth opened her doors to Philip's exiles and rebels. More and more the one country was assuming the role of Catholic champion and the other of Protestant champion.

What would have happened if the former Spanish ambassador had been in England, it is hard to say. His successor, with the bee of an economic blockade buzzing in his head, advised Alva to seize English shipping and goods before he knew that Elizabeth intended to appropriate the treasure. He thus gave her the chance, which she used superbly, of appearing the aggrieved party. He was so beside himself that she put him under restraint in his house, and let him taste of the ignominy meted out to Dr. Man. In the first few months of 1569 war seemed inevitable.

But the facts belied appearances quite ridiculously. Elizabeth held all the trumps. In the game of seizures, apart from the treasure, she gained an immensely richer booty than Spain; and while English merchants and industry, though not unharmed, found a fairly satisfactory market immediately in Hamburg, the stoppage of trade was ruinous to merchants in the Netherlands and Spain. Alva declared war impracticable, and Philip and his Council decided against it; indeed, they prayed that Elizabeth would not discover how earnestly they wanted a settlement, or inflict some new indignity which Philip could not overlook. She was to be treated very gently. The ambassador was told to bear his cross with patience, and Alva, who was contemptuous of him as a meddling fool, peremptorily ordered him to stop his intrigues.

But it was given to few, other than Elizabeth and Cecil, to realize how far she could venture out on the plank without tumbling into the void. Commercial and political relations with France were only less serious than those with Spain; the problem of Mary Queen of Scots was unsolved, and this because of the favour shown Murray's party: is it surprising that English conservatives thought that the climax of Cecilian folly had been reached?

Hitherto, discontent had not come to a head, because no party had been really driven to desperation, and there was no outstanding person, like Condé or Guise in France, round whom it could gather and breed revolt. But Mary, 'the daughter of debate, that eke discord doth sow,' was now in England. History was busy repeating itself, recreating the setting of Queen Mary's reign, even to the imprisonment at Woodstock, Elizabeth now being in her sister's role, Mary Queen of Scots in hers. But if in her sister's day prudence and popularity had been Elizabeth's salvation, prudence was the last quality to be attributed to Mary, and time was to show whether on this occasion the people of England would fain change Queens.

It was a strange company of malcontents that united round Mary. Its strangeness was due to the project of marrying her to the Duke of Norfolk, which had been conceived at the York Conference in October, 1568. In many ways the plan was a happy one, for the root difficulty of Mary's problem was that nobody trusted her, whereas, if she could be subjected to a husband on whom Murray and Elizabeth could rely, her restoration might easily be accomplished. But whatever chance the scheme had was ruined by secrecy and delay. It became a plot, with wide ramifications. The conservative peers resolved to have the marriage, recognize Mary as Elizabeth's successor, resume friendship with Spain by surrendering treasure and property, and withdraw all countenance and help from the Huguenots in France. In other words, they decided to save England from the disaster of war with Spain and France, and solve all its problems by a political revolution. They were not perturbed—they were pleased—that it would involve the overthrow of Cecil and his party of new men. In the good old way Cecil would pay his debt to power by losing his head—another Thomas Cromwell. At first they meant to overthrow Leicester, but he joined forces with them; so did his henchman Throckmorton, who had changed from a friend to an enemy of Cecil's, and though still a stout Protestant, probably thought it prudent to support the Norfolk marriage scheme, seeing that Elizabeth was bent on restoring Mary.

The incongruity of Throckmorton being in such company, was matched at the other end by the northern Catholics, among whom were the Earls of Northumberland and Westmorland, and Leonard Dacres, each with personal grievances against the Government. These Catholics and others in the south had been plotting with the Spanish ambassador. They had long been charmed with flattering notes and encouraging messages from Mary and the exchange of pretty tokens—now a diamond ring, now beads or perfume for the Countess of Northumberland, now a precious stone set in a tablet of gold. If they did not openly say that they wanted to change Queens, they aimed at restoring Catholicism with foreign help, which could hardly avoid ending in the deposition of Elizabeth. Nor could adequate rewards come to them otherwise. Some were broken in fortune, others, including the southern Earl of Arundel, all but bankrupt; and the revenue of Scotland would have made a poor meal for such a greedy crew.

In March and April of this eventful year, 1569, the storm

was blowing mightily against Cecil. On various excuses disgruntled councillors absented themselves from meetings of
the Council; and on Ash Wednesday—it is said—Leicester
ventured to tell the Queen that most, and they the best, of
her subjects thought affairs so badly managed that either
her State must run into danger or Cecil must answer with
his head. While Leicester faced the Queen, and received a
sound rating from his angry mistress, Norfolk, in another
corner of the Chamber, bravely uttered his thoughts aloud
to a fellow-councillor. Thwarted in this approach, the con-
federates—again it is a story needing corroboration—resolved
to attempt a *coup de main* and arrest Cecil. Thrice in April
they steeled themselves to it, but Leicester's loyalty or
prudence was too much for them. He wavered, and threatened to tell the Queen. Then Cecil bent to the wind, made
friends with Norfolk, and moderated his conduct. In any
case the Thomas Cromwell business was out-of-date under
Elizabeth. It was impossible to intimidate her; she was
clement, and she was astonishingly loyal to her ministers.

The cabal now devoted its activities to the marriage of
Mary and Norfolk. Elizabeth had heard of the plan soon
after it was first broached the previous autumn, and spoke
some sharp words to Norfolk; but he had answered, 'What!
should I seek to marry her, being so wicked a woman, such
a notorious adulteress and murderer? I love to sleep upon
a safe pillow. I count myself, by your Majesty's favour, as
good a prince at home in my bowling-alley at Norwich, as
she is, though she were in the midst of Scotland. And if I
should go about to marry with her, knowing, as I do, that
she pretendeth a title to the present possession of your Majesty's crown, your Majesty might justly charge me with
seeking your own crown from your head.' This had stilled
Elizabeth's misgivings, though at the cost of making it very
difficult for Norfolk to reopen the subject.

Leicester assumed the lead of the cabal, aspiring to be a
king-maker, and to reap his reward should Elizabeth die
young. He and his relative the Earl of Pembroke wrote to
Mary about Easter; and at the very time that Elizabeth was
straining to carry through her plan for restoring Mary, they

and their friends were secretly negotiating terms of their own. They meant well; they were quite loyal, except in their intention to impose their settlement on Elizabeth; and this, in their masculine eyes, was a proper proceeding towards a misguided woman. Norfolk, who was beginning to receive sweet letters from Mary and found himself being drawn into deep and dangerous waters, was uneasy at the delay in approaching Elizabeth. These precious conspirators, in fact, dared none of them face her, and Leicester, as ready with excuses as promises, kept waiting for 'the opportune time.' By July they were in something of a stew, and in their anxiety told the secret to Cecil. He kept their confidence. At best he was indifferent about their plan, and sceptical of Elizabeth consenting.

Soon Elizabeth had wind of it. Very wisely she gave Norfolk ample chance to make a clean breast of the business. Calling him to her one day, she asked what news was abroad. None that he heard of, answered Norfolk. 'No?' she said. 'You come from London and can tell me no news of a marriage?' Leaning on the hollow Leicester, and afraid to take Cecil's advice and confess, he let time pass in compromising silence. Then Elizabeth invited him to dine at her table and at the end of the meal gave him a nip, bidding him take good heed to his pillow. Three weeks went by. He was still silent. She sent for him and asked if reports were true. When he replied that she had heard the truth from others, she answered that she had rather hear it from himself. It was a fragment of the truth he told. She commanded him on his allegiance to deal no further in the matter.

Courtiers now began to shun Norfolk, and he was left a prey to changing emotions, fear, pride, anger. He had gone too far with Mary to retire with honour, and unlike Leicester and some of the others, had played with treason and got himself involved in the Catholic insurrectionary movement. Without asking permission, he left the Court, then on progress, and retired to his London house. Elizabeth sent, bidding him return. He answered that he had an ague but would come in four days; instead, he fled the same night to his estates in Norfolk. His action had brought him to the fearful alternative that had been planned, of revolt in company with the northern Catholics. Mary and her friends urged him to be valiant; the Spanish ambassador, to whom it seemed that God was opening a wide door to the great good of Christendom, believed that pusillanimity alone could ruin him. Norfolk tried to get a messenger over to Alva, only to find the ports closed; and instead of the gentry of his county flocking to him, the Papists alone came, while loyal Protestants took precautions even before a letter arrived from Elizabeth telling them to do so. As for Mary, about a fortnight before, two dependable lords had been joined with the pliant Shrewsbury to keep her safe. Elizabeth was intensely awake. She commanded Norfolk to return on his allegiance, and when he pleaded another ague, ordered him to come, if need be in a litter. His courage ebbed away. Dispatching a messenger to beg the Earl of Westmorland not to stir, or his head would be in danger, he set off for Court and was diverted to the Tower which he entered on October 11th. Three other lords and Throckmorton were placed under restraint. Leicester confessed all —or said he did—and was forgiven.

Cecil and most people had an unshaken faith in Norfolk's loyalty. Not so Elizabeth, who had acquired a sixth sense in the matter of plotting. She vowed that she would know the truth. But Norfolk's friends at Court and elsewhere took care that he was advised of everything that went on and prepared against awkward questions. They instituted a secret post in bottles of drink, found means of conveying verbal messages through a hole leading from an adjoining dwelling, while a man of his, passing in under guard to his master's chamber, would cast letters, wrapped in black paper, into a little dark privy from which they were later recovered. Elizabeth impetuously talked of his offence as treason. Cecil sent her the gist of Edward III's statute to show her it was not, and counselled her to scotch the marriage scheme by marrying Norfolk to someone else.

Meanwhile, disturbing news had been coming in from the north, where the countryside had been swept by rumour, picked up at the fairs, spread from mouth to mouth, as pervasive as the wind and as elusive. Who its authors were, what substance was behind it, the authorities could not discover. It followed the fortunes of the Duke of Norfolk, reporting that the naming of a successor was in hand again, the Duke home to his country, other noblemen to theirs, and the realm would soon be in a hurly-burly. One of these nights there would be a rising in favour of Mary and religion; and Protestants were warned by their friends to beware. The Earl of Sussex, who was President of the Council in the North, sent for the Earls of Northumberland and Westmorland. They spoke him fair words; and then rumour died down as mysteriously as it had arisen. Their plans had been thrown into confusion by Norfolk's return to Court and by messages from him, Mary, and the Spanish ambassador, warning them not to rise.

Sussex was for letting well alone, but Elizabeth could not allow sedition to breed and gather renewed confidence from her inactivity. If trouble was to come, better now than at a later time, more propitious for the enemy. She therefore summoned the two northern earls to Court. As the messenger left Topcliff after delivering the Queen's command to Northumberland, the bells of the village were rung backwards, and when he inquired the reason, his guide sighed and answered that he was afraid it was to raise the country. Treason was a dreadful word to men of lineage and property, and gladly would the two Earls have drawn out of the enterprise. But their hot-headed friends and followers were there to persuade, nay compel them; and their wives, too. 'We and our country were shamed for ever,' my Lady of Westmorland exclaimed, weeping bitterly, 'that now in the end we should seek holes to creep into'. A servant told Northumberland that he could not choose but proceed. 'Then,' answered he, 'if it be so, have with you!' Old Richard Norton was there, with his reverend grey head; a man of seventy-one, sheriff of Yorkshire, one of the Council in the North, and Governor of Norham Castle. He bore the cross and a banner on which were painted the five wounds of

Christ—an echo of far-off days and the Pilgrimage of Grace. Seven of his eleven sons rose with him.

> . . . the inly-working North
> Was ripe to send its thousands forth,
> A potent vassalage, to fight
> In Percy's and in Neville's right.

On November 14th the rebels entered Durham Cathedral, tore up the Bible and other books, cast down the communion-table, erected two altars which had lain hidden these many years, and restored the Mass. Elsewhere the people did the same. Altars and holy-water stoups came out from the dunghills and other hiding places, and Protestant books went up in a holocaust: 'Lo, where the homilies flee to the devil!'

They had some thousand foot, armed in the rudest manner, and fifteen hundred or more horse, well-appointed and dangerous. For a time the north lay at their mercy. Sussex dared not give battle, since his Yorkshire levies, with father, son, or brother among the rebels, might desert, as some of the garrison at Barnard Castle, who leapt over the walls to join the besiegers. The moral effect of a defeat would have been disastrous. The rebels marched south towards Mary at Tutbury, from which she was hurried away to Coventry in the nick of time. Not daring to venture much beyond York, nor to attack that city, they returned north again, with the spirit evaporating from their men. A detachment took Hartlepool, deceived by the ebullient Spanish ambassador into hope of help from Alva; others besieged and captured Barnard Castle.

In the meantime, from every quarter in the midlands and the south, levies had been hastily raised, some to go to the Court as a royal guard, the rest marching slowly and painfully north along miry roads. In London the noted walkers in St. Paul's were making a harvest-time of rumour, and the frequenters of 'Papists' Corner' and 'Liars' Bench' looked cheerful, for the tale went that Alva had promised to come and pay his soldiers their wages in Cheapside and make Elizabeth hear Mass at St. Paul's on Candlemas day next.

Another tale told that ten thousand Scots, coming to the Queen's help, had been given such a breakfast by the rebels that it had been better they had not come. But outside the north, the country stood firmly loyal, irrespective of religious belief, and against the numbers and weapons of the advancing army the rebels had not a dog's chance. They broke and fled, without giving battle, and on December 20th, 1569, their leaders crossed the Border to take refuge among Mary's Scottish adherents.

Stern was the vengeance meted out to humble offenders. In every village that had sent men to the Earls, martial law took its toll. Some six hundred were hanged. They cursed their leaders, more fortunate than they, who were reserved for the ordinary process of the law, and for the most part paid for their sins with their property, having fled into Scotland or found friends to intercede for their lives. Elizabeth was disturbed at the palpable injustice of sparing the rich, but it was the way of the world. It was the way of her world also, that instead of quiet thankfulness for victory, Court and army lapsed into a sordid scramble for the forfeited estates of the rebels and the spoil of humble villagers. Leaders eyed one another with jealousy. Leicester's brother commanded the southern force, and his faction at Court poisoned the Queen's mind against Sussex. Gloom settled on Cecil and his friends, for 'faithful councillors' were discredited, and the Queen's one thought was for her moneybags—which indeed were empty—and the immediate necessity of disbanding her army.

While Leonard Dacres was at large, commanding the same sort of tenant-loyalty as Percy and Neville, there was still a kick left in the north. He had been deeply involved in the conspiracy, but largely owing to a quarrel with Norfolk over his inheritance, had kept out of the rebellion. When inquiries revealed his guilt, Elizabeth sent to bring him to Court. It was a commission that her ministers in the north hesitated to carry out; but her cousin, Lord Hunsdon undertook it, and marching to join forces with Lord Scrope, was surprised by Dacres and his men on February 19th. The fight was hot, and Hunsdon's troops only half the number of their opponents, but they gained a brilliant and decisive victory. Dacres fled over the Border to join the other northern leaders. For months these exiles hovered about. Northumberland was taken by the Scottish Regent and was ultimately surrendered to Elizabeth and executed. The rest, when their fortunes sank in Scotland, crossed to the Netherlands to lead a precarious life as pensioners of Spain, perpetually plotting, perpetually hoping, perpetually disappointed, incurably impecunious.

> The sun shone bright, and the birds sung sweet
> The day we left the North Countrie;
> But cold is the wind, and sharp is the sleet,
> That beat on the exile over the sea.

Elizabeth was overjoyed at Hunsdon's victory, and appended a glowing postscript to her official letter of thanks to him: 'I doubt much, my Harry, whether that the victory were given me more joyed me, or that you were by God appointed the instrument of my glory; and I assure you that for my country's good the first might suffice, but for my heart's contentation the second more pleased me. . . . And that you may not think that you have done nothing for your profit, though you have done much for honour, I intend to make this journey somewhat to increase your livelihood, that you may not say to yourself, *perditur quod factum est ingrato.* Your loving kinswoman. Elizabeth, R.' Hunsdon, who had been exchanging a good grouse with Cecil a month before, was exquisitely happy.

CHAPTER XII

THE RIDOLFI PLOT

FROM over the Border came the voice of one—rare among men—who in all these years had not succumbed to Mary's charms: 'If ye strike not at the root, the branches that appear to be broken will bud again, and that more quickly than men can believe. . . . Yours to command in God. John Knox with his one foot in the grave.'

As though to confirm Knox's warning, Rome seized the opportunity of the Northern Rebellion to issue the long-delayed excommunication, depriving Elizabeth, with eloquent preamble and opprobrious epithets, of her pretended title to the Kingdom of England, releasing her subjects from their allegiance, and interdicting obedience to her laws. In some respects, it was a pathetic revelation of Papal impotence. Philip II and Alva were annoyed at it, as was the Emperor, and France bluntly refused to publish it. Issued in February, 1570, and not 'published' in England until May, when it was secretly fixed to the door of the Bishop of London's palace in St. Paul's Churchyard, the Bull came when the Rebellion was already long over. But it remained an incentive to disobedience, however English Catholics strove by argument or sophistry to ignore its injunctions; and for all Elizabeth's earnest desire to maintain her policy of comprehension, it deepened the Protestant and militant tinge of the government by the anger that it aroused.

The Papal Bull was only another incident emphasizing the urgent, perplexing problem of Mary Queen of Scots. In the last year Murray's party in Scotland had been breaking up, and Maitland, the cleverest, had gone over to an intermediate position, before finally deserting to Mary's side. Then, in January, 1570, irreparable disaster befell them: Murray was assassinated. Elizabeth was deeply moved. To add to her worries, Spain and France were pressing her to restore Mary to her throne, and in February Charles IX declared that he would employ his whole forces to effect this. Elizabeth answered bravely, but she was ill at ease. Knowing much of Mary's plotting, and guessing more, she had no illusions about her pernicious duplicity, and wanted her out of the realm, where she was stealing the affections of Englishmen and ruining that clement state of unity and concord, so dear to Elizabeth's heart. She expressed her sentiments in verse:

No foreign banished wight shall anchor in this port.
Our realm it brooks no strangers' force: let them elsewhere
    resort.
Our rusty sword with rest, shall first his edge employ
To poll their tops that seek such change, and gape for joy.

Elizabeth's sense of propriety and prudence still led her to aim at restoring Mary to her throne, but it would have been madness to re-embark on this policy without first redressing the balance of Scottish parties upset by Murray's death. By good fortune an excuse for doing this was at hand, for the leaders of the Northern Rebellion were on the borders with Mary's followers, joining raids into England and waiting for the opportunity of stirring up a new rebellion. She determined to teach these Scottish borderers a salutary lesson. Sussex was ordered to take his army on a punitive expedition, and in April the borders were crossed simultaneously from the East, Middle, and West Marches. They slew and captured, burnt hundreds of villages, and destroyed the castles. It was 'the honourablest journey that ever was made into Scotland, with so few men, with so safe a return.' Elizabeth had put new heart into the King's party —despite Maitland's vow that he would make her sit on her tail and whine. Cecil was pleased with his mistress. Lo! how the sluggard had cast aside her sloth.

On April 29th, Elizabeth summoned her councillors to listen to their advice; free, she said, from any determined resolution herself, and ready to make choice of what she should think meetest for her honour. Cecil and his supporters—a majority of the Council—advised her to help the boy-King's party with money and men; if she restored Mary to her throne, she could have no sufficient assurance for her own safety. Sussex wrote urging her to do something: 'If you be on the Queen's side, take up the matter between her and her subjects quickly. . . . If you be on the other side, bend your force to that end presently. Otherwise, if you suspend longer, I see not how you can be assured of either.'

Elizabeth, still clinging to her old policy, turned to negotiate with Mary. The terms were to be stiffer than ever, symbol of an ever-deepening distrust, and the boy James was to be delivered over as hostage, to be brought up in England. In June Mary's ambassador presented her with some tokens from his mistress, including an inkstand or table-desk on the lock of which was engraved the cipher employed between the two Queens in the old days of amity. 'Would God, my Lord of Ross,' she remarked, 'that all things were in the same state they were in when this cipher was made betwixt us.'

The way prepared, Elizabeth decided to send two councillors to Mary to settle the actual terms of the treaty; and with characteristic wisdom she chose, not Leicester or any of Mary's favourers, but Cecil and another of his party. Cecil was 'thrown into a maze.' 'God be our guide,' he wrote, 'for neither of us like the message.' In the discussions with Mary, there was some haggling over the terms. She suggested in the clause binding her to renounce her claim to the English throne in favour of Elizabeth and her issue, changing the word 'issue' to *lawful* issue.' Elizabeth snorted. 'She may, peradventure, measure other folk's dispositions by her own actions,' she told Cecil; but she compromised by allowing 'lawful' to be inserted before 'husband,' seeing that it was possible in good faith to marry someone already secretly contracted to another; and she gave tit for tat by inserting the word 'pretended' before Mary's title to the succession. Cecil came away thinking that Mary would yield the two or three points on which they still disagreed.

By the end of October, the negotiations were in a state to summon commissioners from the two parties of Scottish nobles, Mary's and the King's. This was the point at which they had stuck before in 1569, and by putting new spirit into the King's party, Elizabeth had risked their sticking again. The risk was inevitable. In February, 1571, the King's commissioners arrived, only to show themselves, as in 1569, set against Mary's restoration. Their opposition led to a final battle on their behalf in the English Council. But Elizabeth was determined to have her way, and wanted the business ended, without further hindrance from Cecil and his 'brothers in Christ.' There was nothing for the commissioners to do but play their last card. They declared that they had no powers to conclude a treaty, and so forced Elizabeth to postpone proceedings until they could summon a parliament in May.

If Mary had been of a less sanguine and more patient nature, if she had ruminated on the lessons of the past, if instead of being an inveterate plotter and fluent liar she had been content with one string to her bow at a time, if, in short, she had been honest over these negotiations—then there is scarcely a doubt that Elizabeth would have restored her, a crippled Queen maybe, but free and a Queen. Instead, she was scheming here, there, and everywhere; whispering one thing in the ears of Spain, and the opposite in the ears of France; writing love-letters to Norfolk, and equally ready to write them to the Duke of Anjou or Don John of Austria; sending encouraging messages to the English rebels; planning to escape; building up a first-class plot to sweep Elizabeth from her throne. In 1569 the negotiations for her restoration had foundered through the discovery of the intrigues associated with the Norfolk marriage. The negotiations in 1570–71 were to be ruined by the Ridolfi plot.

Ridolfi was a Florentine banker, one of those 'bosom-creeping Italians' who lived and did business in London.

The Pope secretly used him as an agent, and it was to him that copies of the Bull of Excommunication had been sent. His business offered a convenient cloak for dealings with the Spanish ambassador, the Bishop of Ross, and others, and like the ambassador, he was a sanguine and crack-brained schemer, ready with childish irresponsibility to put the name of any nobleman or man of worth into a list of potential rebels, and with simple faith compile figures of their followers. If, with the co-operation of Mary, these men could not construct a vast rebellion on paper, nobody could. Ridolfi sent a sample of his handiwork to the Pope in September, 1570: a puff, it seemed, and Elizabeth's throne was gone! The Pope was captivated: he wrote to Mary that he would take her and hers under his wings as a hen its chickens; a dispensation awaited all those who rebelled.

Persuaded by Mary, dragged by Ridolfi, the Duke of Norfolk entered half reluctantly, half willingly into this man's plots. Thanks to the general favour he was in at Court, he had been released from the Tower in August, 1570, and placed under restraint in his own house. He was under a double bond to forsake his old practices: the command given him by Elizabeth a year before, and a submission he wrote in the summer of 1570, binding himself on his allegiance never to deal in the marriage scheme again, nor in any cause relating to Mary. But his most solemn promises were not worth the paper they were written on. He had sent his submission to Mary for her approval before signing it; he continued to exchange letters and presents with her; he lent her money, advised her about plans for her escape, even acted as her counsellor over the treaty for her restoration, advising her to reject certain of Elizabeth's demands. And this, in spite of having taken the councillor's oath to Elizabeth! He was a weak man, cursed with the dignity of England's sole dukedom, lured on by ambition, and too infirm of purpose to withdraw before he was deep in treason.

Ridolfi's plot, as finally evolved in discussions with the Spanish ambassador and Mary's supporters, was as follows: Alva was to be asked to send over a force of six thousand men, or better still, ten thousand, with money and arms for the English insurgents. They were to land at Harwich or Portsmouth and march on London, whereupon Norfolk, with his noble—and impecunious—friends, would rise in revolt. Norfolk was to make straight for Mary, or alternatively seize Elizabeth and hold her as hostage for Mary's safety. The Catholic faith was to be restored, and no doubt it was intended that Mary and Norfolk should rule in England as well as Scotland.

Towards the end of March, 1571, Ridolfi set out to see the Duke of Alva, the Pope, and Philip II. His plot was contained in long instructions from Mary and Norfolk, drawn up by himself: he placed Harwich in the county of Norfolk! The Duke certainly knew the gist of them, and gave his approval. In addition, there were letters of credence. Once more the Duke had been cautious, and had refused to sign the letters, although he let his servant go with the Bishop of Ross, Mary's ambassador, and avow them before the Spanish ambassador. Ridolfi first saw Alva. A soldier and realist, Alva wrote to Philip that if Norfolk and his friends would revolt and hold the field for forty days, it would be sound policy to send over an army; and he would do so. But to send the army first, as Ridolfi asked, would be madness. He did not hide his contempt for Ridolfi, and, taking his measure, warned Philip that the man was a dangerous babbler. In Rome and Madrid, however, Ridolfi fared better. There his plot looked enchanting, and his exuberant mind introduced into it the possibility of slaying Elizabeth.

Ridolfi, in truth, was a babbler. After seeing Alva, he must needs write at once to his friends in England, including Norfolk and another nobleman, telling them that all went well; a message that was not worth the sending, especially as the English government had spies among the exiles in the Netherlands. When his messenger, a servant of the Bishop of Ross, landed at Dover, he was arrested. The noble official who took him, unwittingly covered the treason, for being friendly disposed to Norfolk, in a lax mood he let the incriminating letters be extracted and sent on to the Bishop of Ross. But Cecil—or Lord Burghley, as he must now be called—clapped the messenger in prison, and a spy was set on him, who acted as go-between in a secret correspondence between the prisoner and his master, the Bishop of Ross. In this way, Burghley found out what had happened. Still he was baffled. Ridolfi's letters were in cipher, and addressed to '40' and '30.' He discovered that they were two noblemen, but their names eluded him.

Then a stroke of fortune gave Burghley the clue. At the end of August, Norfolk undertook to convey £600 from the French ambassador to Mary's supporters in Scotland. A Shrewsbury merchant was induced to carry the money to Norfolk's agent in the north of England, but becoming suspicious at the weight of the bag, which did not square with the tale told him, he took it to the authorities. Norfolk's servants were arrested, and the questions put to them, together with the discovery of ciphers hidden in the tiles of his house and letters secreted in other places, enabled Burghley not only to unfold the whole plot, but much that had been going on for the last two years. As the Spanish ambassador was found to be deeply involved, an ignominious end was put to his incessant scheming and unbearable insolence. Summoned before the Council, he was told his sins, and ordered to quit the realm at once, as the Queen could no longer endure his presence. He left England early in January, 1572, with little sympathy from Alva.

On the sixteenth of that month the Duke of Norfolk was brought before his peers in Westminster Hall on the charge of treason. The items were many, the documentary evidence lengthy, and he was allowed unusual latitude of speech, so that the trial lasted from eight in the morning till after eight in the evening, 'which has not been seen in any time.' He was found guilty, and the edge of the axe turned towards him as the Lord High Steward pronounced the terrible sentence of a traitor.

The Duke was popular. He was the premier nobleman of the realm, and in this singularly clement reign, in which as yet no peer had gone to the scaffold, his fate moved many to pity. Two desperate and rather burlesque fellows planned to kill Burghley and the Queen to save him. Despite this, Elizabeth recoiled from signing Norfolk's death-warrant, being too profoundly moved to think merely of her own safety. The execution was expected on January 21st. It was deferred. 'The Queen's Majesty,' wrote Burghley, 'hath been always a merciful lady, and by mercy she hath taken more harm than by justice, and yet she thinks that she is more beloved in doing herself harm. God save her to his honour long among us.' Sometimes when her thoughts ran upon her safety, she was ready to let justice be done; at other times when she thought of Norfolk as her relative, and of his rank, she hesitated. One Saturday, early in February, she signed a warrant for his execution on the Monday. Suddenly, on Sunday late in the night, she sent for Burghley in great distress and insisted on a warrant being made out that night to postpone it. 'God's will be fulfiled,' he wrote, 'and aid her Majesty to do herself good.' His friends were equally upset. Hunsdon was amazed at the Queen's carelessness of herself. 'The world knows her to be wise, and surely there cannot be a greater point of wisdom than for any to be careful of their own estate, and especially the preservation of their own life. How much more needful is it for her Majesty to take heed, upon whose life depends a whole commonwealth, the utter ruin of the whole country and the utter subversion of religion. And if by negligence or womanish pity these things happen, what she hath to answer for to God, she herself knows.' At the end of February there was once more decision, once more recession. On April 9th she signed another warrant. On the eleventh at two in the morning Burghley received a note, written in her own hand, to say that the hind part of her head—the seat of the affections—would not trust the forward side of the same. The execution must be counter-manded. She shrank from the irrevocable stroke of death.

Inevitably, as a result of the Plot, a change came over Elizabeth's attitude to Mary. Ridolfi's messenger was arrested just after she had sent the Scottish commissioners back to Scotland to obtain powers for Mary's restoration. The negotiations were stopped, and when the full extent of the Plot was revealed, Elizabeth abandoned her policy. No longer, she declared, would she talk of restoring Mary, either to rule alone or jointly with her son; never would she allow her to be at liberty, with power to repeat such practices against her. Step by step Elizabeth had been driven from the political theory of the schoolmen of her faith—a theory given full-blooded expression in a remarkable sermon recently preached by one of Mary's supporters, the Bishop of Galloway: 'Saint David was a sinner, and so is she. Saint David was an adulterer, and so is she. Saint David committed murder in slaying Uriah for his wife, and so did she. . . . I doubt not but you consider that no inferior subject has power to depose their lawful magistrates, although they commit whoredom, murder, incest, or any other crime.'

Hitherto, Elizabeth had been careful of Mary's honour —or so, with some justification, she liked to say. After the Westminster inquiry in 1568, she had refrained from any pronouncement against her, and from publishing the charges and evidence brought forward by Murray. She meant to restore Mary and did not want her publicly defamed. Perhaps nothing was more indicative of the revulsion in her feelings after the Ridolfi Plot than the fact that she now allowed Burghley to have Buchanan's *Detection*— a tract telling the story of Mary, Darnley, and Bothwell, as Murray and his party told it—translated, and published in anglicized Scots and Latin for the world to read, with the Casket Letters appended.

Elizabeth announced her change of policy to Mary's party in Scotland, so as to remove from their minds, once and for all, any hope of Mary's return. At the same time, she addressed herself to secure peace and concord in Scotland on the basis of recognizing the King and Regent, and forgetting past squabbles. The task proved hopeless, for Mary and James were only façades for internecine personal and family rivalries. Burghley and his friends were for speeding the pace by using force against Mary's party; but Elizabeth, for one reason and another, preferred the interminable but peaceful way of negotiation.

At first, what with the close restraint under which she was put, and the dismissal of many of her servants, Mary had feared for her life. Death not coming, her self-assurance returned, and with it the tone of an innocent, well-meaning, misjudged and grossly ill-used person. She wrote a series of letters to Elizabeth, culminating in one full of 'uncomely, passionate, ireful, and vindictive speeches.' The earlier were left unanswered, but to the last Elizabeth replied, at the same time giving the Earl of Shrewsbury a long memorial to be read to Mary, reviewing her own and Mary's conduct. She did not mince words. But there were two sides to this question, and at still greater length, in caustic tones, and with many shrewd hits, Mary answered. The gloves were off.

But there was little fear that the person who had recoiled from putting the Duke of Norfolk to death, would of her own will destroy Mary. Mary's ultimate fate depended on public opinion, just as Elizabeth's had done in the days of her sister; not on the opinion of a handful of noblemen, whose names looked imposing in a conspiracy and were really as sounding brass, but on the opinion which, without any appreciable government influence, found overwhelming expression in the Elizabethan House of Commons.

There had been a Parliament in the spring of 1571, called to attaint the leaders of the Northern Rebellion, grant money to meet the cost of suppressing it, and pass acts, including a new treasons bill, to guard against the dangers of the time. Its feeling about Mary was significant. One of the members was Thomas Norton, who a few years before had collaborated in the writing of the well-known tragedy, *Gorboduc*, the fifth act of which was no more than a tract for the times on the subject of the succession, containing a palpable attack on Mary's title. When the Government introduced its treasons bill into this Parliament, Norton had ready a bill of his own, which, without mentioning Mary by name, quite effectively took away the title of her or her heirs to the succession. He realized that Elizabeth would veto it if given the chance, and so to prevent this, proposed to tack it on to the Government's bill. Councillors used all their influence to thwart him, fighting at every stage and helped by Mary's friends; but they were defeated and were compelled to get the more pliant House of Lords, where Mary's friends were many, to draw the sting of the bill for them.

This was the temper of the House before the Ridolfi Plot. What was it likely to be when a new Parliament met after the Plot in May, 1572? The first hint came from the newly-elected Speaker: 'This error has crept into the heads of a number, that there is a person in this land whom no law can touch.' The great business of the session was to make provision for the Queen's safety, and the gracious words of Elizabeth—that she wished the benefits of her realm, extolled by the Speaker, were doubled, trebled, yea quadrupled—were ringing in members' minds when they listened to the tale of Mary's undue dealings, beginning with her claim to the English throne in 1558–59 and ending with the Ridolfi Plot. The tale was very long, the time far spent when it ended, and debate was postponed to the next day. The first speaker—in age superior, though, he modestly declared, in wisdom and understanding the most inferior of that society—had feared to sleep after yesterday's story until something had been done. Mary had been a killer of her husband, an adulteress, a common disturber of this realm. His advice was 'to cut off her head and make no more ado about her'. Cut off her head and the Duke's, the next speaker urged. 'Warning hath already been given her,' declared the third, 'and therefore the axe must give the next warning'. 'Shall we say our law is not able to provide for this mischief? We might then say it hath defect in the highest degree.'

A committee was appointed to sit with a committee of the House of Lords to devise a remedy; but the House went on with its clamour for Mary and Norfolk's heads. Norton made a long speech. If the Duke were not executed, he told his hearers, they could not take Mary's life. It was no use Elizabeth thinking that she could be assured of his loyalty. 'Mercy hath been showed him, and no good followed; submissions have not served, subscriptions have not served, oaths have not served, protestations and detestations have not served.' Men will be afraid to disclose treasons when traitors are suffered to live and revenge themselves on those who betrayed their treasons. As for Mary, her execution 'is of necessity, it lawfully may be done'. 'A general impunity to commit treason was never permitted to any.' Peter Wentworth—an irrepressible character—on this or another day declared that Mary was the most notorious whore in all the world.

The committee came back to report that there were two ways of proceeding: to attaint Mary in the highest degree of treason, or alternatively to take away her title to the succession, at the same time providing that if she renewed her attempts against Elizabeth, she should be attainted. The House chose the first way, and found that the Lords had done the same. Elizabeth intervened, saying that she preferred the second, for she could not with honour attaint Mary without calling on her to answer the charge, and to keep Parliament in being while she sent a committee from each House to hear her answer, would be costly to members and dangerous, since summer and the plague were at hand. The Commons answered that their own danger and expense were as nothing compared with the Queen's safety. With one whole voice and consent they resolved to proceed with the first way; the second they disliked. And, fired by their example, the Lords did the same. From every source of wisdom and authority—the Bible, the Civil Law, and History—members armed themselves with appropriate precedents, texts, and reasons.

Convocation, through its Bishops, addressed the Queen with a multitude of godly arguments. 'The late Scottish Queen hath heaped up together all the sins of the licentious sons of David—adulteries, murders, conspiracies, treasons, and blasphemies against God.' Their hope, as spiritual advisers, was to move the Queen's conscience to proceed with Mary's execution. The two Houses, for their part, addressed themselves to her reason. Persuasive their petition was, and cogent. They appreciated Elizabeth's feelings, her thought that Mary had fallen into her hands from the violence of others, and as a bird followed by a hawk had sought succour at her feet; they appreciated her sense of honour to a sister and a Queen born. But 'threatening words of law' would be of no avail to keep Mary from her malicious intent to overthrow their Queen, nor would they serve to stay traitors from aiding her, for 'such as will not deal in small matters will venture deep for a kingdom, because the reward is great when the service is done.' They described their petition as the call and cry to God of all good subjects against the merciful nature of their Queen.

At 8 a.m. on May 28th Elizabeth received the joint committee of both Houses at Court. No account of her speech survives; yet it must have been a remarkable one, blending eloquence, reason, and tact, for though she had to deny their petition and inflict the cruellest disappointment on them, she did it in words of such loving gratitude that two members of the Lower House were moved to propose sending her thanks for the good opinion she had of them. Peter Wentworth rose and declared that she deserved no thanks.

The House of Commons was in a difficult mood; swayed by great love for the Queen and tempestuous wrath against her enemies. If they could not have the head of 'the monstrous and huge dragon', the Queen of Scots, they were determined to have that of 'the roaring lion', the Duke of Norfolk. They could hardly be persuaded to wait for a few days, and let Elizabeth act without coercion. A victim they had to be given; and so on June 2nd Norfolk was led out to suffer on Tower Hill. He died bravely and repentant, though to the end, in expectation of life, he lied about his acts. There was much good in him. Few documents are so moving as the sweet letter of farewell that he sent to his children. Thus perished the only duke in England, and the first noble victim of the reign. All that day Elizabeth was sad.

Mary would have died, too, had it not been for Elizabeth's compassion and indomitable will. The French ambassador was busy interceding for her life, but from Paris the English ambassador told his mistress that the only reason for Charles IX's concern was his fear that if Mary lived and one day came to the English throne, she would ally with Spain unless he retained her friendship. Execute her, and the French King, for all his words, would rejoice at heart. 'Ah!' exclaimed Charles, when told the details of her plotting, 'the poor fool will never cease until she lose her head. In faith, they will put her to death. I see it is her own fault and folly. I see no remedy for it.' There is not the slightest doubt that Elizabeth could have sent Mary to the scaffold with impunity, and it is just as certain that Parliament and her councillors were right in thinking this the surest and simplest way for Elizabeth's safety and the quiet and security of the realm. The strongest ruler might have sacrificed a tender conscience to such cogent arguments and the tremendous pressure of subjects and statesmen. Elizabeth could not and would not.

With glum faces Parliament, frustrated in its first way against Mary, went forward with the second. It was drastic enough. The bill recited Mary's offences and called on Elizabeth not to bear the sword of justice in vain, but hereafter, when opportunity served, to punish her as she deserved. It took away her imagined title and interest in the English throne, making it a treasonable offence to advocate it, and provided for Mary's trial by English peers in case she plotted against the Queen in future. Even more: it made her responsible for any insurrection in her favour and legalized lynch law against her in such an event. This last clause aroused misgivings in the mind of one member at least. It may have been modified, though probably not: we do not know.

The act passed both Houses. It had been adopted as the milder alternative solely in deference to Elizabeth's personal feelings, but when it came before her on the closing day of the session for the royal assent, she vetoed it. To calm the minds of members, she added to her many gracious words a request that they would construe her veto, given in the traditional form—*La royne s'advisera*—literally; she neither assented nor rejected. But what comfort was that? They saw that Elizabeth could not bring herself even to this measure of severity against Mary. 'The monstrous and huge dragon' was to be left untouched.

CHAPTER XIII

'THE AFFABILITY OF THEIR PRINCE'

PARLIAMENT's fury against Mary Queen of Scots was partly an expression of Protestant feeling, but also a genuine tribute to the popularity of Elizabeth. No Prince has been a greater courtier of the people, nor any actress known better how to move her audience to transports of love and admiration. Save for a fleeting crisis like that over Dudley, Elizabeth's mind was ever fixed on popular favour, at first as an art of government, and later as a profound emotional satisfaction.

The opportunities of showing herself to the people were numerous, for the Court was constantly on the move. Greenwich, Whitehall, Richmond, Hampton Court, Windsor: there was not a year but the Queen could often be seen, like some very human and approachable goddess with her train, going by river or road from one of these palaces to another, or visiting other royal houses or private homes in the near neighbourhood of London. The City was afforded an annual autumn spectacle on the return of the Court to Whitehall, where Christmas was ordinarily kept. It became a ceremonial occasion, when Mayor, Aldermen, and Citizens in their rich finery met the splendid royal procession, and to mutual greetings of 'God save your Grace!', 'God save my people!' welcomed their sovereign back to town. In 1570, after the Northern Rebellion, the anniversary of Elizabeth's accession, November 17th, which had before then been celebrated with ringing of bells, was made a day of national thanksgiving and festival, and continued throughout the reign to be one of the great days of the year.

It was revived in James I's reign, as Elizabeth's name came to connote the peak of national greatness, retained much of its emotional significance for a hundred years after that, and still left its traces during another century. On this day young courtiers displayed their manhood and wit before thousands of spectators, running at tilt in the tilt-yard at Westminster, with all the pageantry and extravagant devices, part of the romance between them and their Queen. After that, preparations were made for the plays and masks that marked the high season of festivity, the twelve days from Christmas on.

Londoners, naturally, had the lion's share of Elizabeth's favours. She kept them bewitched, for it was a secret of power to hold this key to the kingdom. But for those who could not come to City or Court, there were the annual royal progresses. These were the Queen's summer holidays, when, combining business with pleasure, she took the Court on a month's or two months' perambulation through the country, staying at some royal manor or claiming the ready hospitality of the gentry or towns. She loved them, as she had reason to do, for they satisfied her healthy desire for activity and change of air and surroundings, and offered supreme opportunities to her genius in winning the hearts of the people; and if they allowed little or no respite from the business of being Queen, that was no disadvantage, for her work was the very breath of life, and she never seemed to lose her gusto for it.

Officials did not share the enthusiasm. Progresses involved tremendous preparations. Along with the personnel of the Household went hundreds of carts bearing the baggage, including furnishings for the bare houses which often had to be got ready; and it was the reverse of pleasure, in bad weather and on bad roads, to follow after an advance guard of this nature. Ten or twelve miles was as much as the stately procession travelled in a day. Moreover, it was often impossible to find reasonable accommodation for all the Queen's followers, and to add to their trials, Elizabeth had an increasing proclivity to change her mind and upset plans at the last minute. There were many complaints, and

every excuse was exploited to stay a progress, though rarely
with success. In 1571, in the midst of the unfolding of the
Ridolfi Plot, the Council advised her for safety's sake to can-
cel her progress. She would not. Even in the last year of
her life she kept the custom, and two years earlier, in her
sixty-seventh year, when courtiers were grumbling at a
'long progress,' she bade 'the old stay behind, and the young
and able to go with her.'

The Queen either rode on horseback or in an open litter
to be seen by the people who flocked from the countryside
and lined the roads. At the county boundary she was met
by the sheriff and gentlemen who waited on her during her
stay. On one progress into Suffolk and Norfolk the gentry
of the former county bought up all the velvets and silks
upon which they could lay their hands, no matter what the
price, and when he met the Queen the sheriff had with him
two hundred young gentlemen in white velvet, three hundred 'of the graver sort' in black velvet coats and fair chains,
with fifteen hundred serving men, all well and bravely
mounted, 'which surely was a comely troop and a noble
sight to behold'. Not to be outdone, the gentry of Norfolk
'in most gallentest manner assembled and set forward with
five and twenty hundred horsemen'.

There was an extraordinary ease and informality about
the slow procession, Elizabeth stopping from time to time
as persons came to present petitions or say a word to her.
'Stay thy cart, good fellow!' cried Serjeant Bendlowes of
Huntingdonshire to the royal coachman, 'stay thy cart, that
I may speak to the Queen'. 'Whereat her Majesty laughed
as she had been tickled . . . although very graciously, as
her manner is, she gave him great thanks and her hand to
kiss.' The Spanish ambassador described the scene on progress in 1568: 'She was received everywhere with great ac-
clamations and signs of joy, as is customary in this country;
whereat she was extremely pleased and told me so, giving
me to understand how beloved she was by her subjects and
how highly she esteemed this, together with the fact that
they were peaceful and contented, whilst her neighbours
on all sides are in such trouble. She attributed it all to God's

miraculous goodness. She ordered her carriage sometimes to be taken where the crowd seemed thickest, and stood up and thanked the people.'

Whenever a town was visited, there were great preparations:

> No sooner was pronounced the name,
>   but babes in street gan leap;
> The youth, the age, the rich, the poor,
>   came running all on heap,
> And, clapping hands, cried mainly out,
>   'O blessed be the hour!
> Our Queen is coming to the Town,
>   with princely train and power'.

Rubbish was cleared, streets cleaned, houses gaily decked, speeches memorized, perhaps pageants prepared, and last, but not least, a silver-gilt cup purchased to present to the Queen, usually with money inside, varying from twenty to a hundred pounds according to the wealth of the town. Worcester's silver cup, with its cover double gilt, was worth £10 17s. 2d., 'the fairest that might be found in London,' and in it was forty pounds in half sovereigns. Coventry put a hundred pounds in its cup, and Elizabeth 'was pleased to say to her Lords, "It was a good gift, £100 in gold; I have but few such gifts". To which the Mayor answered boldly, "If it please your Grace, there is a great deal more in it." "What is that?" said she. "It is," said he, "the hearts of all your loving subjects." "We thank you, Mr. Mayor," said she; "it is a great deal more indeed."'

At Warwick, after the Recorder had made his speech of welcome, 'Come hither, little Recorder', said Elizabeth, offering her hand to be kissed. 'It was told me that you would be afraid to look upon me or to speak boldly; but you were not so afraid of me as I was of you; and I now thank you for putting me in mind of my duty.' At Norwich, the schoolmaster having to make a Latin speech and seeming nervous, she said graciously, 'Be not afraid!'; and at the end purchased a loyal heart at the cost of a small lie, declaring, 'It is the best that ever I heard; you shall have my hand'.

Moving on, she sent back to ask his name. There was as subtle flattery in her behaviour at Sandwich. Here the magistrates' wives made the Queen a banquet of one hundred and sixty dishes on a table twenty-eight feet long. Not only did she eat without the assay or preliminary tasting, employed as a precaution against poisoning, but also had certain of the dishes reserved and sent to her lodging—unsurpassable compliments, both. Her farewell words to Norwich may be taken as typical of her partings: 'I have laid up in my breast such good will, as I shall never forget Norwich'; and proceeding onward, she 'did shake her riding-rod, and said, "Farewell! Norwich," with the water standing in her eyes.'

Elizabeth visited both Universities, Oxford twice, Cambridge once, and listened to a heavy round of addresses, disputations, sermons, and plays, in Latin and Greek, which must have been insufferable boredom to less cultured courtiers, though she herself went through the routine with patience, nay, with pleasure, and let herself be prevailed upon to answer the Universities in their learned tongues. When one orator praised her many and singular virtues, she modestly shook her head, bit her lips and fingers, and interrupted with disclaimers; but when he turned to praise virginity, 'God's blessing of thine heart,' she called out; 'there continue'. There were rarely any unfortunate incidents, but after the Cambridge visit in 1564 some of the scholars pursued her to the next stage of her journey in order to present a farce for which there had been no time. It turned out to be a scandalous satire on Catholicism, one player representing Bishop Bonner, another being dressed as a dog with the Host in his mouth. Elizabeth rose and left the chamber, outraged, using strong language; and as the torch-bearers followed her, the farce met an ignominious end in darkness.

Elizabeth's descent on private houses was both coveted and feared; coveted for the honour, feared lest there might be some hitch, or the entertainment fall short of expectations. Apparently, there was no need to do more than surrender the house to the Queen's use: the cost of food, even the furnishings, would be provided by the Royal Household. But to do no more than this might be regarded as churlish behaviour, and in one instance certainly was so regarded, at least by courtiers. There are many little incidents to suggest that Elizabeth herself was reluctant that smaller folk should outreach themselves on her behalf, but the extravagant preparations made by wealthier hosts, or by courtiers trying to outdo one another, tended to set a standard that made royal visits an expensive honour. In 1577 a four-days' visit cost Sir Nicholas Bacon £577; a ten-days' visit to Burghley in 1591 cost rather over £1,000; a three-days' visit to Lord Keeper Egerton in 1602 cost as much as £2,000.

Apart from the problem of feeding and housing the Queen and her followers, the host had to have ready some gift or gifts and arrange entertainments. The gifts were often very costly. Visiting Lord Keeper Puckering, Elizabeth on alighting received a fine fan, the handle of which was set with diamonds. Before she reached the house, a man came running towards her, and with an appropriate speech gave her a nosegay in which was a rich jewel with diamond pendants, valued at £400. After dinner there was a present of a fair pair of virginals, and in her bed-chamber still another present—a fine gown and skirt. These were not all. 'To grace his Lordship the more, she of herself took from him a salt, a spoon, and a fork, of fair agate.' Puckering could afford to be extravagant, the fees and perquisites of his office being notoriously great.

The entertainment *par excellence* of the reign was 'The Princely Pleasures' at Kenilworth, where Leicester lavished his wealth and the imagination of professional versifiers in amusing the Queen during a three-weeks' stay in 1575. But other entertainments, if not so elaborate, were in the same vein. In 1591 the Earl of Hertford received the Queen at Elvetham. Though only a three-days' stay, three hundred men were set to work beforehand to enlarge the house, erect a host of out-buildings for the royal train, and dig a pond, half-moon shape, with three islands representing a ship, a fort, and a snail. At her arrival she was saluted in Latin verse by a poet clad in green to signify his joyful thoughts, with a laurel garland on his head and olive branch in his hand, and booted to betoken that he 'was not a loose or low creeping prophet', as some ignorantly thought poets to be. While he spoke, six virgins removed blocks out of her Majesty's way, put there by Envy, and afterwards walked before her to the house, strewing the path with flowers and singing a sweet song of six parts. The next morning the pleasures were ordered, or rather, ruined by English weather: it rained. But in the afternoon the Queen came down to the pond, where Nereus, the prophet of the sea, was seen swimming ahead of five Tritons, 'all with grisly heads and beards of divers colours and fashions', who waded, cheerfully sounding their trumpets. After the Tritons came Neptune and Oceanus drawing a pinnace, in which were three virgins playing cornets, a nymph named Neæra, and three singers—answered in the form of an echo from two other boats—and lastly, two jewels for the Queen. At a sign, Silvanus and his followers came forth out of a wood, to provide another oration and a diversion.

The next morning, when Elizabeth opened her casement window, she was greeted by three musicians, disguised in ancient country attire, singing the lovely lyric of Coridon and Phillida:

> In the merry month of May,
> In a morn by break of day,
> Forth I walked by the wood side,
> Where as May was in his pride.
> There I spied, all alone,
> Phillida and Coridon.
> Much ado there was, God wot!
> He would love, and she would not.

That evening there were fireworks from the three islands in the pond. 'First, there was a peal of a hundred chambers discharged from the Snail-mount; in counter whereof, a like peal was discharged from the Ship-isle, and some great ordnance withal. Then there was a castle of fireworks of all sorts, which played in the fort. Answerable to that, there was in the Snail-mount a globe of all manner of fireworks, as big as a barrel. When these were spent on either side, there were many running rockets upon lines, which passed between the Snail-mount and the castle in the fort. On either side there were many fire-wheels, pikes of pleasure, and balls of wild fire, which burned in the water.' During this display a banquet was served by two hundred gentlemen, the dishes numbering a thousand and being all in glass and silver.

On the last morning, the Fairy Queen and her maids saluted the Queen at her rising. And then came the departure, when the ditty of 'Come again' was sung:

> O come again, fair Nature's treasure,
> Whose looks yield joys exceeding measure.
>
> O come again, Heaven's chief delight,
> Thine absence makes eternal night.
>
> O come again, world's starbright eye,
> Whose presence doth adorn the sky.
>
> O come again, sweet beauty's sun:
> When thou art gone, our joys are done.

Done their joys were! The Earl was left to foot the bill and count the silver and dishes and all manner of movables, for the passing of the Queen's followers was apt to resemble that of a plague of locusts.

The slow cumbersome character of a progress, together with constant political uncertainty, domestic and foreign, prevented Elizabeth from going very far afield. She visited Dover, Southampton, Bristol, Worcester, Stafford, Norwich, but a circle through these places represents the limits of her travels. There was a proposal to visit Shrewsbury: it came to nothing. In 1562 she was to have met Mary at York, and in 1575 was anxious to visit this city; but 'the inly-working North' was never stirred by the emotions of an Elizabethan progress. It was left to its own loyalties and the romantic appeal of a rival, captive Queen. It was a pity, but unavoidable. Accounts of these progresses, with their curious entertainments and equally curious verse, with their inimitable royal touches, and sometimes with unrehearsed incidents like that at Kenilworth, when a savage, tamed at sight of the Queen, in token of submission broke a tree that he carried and cast the top away, narrowly missing Elizabeth's horse and causing it to rear with fright: 'No hurt, no hurt!' she cried—such accounts were printed as pamphlets, carrying to a wide audience the flavour of the occasion and the gratifying appeal of a Queen of whom Englishmen could be mightily proud and fond. The press and propaganda were powerful auxiliaries in this choice romance.

At Court there were regular spectacles to which it was easy for any gentleman to get access. Each Sunday there was a ceremonial procession through the rooms of the Palace to the Chapel, and the Presence Chamber was usually crowded with spectators to many of whom Elizabeth would say a few gracious words as she passed along. Lord Herbert of Cherbury, as a young man, came to Court on such an occasion, at the end of the reign. 'As soon as she saw me,' he tells, 'she stopped, and swearing her usual oath, "God's death!", demanded, "Who is this?" Everybody there present looked upon me, but no man knew me until Sir James Croft, a Pensioner, finding the Queen stayed, returned back and told who I was, and that I had married Sir William Herbert of St. Julian's daughter. The Queen hereupon looked attentively upon me, and swearing again her ordinary oath, said, "It is a pity he was married so young," and thereupon gave her hand to kiss twice, both times gently clapping me on the cheek'.

While the Queen was at service in the Chapel, the spectators could watch the ceremonial laying of dinner in the Presence Chamber, to the accompaniment of trumpets and kettledrums. The articles—table-cloth, salt-cellar, etc., as well as food—were brought in by attendants preceded by an usher with his rod, all of whom knelt three times before the Cloth of State, on entering and retiring. A lady-taster gave each attendant a morsel of the dish that he bore, this being the assay; and then, when everything was ready, a number of the Queen's maids appeared and solemnly carried the food into an inner, private apartment, for it was rarely, and only on great festival or state occasions, that Elizabeth actually fed in the Presence Chamber, before spectators. She was abstemious over food and drink.

In the Presence Chamber Elizabeth graced the general body of courtiers with her presence at various entertainments, including dancing, of which she was fond; in the Privy Chamber she talked or played cards or chess with councillors and the privileged great having access there; in her Withdrawing Chambers she became, so far as she could, a private person, and in addition to her ladies, passed the time with a very small intimate circle, who from one point of view were personal friends, but from the point of view of those without were 'favourites'. All monarchs had 'favourites'. How could it be otherwise? The anomaly in Elizabeth's reign was the difference in sex, and this was emphasized by the romantic note which the language of intimacy assumed. It betokened neither a lustful disposition, nor a callous heart; and though the amorous way in which men addressed her may seem highly suspicious, the staggering promiscuity of Elizabeth's 'love' mocks at such fond credulity. Sir Thomas Heneage sent her a bodkin and pendant with the message, *Amat iste sine fine*—'This man loves you without end'. She sent him answer that as these were his words to her, so hers to him were, 'I love *sine fine*', giving him 'ten thousand millions of thanks' and promising to wear his pendant on that ear 'that should not hearken to anything that should anyways hurt him that sent it'. 'Knowing that her Sanguine—presumably a nickname—was far in the cold north country where no butterflies were', she sent him a mother-of-pearl butterfly to play with. The quality of the 'love' may be gauged by the fact that she told him to hasten back to his wife and bring her to Court.

All Elizabeth's close friends seem to have received nicknames. Leicester was her 'Eyes', and ornamented his letters with a pair of eyes. Christopher Hatton, who was entering the fortunate circle of intimates in the late 'sixties, was her 'Lids', and employed a cipher which may have been a crude representation of eyelids. 'Adieu, most sweet Lady', he ended a letter. And then, with a play on the initials of *Elizabetha Regina*, went on 'All and EveR yours, your most happy bondman, Lids'. Later he became her 'Mutton', or 'Bell-wether'. On one occasion, fearing that Sir Walter Raleigh, nicknamed 'Water', was displacing him from Elizabeth's affections, he sent her what one imagines was a sweet, reproachful letter along with some 'tokens', including a diminutive bucket, signifying Raleigh. She sent a verbal answer, 'that if Princes were like Gods (as they should be) they would suffer no element so to abound as to breed confusion'. The beasts of the field were 'so dear unto her that she had bounded her banks so sure as no water or floods could be able ever to overthrow them'; and for better assurance unto him that he should fear no drowning, she sent him a bird—a dove—'that, together with the rainbow, brought the good tidings and the covenant that there should be no more destruction by water'. Further, she willed him to remember she was a Shepherd, and then he might think 'how dear her Sheep was unto her'. The dark-featured Walsingham was her 'Moor'. Burghley was her 'Spirit'. 'Sir Spirit', she wrote to him playfully, when he was in one of his blue moods, 'I doubt I do nickname you, for those of your kind (they say) have no sense; but I have of late seen an *ecce signum*, that if an ass kick you, you feel it too soon. I will recant you from being my spirit, if ever I perceive that you disdain not such a feeling. Serve God, fear the King, and be a good fellow to the rest'. Don't be 'so silly a soul', she went on, 'as not to regard her trust, who puts it in you. God bless you, and long may you last. *Omnino*, E.R.'

It is difficult to convey a proper appreciation of this amazing Queen, so keenly intelligent, so effervescing, so intimate, so imperious and regal. She intoxicated Court and country, keyed her realm to the intensity of her own spirit. No one but a woman could have done it, and no woman without her superlative gifts could have attempted it without disaster. In part instinctive, it was also conscious and deliberate. 'Her mind', wrote her witty godson, Sir John

Harington, 'was oftime like the gentle air that cometh from the westerly point in a summer's morn; 'twas sweet and refreshing to all around. Her speech did win all affections, and her subjects did try to show all love to her commands; for she would say, "Her state did require her to command, what she knew her people would willingly do from their own love to her" . . . Surely she did play well her tables to gain obedience thus, without constraint. Again, she could put forth such alterations, when obedience was lacking, as left no doubtings whose daughter she was'. Harington tells how she would covertly search out the minds of her councillors, talking to Burghley till late at night, and then calling in another councillor, and so on; and afterwards compare their real thoughts with their utterances in council. 'Sir Christopher Hatton was wont to say, "The Queen did fish for men's souls, and had so sweet a bait that no one could escape her network" . . . I have seen her smile—sooth, with great semblance of good liking to all around—and cause everyone to open his most inward thought to her; when, on a sudden, she would ponder in private on what had passed, write down all their opinions, draw them out as occasion required, and sometimes disprove to their faces what had been delivered a month before. . . . She caught many poor fish, who little knew what snare was laid for them'.

Elizabeth was exceedingly human, and was always letting impulse break through regal formality, which she regarded as made for her, not she for it. Glowing postscripts scribbled at the foot of formal letters to convey her gratitude or remind a distant servant of her affection: there were numerous touches of this kind, and we know their miraculous healing power. Or she might scribble a political letter, unbeknown to her officials, as she did to Sir Henry Sidney in Ireland in 1565. 'Harry', it began; and went on in her most euphuistic style, like the utterance of some oracle, ending, 'Let this memorial be only committed to Vulcan's base keeping, without any longer abode than the leisure of the reading thereof, yea, and with no mention made thereof to any other wight. I charge you, as I may command you. Seem not to have had but Secretary's letters from me. Your loving mistress, Elizabeth R.' Fortunately, Penshurst and not Vulcan kept the letter. Or she might interrupt a speech or sermon. At the end of one parliament, when the Speaker had made a long-winded speech and Lord Keeper Bacon was rivalling him in the answer, Elizabeth told him to cease. In his text of the speech Bacon writes: 'Hereafter followeth that I intended to have said if I had not been countermanded'. In contrast, at the beginning of another parliament, after confirming the election of a new Speaker and listening to his happy and eloquent oration, as she passed she pulled off her glove and gave him her hand to kiss, and using a figure of archery, said, 'You, sir, you are welcome to the butts, sir', and laid both her hands about his neck, and stayed a good space, and so most graciously departed; and in her Privy Chamber after, amongst her ladies, said, 'she was sorry she knew him no sooner.'

Preachers who overstepped discretion, sometimes found themselves sharply pulled up. Nowell, Dean of St. Paul's, preaching a Lenten sermon before a large congregation at Court in 1565, inveighed against a recent Catholic book dedicated to the Queen, and then went on to attack images and idolatry, an attack which in the circumstances was palpably meant for the crucifix in the royal Chapel. 'Do not talk about that', Elizabeth called out; and as he went on, not hearing her, 'Leave that', she cried, raising her voice, 'It has nothing to do with your subject, and the matter is now threadbare'. In 1596, when Elizabeth was in her sixty-third year—the grand climacteric, very much feared in those days—Bishop Rudd, encouraged by previous praise and Whitgift's report that 'the Queen now is grown weary of the vanities of wit and eloquence wherewith her youth was formerly affected, and plain sermons which come home to her heart please her the best', chose for his Lenten sermon the text, 'O teach us to number our days, that we may incline our hearts unto wisdom'. Having spoken awhile of some sacred and mystical numbers, as 3 for the Trinity, 3 times 3 for the heavenly Hierarchy, 7 for the Sabbath, and 7 times 7 for a Jubilee, he came to 7 times 9 for the grand climacterical year, and Elizabeth seeing the trend of his sermon grew troubled. The Bishop noticed this, and tried to save himself by treating of some more plausible numbers, as 666 making Latinus, 'with which, he said, he could prove the Pope to be Antichrist', and also of the fatal number 88. But at the end of the service, the Queen opened the window of her closet and told him plainly that 'he should have kept his arithmetic for himself'. 'I see', said she, 'the greatest clerks are not the wisest men': a pertinent saying, for it was the height of folly to play on the fears that were entertained about her death.

In the sorrows of others the Queen was a woman. When the Earl of Huntingdon died she had the news kept from his wife and moved suddenly to Whitehall in order to break the blow by her own ministration of comfort. When Lady Norris lost a son in Ireland, 'My own Crow', she wrote to her, 'Harm not yourself for bootless help, but show a good example to comfort your dolorous yoke-fellow. . . .' And when two years later the same service took the lives of two more sons, she wrote to both father and mother: 'We couple you together from desire that all the comfort we wish you may reach you both in this bitter accident. We were loth to write at all, lest we should give you fresh occasion of sorrow, but could not forbear, knowing your past resolution in like mishaps, and your religious obedience to Him whose strokes are unavoidable. We propose ourselves as an example, our loss being no less than yours'. In 1595, when the Earl of Hertford took steps to set aside the declaration of invalidity against his marriage with Lady Catherine Grey and was imprisoned in the Tower for his dangerous action, Elizabeth wrote to his second wife, who was distraught with anxiety. 'Good Francke,' she began, and bade her not to think the crime 'more pernicious and malicious than an act of lewd and proud contempt against our own direct prohibition'. 'It is far from our desire to pick out faults in such as he. Being slow to rigour towards the meanest, we will use no more severity than is requisite for others' caution in like cases, and then shall stand with honour and necessity. . . . For a farewell, you are to observe this rule, that seeing griefs and troubles make haste enough, unsent for, to surprise us, there can be no folly greater than by fearing that which is not, or by over grieving for that which needs not, to overthrow the health of mind and body'.

Another very human glimpse of the Queen is in a note which she sent to her godson Harington, then a boy, accompanying a copy of her speech to the Parliament of 1576: 'Boy Jack, I have made a clerk write fair my poor words for thine use, as it cannot be such striplings have entrance into parliament assembly as yet. Ponder them in thy hours of leisure, and play with them till they enter thy understanding; so shalt thou hereafter, perchance, find some good fruits hereof when thy godmother is out of remembrance; and I do this, because thy father was ready to serve and love us in trouble and thrall'—a reference to the days of her sister, Mary.

Elizabeth's courtiers and advisers found her humours difficult. She had foibles: good health was one. Most of her life she enjoyed remarkable health and hated to be ill or even thought ill. In 1577 she several times commanded Leicester to write to Burghley, then at Buxton, asking him to send her some of the medicinal water from there. When it arrived, she mistrusted 'it will not be of the goodness here it is there'; though the truth was that she had been told people were talking of it, 'as though her Majesty had had some sore leg'; and she was half angry with Leicester now for writing to Burghley! In 1578 a tooth was giving her pain, and needed to come out, but because the Queen 'doth not or will not so think', her physicians were afraid to tell her. In 1597 she had 'a desperate ache' in her right thumb, but the gout it *could* not be, it *dare* not be; in fact, she had no ache, but she would not sign letters!

A person of such vivacity and wilfulness was in the nature of things trying at times. Her eyes were everywhere, faults were numerous, and she was exacting. Efficiency she would have, or know the reason why. And her very freedom with those around her called for sharp tugs on the rein to remind them that she was mistress. When Lord Hunsdon, her cousin, took advantage—as others did—and overstayed his leave from his post at Berwick, his son wrote to him that Elizabeth 'grew into a great rage, beginning with, "God's wounds! that she would set you by the feet, and send another in your place if you dallied with her thus, for she would not be thus dallied withal"'. But when all is said of her passionate outbursts, they were usually little more than flashes of summer lightning. Sir John Harington, whose freshest memories were of her last years, when worry fretted her temper, says: 'When she smiled, it was a pure sunshine that everyone did choose to bask in if they could; but anon came a storm from a sudden gathering of clouds, and the thunder fell in wondrous manner on all alike'.

CHAPTER XIV

RELIGIOUS PASSION AND POLITICS

In Burghley's ever-recurring memoranda, criticizing his mistress's policy, one item was rarely absent: her failure to marry. Naturally enough, gossip, fastening on this strange and disturbing fact, often tried to explain it by surmising that Elizabeth was incapable of bearing children; just as it rounded off its tales about Leicester and the Queen by bestowing one or two children on them. The tongue is an unruly member. Ben Jonson knew this surmise and added a few lewd details to give it an air of reality when he talked and drank with Drummond of Hawthornden, his story being like the occasion, quite irresponsible. When the French king was a suitor for Elizabeth's hand in 1566, his ambassador asked her physician about the talk of sterility. He pooh-poohed the story: 'If the King marries her', said he, 'I guarantee ten children; and no one in the world knows her constitution better than I do'. Burghley and others had at least a tenth of the physician's confidence. They wanted an heir to the throne, and did not doubt that marriage would provide one.

The question of marriage was a choice of two evils. Differing in temperament, imagination, and policy, the Queen had preferred the one, her minister the other. In consequence, the Archduke Charles's suit had been allowed to lapse. But since those days the presence of Mary Queen of Scots in England had lent new emphasis to the marriage argument, for it was obvious that Mary drew immeasurable strength from her claim to the succession. Let Elizabeth produce an heir, and at once her rival's attraction would fade. Even foreign princes would be less interested in her. As it was, men feared to offend the future sovereign of England. Leicester, for example, was for putting her to death after the Ridolfi Plot, but he was very anxious that she should not know him for an enemy. Where much was at stake it needed courage and conviction to be single-minded in loyalty to Elizabeth. 'See you not', declared a Catholic manifesto to the Irish, 'that she is without a lawful heir of her own body, who may either reward her friends or revenge her enemies?' Slay her, and most people would hasten to make their peace with Mary. A child would be Elizabeth's shield and buckler, preserving the loyalty of her people and saving her from the assassin's blow.

After the Northern Rebellion the argument was too plain to be ignored, and as England had no allies, while Spain, France, and the Pope were unfriendly, the alliance that marriage would bring was another point in its favour. In August, 1570, spurred on by the close of the third civil war in France, which left that country free to be a nuisance to England, Elizabeth sent an envoy to try and revive the old suit of the Archduke Charles. He was still at liberty, but would no longer rise to the bait, and in fact soon married elsewhere and became a persecutor of Protestants. That chance was gone. However, Catherine de Medici had three sons. One, the King, had been a suitor of Elizabeth's. He also was a lost chance; he was married. The second, the Duke of Anjou, was not quite nineteen years of age, Elizabeth being thirty-seven. But the disparity of age was amply covered by a crown—and such a crown, the best of fortunes! It was Catherine's fond ambition to see her children, each on a throne, this daughter of an Italian banking-house being very much a *parvenu*. Moreover, the marriage was attractive to France from a political point of view, since the prospect of England allying with Spain was a bugbear of theirs, as the opposite alliance was Spain's bugbear. Also, the time was particularly propitious for an English alliance. Peace had brought into power, not the Guise party, hostile to Elizabeth and violent in its hatred of the Huguenots, but the *Politiques,* or moderate Catholics, who preferred to unite the religious factions and follow a national anti-Spanish policy.

So, in the autumn of 1570, negotiations were set on foot for a marriage between Elizabeth and the Duke of Anjou. Apparently, there were no dregs of Elizabeth's old passion for Leicester left to disturb her resolution. The romance had sobered down into a sentimental friendship—a sweet memory of the past, and no more. She was entirely the Queen in this wooing. She was probably sincere in her resolve to marry, convinced by the urgent reasons for it; but she soon came up against the old obstacle of religion, and once more had to balance the perils of childlessness against the danger of provoking civil strife by allowing her husband to retain his Catholic worship. She decided as before, with Burghley and others deploring as before. The negotiations foundered.

Catherine de Medici was upset at Anjou's religious obstinacy, the more so because he was her favourite child. But despair was unnecessary for was there not another son, the Duke of Alençon? He was three years younger than his brother and more than twenty years younger than Elizabeth. Catherine offered him, pointing out to the ambassador his sprouting beard. She took to reckoning the number of their children; two boys, lest the one should die, and three daughters with whom to make alliances. Alençon was not a beauty. Smallpox had ruined his features. 'The pock holes', an English ambassador wrote, 'are no great disfigurement of his face because they are rather thick than deep or great. They upon the blunt end of his nose are great and deep, how much to be disliked may be as it pleaseth God to move the heart of the beholder'. 'When I saw him at my last audience, he seemed to me to grow daily more handsome'. It pleased God at the moment to move Elizabeth's heart without beholding. She sent word that the difference in age was too great: really, it was 'the delicacy of her Majesty's eye' and, as she confidentially remarked, 'the absurdity that in the general opinion of the world might grow' if she married this ill-favoured, pock-marked boy after refusing so many suitors of great worthiness. She let the suit drag on in a desultory way, but in fact Alençon was put on the shelf for his beard to sprout a little more, perchance to grow daily more handsome, and for the shock of the transition to this strange little man to pass off.

Marriage or no marriage, Catherine and Elizabeth both wanted an alliance, and after much negotiation, in which Elizabeth got the better of the bargain, they concluded the Treaty of Blois in April, 1572. It was primarily a defensive treaty against Spain, and perhaps, with apologies for an abuse of terms and a naïve misrepresentation of Elizabeth's mind, may be called a diplomatic revolution. Certainly it was significant to find England allying with France against the ruler of the Netherlands; the challenge to Spain was slowly unfolding itself. But the value of the treaty to Elizabeth was that it ended her dangerous isolation and paralysed French interference in her dealings with Mary and Scotland. She did not regard it as precluding or hindering a settlement of her differences with Spain, and in the last stages of the treaty Burghley was speaking soft words to the Spanish agent in England. One day as this man was going home in a boat, he saw the Queen approaching her palace in a barge, in which as the day was fine she had been taking the air in company with Leicester and many other gentlemen. He joined a great number of boats following the royal barge, and made his bow to the Queen as the rest did. Noticing him, she discovered who he was, and to the surprise of everyone, he 'being such a humble person', called out in Italian and asked very gaily and graciously if he came from the Court and had seen Burghley. She said a few more words and bade him farewell, waving her hand with many signs of pleasure and favour.

In the same month as the Treaty of Blois, the revolt in the Netherlands, which had been more or less suppressed by Alva's merciless hand, broke out again. Elizabeth covertly let the refugees, who in the last four years had fled in hundreds to England, return to their country to help in regaining its liberty. It was the opportunity for which the Huguenots and Politiques in France were waiting, to lead their nation in war against Spain and extend the boundaries of French territory. They won over their King. Immediately the limitations of Elizabeth's friendship became evident. She could not tolerate France in the Netherlands, controlling English trade and destroying her sovereignty on the narrow seas. Better far the Spaniard. Sir Humphrey Gilbert went over to help the rebels with a company of volunteers, pretending to go without the Queen's knowledge and against her will, yet with secret instructions to hold on to Flushing and keep the French out of that port at all costs.

The situation filled Catherine de Medici with alarm. France seemed to be heading straight for disaster; war with Spain, and at best, unfriendly neutrality from England. And the blunder was due to her son, Charles IX, escaping from her tutelage and succumbing to the influence of the great Huguenot leader, Coligny. Her jealousy led to the terrible tragedy of the following August. In that month almost all the Huguenot nobility were assembled in Paris, along with the rest of the French nobility, to witness the marriage of their leader, the young King Henry of Navarre, to Catherine's daughter. It was an exceedingly dangerous gathering in the state of religious and political passions, and yet Catherine, in her maternal lust for power, foolishly chose the occasion to arrange with the Guise party for Coligny's assassination. Panic and desperation seized her when, instead of being killed, he was only wounded. Here was the whole body of the Huguenot nobility, now crying out for revenge, presenting as it were a single head that could be struck off at a blow. It was too obvious an opportunity not to have been foreseen. The idea was in the air, and Catherine grasped at it as an escape from her terrible position.

Coligny was wounded on August 22nd. By the night of the 23rd, the Eve of St. Bartholomew, Catherine had made plans with Guise and others and won over the King. With dawn the killing began. The tocsin was rung and the mob joined in the massacre. Every Huguenot on whom they could lay their hands, noble or simple, man, woman, or child, was murdered and many a grudge satisfied as well. The streets ran with blood and the river was full of corpses, naked and horribly disfigured. One man, a butcher by trade, boasted that he killed four hundred that day. By midday two thousand had been slain and the killing went on for two more days. As the news sped through the country, the Catholics rose in many towns and followed the example of Paris. At Lyons some seven or eight hundred were killed, at Orleans five hundred. In all, three or four thousand probably perished in Paris and as many elsewhere.

Protestant opinion was stirred to profound anger, and following the news, fanning passion still more, came the first of the hundreds of refugees who fled to England from the terror. Even the friends of France in a moment became its violent haters. A word of extenuation, and swords left their scabbards. Londoners held meetings, and along with less responsible preachers called for retaliation on their own papists. The staider bishops poured out their fears and counsels in letters to Burghley: deprive all Catholics of their weapons, they urged; remove them from the Queen's presence, set a strong guard of Protestants about her, watch the City and the Tower, make a firm league with the Protestants in Scotland and Germany; Almighty God has oft called upon us and showed his favourable countenance, and yet we heedlessly despise his counsel; God send to the Queen's Majesty ears that she may hear, and a teachable heart that she may understand. The belief in a Catholic League to exterminate Protestantism gained new and terrifying confirmation. It was only natural for Protestants to believe that the Massacre had been long premeditated and planned in collaboration with the Pope and Spain. The English coast was put in a state of defence, the navy ordered to sea with speed, and all was vigilance.

When the French ambassador asked for an audience to convey the official explanation of the Massacre, Elizabeth kept him waiting three days, and then, surrounded by many of her councillors and the chief ladies of the Court, received him in dead silence. Advancing a few paces, with a sad and stern, yet not unfriendly face, she let him salute her, and leading him aside to a window-recess listened to the pathetic but diplomatic lies that were meant to cover the King's action. Her reply was dignified, accepting the explanation, but rather as it became her to accept a King's word, and not extenuating the vile criminality of the deed one whit. Break with France she dared not; condone the Massacre she would not.

In the general alarm, all men cried out against that 'dangerous traitress and pestilence of Christendom', Mary; with additional reason, because the Massacre had brought back into power her relatives, the House of Guise, whose name was a byword for danger. The Bishop of London urged Burghley 'forthwith to cut off the Scottish Queen's head'; Archbishop Parker gave the same advice in less direct language. An anonymous correspondent of Leicester's disclosed 'the common voice, lamentation, and fear of good subjects' in six closely-written eloquent pages: 'For God's sake, my Lord, let not her Majesty in these great sorrows forget the greatest danger. Let her Highness be prayed to remember conscience and eternity.' Let her not bring on England murders, rapes, robberies, violence, and barbarous slaughters, and the damnation of so many seduced souls by the advancement of papistry; 'and all for piteous pity and miserable mercy in sparing one horrible woman, who carries God's wrath where she goes'. 'Surely never Prince deserved so well to have loving subjects as our Queen hath'. 'Shall we not trust that her Majesty, our mother, will not stick to command to kill a toad, a snake, or a mad dog whom she finds poisoning her, gnawing the throats of her infants, and presently threatening the same to herself?'

What the pressure of Elizabeth's most influential councillors was we can imagine, not say. The crisis brought the Queen to this concession that, while she was not prepared to put Mary to death herself, she would send her to Scotland to be executed there for complicity in Darnley's murder, if sufficient security were given that she would not be kept alive. Burghley's brother-in-law was hastened off to Scotland with this as a secret mission, known only to the Queen, Burghley, and Leicester, and later to Bacon. The suggestion was to be made as coming from certain councillors, and on no account was Elizabeth's name to be mentioned; obviously in case of failure. The Regent and those he consulted were willing, but on conditions; among others, that an English army be present at the execution and afterwards turn the remnant of Mary's followers out of Edinburgh Castle.

But two months having passed since the Bartholomew Massacre without the skies falling on her, Elizabeth seems to have inclined to mercy and become difficult. The question, however, was decided for her, since with the news of the Regent's conditions—which were regarded as impossible—came news of his death. That ended the business, at any rate for the time being. Burghley opened his soul to Leicester: 'God send her Majesty strength of spirit to preserve God's cause, her own life, and the lives of millions of good subjects. . . . God be merciful to us'. The following April he found a little solace, for Elizabeth sent a force to capture Edinburgh Castle and with its fall Mary's party in Scotland was destroyed.

All things seemed to be working together to make a crusade of Elizabeth's reign. The memory of St. Bartholomew was added to the memory of the martyrs in Queen Mary's reign, which had been kept fresh and poignant for Elizabethans in the woodcuts and text of Foxe's *Book of Martyrs*. The anger of English Protestants against Catholicism, and their devotion to the Queen, whose life seemed the only sure foundation of their faith, were both taking on a deep and passionate quality. The days were past when in alehouse and village lewd stories were bandied about with impunity, and at Doncaster, if the magistrates had only let them, the people would have torn a man in pieces for slandering her.

This intense feeling—the spirit of England for the next few decades—was to find perfect expression in the Council owing to the political changes that followed the death in March, 1572, of the Lord High Treasurer, the Marquis of Winchester—the old, old, very old man of English politics, who was eighty-seven years of age, and 'in his lifetime did see the children of his childrens' children grown to the number of one hundred and three, a rare blessing of God to men of his calling'. Burghley was given his office, vacating the Secretaryship, whereupon a return was made to the practice of having two Principal Secretaries. The second of these, appointed in December, 1573, was Francis Walsingham, a man about the Queen's age and related to her through his stepfather. He had been educated at Cambridge in the keen Protestant circle there, and had fled abroad in Mary's reign, returning with the mentality of the religious *émigré*—a sense of the everlasting struggle with the powers of darkness—which had been still more deeply impressed upon him by passing through the Massacre of St. Bartholomew as resident ambassador in Paris. He was the embodiment of the crusading spirit, a serious and sombre-looking man. 'Surely', he wrote of the Spaniards, 'hardly will there follow any thorough reconciliation between us unless we may be drawn to one unity of religion, for Christ and Belial can hardly agree'. 'What juster cause can a Prince that maketh profession of the Gospel have to enter into wars than when he seeth confederacies made for the rooting out of the Gospel and religion he professeth? All creatures are created to advance God's glory; therefore, when His glory is called in question, no league nor policy can excuse if by all means he seek not the defence of the same, yea, with the loss of life'. Walsingham did not say, but presumably God would provide; otherwise it is certain that his policy would quickly have bankrupted the State.

When Walsingham entered politics it was under the patronage of Burghley, but he soon drew closer to Leicester who began to settle down as the leader of the radicals, with Walsingham as his familiar spirit. The emergence of this party to the left, made Burghley incline a little to the right. He was still a brother in Christ, making his lamentations over the Queen with the rest, but an older brother—he was over fifty—and not so shrill as the younger brethren. Age brought the spirit of resignation, and his new office of Lord Treasurer a better appreciation of thrift. Possibly there was a dawning respect for the Queen's judgment. At any rate, in spite of woeful cries from time to time when their moods or policies crossed, a wonderful intimacy and trust was developing between the two. 'No prince in Europe had such a councillor as she had of him', Elizabeth declared. If he was away from Court, as gout in these days sometimes kept him, it was hard to get business through, for she would do nothing perfunctorily and trusted no one as she did him. In the autumn and winter of 1572 the Secretary, Sir Thomas Smith, was driven to distraction by the difficulty of getting documents signed or decisions made in Burghley's absence. And Leicester was scarcely more fortunate. She was willing enough to listen to his opinion, talk to and fro what was best to be done; she let him prate about the necessity for a prince, 'yea the wisest', to trust her faithful councillors; if she had only believed them she would have been saved from the disasters that now seemed imminent; but though the question, according to Leicester, was one in which hours were days, and days years, and too many gone already, she would decide nothing until he had written for Burghley's advice. And after receiving this advice, she went her own way. As a councillor put it: 'If we prosper, it must be as our custom is, by miracle'.

There was no greater tribute to the tolerance, sagacity, and masterful nature of Elizabeth than her choice of such ministers as Walsingham. She chose them for their ability, their honesty, and their unshakable loyalty. Even in their intensity they were the expression of the England she was nurturing, and if like thoroughbreds they were hard to ride, she was a perfect horsewoman. Like them, she coveted glory, but thought it true glory to maintain the good yeoman, living in the temperate zone betwixt greatness and want, who wore russet clothes but made golden payment, having tin in his buttons and silver in his pocket. With a lively sense of the limitations of English resources, she preferred to trim the country's sails to the winds when and how they blew, rather than set them at once for a storm that might not come.

It is little wonder that Elizabeth's statesmen wrung their hands over what seemed her folly, for the outlook was very ominous. In the Netherlands, at Rome, and in Spain there were Catholic refugees, some of whom had fled for religion's sake at various times since the beginning of the reign and recently had been joined by the exiles of the Northern Rebellion, under whose influence they became a company of plotters, brooding upon a single idea, 'the Enterprise of England'. They lived for the day when the Pope and Philip of Spain would send an army to turn that wicked woman and 'she-devil' of England from her throne, put the devout Mary in her place, and restore the Catholic faith along with their fortunes. These men developed the revolutionary's or *émigré's* mind. The wish was father to the thought, their judgments were warped, their notions about the government and people of England quite fantastic; they were as optimistic about the ease with which Elizabeth could be overthrown as Ridolfi had been. At Rome their plots were naturally welcomed, for the Bull of 1570 deposing Elizabeth still awaited execution; and in the years following Bartholomew the Papacy was constantly trying to commit Philip II to the 'Enterprise' and launch an invasion of England. Indeed, if Elizabeth had cared to proceed with all rigour against Catholics, on the ground that their faith, by involving adherence to a public and dangerous enemy of the State, was incompatible with loyalty and good citizenship, she would have been amply justified by the activities of the Papacy. It was not only Walsingham and Protestant zealots who thought that politics should be stated in the simple terms of a battle between Christ and Antichrist.

As for Philip, he sympathized with the 'Enterprise' as he had done with the Ridolfi Plot. He had good cause. If he sheltered Elizabeth's malcontents and rebels, she did the same for his, letting them slip back to the Netherlands to reinforce the rebel army, or send money, or use her ports. It was a common bruit on the continent that by feeding the factions in other realms she was the real cause of all the troubles. She was the most notorious Prince in Europe, as honoured by those whom Philip detested as she was feared by those with whom he sympathized. He was afraid, as were many others, that while she continued on the throne of England there would be little chance of a satisfactory peace in the Low Countries. At the same time, he respected her skill, and was still more afraid that if he moved against

her she would promptly join with France. It was a dilemma; but a dilemma from which there was an escape in
the person of Mary Queen of Scots. France was not likely
to interfere with a Spanish attack upon England, if the object was to make Mary Queen. No wonder that Elizabeth's
subjects regarded her mercy to Mary as a dangerous, quix-
otic sentiment! If, as her statesmen and parliament urged,
she had executed her in 1572—why, then the 'Enterprise'
for the next decade or more would have remained the vain
babbling of a few exiles and a pious aspiration of some
clerics: even the hope of a sympathetic rising in England,
which was an integral part of it, would have practically
faded away.

It is in the light of Philip's actions that Elizabeth's foreign
policy must be judged. Though he agreed to help in financing an invasion of England, and actually sent half his sub-
vention to Rome, doubts and fears immediately assailed
him, he began to counsel delay, and at last withdrew. All
the advantage to be gained from the uncertainty of his
slow, cautious mind and the paralysing rivalry of Spain and
France would have been thrown away in an aggressive
policy. Philip would have been forced into war, and it is
hard to say what the result would have been: certainly,
financial and economic disaster for England at this time.
The situation was peculiarly suited to a policy of opportunism, and Elizabeth peculiarly suited to the policy. Here was
the miracle from which England drew its customary good
fortune. 'The Lord above is working for the preservation of
his own', wrote Burghley's brother-in-law; and in an age of
faith it passed for a satisfactory explanation.

In the years from 1572 on this opportunist policy ran a
bewildering course. Fearing to revert to the isolation from
which the Treaty of Blois had rescued her, Elizabeth re-
sponded—though, in view of the Massacre of St. Bartholomew, with just the right amount of coolness and restraint
—to Catherine de Medici's desire for continued friendship.
She accepted—with some caustic remarks—an invitation to
be godmother to Charles IX's baby daughter, and let the
Alençon marriage suit be revived, to linger as an option on

a closer alliance in case of necessity. Yet at the same time she lent secret aid to the Huguenots who were again in revolt, deeming it essential to maintain the balance of parties in France and keep the House of Guise from ruling the roost. There was no knowing how French policy would ultimately develop as a result of the Massacre, and therefore on the principle, 'When in danger from one country, play the other against it', she drew closer to Spain, re-opening negotiations to settle their differences and restore trade relations, which had ceased since the seizure of the treasure in December, 1568. In this, the Duke of Alva went more than half way to meet her, and did his forceful best to wean Philip from the folly of listening to advisers who were Walsingham's crusading opposites. What would it profit him, Alva asked, if for the sake of encouraging English Catholics he lost the Low Countries? It was quite possible, as Philip feared, that English pirates, treaty or no treaty, would continue to prey on Spanish commerce, and English Protestants send secret help to the Netherland rebels: but this would be less dangerous than open support. Drake had gone off in May, 1572, on a marauding voyage to the Spanish Main: it was a fair equivalent, Alva thought, for the Ridolfi conspiracy. In short, he swept aside the King's objections to a treaty, arguing that it would be dangerous to have war, or the expectation of war with England; and by the spring of 1573 the terms of the treaty were arranged and trade began again between the two countries.

Although Elizabeth's attitude to the Revolt of the Netherlands displayed baffling moods and changing tactics, she had clear principles. As rebels, and nothing more, she had no sympathy for William of Orange and his supporters. As Protestants—though it is well to remember that even in the two provinces that were the centre of the Revolt there was a Catholic majority—she felt sympathy, but not of the kind to justify supporting them. The political principle of the age was *cuius regio eius religio*: it was the business of the Prince to determine the faith of his subjects. She did not think of protesting against the persecution of Spanish heretics or Italian heretics: nor for that matter did Walsingham and his friends, and Elizabeth was therefore much clearer-minded in regarding the problem frankly as one of politics, instead of letting religion confound her judgment. What did it matter to Philip, she asked an ambassador of his, if the Netherlands 'went to the devil in their own way?'

Politically, the Revolt touched English interests in two ways. First, there was good reason to fear that if Philip overcame the rebels, he would turn his arms against Elizabeth in support of the Catholic 'Enterprise', striking at her from the Netherlands. Secondly, if France managed to compose her own religious troubles, she might respond to the appeal of the Dutch rebels for help, with the object of annexing the Low Countries. A policy was needed to meet both dangers, and the one Elizabeth followed—and for all her apparent opportunism, followed with extraordinary steadiness—was the same in principle as that she adopted for the Scottish problem at the beginning of her reign. She wanted to maintain Spanish sovereignty in the Netherlands: this would keep out the French. But she would maintain it with the native nobility and local liberties so strong that Spain would be unable to use the country as a base against England. She had closed the postern gate of Scotland against her enemies. She was now aiming at closing the strategic sea-gate of Flanders against them.

It was of course essential to keep the Revolt going until Philip tired of it and became tractable. But for the time being Elizabeth could rely on the adventurous spirit and sympathy of her people to furnish the rebels with volunteers and subscriptions. The Netherlands became a military academy where Englishmen learnt the art of war, as privateering in the Channel and on the Spanish Main was a school of seamanship. In this way England reaped the advantages of war without its cost; and the Queen was able to observe the proprieties of her treaty with Philip. When in November, 1573, Alva gave place to a milder Governor, sent—though without the necessary concessions—to make peace, she pressed forward to mediate.

In the spring of 1574 there came a gathering of clouds with the death of Charles IX. On this luckless youth, who had escaped but once from his mother's leading-strings, had fallen the nominal responsibility for the Massacre of St. Bartholomew; and popular story, with its instinct to point a moral or adorn a tale, gave him a fitting death, troubling his nights and his days with hideous dreams of massacred corpses that mocked at him with their bloody faces. He was succeeded by his brother Henry III—the Duke of Anjou, once Elizabeth's suitor, and since those days the darling of the Guise party. Elizabeth feared the worst from such a King, and accordingly struck the chords of Spanish friendship with vigour: 'You understand full well—old wine, old bread, and old friends should be valued, and if only to show these Frenchmen who are wrangling as to whether our friendship is firm or not, there is good reason to prove outwardly the kindly feeling which inwardly exists'. But her tune changed when it became evident at last that Henry III was adopting the moderate ways of his mother. Elizabeth now felt herself free to follow up her attempts at mediation in the Netherlands, with threats. She told an envoy that she would never allow Spaniards to impatronize themselves in that country. She knew very well what sort of neighbours they were. They imagined that they could draw a girdle round her realm; that they had only to do with a woman and a nation of women who could be conquered by a handful of Spaniards. Her father would never have let them go so far, and woman though she was, she would know what to do. Having let her threats sink in, she tried the opposite art a month later; bade him sit down, overwhelmed him with fine compliments, and urged him to speak his mind freely; not a living soul, no, not even her own chemise should know what he said, for though she was a woman and on that account might be thought a blab, yet she was a Queen, which had taught her the virtue of secrecy.

Philip was tired of the Revolt, alarmed at the drain on his resources, and really wanted peace, although he stuck at conceding religious liberty to the rebels. But peace was still far off when the new Governor died in March, 1576, and in his place the King chose his illegitimate half-brother,

Don John of Austria. It was an arresting choice. Don John was a young man, who five years before, at the age of twenty-four, had won universal fame as the victor of Lepanto, a naval battle with the Turks as renowned in its day as Trafalgar in modern times. Before that he had gained his laurels in war with the Moors of southern Spain. He was the most romantic figure of his time, something of a dreamer, a hero whose head had been turned by a famous exploit; a knight-errant and an Emperor's bastard in search of a kingdom. His name had been mentioned as a possible husband for Mary Queen of Scots as early as 1569, and many, including himself, had seen in him the ideal leader for the 'Enterprise' against England. He went to the Netherlands to offer concessions and make peace. But it was not this that he cared about. Philip had consented that once peace had been made, he should transport his army to England, free Mary Queen of Scots, and acquire a Queen and a kingdom for himself.

Alas! The Netherlands, like Ireland, were the grave of reputations. While he delayed in Italy and Spain, the Spanish troops in the Low Countries mutinied and ran amuck, ending by sacking the city of Antwerp. Their excesses drove the provinces into alliance, so that Don John arrived to find, not two provinces but the whole country in revolt. The new situation demanded more active diplomacy on Elizabeth's part. She guessed correctly at Don John's secret schemes, and immediately lent the rebels £20,000 and promised to guarantee a loan of £100,000—half her ordinary annual revenue—should it be needed to cashier the Spanish troops and send them home; but they were to depart by land and not by sea, for this would merely be inviting an attack on England. Within a few months of his arrival in the country, Don John was forced to see his troops leave as Elizabeth wished. The first round had gone in her favour, and if there had been real unity of purpose in the rebel leaders, Spain would have been driven to concede the terms of a lasting peace.

United in purpose the rebel leaders were not; the peace was partial and did not last, and Don John recalled his

troops from Italy, and renewed his thoughts of the 'Enterprise' against England. In this he was encouraged by the
Papacy, which lent all the support it could to his plans,
and by the Duke of Guise who was anxious to join with
him. Elizabeth's enemies were all drawing together; and
the close of another civil war in France in September, 1577,
not only freed the Duke of Guise to aid any movement
against her, but—what she feared just as much—set the
French King free to do as he wished. The climax came in
the New Year when Don John's troops won a signal victory
over the rebels. The situation was alarming. 'These are the
signs preceding the end of the world', wrote an English Puritan to a foreign brother. 'Satan is roaring like a lion, the
world is going mad, Antichrist is resorting to every extreme,
that he may with wolf-like ferocity devour the sheep of
Christ.' Elizabeth's advisers urged her to send both men and
money to the Netherlands. She herself was ready with her
purse, ready with brave words, and ready if necessary with
brave actions. But to enter on war was to give hostages to
fortune. Her instinct was to gamble on avoiding it; and
when the alternative presented itself of hiring mercenaries
under the leadership of a German prince to help the rebels,
rather than commit her country to war she chose this way,
to the sorrow of her councillors.

Events justified Elizabeth. The situation was not as desperate as it seemed, and it would have been folly to provoke
war, perhaps even to provoke France into aiding Don John
through fear of her intentions. Philip wanted peace. His
finances were still floundering after the state bankruptcy of
September, 1575. He had turned against the 'Enterprise' of
England, and even begun to suspect his brother of disloyalty. Early in 1578 he sent Bernadino de Mendoza to England to revive the embassy, closed by the expulsion of the
Spanish ambassador in January, 1572. As for Don John, his
sensitive spirits were drooping. Everything had gone wrong
with him. He had lost credit in the Netherlands; his favourite secretary had been murdered in Spain, and murdered—though this he did not know—with the connivance
of the King; he had been woefully starved of money and

his troops inadequately reinforced; he was distrusted. Out of such misfortunes he could scarcely conjure victory, much less the conquest of England. The final blow came with a check to his arms in August, 1578. In his low state he was unable to throw off a fever that took him, and on October 1st died. Two months before, Leicester had written to Walsingham—one worn-out soul to another—groaning over their mistress: 'Our only Queen, whom God alone I see must now defend and uphold by miracle'. Don John's death was the miracle: 'God dealeth most lovingly with her Majesty', wrote Walsingham, 'in taking away her enemies'.

CHAPTER XV

A LAST EFFORT AT MARRIAGE

To the grief of her principal advisers, the more Elizabeth had to do with the Netherland rebels, the less she liked them. She lent them money: repayment would be at the Greek Kalends. She offered her unmatched credit in the money market as a cover for theirs: they violated the conditions of the offer and tried to overreach her. A fine prospect, she thought, to enter into partnership with a faction-ridden, untrustworthy company who were demanding from Philip peace conditions so preposterous that there could be no end to war except by overwhelming victory, such as only a simpleton or God could have foretold in 1578! Helping them was a case of pay, pay, pay!

In this mood councillors found Elizabeth quite unmanageable during the months preceding Don John's death. She consulted them as little as she dared. Leicester dealt plainly, boldly, and faithfully with her. She listened patiently, then went her own way, while he threw up his hands in despair: 'God only now must defend her and us all'. Burghley grieved over their lot, which was 'to behold miseries coming and to be denied remedies'. 'You must be contented', wrote Secretary Wilson, 'and make of necessity a virtue, and say with yourselves that this world is not governed by wisdom and policy, but by a secret purpose or rather fatal destiny'. 'The lamb shall be committed to the wolf, and what will follow afterwards but utter ruin and destruction to this land?' Walsingham swelled the chorus: 'Our remedy must be prayer, for other help I see none.'

While her ministers prophesied calamity, Elizabeth was in fact veering round to a new course. She was beginning to perceive an escape from her perplexities in the Duke of Alençon. This restless young man, a thorn in his brother's side with his propensity for making mischief in France, had turned his thoughts, after the advent of peace and idleness at home, to the prospect of carving out a fine patrimony for himself in the Netherlands. Beggars as they were, the rebel leaders were indeed fortunate in having his terms— those of an irresponsible adventurer—to play against Elizabeth's. He asked no more than to be given a title and let fight at his expense. For a time his activities troubled Elizabeth, and even made her ready to send over an army and cast aside financial prudence, if they augured French hegemony in the Low Countries. But she soon discovered that he was playing a lone hand. So far from being behind the adventure, his brother, Henry III, was torn between anxiety at its possible consequences and relief at being rid of a domestic nuisance. Nothing would have pleased the King more than to transfer Alençon and his escapades to Elizabeth by marrying the two. Now marriage—or at any rate courtship—was in Alençon's mind also. He realized that Elizabeth's fears stood between him and his adventure, and moreover, being in need of money to maintain an army, recognized that his credit would rise considerably as the prospective King of England. To Elizabeth courtship had been a present help in time of trouble, and she was not averse to using it again. If she could keep Alençon dangling as her suitor, she would be able to put off, perhaps even to avoid, the evil day of war with Spain. At worst, should things go seriously amiss, she could marry him. At best, he could do his wooer's service as her catspaw.

In this diverting, if unpropitious way began the second Alençon courtship. The first had dragged along, without any enthusiasm on Elizabeth's side, until it had fallen asleep two years before, in 1576. There seemed no reason why the second should not do the same. Walsingham expressed his masculine disgust at the stale and sickening spectacle. Would to God her Majesty would forbear, he wrote: 'No one thing hath procured her so much hatred abroad as these wooing matters'. But there was a new factor in this courtship. Alençon was conducting it himself, and with a dash that threatened to sweep Elizabeth off her feet. If she would marry him, he wrote, she would gain the six works of mercy and restore a languishing life which existed only for the service of the most perfect goddess of the heavens. Perhaps—who could tell?—if glowing words and amorous advances could charm away a mean figure and bulbous, pitted nose, the virgin citadel of the Queen might yet capitulate. For all their twenty years' difference in age these two high-spirited souls promised an inflammable conjunction.

In January, 1579, Alençon sent over to do his wooing his 'chief darling,' Jean de Simier, Baron de St. Marc, 'a most choice courtier, exquisitely skilled in love-toys, pleasant conceits, and court-dalliances'. Being in Elizabeth's chamber one morning, he stole her nightcap, and, with her leave, sent it to Alençon to join another trophy, one of her handkerchiefs. Like master, like servant: the double battery of ardent letters from the one and ardent words from the other, combined with the Queen's own propensities, produced the love-game *in excelsis*. Court and people were startled. Some muttered that Simier was employing love-potions and other unlawful arts; scandal took note and whispered that he had won his way not only to her heart but to her body. The two were like twin souls. Making play of his name, she gave him a nickname—'her monkey', and he signed himself *'à jamais le singe votre'*: he was 'the most faithful of her beasts.' She was never happier, never in better humour, as courtiers noted by her gestures, than when in his company.

The courtship took on a serious complexion, and in March-April the Council was engaged in long discussions, trying to formulate its advice to the Queen. Its members fell asunder into two parties, as before. Walsingham led the more zealous brethren in opposition; Burghley and Sussex were still in the van for marriage. The former produced ten objections, the latter seven benefits plus eleven perils. Some of the objections were remote, others irrelevant, as the difficulty of satisfying Elizabeth's taste in men, for, as it was pertinently said, the hearts of kings are in God's keeping, not their councillors'. Naturally, the old religious objection cropped up, but it was far less grave than before, for Alençon was no *dévot;* he had fought with the Huguenots and was now with the Dutch rebels, though, being heir presumptive to the French throne, he was compelled to remain a Catholic.

There was one objection, new and prominent—the Queen's age. She was forty-five and would be forty-six before she married. To have a first child at that age, Walsingham and his party argued, would be extremely perilous. An ambassador—an unreliable retailer of gossip, although in this instance he may be right—says that she held a consultation of doctors to decide whether she could hope for children, and they saw no difficulty. Burghley and his supporters cited the example of the last Duchess of Savoy, a woman of sallow and melancholy complexion and in all respects far inferior to her Majesty, who was older when she married, yet gave birth to a goodly prince. There were many other cases. Elizabeth, they declared—the description was for her eyes—was 'a person of most pure complexion, of the largest and goodliest stature of well-shaped women, with all limbs set and proportioned in the best sort, and one whom, in the sight of all men, nature cannot amend her shape in any part to make her more likely to conceive and bear children without peril.' The French ambassador was equally confident. Elizabeth was never prettier nor more beautiful, he wrote. There was nothing old about her except her years, and those born under her constellation were never sterile and rarely died without heirs. He had himself seen in his house one of the wonders of the world —an Englishwoman, his neighbour, fifty-six years old, who was eight months gone with child. Yet in England it was not thought strange, but natural to all their women of good physique and temperament.

Discussion of the terms of marriage went forward, and Alençon was invited to come over for inspection. The betting in London was two to one against his coming and three to one against the marriage. The Puritans in the City, probably encouraged by their friends at Court, were working up a formidable opposition. In January books against a French alliance had been found in the Queen's chamber. Now, the preachers were choosing their texts to inveigh either covertly or openly against the marriage. They did not spare the Queen's own ears, and on one occasion she rose and swept from the service in the middle of the sermon. She was compelled to issue a ban on texts that lent themselves to this manner of preaching. Simier, however, had every good hope. He declared that he would merely wait to say more till the curtain was drawn, the candle out, and his master in bed. English gentlemen at Milan were ordering sumptuous attire in anticipation of the wedding.

Alençon, unlike the Archduke Charles, was too astute and impetuous to let dignity impede his fortune, or dally away time over negotiations. Ignoring his brother's cautions, in the middle of August he slipped over to England, heavily disguised. No one at Court knew—or was supposed to know—that he had landed, except the Queen and Simier. Arriving in the latter's chamber early in the morning, while Elizabeth still slept, he could hardly be restrained from rushing straight to kiss her hand. Simier wrote her a note saying that he had put his tired master between two sheets: 'Would to God it was by your side'. Alençon certainly had a way with him. Age had improved his looks a little; vivacity did the rest. Elizabeth told him that he had been represented to her as hideous, hunchbacked, and deformed, but she found him the reverse and most handsome in her eyes. Thirteen days and thirteen nights of continuous love-making ensued, with mutual vows and fine promises. They exchanged valuable presents, and she added him to her list of pet beasts, giving him the nickname of her frog. The days hastened by; he took his leave. Simier wrote that his master had spent the last night in sighs and moans and had got him up early to talk of the Queen's divine loveliness and swear a thousand oaths that without hope of seeing her again soon, he could not live. Alençon himself wrote four letters from Dover, three from Boulogne, declaring that he was desolate, doing nothing but wipe away the tears that fell uninterruptedly from his eyes. He was the most faithful and affectionate slave in the world, and as such kissed her feet from the coast of that comfortless sea.

But the hostile murmur in London and elsewhere grew alarmingly. The same spirit seemed abroad that had opposed the marriage of Philip and Mary in the past, and the Spanish ambassador thought he saw revolution in the offing. In September a tract was secretly printed, scattered about the City and distributed in the provinces, entitled 'The Discovery of a Gaping Gulf whereinto England is like to be swallowed by another French marriage, if the Lord forbid not the banns by letting her Majesty see the sin and punishment thereof'. The author was John Stubbs, a country gentleman trained in the law, whose sister was married to the leading divine of the Puritan party. The violence of a hot-headed professor of religion, the prejudice of an Englishman, the concern of a loving subject, spoke in outrageous language. Let Alençon's Mass be brought to England, Stubbs wrote; it would be as wildfire that all the seas could not quench, working havoc on the church here and abroad. His House was rotten with disease, sealed with visible marks of divine vengeance upon their carcasses for their manifest cruelties. It was a French trick to seek this marriage so eagerly now, at the very time of most danger to Elizabeth for child-bearing. If only her Majesty would call her most faithful and wise physicians, adjuring them on their conscience, their loyalty, and their faith to the whole land, to speak without thought of pleasing or displeasing any, they would tell her how fearful was the expectation of death.

Elizabeth was passionately angry. With reason: a nation with whom it behoved her to remain friendly had been insulted, her guest slandered, and her people provoked to discontent 'like as by a trump of sedition, secretly sounding in every subject's ear'. She issued a long proclamation which the authorities were told to read to the City companies, and the bishops to their clergy. A preacher was put up at St. Paul's to extol the Queen's government and assure his hearers that as she had been bred and brought up in Christ, entered and reigned by Christ, so she would live and die in Christ. 'The people seemed, even as it were with a shout to give God thanks' for this assurance; but 'they utterly bent their brows at the sharp and bitter speeches which he gave against the author of the book', whom they regarded as one that feared God and dearly loved her Majesty. It was the same with the Bishop of London's clergy. When the Bishop praised the Queen they wept, and drew down his tears for company; but some insisted that they must move their flocks to prayer and fasting against the peril that beset her, with the result that the Bishop was afraid to bring too many of them to hear his admonitions, lest Londoners should learn of the grudging and groaning in the country and become worse.

Stubbs together with his printer and publisher were arrested, tried—significantly enough—under an act passed to protect Philip when King of England, and condemned to lose their right hands and be imprisoned. Measured by the offence and the age the sentence was not vicious, but it was certainly tactless and unmerciful. Some thought it illegal, and a judge who denounced it, together with a lawyer who openly bawled out his opinion—both, a few years before, obstreperous parliamentarians—were imprisoned. Elizabeth's good sense had deserted her. She pardoned the printer, but the other two had to suffer. At the scaffold each made a loyal speech to the people, Stubbs ending with a pun: 'Pray for me,' he begged, 'now my calamity is at hand'; and when his right hand had been cut off, he took his hat from his head with his left, cried 'God save the Queen!' and swooned. The publisher lifted his bloody stump; 'I have left there a true Englishman's hand,' he cried, and went away very stoutly and with great courage. A deep silence pervaded the multitude of spectators.

Parliament was to meet on October 20th to conclude the marriage, but Elizabeth decided to prorogue it for a month as it was only too clear, from the state of public opinion, that the Commons would get out of hand and perhaps wreck everything. At the beginning of October she ordered the Council to give her its advice. There was a wordy struggle, lasting several days: it is said that they sat one day from 8.0 a.m. till 7.0 p.m., without stirring from the room. Walsingham was absent, but seven councillors, including Leicester and Hatton, were against marriage, five, under Burghley's pertinacious leadership, for it. At first they decided merely to tell the Queen the pros and cons, leaving the choice to her wisdom, 'with the assistance of God's spirit.' Then, possibly under Burghley's persuasion, they altered their decision and resolved first to ask her what her own inclination was, whereupon they would come to some resolution themselves.

It presaged the failure of the marriage, for whatever Elizabeth's immediate reaction might be, her instinct was too sound to proceed in face of a divided Council and hostile people. When a deputation of four waited on her in the morning with the Council's message she broke down, shed many tears, and reproached them for any disposition to doubt that it would be best for her and the realm if she married and had a child of her own body to continue the line of Henry VIII. She cursed her folly in letting them discuss the subject; but she had expected a universal request to marry, not doubts. Too upset to decide anything at the moment, she asked them to see her again in the afternoon. By that time she was more composed and argumentative, and trounced the opponents of the marriage, which she defended at length. They returned to their colleagues, and the next day came together to offer her their support, moved, they said, by two reasons—that she appeared to want marriage in order to have issue, and that she had said she would have Alençon or no one, and did not mislike him. Once more she trounced her opponents, but what she meant to do, she would not say.

So the cup of marriage was dashed from Elizabeth's lips. It was her last chance. In a sense it was the only chance that she had had. Leicester she would have married, if the evil results of the step had not been obvious. She preferred her career to him. The Archduke Charles she had not seen, and could not bring herself, either on grounds of political prudence or personal inclination, to wed the unknown. Had he, like Alençon, risked his dignity and come to see her, the odds are that the imperial votaress would have been as loth as she was now to pass on 'in maiden meditation, fancy free'. Necessity is a persuasive mistress, and perhaps it is not strange that at the age of forty-six she who had a nice eye for handsome men found Alençon's wit more than enough to excuse his bodily shortcomings. Her motives were probably mixed. She was convinced by the political argument, as Burghley and others expounded it, although it had not seemed to move her very much until Simier came to woo, and his master after him. With Alençon the religious difficulty, which had proved a stumbling block in the Archduke's negotiations, was as slight as it possibly could be with a Catholic husband; and she was probably right in thinking that little or no harm need come of it. But political motives were not all. Hard as it is to look into the heart of this supreme deceiver, there seems to have been a genuine—and pathetic—desire for marriage and a child. Otherwise, her passionate breakdown before four of her most intimate councillors, which we cannot dismiss as acting, would be an enigma. As to the possibility or risk of a first child at her age, the relevant fact is not modern medical opinion, but her belief, a belief which her most devoted servant, Burghley, shared with his whole soul.

The brush with the Council really ended the marriage, but Elizabeth was in the same wayward mood afterwards that she had been in when she wanted to marry Leicester, long ago. Walsingham spoke to her: she told him to be gone; he was good for nothing save to protect Puritans. She railed at the godly Knollys: Might she not, like others, she asked, desire to have children? Hatton, too, came in for a good drubbing. She drove or banished the critics from her presence, Walsingham and Leicester for two or more months.

It was on Leicester, naturally enough, that the full vials of Elizabeth's wrath were emptied. At this critical juncture Simier and the French ambassador revealed to her, what no one else at Court had apparently dared to tell, that he was married. He had married, a year before, Sir Francis Knollys's daughter, the widowed Countess of Essex, concerning whom London gossip, at the end of 1575, had been saying that, during her husband's absence in Ireland, she had had two children by Leicester. She was not Leicester's only amorous adventure. He had had a son by Lady Sheffield in 1574, and was said to have been secretly married to her the previous year, but had now repudiated her. It is perhaps futile to guess at the motives for Elizabeth's anger. She may have known something of his relations with Lady Sheffield; she may have heard the scandal about Lettice Knollys; she may even have felt an unreasoning, possessive jealousy. But the secrecy of Leicester's marriage was a definite slight to her as Queen, and, also, here was he denying marriage to her while slyly enjoying it himself. Her anger was open and devastating. In sorrow for himself, Leicester complained to Burghley: he had lost youth, liberty, and all his fortune reposed in the Queen, towards whom he had carried himself, he wrote, 'almost more than a bondman many a year together, so long as one drop of comfort was left of any hope'. In a sense he was right. He had competed with princes, staked his throw on the most glittering of all prizes, and lost. 'Empty words, grinning scoffs, watching nights, and fawning days'—the lot of those who loved 'pride of life, the Court's vanity, ambition's puffball'—he had known. But he had his reward, in power, influence, and princely extravagance; and as for love—if that word be profaned—he had taken his comfort.

The battle over Alençon went on. Elizabeth seemed determined to marry. But it was no use acting like the ostrich which buries its head in the sand. Driving her opponents from Court simply made their absence a reproach to prudence, and with Elizabeth, prudence in the long run was fairly sure to prevail. Parliament was prorogued from November to January; yet such was her irresolution that the order was given, rescinded, and given again, all in one day. Then the articles of marriage were signed; but there was a proviso granting her two months' grace in which to win over the people, and opening an easy way of escape. At the end of November Simier departed, leaving sweet memories behind but no persuasive tongue; and sentiment rapidly wilted. When January 1580 came, Parliament was once more prorogued, and by the end of the month Burghley was sadly compelled to recognize that the battle was lost. The line of Henry VIII was now doomed to extinction. The future stood sharply and disturbingly defined as a gamble on the Queen's life, on the possibility of her outliving Mary Queen of Scots. In the discussions on the marriage, some councillors had definitely argued that her constitution was sound enough to make this probable; they thought that she might even outlive Alençon. And two years later, a foreign visitor, with no reason to pervert the facts, remarked how much younger she seemed than her age.

The urge to marry was stifled, but the purely political considerations which had made both Alençon and her enter upon their second courtship retained their force. They kept the game going. For Elizabeth it was still both a way out of the perplexing problem of maintaining the Netherland rebellion, and an option on a close alliance with France in case of need. As the months went by, the need seemed very near. In the Netherlands, Don John's death turned out to be the reverse of a providential accident, for he was succeeded by one who was as able a diplomat as he was a general, the Prince of Parma. In seven months, he was able to recover for Philip the allegiance of the southern or Walloon provinces, and if the Revolt was not to collapse, foreign aid was as necessary as it had ever been. The rebels now went a step farther in their intransigeance, repudiated their allegiance to Philip, and offered Alençon the sovereignty of their country. The prospect of peace in the Netherlands, the goal at which Elizabeth aimed, receded, while Alençon's new title disturbed her. War approached nearer. But for the time being she settled down to her former policy of using Alençon as her catspaw, he, for his part, still finding his value enhanced as her suitor.

The question remained, how long could Elizabeth go on with impunity, fostering trouble for everyone else and escaping it herself? If the Papacy could only fire Philip with a little of its zeal for the Holy War, the answer would be, 'Not long'.

Papal zeal had already prepared two expeditions to be launched against Elizabeth in Ireland, where the combination of national and Catholic feeling in a people of simple and rude ways of life inhabiting a country of bogs and woods, presented a problem which from the financial as well as the military point of view was harassing in the extreme. The first Papal expedition set out from Italy early in 1578 in a rotten ship, with soldiers who wanted to run away, led by a plausible, disreputable adventurer and renegade, Thomas Stukely, who was reputed to be a bastard of Henry VIII's. Arriving in Portugal, Stukely took himself and his men off with the young King on a madcap crusade in Africa, where he had both his legs shot off in the terrible disaster of Alcazar, and so passed out of history into Romance, as the Dick Turpin of his day. The second expedition actually reached Ireland, in July, 1579. It was led by a scion of an Irish noble family, and equipped with a holy banner and a papal agent, who was a distinguished English priest, the bitter foe of his country. A mere handful of men, it was quite negligible in itself though not without a mischievous effect in stirring up fresh risings, while, coming from abroad, it seemed like the first beginnings of intervention which might ultimately make a second Netherlands of Ireland. Sure enough, a year later, in September, 1580, reinforcements arrived, to the number of about six hundred with a plentiful supply of weapons for the Irish. They had short shrift. In two months they had been besieged, forced to surrender unconditionally, and slaughtered, almost to a man. They had come in the name of the Pope: the Lord Deputy refused to recognize the right to levy war in one who had no authority from God or man, but was 'a detestable shaveling, the right Antichrist and patron of the doctrine of devils'.

Philip II had been far from happy at the thought of provoking Elizabeth to anger with these petty goads, but he had allowed the reinforcements of 1580 to be organized in Spain, and there was a sprinkling of Spaniards among the

Italians who comprised the expedition. Perhaps he abandoned caution to this extent owing to the news, which reached Europe in the late summer of 1579, of Drake's successful passage through the Straits of Magellan and the unexampled plunder that he had taken, sailing along the Pacific coast of South America. In England, those who had shares in the voyage were beside themselves for joy, and Londoners, all agog with excitement, could talk of nothing else but going out themselves to join in the game of plunder. Piracy was a not ungentlemanly calling, and to these zealous Protestants, who bought coloured pictures entitled 'The Three Tyrants of the World', with portraits of the Pope, Nero, and the Turk, Spain was fair game. Only the merchants who traded with Spain were sad.

Elizabeth watched the year 1580 unfold itself, with legitimate anxiety. Another grave event was at hand in the succession to the crown of Portugal. The young King, like Stukely, had been killed at the battle of Alcazar, and, as he left no children, his great uncle, an old man and a cardinal, had come to the throne. He was dying, and Philip II, who had the best claim to the succession, was busy preparing an army and fleet to enforce it. It was bad enough to see Philip annex Portugal and its colonies, but Elizabeth also feared that the fleet which he was preparing would be turned against her. Early in 1580 in England men were being mustered and the fleet put in readiness as a precautionary measure, and the Queen at an interview halfjokingly welcomed Mendoza, the Spanish ambassador, by demanding if he came as a herald to declare war. In July Philip's army overran Portugal. Close on this news, came the reinforcements from Spain for the papal expedition in Ireland. In the same month Drake arrived home with his fabulous booty, after sailing round the world.

If at this terrible moment, when it seemed sheer lunacy to sting Spain into madness, Elizabeth had taken fright and sacrificed Drake to placate Philip, it would have been excusable. But relying on France, which was alarmed at the annexation of Portugal, and having Alençon in reserve should the Heavens fall on her, she gambled, with a brave defiant face. She demanded from Mendoza an explanation of the presence of Spaniards in Ireland, thus taking the wind out of his sails over Drake; and for months refused to see him, on the plea that Philip had not sent her a letter of apology—a fine thing, as Philip remarked, seeing that she herself had been helping the Dutch rebels, without apologizing, for years! Philip found her unscrupulous tactics, as Mendoza did, very disconcerting, but they served her purpose, which was to make a hero of Drake and if possible save his booty. She sent an order that he was to be allowed to abstract ten thousand pounds' worth of the plunder, 'the leaving of which sum in his hands is to be kept most secret to himself alone'; thus if she were forced to return the booty, he would still have his reward. She had him at Court, delighted in his talk, and on New Year's Day wore a crown that this 'right *magnifico*' had given her, set with five splendid pilfered emeralds. On April 4th she went to Deptford to visit his ship, the *Golden Hind*, told him playfully that she had a gilded sword there to strike off his head, and requested the French ambassador to knight him. The ambassador secured a trophy on this occasion, which he afterwards sent to Alençon to add to his collection—a purple and gold garter of the Queen's, that had slipped down and been picked up by him. She put it on again in his presence, but later restored it to him as fair prize.

It was also in the year 1580 that the first Jesuit missioners landed in England, to win back the people to the old faith. As early as 1568 one of the exiles had founded a seminary at Douai in the Netherlands to meet the need for educating English Catholic youth, the purpose of which gradually shaped itself as a training college for secular priests. In 1579 another college was founded at Rome, passing under Jesuit management. Its scholars were definitely pledged to return to England 'for the salvation of souls,' and their education was carefully directed to this missionary object. As the struggle with the English Government developed and it became evident that the fate which awaited them was the terrible death of a traitor, they were taught in their Spiritual Exercises to contemplate martyrdom and live imaginatively through the humiliations and horrors of arrest, trial, and execution, until death—yea, the traitor's death—had lost its sting, and they could woo it as the glorious way to the martyr's crown. The best of these students were filled with the purified spirit of the Counter-Reformation and fired by a great cause to the point of self-oblivion, like the Protestant martyrs in Mary's reign. St. Philip of Neri was accustomed to salute them in the streets with the words, 'Salvete flores martyrum!' and their college acquired the name of the Seminary of Martyrs.

From 1574 on, a steadily increasing stream of missionary priests had flowed from the Douai seminary into England, the coming of the Jesuits in 1580 being merely the broadening of that stream. But the Jesuit Mission aroused extraordinary alarm, partly owing to renewed belief in a Holy League against England; partly because the missionaries came direct from the Pope, 'the most capital enemy of the Queen and this State,' to whom their Order was bound in a specially close way; partly through the distinction of their leaders, Parsons and Campion—the latter a cultured, saintly man, the former politically-minded, irascible, an able organizer, and trenchant controversialist. Their mission was to save souls. They were forbidden to meddle in politics; or rather—for the leaders of Catholicism were incorrigible plotters—they were forbidden 'except, perhaps, in the company of those whose fidelity has been long and steadfast'. The loophole was enough for a man like Parsons. A year later it had to be closed, as it proved too dangerous. There was an obvious obstacle in the way of 'such holy, peaceable, and sweet endeavours of orderly good men'—the papal Bull of 1570. To avoid the political complexion that this would have given to the mission, the Jesuit fathers were empowered to relieve Catholics of obedience to the Bull, 'while things remain as they are'; in other words, their converts could be loyal to Elizabeth, until, but only until, someone was found to carry out the Papal sentence of deposition against her. Put from Elizabeth's point of view, the missionary priests were to win over Englishmen to a contingent disloyalty.

The Government's answer was to destroy the priests as traitors. The Spirit of Pity hovers over the victims, but Justice also has its place. Some priests undoubtedly dabbled or even waded deep in treason; most were concerned only with the salvation of souls, and tried to maintain a distinction between religion and politics, although in the conditions of Elizabethan England, it must have required unusual discretion really to live up to their intentions. The tragedy of their position was that the Pope himself, his ministers, the founder of the Douai seminary, and other leaders of their Church, with their medieval conception of the Holy War made the distinction quite impossible. In all but name the Papacy was at war with Elizabeth; worse, it was prepared to encourage its adherents to murder her. In December, 1580, the Papal Secretary replied as follows to an inquiry made in the name of certain English Jesuits: 'Since that guilty woman of England rules over two such noble kingdoms of Christendom and is the cause of so much injury to the Catholic faith and loss of so many million souls, there is no doubt that whosoever sends her out of the world with the pious intention of doing God service, not only does not sin but gains merit.' The efforts of the Papacy to bring about the 'Enterprise of England,' of which at this very time there was a pitiful manifestation in the Irish expedition, were unceasing. Those efforts always contemplated and relied upon support from a Catholic rising in England itself. Hence, the missionaries were in effect engaged in facilitating the destruction of Elizabeth.

The work of the priests went on, with striking success. Moving about the country in disguise, hidden now in this gentleman's house, now in another's, spied upon, hunted, till fear itself took away all fear, they inspired Catholics with their own fervour, restored discipline, and banished the uncertainty and compromise of twenty years. Their work was fatal to the hope that had prompted Elizabeth's policy of peaceful absorption into the Anglican church; it inflamed Protestant opinion; the note of Puritan nationalism became more strident. In the parliament which met at the beginning of 1581, with the Catholic menace for its chief business, the Commons were moved by a spirit of vengeful anger and proud confidence; anger against the Pope and those whom he had lately sent hither, 'a sort of hypocrites, naming themselves Jesuits, a rabble of vagrant friars newly sprung up and running through the world to trouble the church of God'; confidence in how little the Pope's curses could hurt true Englishmen and how little his blessings could save his followers from that punishment which they were able to lay upon them. They would have gone to any length in defence of their faith and their Queen; 'a princess', as one speaker said, 'known by long experience to be a principal patron of the Gospel, virtuous, wise, faithful, just, unspotted in word and deed, merciful; . . . a Queen, besides, of this noble realm, our native country, renowned of the world'.

It would have been easy to let this spirit in Council and Parliament run away with policy; it was difficult to prevent it. The laws passed were drastic; and in times of crisis, they were more or less rigorously enforced. But there was a statesmanlike difference drawn between the laity and the priests, and between being and becoming a Catholic; nor was moderation absent from the application of the law. There can be little doubt that this was largely due to the Queen herself, whose mind, with its secular view of the problem, its dislike of bloodshed, and its relative tolerance, was essentially modern. Her sister Mary, a Catholic first and an Englishwoman afterwards, had fought Protestantism as heresy, in accordance with her religious instincts, using the ecclesiastical courts and the stake. Elizabeth persecuted—if that word must be used—in the name of patriotism, through the secular courts and with secular punishments. She had a profound belief in the loyalty of the people to her, and self-pride was involved in her attitude. Councillors were constantly complaining of her lenity. 'Nothing in this world grieveth me more', wrote Leicester to Walsingham in September, 1582, 'than to see her Majesty believes this increase of papists in her realm can be no danger to her. . . . If she suffer this increase but one year more, as she hath done these two or three years past, it will be too late to give or take counsel to help it.'

Threatened at home, threatened as she now was by a new turn of events in Scotland, threatened from abroad, Elizabeth had to cling to France and Alençon to prevent the Catholic storm from completely encircling and overwhelming her. She went about it in her own peculiar, variable way, nonplussing even Burghley, and driving Walsingham to distraction with her tergiversations. 'If you mean it . . .' he wrote of the marriage. 'If you mean it not. . . .' In reality, she would now have preferred an alliance with France, without the marriage, leaving Alençon dependent on his brother. But the King and Catherine de Medici were not to be caught in that way. What they wanted was to pin the elusive Elizabeth down by marriage, saddle her with Alençon's adventures, and if possible let her pay the price of war with Spain; not, as they feared, be pushed into war themselves and then left in the lurch. Catherine actually tried to persuade her son to forsake England for Spain and marry a Spanish bride. Elizabeth thereupon blew warmly upon the courtship. Escape from it she could not—at least, not without too grave risks. And so it went on.

Alençon himself wanted marriage, or failing that, money, and the best way to get either was to slip over to England: if Elizabeth would not marry him he could at least make her pay to be rid of him. In May, 1581, he embarked at Dieppe, full of eagerness; but the sea raged, he was very sick, and the boat was driven back to port—misfortunes, he wrote, which needed the eloquence of a better orator than he to describe. In July, Elizabeth wrote him a tender, loving letter to say that she could not marry him: 'though her body was hers, her soul was wholly dedicated to him.' A month later she sent a loan of £30,000 to help finance his Netherland adventure; but it was inadequate. His brother would not help him and he was in desperate straits. And so, at the end of October, he again slipped away to visit the Queen, whose lovely garter he still cherished as the talisman of victory, and at whose feet he would fain consecrate all his trophies. He was sorely buffeted by the waves, but this time managed to reach England. Elizabeth wrote to Burghley: 'Let me know what you wish me to do.'

Sober business, combined with persuasive, and rather ridiculous wooing: thus the days passed. Alençon wanted Elizabeth to finance his Netherland adventure. She entered into a qualified agreement to do so, provided his brother also helped. Coupled with this—and preceding it—was a clause binding Alençon to champion the anti-Guise cause in France, again with her support. It was an astute move. Nothing could have been better calculated to keep the French King from siding with Elizabeth's enemies, for as heir to the throne Alençon enjoyed the same kind of influence among Frenchmen—only, much greater in degree—as Mary Queen of Scots had enjoyed in England; and Henry dreaded his brother's interference in French politics. Indeed, in this agreement with Alençon, Elizabeth had brought off a masterly diplomatic victory. She had outwitted Henry III and Catherine de Medici, got the substance of an alliance with France—and was still unmarried.

Probably Elizabeth's one idea now was to avoid marriage. Despite Catherine de Medici's calculated optimism, she could no longer hope for children, and English Puritans were still vociferous in their opposition: Thomas Norton, 'the great parliament man', got himself into trouble for letting his zeal outrun discretion on the subject. But the one thing Elizabeth dared not do was to let Alençon depart disgruntled. And 'François the Constant' still professed himself to be longing night and day to sleep in the great bed and show what a fine companion he could be. On November 22nd, walking in the gallery at Whitehall, with the French ambassador and other company, Elizabeth kissed him, drew a ring from her finger, and announced that she would marry him. Whether 'the force of modest love in the midst of amorous discourses' had carried her farther than she intended; whether, as was said, she spent the night among her weeping and wailing gentle-women in doubts and cares, it is impossible to know. Probably not, for the promise to marry was made upon conditions which the French King was expected to refuse, and even should Henry III call Elizabeth's bluff, she could raise the terms still farther. The announcement in the gallery saved Alençon's face. He could depart, a little nearer being her husband, and with his credit in the money market strengthened, just as a favourable rumour on the Stock Exchange to-day sends up sagging shares.

But Alençon, having manœuvred Elizabeth into an awkward position, was determined to press forward to complete victory. A battle of wits and wills followed, fought in amorous terms. Elizabeth promised Alençon a loan of sixty thousand pounds, half to be paid fifteen days after his departure, the rest within fifty days after that. He was to have gone, with this as his solatium, in the middle of December. He stayed on. At the end of the month he had ten thousand pounds paid him at once. Still he stayed on. At last, on February 1st he was got away. The Queen and the whole Court accompanied him as far as Canterbury. At Rochester she showed him her great ships, a spectacle which moved the French lords and gentlemen to confess 'that of good right the Queen of England was reported to be Lady of the Seas'. Three war-ships were appointed to take him from Sandwich to the Netherlands, together with a train of a hundred gentlemen and three hundred serving men, with Leicester, Howard, Hunsdon, and many distinguished courtiers. Had he in fact been the King of England, Elizabeth could not have honoured him more. According to the Spanish ambassador she pretended grief at his absence and declared that she would give a million to have her frog once more swimming in the Thames instead of the stagnant marshes of the Netherlands.

The two continued to exchange affectionate letters and Alençon to press for the marriage, but to press also for the rest of his loan. For a time Elizabeth kept the courtship going, now encouraging, now obstructive. At last it died away like the sunset glow. It had served her purpose, for she had succeeded in keeping out of the Netherlands, and had frightened Philip with the prospect of an Anglo-French alliance. In August, 1581, Philip had written, threatening her with war; two months later he offered forgiveness for all past offences and a renewal of the old friendship. The sky cleared a little. French policy took a more active turn against Spain, and the King actually sent his brother money, whereupon Elizabeth sent no more of hers. In Scotland, also, events took a more favourable turn.

But in January, 1583, there came a set-back when Alençon foolishly tried to seize the town of Antwerp from his Dutch allies, failed, and ignominiously fled the country. Still bent on her old policy, Elizabeth tried to patch up the quarrel. She was trying when on June 10th, 1584, Alençon's adventures ended in fever and death. As her councillors had foretold, she had survived her wooer. For three weeks on end not a day passed without tears. 'Melancholy doth so possess us,' wrote Walsingham, 'as both public and private causes are at a stay for a season.' To the French ambassador she described herself as a forlorn widow. 'She is a Princess', he remarked, 'who can act any part she pleases.' But his cynicism, on this occasion, was mistimed. Elizabeth had indeed exploited Alençon without scruple, but this ugly yet most congenial and constant of suitors had a real place in her affections. He had been her last hope of children. She wept for herself.

CHAPTER XVI

THE TRAGEDY OF MARY

MORE than ten years had now gone by since Protestant anger, provoked by the Ridolfi Plot and the Massacre of St. Bartholomew, had blazed out against Mary Queen of Scots —'the bosom serpent,' as Walsingham called her. These years she had spent in the custody of the Earl of Shrewsbury, chiefly at Sheffield Castle, with occasional moves while the place was cleansed of the foulness resulting from the evil sanitary conditions of the day. Her life was subject to trying restrictions: all correspondence was supposed to pass through Shrewsbury's hands; whenever she went out, he accompanied her with a guard; every night soldiers kept their stations within and without the house, and watch was set in the villages near by; any stranger in the district was suspect, and no one was allowed to enter the house or speak to her without permission and supervision.

But within the limits set by these necessary precautions against escape and plotting, Mary was treated with respect and generally with indulgence. She sat and dined under a cloth of state, as a Queen; she was allowed her own household, gentlemen, gentlewomen, and domestic servants, chosen and paid by her and loyal to her; and the cost of their and their mistress's diet was borne by Elizabeth, which together with the maintenance of Shrewsbury's household amounted to fifty-two pounds per week, no small sum. Saved this expense, Mary was better able, from the dowry settled on her as Queen dowager of France, to make payments to the most pernicious of the English Catholic exiles, maintain secret intelligence with Elizabeth's enemies, and seduce the simple villagers in her neighbourhood with lavish alms. Her health was not good. She was still troubled with an old complaint, a pain in her side; and as middle age crept on she fell a victim to rheumatism and lost her good figure. Several times she was allowed to visit Buxton to take the cure at the baths there. Though her great love of hunting remained, latterly she was often unable to sit a horse, or indeed to walk, and her time was spent embroidering, or with her collection of little birds and pretty lapdogs. She set siege to Elizabeth's heart with gifts of her needlework and other presents, which were at first received kindly and 'tokens' given in exchange, until the practice became embarrassing, and Elizabeth sent word that 'persons who begin to grow old willingly take with two hands, but give only with one finger'.

It might have been a tolerable life for anyone of a placid nature, but not for Mary. She had, as she said, a great heart; her passion was unassuageable. After so many disappointments and so many years of captivity, she could still declare that she would not leave her prison save as Queen of England; and despite the danger into which plotting had led her, she persisted in the habit, intriguing everywhere and with everyone who could serve her interests, pledging herself to the Pope, to Philip II, to the King of France, to Elizabeth, and all simultaneously, with complete lack of scruple. According to the practice of the age, she was no doubt entitled, as a Queen, to do this. Morals need not enter into the question, but simply prudence. She wrote far too much and too impetuously, committing her fate to the risks of secret correspondence, though spies were everywhere, she herself handicapped by captivity, and the English government's intelligence service the subtlest and most efficient in existence. Her flagrant lies and her malice confronted Elizabeth in letter after letter, intercepted, or copied by spies. They afforded the most damning answer to all her pleas for better treatment.

Archbishop Parker's sage remark—'Our good Queen has the wolf by the ears'—was if anything truer now than when it was first uttered. Elizabeth was past the age for children, and though Mary's health was giving way, while hers was good, life after all was a gamble. Courtiers and statesmen lived under the shadow of a great fear, with their eyes anxiously on the future. Sir Christopher Hatton sent word to Mary that if Elizabeth died he would immediately come with the guard and release her. Burghley, who had bent to many winds, cultivated a reputation for moderation. Even the dour and steadfast Walsingham took pains to let her know that he was not her enemy. These men were not false. They would gladly have had Mary put to death if Elizabeth would have countenanced it. Shrewsbury, too, steered a course between the present and the future. His family, less loyal than he, and succumbing to Mary's many attractions, amused her by deriding their Queen. The Countess of Shrewsbury, who was the notorious Bess of Hardwick, an incorrigible intriguer with the tongue of an adder, told malevolent tales of Elizabeth, spiced with gossip's foulest inventions: of her insatiable, predatory lust, practised with Leicester, Simier, Alençon, Hatton, and others; of her cruelty and foolish vanity—how, for example, she delighted to be told that it was impossible to look her fully in the face, as it shone like the sun!

It is little wonder that in Shrewsbury's household Mary found it easy to send and receive letters secretly. When in 1581–82 the Catholic exiles were busy reconstructing the 'Enterprise' against England, negotiating with the Pope, Philip, and the Duke of Guise, and intriguing in Scotland in the hope of launching the invasion through that country, Mary was able to take her share in the plotting, maintaining active intelligence with the principal people concerned. Her hopes rose, especially over Scotland, which had at last broken the close connection with England, synonymous with her captivity. Nor did hope fail her when, like a meteor that had flashed across the sky and spent itself, the contriver of this political revolution, Esmé Stuart, fell from power in 1582 and returned to France to die. For, amidst the faction strife that followed his fall, a new figure was intruding into Scottish politics—the youthful King, James

VI, now in his late 'teens, and anxious, so far as his timorous nature would allow, to take the reins of power from the nobility.

Mary had not seen her son since the fateful days of the Bothwell marriage; he had no childish recollections of her to which she could appeal; and he had been educated by the scholar who had prepared the famous *Detection,* indicting her with the murder of his father. Nevertheless, she had a mother's confidence in his filial loyalty, and if her simple faith proved to be justified, then sooner or later she would be able to confront Elizabeth with a combined demand from herself and James for her release, a demand, the moral power of which Elizabeth would find it hard to resist. And so James appeared on the political horizons of both Mary and Elizabeth, as yet an enigma.

According to the brother of Mary's French secretary, who gave a penetrating account of him about this time, James was 'an old young man,' very learned, quick to grasp a point and fond of argument; having an excellent opinion of himself, despising other princes and quite unaware of his relative poverty and insignificance, hating to be surpassed by anyone in anything he did, desirous to be thought brave and to be feared, but really a coward. He was inordinately fond of hunting, like his mother, and neglectful of affairs, though he complacently excused himself by claiming that he could dispatch as much business in one hour as others in a day, since he watched, listened, and spoke simultaneously; in fact, could do five things at once. He was loud of voice and weak of body, restless, for ever walking up and down with an odd, erratic gait. He was too fond of favourites. His manners struck this Frenchman as very rude and 'uncivil.' In short, he was rather more and a great deal less than the simple, loving child whom Mary pictured.

Oddly enough, Elizabeth and her statesmen believed in Mary's reputed influence over her son. So probably did Mary herself, and she fostered it in Elizabeth by declaring —at best an exaggeration—that James had agreed to associate himself with her in the crown of Scotland, thus recognizing that her abdication of the throne at Loch Leven had been invalid. If true, it was a menace to Elizabeth. Yet at the same time it offered a welcome opportunity.

Elizabeth perceived and welcomed in the supposed relations of mother and son the chance of a humane solution to the problem of Mary. She saw the possibility of granting Mary her liberty in some way to be agreed upon, provided that James entered the English political circle, and that France, which had always been solicitous about Mary's welfare, stood as joint guarantor with James for her good conduct. If attainable—and Elizabeth had excellent bait in the form of her goodwill over the English succession—the policy was extremely attractive. It promised to unite England and Scotland, probably France as well, in a common front against Elizabeth's enemies, depriving them of 'the principal and only foundation' upon which their hostile schemes rested—the captive Mary. Who could say? perhaps in face of such a combination, Philip might even be driven to conciliation in the Netherlands. In fact, there was no end to the material which the plan provided for building castles in Spain.

Thus began an eleventh-hour attempt to avoid tragedy. There were two difficulties in the way. The first was one over which an angel would have wept: the old, old problem of trusting Mary's oaths and promises, or finding some reliable security for her behaviour. There was little trouble in getting her to agree to terms. She was content to stay in England for the present, under some slight surveillance, and with a limited range of freedom, leaving the government of Scotland to her son and merely sharing the title with him. But her surprising docility is easily explained, for the Spanish ambassador had urged her to stay in England, ready to place herself at the head of the Catholic invading army when it came. From his point of view—perhaps from hers—the new treaty was only a means of striking Elizabeth down with greater certainty. Throughout the negotiations Mary maintained her plotting. In a way, this was understandable, for the Pope, Philip, and other parties to the 'Enterprise' were interested, not in her liberty on conditions favourable to Elizabeth and Protestantism, but in Elizabeth's overthrow. To alienate them seemed folly, since they provided a second string to her bow. Should the Catholic army land in England before the treaty with Elizabeth was concluded, Mary would certainly declare for the army. Should the treaty come first—who can tell whether her intrigues would cease? Charity itself dare not venture beyond an interrogation.

The second difficulty was the response of James and Scotland. As 'a loving son', James said that he desired to further his mother's liberty; but it was obvious, when he was frank or driven to answer precise questions, that he himself came first, while Mary could have the remnant of his charity. His paramount thought was to maintain his crown and authority, even to edge his mother out of the English succession; he denied hotly having concluded an agreement to associate her with himself in the Scottish crown. Beguile her with contrary sentiments he might, but this was only out of fear lest the 'Enterprise' should be turned against him as well as Elizabeth. The government of Scotland, at the moment, was in the hands of Anglophil noblemen, entirely opposed to any association of Mary in the crown. They feared that if granted her liberty, she would merely commence intriguing in Scotland, and restart the old troubles there. Nor—significantly enough—when this English faction was overthrown, were their successors, from whom Mary expected favour, much different in their views, for she could be as unmitigated a nuisance to them as to Elizabeth. In short, Scotland did not want her.

Elizabeth had got as far as defining the terms of the treaty with Mary and had ascertained the views of James and his chief advisers when the English faction in Scotland fell from power. Naturally she held up the treaty to watch how Scottish policy developed. Mary was upset. In her impetuous way she declared that it merely confirmed the mistrust that she had felt all along. This was in August, 1583. Before the negotiations could be resumed, with epic fatality another plot—the Throckmorton Plot—had come to light. The time was fast approaching when the fearful wrath of a nation would intervene and cut this Gordian knot.

In May, 1582, a messenger sent by the Spanish ambassador to Scotland, disguised as a dentist, had been stopped near the Border. He had managed to bribe his guards and escape with his baggage, but, as luck had it, left behind a looking-glass, hidden in the back of which were found letters that revealed the existence of the 'Enterprise.' Walsingham set himself to get to the bottom of it. He intercepted letters from the French ambassador to a French agent in Scotland, opening and closing them again with the seals intact; then he corrupted the Italian courier who carried letters back. In each instance he drew a blank; inevitably, because France was not a party to the 'Enterprise'. Ignorant of this, Walsingham persisted. He procured a spy in the French embassy, and through him corrupted the ambassador's secretary.

As a result, Walsingham came to tap a regular secret correspondence that Mary carried on with the ambassador, in addition to her open correspondence that passed through Shrewsbury's hands. Though the 'Enterprise' was not referred to in her letters, it being dependent on France's rival, Spain, they were damaging enough, in all conscience. There must have been a grim humour in reading them. For example, Mary suggested to the ambassador that, in the event of reliable means of communication failing, he should write on paper or thin white cloth in alum, soaked in a little clear water twenty-four hours beforehand: the writing was invisible, but when dipped in water it appeared, white and clear enough to be read. Or he could write between the lines of books, using only every fourth page, and having green strings put on the volumes that had been so treated. If he used cloth, he should see that the length always measured an odd half-yard to distinguish the piece. Again, letters might be stuffed into high-heeled slippers in place of cork, or spread between the wood of trunks and coffers. Walsingham read these suggestions. Did he think that one day he might trap Mary through her trust in such furtive tricks?

So far as the 'Enterprise' was concerned, it was the wrong trail; but fortune favoured Walsingham. He learnt that Francis Throckmorton—a Catholic nephew of Sir Nicholas —visited the French embassy by night and was a chief agent of Mary's. Spies were employed, who for six months tracked this man from place to place. Then in November, 1583, two gentlemen were sent to arrest him at his London house. He managed to dash up the stairs, destroying a letter to Mary as he went, and to get a casket of fatal documents conveyed to the Spanish ambassador; but papers were found containing a list of Catholic noblemen and gentlemen and of havens where foreign forces could land, and though at first he withstood the rigours of examination and even the torment of the rack, his courage at last gave way. 'Now', he moaned, 'I have disclosed the secrets of her (Mary) who was the dearest thing to me in the world'. And as he moved away from the place where he sat by the rack, he muttered, 'Chi a perso la fede, a perso l'honore': faith broken, honour lost.

Throckmorton had been one of the principal advisers concerned with the 'Enterprise', had discussed the plans with the Spanish ambassador, corresponded with Mary, and acted as agent for her letters. All these activities he disclosed. The conspiracy looked extremely alarming, involving, as it did, various noblemen and gentlemen, some of whom fled at the news of his arrest, while others were taken and lodged in the Tower. In January, 1584, Mendoza, the Spanish ambassador, was summoned before the Council, accused of his misdeeds and told to leave the country in fifteen days. He tried bluff, without effect, and the last representative of Spain in Elizabethan England took his leave, declaring that as he had failed to satisfy the Queen as a minister of peace, he must in future try to satisfy her in war.

A project like the 'Enterprise', however, was a slow business, subject to the caution and finance of princes, and liable to be betrayed long before it could be realized. In

contrast, assassination could be secret, swift, and no less effective, appealing in consequence to the impatient and forlorn of hope. It was an old question in the Schools whether
tyrannicide was lawful, and Rome had recently pronounced
in its favour by offering its blessing to the person who should
slay Elizabeth. It is notorious that striking and peculiar
crimes, once attempted, move others to imitate them. And
so it proved in this instance. In March, 1582, William of
Orange, who after Elizabeth was the greatest obstacle to
the Catholic faith, was shot by an assassin and lay between
life and death. Then, in England, just before Throckmorton's arrest, a young Catholic gentleman of Warwickshire
told his friends that he was going to London to shoot the
Queen with his pistol, and 'hoped to see her head set on
a pole, for she was a serpent and a viper'. He set out alone,
blabbed of his intention *en route*, and arrived at the Tower
instead of the Palace. Probably he was a little mad, but if
he had not also been loose-tongued it would have been no
disqualification for his task. Immediately on top of his frustrated plan came Throckmorton's revelations, and the country was still under the excitement of them when on June
30th, 1584, another attempt was made, this time successfully, to kill William of Orange.

To fan alarm still more—if that were possible—two
months later came further revelations of the wide-flung
conspiracy against Elizabeth, when the Dutch authorities,
probably at a hint from Walsingham, intercepted a vessel
bound for Scotland on which was the Jesuit Creighton, a
person deep in the conspiracy. As he was about to be taken,
he tore up and threw overboard a paper describing the 'Enterprise' in detail, but providentially the pieces were blown
back on the deck, collected, and carefully fitted together.
Creighton was sent to England, and there confessed what
he knew.

Is it any wonder that a wave of passionate indignation
swept over Protestant England? The previous winter, as
Elizabeth went from London to Hampton Court, throngs of
people had come to see her pass by: kneeling on the ground
they wished her a thousand blessings, and prayed that those

who meant her harm might be discovered and punished as they deserved.

But the galling fact was that as long as Elizabeth remained squeamish about taking Mary's life, disloyal Catholics had little to lose and everything to gain by violence. Were Elizabeth to be slain, chaos would follow: there would be no Council, no judges, no royal officials anywhere, as their commissions died with the monarch; no one would be entitled to avenge her murder; in all probability Mary would succeed to the crown with impunity. In October, the Council took steps to meet this monstrous situation. They drew up a Bond of Association, pledging its signatories, in the event of an attempt being made on Elizabeth's life with a view to advancing some person to the throne, not only to disallow that person's succession, but to kill him—or, we should say, her—by any means they could. The Protestant cause stood personified in Elizabeth, the Catholic in that nameless person whom everyone could identify. Violence was to be met with violence, lynch law to answer Rome's sanction of assassination. Copies of the Bond were sent to the counties and towns for the principal gentlemen and others to join the Association if they so wished. The response was fervent, so fervent that it needed courage to remain out, although there were devoted Protestants who recoiled from its lawlessness and refused to join. In Yorkshire over 7,000 seals had been appended by the end of November, and more were added till they were enough to fill a good big trunk. At Coventry the citizens formed an Association and sent up a loyal address with 201 seals and signatures to it.

To renew the negotiations for the treaty with Mary in the temper of the year 1584 was an amazing thing for Elizabeth to do. Yet renewed they were, only to drag along drearily owing to the confusion of Anglo-Scottish relations. Despair, anger, and a reckless foolishness seized Mary. Time and again, when talking to English officials, she called God to witness and vowed the most solemn oaths that she knew of no conspiracy against Elizabeth nor would consent to any; but her soul was no sooner forsworn, than she was

writing to the conspirators to launch the invasion without
thought of the peril to her. Told of the Bond of Association,
she offered to subscribe it: nevertheless, two days later she
bade her friends go forward with the 'Enterprise', whatever
became of her, whether Elizabeth made a treaty with her
or not. When this last letter was written, early in November,
the treaty was actually under way again, and Mary's secretary was setting out for the Court, there to join with an
ambassador from James.

Had James really desired and been able to associate his
mother in the crown of Scotland, at the same time making
an alliance with Elizabeth, nothing seems clearer than that
the treaty would now have been concluded. English statesmen, drawing up the pros and cons, found the arguments
for it outweigh those against. Elizabeth herself broke a vow
that she had made fourteen years before, and wrote to
Mary in her own hand.

Mary believed in her son. She also trusted his ambassador, who belonged to her party and was deep in her perilous secrets. But perfidy was no monopoly of hers. Son and
ambassador were both playing her false. James wanted an
alliance with Elizabeth, but he did not want to share his
crown; nor, indeed, did he want his mother set free. That
was the shattering truth, and it could no longer be hidden.
Infamous James's conduct may have been: alas! politically
it was very wise. Mary's fury could not be restrained. She
threatened her son, denounced his ambassador as 'worthy
to be baptized a lying knave'. In truth, her last hope of
redemption was gone. Conspiracy had her in thrall; the
shadow of the block loomed over her.

In late November, while these treaty negotiations were
proceeding, Parliament had met. The Commons undertook
the chief business of the session, which was to provide for
the Queen's safety, with a burning passion and devotion
that revealed the magic hold of Elizabeth over her people.
They were determined that, come what might, no conspiracy should profit either Mary or James. They proposed
to legalize the Bond of Association, with its irresponsible
blood-hunt, and thus incorporate in the English statute

book the most utterly lawless provision that it has probably ever been proposed to place there. There was no mistaking their deadly purpose against Mary, and well would it have been for her if she had recognized in this, and not in the fevered dreams of conspirators and *émigrés,* the true voice of the nation.

Some members, however, were troubled in conscience by the proposal, as they had been by the Bond. Torn between their scruples and their loyalty, they sat in sad silence. It was enough. Elizabeth, too, was uneasy. She interfered, asking that nothing should pass which violated any fundamental principle of justice, or offended the conscience of any of her good subjects, or would not abide the view of the world, friends and enemies alike. She ordered that no one was to be made to suffer for another's fault: in other words, that Mary must be proved to have been an accomplice to a plot before vengeance was wreaked on her. The act was therefore redrafted. It was less moderate than Elizabeth wished, but it did introduce a tribunal to try and judge Mary before permitting anyone and everyone to pursue her to the death. The Bond of Association was modified to conform with it. An act was also passed to destroy the Catholic mission in all its stages. Jesuits and priests ordained abroad were ordered to quit the country in forty days, after which their presence in England would be treason; and a number of priests, some of them condemned traitors, were taken from the prisons and deported to France.

Truce with the Catholic authorities abroad was out of the question. And before the Parliament ended, the lengths to which some ecclesiastics were prepared to go in their war with the wicked Jezebel of England received further confirmation in the confessions of Dr. Parry, a Member of Parliament, who had been plotting to murder Elizabeth. Parry had been acting as a spy for the English government, and it is very difficult to say whether he really intended to kill the Queen or was playing a game of his own, as *agent provocateur.* At any rate, it is certain that Rome gave its approval and blessing to his plan, and Mary's agent in Paris also urged on the deed. The anger of the House of

Commons was terrible. They thought a traitor's death, gruesome as it was, too good for Parry, and petitioned Elizabeth to let them devise a more horrible end, to be inflicted by Act of Parliament. Some members were for immediately reviving the proceedings against Mary's life that had been started in the parliament of 1572. Both proposals, however, were stifled.

The alarm about conspiracy and assassination now subsided for a season. In January, 1585, Mary was moved to Tutbury Castle in Staffordshire, and in April the stern Puritan, Sir Amias Paulet, arrived to be her new custodian, a man used to converse with princes, having been Elizabeth's ambassador at the French Court, but one whom neither endearment nor reward could corrupt. It was indeed a change from the lax days of Shrewsbury and his household: new servants, new discipline. Mary's secret post was completely stopped; and letter after letter from the conspirators abroad accumulated in London, waiting for some device which would elude Paulet's eternal vigilance. Meanwhile, Mary's restless spirit found an outlet in floods of querulous talk; she cried vengeance against her enemies.

During the year of 1585 Elizabeth was chiefly concerned with the negotiations for a league with James, and with deciding what was to be done about the Netherlands, where the death of William of Orange had removed the only person capable of holding the intensely self-interested and faction-ridden provinces together. She was as reluctant as ever to ally with 'an ungrateful multitude, a true mob', as she once called them, and she would have preferred joint intervention with France. But in France, Alençon's death had left the Huguenot leader, Henry of Navarre, the successor to the throne, and against such a prospect the Catholic-Guise party had formed a league, with Spain to back them. The symptoms of the old disease of civil war were reappearing, and the French King dared not go adventuring in the Netherlands. Elizabeth was left with no choice. By August, 1585, she had made a treaty with the rebel states and was sending over the first drafts of her army. Quite as much as military aid, someone of outstanding authority was needed to hold them together, as William of Orange had done. Leicester had long cast himself for this role, and with many misgivings Elizabeth gave her consent. She showed herself as variable as the wind over her decision; and the situation was not improved by her health, which, probably owing to her climacteric, was then poor. One night she 'used very pitiful words', begging Leicester not to leave her, since she was afraid that she would not live long. The bout passed, her humour changed: at last, at the beginning of December he managed to get away. The plunge had been taken. After twenty-seven years of but slightly interrupted peace, Elizabeth had embarked upon war—not, however, in name; nor, truth to tell, in purpose.

War now threatening England, it became more imperative than ever to keep touch with Catholic conspiracies. Once again fortune was kind. In this very month of December, 1585, a certain Gilbert Gifford, who had been trained for the priesthood abroad and was in minor orders, was sent to England by Mary's agent to try and reopen secret communication with her, a task for which his parentage—that of a good Staffordshire family, living close to Mary—seemed to fit him. He was arrested on landing, and being a man of weak, unpleasant character, consented to play the spy for Walsingham; not the first, nor the last, of his kind. His mission suggested his service: he was to go ahead and open a 'secret' way for Mary's letters, which Walsingham would tap. There was no simpler or surer method of discovering plots, nor any device more likely to bring Mary herself into danger.

On December 24th, Mary was moved from Tutbury to Chartley, a moated house belonging to the young Earl of Essex, some twelve miles distant from Tutbury. Here the trap was set; a very ingenious trap, perfectly calculated to fool Mary, with her fond trust in padded shoe-heels and the like. Chartley had to obtain its supply of beer from a brewer at Burton; and this man was induced, presumably by Gifford, to convey Mary's letters, packed in a small waterproof case which was slipped through the bung-hole of the beer keg, the ingoing post travelling in the full kegs, the outcoming in the empty. At first, the brewer, for all he knew, was acting in perfectly good faith; nor was he ever told of Gifford's treachery. But Mary's keeper, Sir Amias Paulet, very soon thought it prudent to have him consciously play Mary false, since otherwise there would be no knowing what use the secret post might be put to, nor would there be any effective control over Gifford.

When finally organized, the post worked usually as follows. Letters from Mary's correspondents abroad reached England in the French ambassador's official packet—a gross abuse of diplomatic privilege. They were handed by the ambassador to Gifford or a substitute of his who took them to Walsingham, and then rode leisurely towards Chartley, where they were to be restored to him. Meanwhile, Walsingham gave them to a remarkable, if unlovely servant of his, one Thomas Phelippes, a small, lean, yellow-haired, short-sighted man, with pock-marked face, an excellent linguist, and, above all, a person with a positive genius for deciphering letters. Phelippes deciphered and copied them. They were then sent to Paulet, who restored them to Gifford, who took them to the brewer. The brewer—unknown to Gifford—brought them back to Paulet, who after making sure that the packet remained the same, returned them, and they went to Mary in the next delivery of beer. The return post went through the same process in the reverse order. The brewer—'the honest man', as he was nicknamed —'played the harlot' egregiously. Most handsomely paid by Mary, he probably also pocketed part of the money that she gave him for Gifford. In addition, he was paid by Walsingham, but still had the effrontery to demand a higher price for his beer!

Mary received the first letters through this post on January 16th, 1586. She was delighted. Poor soul! she had been cut off from all secret correspondence for a year, and had received no foreign news—she said—since December, 1584. Quickly lulled into a sense of perfect security, she ordered all the letters that had been waiting at the French ambassador's since the days of the Throckmorton Plot, to be sent through to her. They numbered twenty-one packets, great and small, containing the secrets of the 'Enterprise'. She spent weeks writing her answers. 'Monsieur Ambassador', said Elizabeth at this time to the French ambassador, 'you have much secret communication with the Queen of Scotland, but, believe me, I know all that goes on in my kingdom. I myself was a prisoner in the days of the Queen, my sister, and am aware of the artifices that prisoners use to win over servants and obtain secret intelligence'. Was it a hint, an indiscretion, or subtle bravado?

Close on the inauguration of the secret post came the crucial and probably inevitable test of Mary's discretion. It so happened that a group of young men were planning to murder Elizabeth as the opening move in the 'Enterprise'. The leading spirit was a priest named Ballard, vainglorious, fond of good company, irresponsible, and altogether extravagant: abroad, he declared that 60,000 English Catholics were ready to rise in rebellion; in England, he promised the help of 60,000 foreign troops; both statements were absurd. Ballard brought into the plot a young Derbyshire gentleman of good fortune, Anthony Babington, once a page in Shrewsbury's household, and acquainted with Mary, a man better fitted to muse on philosophy than play the hero. Foreseeing immortality, he commissioned a painter to draw the portraits of himself and the rest of the little band who were to slay the Queen, 'as a memorial of so worthy an act'. Another conspirator was John Savage, a simple soul, very earnest about a vow that he had taken to kill Elizabeth. He had already been earnest about it for eight months; and when, a few months later, on the first alarm of the conspiracy being discovered, Babington came to him and asked, 'What remedy now?' 'No remedy now,' he replied, 'but to kill her presently'. 'Very well,' said Babington; 'then go you unto the Court to-morrow, and there execute the fact.' 'Nay,' said Savage, 'I cannot go to-morrow, for my apparel is not ready'. Gilbert Gifford was on the fringe of the conspiracy, encouraging Savage to fulfil his vow—with what motive, one cannot say: certainly it would be foolish to imagine that Walsingham set him to play the part of *agent provocateur*.

There seemed to be a demoniac fate in all Mary's story. On June 25th, just when the plot was coming to a head, with Babington cast for the leader, Mary happened to write to him—a letter in no way connected with the plot. Babington replied. He told her what was afoot—that six gentlemen were to slay Elizabeth, while others would hasten to Chartley to rescue her, and a foreign force invade the country—at the same time asking for advice and the promise of honourable reward for the six heroes who were to undertake 'that tragical execution'. The letter duly came to Walsingham. A death-trap for Mary, Walsingham could risk no hitch in its successful working. Phelippes the decipherer was therefore sent down to Chartley with the letter, there to await Mary's answer. First came a brief acknowledgement, with promise to answer more at length. Wrote Phelippes, 'We attend her very heart at the next'. Nor was he disappointed. On July 17th the answer was written. It was an exceedingly long letter, warmly welcoming the plot and the slaying of Elizabeth, and offering plentiful advice. Damning enough if read by itself, it was fatal when read in conjunction with Babington's letter; and unless Elizabeth proved obstructive, Mary's head was already as good as off. Phelippes deciphered the letter and sent a copy to Walsingham, endorsed with the postmark for excessive speed —the gallows!

If Walsingham had now let well alone, he would have robbed the old-fashioned but exploded case for Mary of a specious argument. Instead, he forged a postscript to Mary's letter, asking Babington for the names of the six gentlemen who were to kill Elizabeth. His object was simple and excusable. He wanted irrefutable evidence to convict the assassins. Had all gone as he planned, he would have received the reply, retained it, and immediately rounded up the conspirators. As it was, Babington delayed sending the names, and Walsingham was forced to strike before he was ready.

On August 2nd—pathetic confidence!—Mary wrote to a

confederate abroad to say that the secret post was now, thank God, so safely established that he could write to her whenever he pleased. Two days later Walsingham made the first of his arrests, and, a few days after, Mary was invited out to hunt, met by a troop of horsemen, and led to a neighbouring house, while her two secretaries were made prisoners and all her papers at Chartley seized. Among the papers—it is said—were found letters from certain English noblemen, full of expressions of love and respect; but these Elizabeth concealed in silence, 'according to that motto which she used, *Video et taceo,* that is, I see, but say nothing.'

When the conspirators were apprehended, the citizens of London rang their bells, lit bonfires, made merry in the streets, sang psalms, marched about with tabor and pipe, and gave many a shout, 'that the air rang withal'; for if ever subjects worshipped their sovereign, they did Queen Elizabeth. Deeply moved, she wrote them a superb declaration of her love; whereupon their joy and emotion were redoubled. It was as though England had escaped a new St. Bartholomew. 'These hellish priests', wrote a correspondent of Walsingham's, 'are the poisoners and infectors of all the wicked ones in England. Cut off them, and then both treasons and disloyal attempts have lost their taste'. On September 20th, Babington and six of the principal conspirators were placed on hurdles and drawn through the City from Tower Hill to St. Giles's Fields, where a scaffold had been erected and a pair of gallows 'of extraordinary height, as was that whereupon haughty Haman was hanged for his ambition'. They suffered the full horrors of the traitor's death. The next day another seven were executed, but, at Elizabeth's command, were allowed to hang until dead before being mutilated. Then came a spate of rhymes, ballads, and pamphlets. In city and country the ballads 'were chanted with no less alacrity and courage of the singer, than willingly and delightfully listened unto of the hearer; so that, what by one mean and what by another, all England was made acquainted with this horrible conspiracy'.

'Amias, my most faithful and careful servant,' wrote Elizabeth to Paulet, 'God reward thee treble-fold in three double for thy most troublesome charge so well discharged'. And then, referring to the new restrictions on Mary: 'Let your wicked murderess know how with hearty sorrow her vile deserts compelleth these orders; and bid her from me ask God forgiveness for her treacherous dealings'. Throughout the country there was a sense of imminent peril. The alarm was raised that Frenchmen had landed in Sussex; a week or so later, a Spanish fleet was reported to have put into a French port. Hawkins was sent to sea to patrol the coasts, and Lords-Lieutenant were appointed in each county to muster troops, make ready the beacons, and round up Catholic priests. Elizabeth had given order that in the trial of Babington and his fellows Mary was to be alluded to as little as possible, lest if her case were made to look desperate, her partisans might be driven to some reckless deed.

Desperate Mary's case was. Academically it could of course be argued that a sovereign prince, as she claimed to be, was answerable to God alone, and subject to no law. Elizabeth's civilian lawyers dealt with that argument at great length, and to their own satisfaction. But the echoes of the controversy may be left to keep ghostly company with King Charles's head, since what really mattered was on the one hand political necessity, and on the other the cloak of legality—valid or invalid—provided by the late Parliament in the Act for the Queen's Surety, under which Mary was to be tried. The Council wanted to lodge her in the Tower. Elizabeth refused to agree, and she was taken to Fotheringay Castle in the county of Northampton. Nothing could exceed the care with which the commission for her trial was prepared. Judges and learned counsel deliberated long over its wording, and Elizabeth exhausted everyone's patience with her contrariness. 'I would to God', wrote Walsingham, 'her Majesty would be content to refer these things to them that can best judge of them, as other princes do'. The actual writing of it, since it was to be a memorial 'to continue in after ages', was committed to an old clerk, who alone in this age of declining penmanship could write perfectly in a set hand.

On October 11th, the commissioners—thirty-six peers, privy councillors, and judges, some of whom had been Mary's friends, whose letters, it may be, were among those avowals of love and respect seized at Chartley—arrived at Fotheringay for the trial. Mary stood resolutely upon her privilege as a sovereign, anointed Queen; but after two days of incessant argument, in which the events and mutual recriminations of past years were traversed, she consented to appear before the court, without however yielding to its jurisdiction. The trial would amaze and shock a modern lawyer, but it was conducted according to the normal procedure of the day and with less animus and more substantial proof than many another trial of its kind. There can be no doubt whatever that Mary had been privy and consenting to a plot to assassinate the Queen and to bring an invading army into England. She frequently, vehemently, solemnly denied any knowledge of it: that was natural, for she was fighting for her life. But her denials were and are worth nothing against the evidence of Babington and her two secretaries—not to mention the story of the secret post, which was carefully concealed as was the forged postscript. In accordance with unswerving practice, she was not allowed counsel, but she defended herself with spirit, eloquence, and ability. Voluble and impassioned, she was yet very dignified. And then, when the fierce debate was over, with characteristic suddenness, her mood changed. She vowed devotion to Elizabeth, was all sweetness and forgiveness to the commissioners; and as she passed the judges and prosecuting counsel, she said with a smile, 'God forgive you lawyers, for you are so sore fellows. God bless me and my cause from your laws, for it is a very good matter that they cannot make seem bad'.

The court would have proceeded to judgment, but Elizabeth had been left, a prey to doubts and misgivings, while Burghley, Walsingham, and other councillors were at Fotheringay. At dead of night—the hour when her resolution collapsed in the case of the Duke of Norfolk—she summoned her Secretary and bade him tell the commissioners to suspend judgment and return to London. On their return her resolution stiffened; and the commissioners met again, reviewed the evidence, and proceeded 'with one assent' to adjudge Mary guilty.

On October 29th Parliament assembled. Knowing full well what pressure it would exert upon her, Elizabeth had been opposed to calling it: for the same reason the Council had insisted. It was altogether an extraordinary session: the Queen remained away, and normal business was abandoned so that all thought might be given to the great cause. As in 1572, Lords and Commons decided on joint action. After hearing the evidence, they agreed, with complete unanimity in each House, to petition for the immediate execution of Mary; and on November 12th a deputation waited on Elizabeth at Richmond to present the petition, reinforced by arguments from the Lord Chancellor and the Speaker.

Elizabeth's answer drew tears from many eyes. The depths of God's great benefits to her, she said, were bottomless. It was a miracle that she still lived; yet she did not so much thank God for that, as for the fact that after twenty-eight years' reign she did not perceive any diminution in her subjects' love for her. 'For your sake it is', she went on, 'that I desire to live.' 'I take no such pleasure in it that I should much wish it, nor conceive such horror in death that I should greatly fear it; and yet I say not, but if the stroke were coming, perchance flesh and blood would be moved with it and seek to shun it. I have had good experience and trial of this world: I know what it is to be a subject, what to be a sovereign, what to have good neighbours, and sometimes meet evil willers. I have found treason in trust, seen great benefits little regarded.' It had been, it still was, she declared, her grievous thought that one of her own sex, estate, and kin should be consenting to her death. She bore Mary no malice. After the discovery of the conspiracy, she had written secretly to her in order, if she would confess all, to cover her shame and save her from reproach. Mary had steadfastly denied her guilt. Even now, if she thought she would truly repent, she would most willingly pardon and remit her offence. The deputation was dismissed with promise of a message.

When the message came, it was to ask whether some way could not possibly be found other than taking Mary's life. Both Houses, again with unhesitating unanimity, concluded it could not; and on November 24th they came to Richmond, prepared with 'invincible reasons', to show that neither by expectation of a change of heart in Mary, nor by safer guarding of her person, nor by her word or oath, nor by hostages from other princes, nor by her banishment, nor by revocation of the Bull of Pius V, nor yet by the bonds or word of a prince or of any or all the princes, her allies, nor by any other way or means whatsoever, other than the speedy execution of Mary, could true religion, the Queen's life, and the realm be secure. 'Full grievous is the way', answered Elizabeth: 'that I, who have in my time pardoned so many rebels, winked at so many treasons . . . should now be forced to this proceeding against such a person'. What, she asked, will my enemies not say, 'when it shall be spread, that for the safety of herself a maiden Queen could be content to spill the blood, even of her own kinswoman?' She would give no decision: deeds, not words, must answer their demand. And so, she asked them to be content with 'an answer-answerless'. This Parliament, Burghley bitterly remarked, will be nicknamed 'a parliament of words'. But the pressure on the Queen was great, and on December 2nd, when Parliament was prorogued till the following February, Elizabeth promised to publish the sentence against Mary, a promise she immediately fulfilled, to the inexpressible joy of Londoners, who again rang their bells, lit bonfires and sang psalms.

Meanwhile, Mary was at Fotheringay—according to Paulet, 'utterly void of all fear of harm', and plaguing him with 'superfluous and idle speeches'. On November 16th, Elizabeth sent to warn her of the sentence against her, of Parliament's petition, and the possibility of death. She did not flinch. No repentence, no submission, no acknowledgement of her fault, no craving for pardon could be drawn from her. She sat down to make her appeal to the world and posterity in eloquent and impassioned letters. She was playing her last act, still with a great heart, still without scruple. Her declarations to the Pope, though written in the solemn, confessional mood of death, are, some of them, sorry lies. And yet there was a sound instinct in the presentation of herself as a martyr for the Catholic faith. The Catholic struggle in England had been personified in her. She wished to die in that role. When Paulet took down her cloth of state, she now being a woman dead to the law and incapable of all dignities, she set in its place pictures of Christ's Passion, and a Cross.

How happy would Elizabeth have been if she could have found any elation in the part that she had to play! Its necessity she probably recognized, but she shrank from the deed and the infamy of it. We princes, she told Parliament, are set on a stage in the sight of all the world; a spot is soon spied in our garments, a blemish quickly noted in our doings. Mary's death could not be a domestic incident: ambassadors from the French King and James of Scotland were at Court to remind her of that. It was only a few months since James had finally concluded a league with Elizabeth, and his vigorous intercession for his mother's life seemed at first to threaten the invaluable alliance. But Master James was still first and foremost interested in Master James; and very broad hints about jeopardizing his succession to the English throne, brought a remarkable private letter from him to Leicester: 'How fond and inconstant I were if I should prefer my mother to the title, let all men judge. My religion ever moved me to hate her course, although my honour constrains me to insist for her life'. His people were also a constraint, for the Scots, who had once cried 'Burn the whore!' were irate at the thought of Englishmen ridding them of their outcast Queen.

In January a curious plot against the Queen's life was revealed, involving the French ambassador and his secretary. Possibly it was a trick to put an end to the ambassador's intercessions, and to frighten Elizabeth. Whatever it was, the suspense was becoming intolerable and dangerous. At the turn of the month and through the first days of

February, rumour swept like wildfire through the country: that the Queen of Scots had broken out of prison, London was on fire, thousands of Spaniards landed in Wales, and so on. Precepts and the hue and cry ran from place to place, from out of the north into the south and down to Cornwall. Every man was in arms, the roads guarded; the country stood wondering, but its loyalty proved unshakable.

Elizabeth could hesitate no longer. On February 1st she signed the death warrant. Walsingham was sick, and the second Secretary, William Davison, who had been appointed to the office only on September 30th, was in attendance. She bade him tell Walsingham the news: 'The grief thereof will go near to kill him outright!'

Elizabeth had more to say. There were two ways of putting Mary to death—judicial execution, and assassination. The Scottish ambassador, Leicester, and others had apparently urged the latter way, and one, Wingfield, was prepared to do the deed. The Oath of Association gave moral sanction; and a pardon was promised to cover legal difficulties. As Davison was leaving with the signed warrant, Elizabeth suddenly caught at this alternative, and ordered Walsingham and him to write to Paulet to sound his disposition. 'God forbid,' Paulet answered, 'that I should make so foul a shipwreck of my conscience'. And charity has forgotten Paulet's Oath of Association in the nobility of this sentiment. Elizabeth commented caustically on the 'niceness of those precise fellows' who had taken an oath to lynch Mary and were clamouring for her death, but must thrust the odium of it on their Queen, who did not desire it. There were in fact two minds, one of the puritan or godly-inclined, the other of the politically-inclined. The former we understand; the latter has so changed as to elude us. The politically-minded—and they included all sovereigns —were inexpressibly shocked at the idea of subjecting an anointed prince to judicial trial and execution: murder was far preferable. The Count of Aremberg, one of Parma's *entourage*, talking afterwards of Mary, said that 'it had been better done to have poisoned her or to have choked her with a pillow, but not to have put her to so open a death'. It was the opinion of the King of France and of others.

In signing the death warrant Elizabeth had gone as far as she was prepared to go. She expected someone else to take the responsibility and the blame for dispatching it; and the wretched Davison, perceiving that it might fall to him to be made the scapegoat, spread the responsibility to Burghley and other councillors. They quietly sent the warrant off.

Tuesday, February 7th, 1587, Mary received warning that she was to die the next morning. She showed no terror. She denied complicity in the Babington Plot, inferred that her death was for her religion, and forgave her enemies, in the full confidence that God would take vengeance on them. Much of the night she spent in prayer. About 8 a.m. the sheriff and his company escorted her to the Hall of the Castle, where arrangements had been made for the execution. She was dressed all in black, a veil of white lawn over her hair, a crucifix in her hand, her beads hanging from her girdle. She was forty-four, and, save for the fleeting days after her escape from Loch Leven, had been a prisoner for just on twenty years. The charm of youth was gone; she was corpulent, round-shouldered, fat in the face, and double-chinned; her auburn hair was false.

She wept much at parting from her servants, but was unappalled at the sight of the scaffold, draped in black. 'My good servant', she said to one, 'thou hast cause rather to joy than to mourn, for now shalt thou see Mary Stuart's troubles receive their long-expected end'. With well-meant zeal the Dean of Peterborough exhorted her to change her faith and win salvation: 'The hand of death is over your head, and the axe is put to the root of the tree, the throne of the great Judge of Heaven is laid open, and the books of all your life are spread wide, and the particular sentence of Judgment is at hand'. 'Master Dean', she said, as soon as he began, 'trouble me not; I will not hear you; I am resolved in the Roman Catholic faith'. He strove to proceed, but she cried out again vehemently, 'Peace, Master Dean; you have nothing to do with me, nor I with you'. While he prayed, she read her own Catholic prayers in a loud voice, tears flowing from her eyes. The two executioners helped her to disrobe: with a smile she remarked, 'I was not wont to have my clothes plucked off by such grooms'. Quite quietly she laid her head on the block, repeated '*In manus tuas, Domine*', and with perfect fortitude met her death. As the executioner lifted up her head, the lawn dressing and wig slipped from it, revealing her grey hair 'polled very short', save for a lock at each ear. 'God save the Queen!' he cried; 'Amen!' answered the people. 'So perish all thy enemies, O Lord!' added the Dean. 'Amen!' shouted the people. 'This be the end of all the enemies of the Gospel and her Majesty!' said the Earl of Kent; 'Amen!' again cried the people. One of her little dogs had crept under her clothes; it now came and lay between her severed head and her shoulders, in the blood.

'The day being very fair', wrote the Dean of Peterborough, 'did, as it were, show favour from Heaven, and commended the justice. The eighth day of February that judgment was repaid home to her, which the tenth of the same month, twenty years past, she measured to her husband'.

When the news reached London, instantly all the bells were rung, guns discharged, fires lighted in the streets, and there was feasting and merry-making. The citizens asked the French ambassador to give them wood for their bonfires, and when he refused lit an immense fire in front of his door. Elizabeth in contrast was grief-stricken. She could neither eat nor sleep. Pity that with her womanly sorrow she could not maintain the tragedy at its sublime level! But she had to play the politician. Her position was not unlike that of Catherine de Medici after the Massacre of St. Bartholomew: she had to resort to miserable subterfuges to turn the infamy of the deed from her—or turn it sufficiently to maintain her alliances with other sovereigns. 'I never saw a thing more hated by little, great, old, young and of all religions', the English ambassador in France wrote, 'than the Queen of Scots' death, and especially the manner of it. I would to God it had not been in this time'.

In Scotland the people were terribly incensed, and many cried for war. Libels were set up in the streets against James and his Anglophil ministers, and odious epigrams on 'Jezebel, that English whore'.

Neither Henry III nor James VI wished to be driven from their friendship with Elizabeth by popular clamour; and yet, for their honour's sake, they needed some sort of personal exculpation from her. Elizabeth had probably foreseen this and prepared for it by leaving the dispatch of the death warrant to others. She now declared that she had never meant to send it, that Davison had acted improperly in showing it to other councillors, and they in dispatching it. Perhaps she persuaded herself into believing her story; her mind had never been free from doubts, and had the sending of the warrant waited on her explicit orders, she would probably have revoked it again and again, as she had done with the Duke of Norfolk's warrant. Perhaps on the other hand she was doing no more than play a part, though if so, she entered so warmly into it that Burghley and her other victims seem to have been deceived. In any case, her wrath—real or fictitious—descended on those who had sent off the warrant; more heavily on Burghley, most heavily on Davison.

With this sorry story for her defence, Elizabeth wrote to James. So far, so good, one of his chief ministers, a friend to the English alliance, answered: 'If the Queen follow forth this course to excuse herself, and give some proof of it, without doubt the King shall love her and honour her before all other princes. . . . But, to confirm it to be true—I speak plain language—*necesse est unum mori pro populo*': in other words, to save the league with Scotland there must be a scapegoat. The victim was Davison. He was tried in the Star Chamber, and sentenced to imprisonment during the Queen's pleasure together with a heavy fine. He remained in the Tower—probably with ample freedom—for eighteen months, being released just after the defeat of the Armada, that is, as soon as Elizabeth could afford to take a more independent attitude towards Scotland. His fine was apparently remitted; he even kept his fee as Secretary till his death, and did not go without reward.

So ends a story over which Fate and Pity preside. There was no way out of Mary's tragedy of passion and politics other than the pathetic way of death. Its justification was the subsequent history of the reign. The Catholic cause lost its peculiar menace, as the obvious heir to the throne was now James of Scotland; and however uncertain his Protestantism might sometimes seem, or however troublesome his political scheming, he was not Mary. Parsons and other Jesuits transferred their hopes to Philip II's daughter, but in doing so split Catholic ranks. Any reasonable hope of a Catholic rebellion in England vanished, for when it came to fighting Spaniards—as it was to do in future years—all men were Englishmen. And so religion and politics were disentangled a little; very little at first perhaps, but the beneficent idea of toleration was born. Out of darkness came forth light.

CHAPTER XVII

WAR

ELIZABETH was now fifty-three years of age, and had reigned twenty-eight years. Relentless time had been at work. Many of the servants and friends of her youth were dead. Mistress Ashley had gone, long ago—'What a heretic she was!'—and few of the Cambridge humanists remained: Ascham was dead, and so were Nicholas Bacon, Thomas Smith, Thomas Wilson, Walter Haddon, Mathew Parker, James Pilkington—these and others who had gathered about the pupil of their friend, Ascham, and devoted themselves to the construction of the Elizabethan Church and State. Time's unpleasant hand was on the three outstanding men who still were with their mistress to face the approaching crisis of the reign. Leicester had grown stout and lost the sharp precision of his features; his beard and moustache straggled; he was a little bloated. Cecil was an old greybeard, groaning with the twinges of gout, and often from Court; an elder statesman, wise in judgment, still capable of tremendous work. Walsingham was a martyr to the stone, and he too could no longer be so assiduous in attendance; but his nature was as ardent as ever, his grasp of affairs did not falter, nor his cunning fail.

To the Queen herself, Time had been kinder. She was again in very good health, walking or riding, as her custom was, every fair day. Torpid neither in mind nor body, she renewed her spirit in the youthfulness of a Court that was constantly refreshed by new recruits. She had no tendency to stoutness, had not as yet became angular, and the impression that she made upon an observer at this time was of one who had been beautiful when young. Age enhanced rather than diminished her remarkable dignity. Sitting, dressed in white in her golden state coach, she 'appeared like a goddess such as painters are wont to depict'. Her reign had silenced the old blast of the trumpet against the regiment of women. Hated by her enemies, feared or loved by her subjects, at times the utter despair of her councillors—she might be all these, but no one could deny her success. 'She certainly is a great Queen', said the new Pope, Sixtus V, 'and were she only a Catholic she would be our dearly beloved. Just look how well she governs! She is only a woman, only mistress of half an island, and yet she makes herself feared by Spain, by France, by the Empire, by all'.

The disparity between Elizabeth's resources and her achievements, which impressed Sixtus V, was the miracle of her age. It was dependent on the rarest combination of inherited qualities, the popular arts of her father and the financial prudence of her grandfather. Without the former she would have been unable to fire her subjects with a devotion that turned her reign into a kind of romance. Without the latter she would have failed to feed or pay her soldiers and sailors; and upon an empty stomach romance soon wilts.

For all its drabness and difficulty, finance is the essence of Elizabeth's story. Her ordinary revenue—from crown lands, customs, etc.—amounted in the first twelve years of her reign to about £200,000 per annum, and in the last decade to about £300,000—a sum, after making allowance for the difference in the value of money, ridiculously small, and nothing approaching the revenue of her rivals, France and Spain. Financially, England was not a great power. Out of the ordinary revenue Elizabeth had to maintain herself, her Court, and the whole system of government. In a separate category fell what was called extraordinary expenditure, the chief items in which were fortifications and war. Here the Crown was entitled to call on parliament to come to its aid with taxation; but here only, for the normal cost of government was regarded as the private concern of the sovereign, just as much as the financing of a nobleman's household and estate was the nobleman's concern. Taxation was not a normal but an abnormal incidence on the country; and any sovereign, who, like Elizabeth, looked to popularity as the source of her strength, had to bear this in mind. Over the whole reign parliamentary taxation averaged rather less than £80,000 per annum; for the first thirty years, it averaged little more than £50,000. Thus, until 1588 Elizabeth had a total average income, ordinary and parliamentary, of not much more than £250,000 a year, out of which to uphold her royal magnificence, run her government, fight her few battles, and play paymaster to Protestant Europe.

Even before the war period began, the extraordinary expenses were frightening. There was a debt from Mary's reign of about £200,000; then, in 1559–60 came the cost of expelling the French from Scotland, and in 1562 that of the disastrous expedition to France. The two campaigns plus the debt totalled approximately £650,000; and these, though far and away the main, were not the only items. In other words, extraordinary expenses alone, in the first four years of the reign, fell not far, if at all, short of three years' income, both ordinary and parliamentary. Manifestly, they could not be met out of income, nor, with prudence, out of capital; though, in fact, considerable sales of crown land were effected.

To-day the problem would be met by the national debt. There was no such way open to Elizabeth. In this respect —providentially!—England was less modern than France and Spain, where, in the days when Henry VIII was wallowing in his father's legacy and afterwards in the spoils of the monasteries, and was relatively immune from distress, the monarchs had hit upon the device of raising money by creating *rentes*, or permanent annuities—a form of crown debt by means of which they could keep on tapping the wealth of their subjects, diverting money from economic enterprise into the prodigal ways of war and royal extravagance, until they could no longer pay the interest they owed, and defaulted, spreading ruin about them. Having no system of *rentes* to tempt her along the rake's progress, Elizabeth had to have recourse to short-period loans, raised at Antwerp. They were a worry and a danger. The interest was heavy, they were hard to renew or replace, and as the City of London usually stood guarantor, the goods of English merchants lay under the threat of seizure in the event of default. Hence a desperate anxiety to be rid of the incubus of debt.

A sense of economy was inbred as well as inborn in Elizabeth. Her income before she came to the throne had been small, and the financial straits of her early years as Queen compelled her to continue watching her charges closely. She managed, in spite of the rapidly falling value of money in her time, to cut down ordinary expenditure to about £135,000 per annum, thus leaving a surplus from her ordinary revenue to help liquidate her debts. And she did this without impairing the efficiency of government or casting the gloom of poverty over the Court, the splendour of which was the nation's pride and the monarch's dignity. Having got her finances into healthy order, she kept them healthy, notwithstanding the further heavy burdens that fell on her—as £93,000 to suppress the Rebellion in the North, half a million for two Irish rebellions in 1573 and 1579, and lesser, though far from negligible payments, like those to Alençon.

It was essentially a personal achievement, not managed without constant vigilance and an attitude towards additional expenditure that made ministers fear to mention 'charges' and commiserate with one another often and passionately. Parsimony is not a popular virtue. God loveth a cheerful giver, and we are His children. But there was no arguing with inexorable facts. Any relaxation on Elizabeth's part would have swept away her resources before a flood of demands. First, there was Walsingham, with his earnest lament that the Queen 'greatly presumeth on fortune which is but a very weak foundation to build upon. I would she did build and depend upon God'—that is, upon Walsingham's own profligate impulses: to-day, to pension the Scottish nobility and give James what he asked, rather than call the young rascal's bluff, which Elizabeth did; to-morrow, to smash Philip in the Netherlands, regardless of cost and other difficulties; the next day, to smash him at sea; another, to lavish all on Henry of Navarre. Many had Walsingham's disease, even Burghley sometimes taking the infection.

On the domestic front, there was that illustrious Order of Mendicants, the Court and nobility. Its members begged incessantly as they spent immoderately. The Queen had to help many with gifts and loans, for she could hardly let the nobility sink in ruin. Burghley's son-in-law, the Earl of Oxford, having galloped through his estates with princely extravagance and folly, had to be given an annuity of £1,000 by Elizabeth, paid quarterly. In 1579 Leicester owed her £21,000 for loans; and there were always people—courtiers, ambassadors, officials—craving and receiving this sort of indulgence, and in the end, perhaps defaulting. Begging for honours, begging for lands, begging for office! Every post, as it fell vacant—nay, on the rumour that its occupant was likely to die—provoked fierce competition. One unfortunate, attributing his ill-luck 'during the two first triplicities or progressions of his life' to 'the froward influences of the heavenly bodies', told Burghley of his woes: 'He sued, but the door was locked; he knocked too late, and so slept with the five foolish virgins'. Quite early in her reign, Elizabeth spoke of the insatiable cupidity of men. Experience confirmed her reflection.

Difficult as it was to make both ends meet, it would have been impossible without that strange system whereby most activities, from government to Drake's expeditions, were financially joint ventures of sovereign and subject. As in modern hotels, where the 'tipping' system still prevails, wholly inadequate salaries were left to be supplemented by fees and *pourboires*, a demoralizing custom which held equally in the private economy of noblemen's households. The unpleasant mendicancy and ineradicable corruption of the age must in large measure be set down to it, Queen, courtiers, and servants being the victims of a pernicious system, for which there was no real remedy. England had grown rich in the days of peace and prosperity, but the monarchy—still personal rather than national—had not been correspondingly strengthened. It could not tap the new wealth properly, partly because of the tradition that taxation was exceptional, partly because of the social forces that turned the assessment of taxes into a farce and rendered them inequitable and therefore burdensome.

No national debt; no long-terms loans; annual income a quarter of a million, increasing under stress by a further sixty per cent: only with this in mind can the story of the war period be appreciated.

Elizabeth faced the prospect of war with Spain in the autumn of 1585, when she sent Leicester with an army to the Netherlands, and when, following the seizure of an English cornfleet in Spanish ports, she let loose Drake on a marauding expedition to the West Indies. Neither constituted a formal act of war in her eyes; rather, the first was a precaution against an intolerable menace to England, while as for Drake, 'the gentleman', she said, 'careth not if I should disavow him'. Philip's patience stretched very far; she still hoped that he would prefer to make terms with his Dutch rebels and resume friendly relations with her, rather than add to his many burdens by war with England and the loss of an important trade connection. Elizabeth knew the limits of her resources, and was not so simple as to imagine that having once entered on war, she could choose when to withdraw. She was a woman. She had no lust for glory at the cost of her own ruin, commercial and industrial stagnation, and social distress. Consequently, when the Dutch envoys offered, nay pressed upon her the sovereignty of the rebel States, she flatly refused it. She did not wish to make war inevitable.

This, however, was exactly what Walsingham and Leicester did wish. And while Elizabeth proposed, Leicester disposed. Within a few weeks of his arrival in the Netherlands, without sending a word of his intentions to the Queen, he accepted the title and office of supreme civil and military authority, thus violating his instructions, jeopardizing his sovereign's policy, and—perhaps most galling of all —making a mockery of the eloquent pamphlet, published in

several languages, in which she declared to the world her
desire for peace, and her intention to seek neither territory
nor authority in the Netherlands. Her wrath burst like a
thunder-clap. To make matters worse, she was told that
Lady Leicester, whom she loathed, was about to join her
husband, 'with such a train of ladies and gentlewomen, and
such rich coaches, litters, and side-saddles, as her Majesty
had none such, and that there should be such a court of
ladies as should far surpass her Majesty's court here'. With
great oaths she angrily exclaimed that 'she would have no
more courts under her obeissance but her own'.

Burghley, Walsingham, Hatton did their utmost to calm
the Queen. In vain. She stormed at 'a creature' of hers, 'a
man'—as she wrote to Leicester himself—'raised up by our-
self, and extraordinarily favoured by us above any other
subject of this land', treating her with such contempt. She
gave peremptory orders that he was to renounce the title
as publicly as he had assumed it. Councillors delayed the
messenger, until her wrath cooled slightly, and his instructions were modified. On reaching the Netherlands, he ventured to modify the modification. 'Jesus!' she angrily wrote
to him, 'What availeth wit when it fails the owner at greatest need? Do that you are bidden and leave your considerations for your own affairs. . . . I am assured of your
dutiful thoughts, but I am utterly at squares with this
childish dealing'. A messenger told her that Leicester was
ill: she softened at once. Burghley maintained his pressure,
and threatened to resign. At last she calmed enough to realize that the harm was done and that public renunciation
of the title would spread dismay and confusion through the
rebel States. The trouble passed. But she forbade the Council to discuss Netherland affairs without her order, and kept
control of them in her own hands.

It was a sorry beginning to a sorry story. Finance was
the next worry. Elizabeth had been compelled, by the disastrous trend of the Dutch struggle, to pledge herself to
greater aid than she intended. She promised to maintain a
force, numbering, with certain garrisons, 6,000 foot and
1,000 horse, and costing £126,000 per annum. On the

basis of her revenue, and always remembering that she had both to anticipate the Armada—which cost her £161,000— and the need of the Huguenots for her help, it is quite obvious that she could not afford to exceed her commitment: indeed, it was foolhardy to have gone so far. Actually, she paid every penny that she had promised, and a little more. And yet, to her alarm and flaming disgust, she found that her soldiers were unpaid and considerable sums still owing from her.

There was a double explanation. First of all, in addition to the army in her pay, there was an English army in the pay of the States. Now the States were notoriously bad payers. Their commitments far exceeded their taxing powers, though probably not their wealth, as their patriotic and belligerent merchants were doing fine business, selling supplies at extortionate prices to all armies, including the enemy's. The English in their pay starved, and to keep them alive Leicester diverted part of Elizabeth's money to them. In other words, his position as Governor of the Netherlands made him a conduit along which English treasure passed into the abyss of Dutch bankruptcy. A consoling spectacle to Elizabeth, who believed in spending what she could afford, and paying what she owed!

Nor was this all. The army system lent itself with fatal facility to the corrupt inclinations of the time, soldiering being an ancient trade with traditions from the free, commercially-run companies of medieval days, when the captain hired out himself and his company, and armed, clothed, and fed his men, for so much per day. Payment was still made to the captain, whose one idea, often enough, was to get rich quick, or, if a 'Court-Captain', to desert his men in the trying winter season and flaunt himself at Court. He kept as much of the company's pay in his own hands as he could. There were certain deductions which were supposed to be made from the nominal amount of the pay: for shortage in the number of the company, and for arms, clothes, and food if they were supplied in part or whole by the Queen. The captains had their hallowed devices for dodging these. Their men melted away like the snows in spring,

but on muster-day they lent one another men to appear in
something like full strength. Everyone seems to have been
in the game—even Leicester, who had a troop of horse from
which to profit. One of his first acts was to increase his own
pay from £6 to £10 13s. 4d. per day, and raise officers'
pay all round, thus upsetting Elizabeth's financial calcula-
tions, and incidentally, breaking the terms of her treaty. It
was imprudent, to say the least; but Leicester was loftily
indifferent to prudence, and not too nice about duty.

Elizabeth thundered away at this laxity and corruption.
It is 'continually alleged', she wrote, 'that great sums are
due; yet why such sums are due, or to whom they are due,
and who are paid, and who not paid . . . is never certified'.
Each accused the other, and Leicester accused everyone.
She called for accounts; none came, and she refused to send
more money. Harrowing tales were written of the soldiers'
suffering. She only became the more determined to stop the
misappropriation of her treasure, and see the common soldier paid his proper wage. Learning that some disbanded
troops had been paid nothing, though their captains had
been paid in full, she immediately instituted an inquiry and
set up a committee of appeal and award for the men in
every county.

No sovereign could have been more sensitive about her
popularity, and the people were already beginning to murmur against the war. There was the constant drain of men;
there was also the tyranny and corruption that attended
recruiting. The local Justice of the Peace and his servants,
who 'pressed' men for service, only too often seized the opportunity to vent their spite or line their pockets. Some years
later, a candidate for parliament, who was 'pressing' men on
the eve of the election, was accused of levying only his
rival's supporters; while, instead of taking only twelve from
his district, he took forty and released the surplus for a consideration. One man, who was able-bodied, bought his discharge for twenty shillings. A certain John ap John, though
lame, impotent, and maimed, had to go to the wars, since he
had no money. The muster scene of Shakespeare's *Henry IV*
was good burlesque on the age.

Elizabeth was sick at heart over the whole business. 'It is a sieve', she exclaimed, 'that spends as it receives to little purpose'. There was scarcely a bright spot. She herself was spending the utmost that she could safely afford, the States were committed far beyond their resources. And yet, with a joint effort that could not possibly be sustained, the military result was a number of striking losses and no comparable gains. The future promised only disaster, and with English trade at a standstill and unemployment rife, she put out feelers for peace. Negotiations were actually proceeding with the Prince of Parma when the Armada was in the offing. Englishmen thought that she was being fooled; Spaniards were afraid that the peace-talk was 'an artifice of that exceedingly clever woman'.

But Philip at last was being driven into an effort to crush the wasp that stung him. His caution forsook him when invited to co-operate in the Babington conspiracy. 'As the affair is so much in God's service', he wrote, 'it certainly deserves to be supported, and we must hope that our Lord will prosper it, unless our sins are an impediment thereto. . . . Perhaps the time at length has arrived when He will strike for His cause'. Already, as he wrote, the conspiracy was exposed and its leaders condemned to die. Nevertheless, Spain was stirring. Her ports were active with the preparations of a great Armada.

There were sagacious landsmen, like Pope Sixtus V, who were not so sure that the mighty power of Spain would prevail against Elizabeth's petty kingdom, set like an impregnable fortress in the sea; but even they did not realize the significance of the struggle that was now approaching. It was to be a contest between tradition and progress, between a country that wore the laurels of the last famous seafight with the oared galley of the Mediterranean, and a country which, having no traditions but great opportunities, had been in the van of change and discovered the art of modern naval warfare. So completely was Spain dominated by the Mediterranean, that while Philip possessed a strong fleet of galleys, he had no royal navy of ocean-going vessels until he acquired the Portuguese navy in 1580. And even then, the traditions of galley warfare, concentrating on grappling with the enemy, boarding him, and fighting a land-battle at sea, controlled the tactics of his fighting ships, their unwieldy design, and the employment of soldiers for the fighting.

The contrast with England was striking. Here, the galley, which was not suited to the English seas, had never taken hold. No sooner was the modern navy established than its founder, Henry VIII, hit upon the revolutionary idea of mounting broadside guns in his ships; and gradually the tubby, unwieldy vessels of the time were displaced by others of more slender shape. Together, these changes permitted a new form of warfare, dependent on the sailing qualities of the ship and the range of its heavy guns. Rapid progress was made, especially in the hard school of privateering, where success went to superior sailing powers and better guns, and where, by sheer necessity, sailors had to fight as well as navigate their ship. To men like Drake and Hawkins the amazing potentialities of the new ships and the new warfare were a commonplace of experience; and fortunately for England, Elizabeth was intelligent and adaptable enough to use their experience. Hawkins was made Treasurer of the Navy in 1577, and the care of the Queen's ships placed in his hands, with wholly admirable results. Corruption was rooted out, scope given to new ideas. Drake was very much in Elizabeth's favour, not less because he was a free lance who did not mind having his actions disavowed in the interests of diplomacy. These men had not a shadow of doubt that they could beat the Spaniard. And no one was better able to hazard a prophecy.

But there was an Achilles' heel. Elizabeth's path to financial ruin, unlike Philip's, was bound to be steep. She could not afford to keep her navy mobilized and her people in arms, waiting while Spain dallied. The Lord Treasurer, Burghley, was in desperation for lack of money, and on the very day that the Armada reached the entrance to the English Channel, was to utter a prayer that if peace could not be had, the enemy would no longer delay. Perhaps the financial problem was not altogether a misfortune. Anyhow, it reinforced Drake's contention that attack was the best form of defence, and allowed him to try the strategy that was to embed itself in English naval tradition.

In April, 1587, Drake set out, with a small but choice squadron of ships, to seek the Spanish fleet in its own ports, do what damage he could, and prevent its various elements from assembling at Lisbon, from which the Armada was to start. It was a campaign of genius, without flaw. He sailed to Cadiz, and setting all the old-fashioned rules of war at defiance, entered the harbour in face of forts and galleys and destroyed thousands of tons of shipping together with a vast quantity of stores. In his own words, he had singed the King of Spain's beard: he had also demonstrated that even when the English ships lay becalmed, their long-range guns made galleys impotent against them. After Cadiz, he seized Cape St. Vincent, using it as a base to prevent the assembly of the Spanish fleet at Lisbon, and so throwing the enemy's plans into utter confusion. Then he appeared off Lisbon, and though the port was too strong to be attacked, rode there at anchor, defying the Spaniards with calm insolence. His final exploit was off the Azores where he captured a rich carrack homeward bound from the East Indies, with goods to the value of £114,000. Even as he put into Plymouth with his prizes, his strategy was at work, for the Admiral of the Armada, not knowing where he was, set sail on a wild-goose chase to the Azores to save the treasure fleet of the Spanish Main from a danger that did not exist. To this day Drake's campaign 'may serve as the finest example of how a small well-handled fleet . . . may paralyse the mobilization of an overwhelming force'.

'Just look at Drake,' cried Sixtus V in admiration. 'Who is he? What forces has he? . . . We are sorry to say it, but we have a poor opinion of this Spanish Armada, and fear some disaster'. 'El Draque,' the dragon, were words of terror to Spaniards. They declared that he was a devil and no man; that he worked by a familiar; in his cabin was a magic mirror which revealed his enemy's ships and all that went on aboard them; he could loose or bind the winds at his pleasure. 'The King,' said others, 'thinks and plans while

the Queen of England acts, and acts in earnest'. Philip was
a pitiable figure: sixty-one years old, troubled with gout
and a cataract in the eye, borne down with work and worry.
Between prayers and business, he was never idle, anno-
tating dispatches, signing innumerable documents, writing
minutes and orders. Like Elizabeth he was an autocrat, but
without the capacity to make proper use of others. His ministers were ciphers, and policy waited on the congestion of
routine business in his slow hands. But he was aroused by
the attack on Cadiz. No reasoning could stop him from insisting that the Armada must sail that year. Yet it was impossible: Drake had effectually scotched invasion in 1587.
And so the heavy financial burden of delay fell on Philip,
while Elizabeth prudently kept the greater part of her fleet,
immobilized, in dock.

There was a prophecy, long rife among Englishmen, that
1588 was to be a year of wonders. It proved to be the year
of the Invincible Armada. Philip's preparations were still
going on, confusedly, when in February he suffered an irreparable blow through the death of his able, if aged Admiral. 'God', was his resigned comment, 'had shown him
a favour by removing the Marquis now rather than when
the Armada was out at sea'; and he appointed a new commander. The moment was an extraordinarily favourable one
for Drake to have repeated his exploit of the previous year,
with quite ruinous effect. But Elizabeth was just then sending her peace commissioners to negotiate with Parma, and
military considerations, probably quite properly when all
the circumstances are considered, were sacrificed to political. The war-party was furious. 'Sir,' wrote the Admiral,
Lord Howard of Effingham, to Walsingham, 'there was
never, since England was England, such a stratagem and
mask made to deceive England withal as this is of the treaty
of peace. I pray God,' he went on, alluding to Burghley,
'that we do not curse for this a long grey beard with a white
head'.

As the day for sailing drew near, Spain gave itself up to
prayer, the King being on his knees before the Sacrament
two or three hours every day. In the middle of May the

Armada got away. The country was 'full of processions, austerities, fasting and devotion'; day and night Philip passed in prayer, miserable from gout in his hand. Then came the first news: the fleet had been scattered by a storm and damaged, and was reassembling in Corunna.

In England, meanwhile, all had been activity; impounding Catholics—the gentry in private houses, others in prisons —mustering, training, and arming the people to resist a landing, mobilizing the fleet, and ordering the several ports, subject to the burden known as ship-money, to supply additional vessels. Drake was vice-admiral to Lord Howard, Hawkins and Frobisher had commands; and, as Howard proved to be supple-minded, the new school of seamanship dominated the fleet. At Court there had been a conflict between old ideas and new, but in the end the new had prevailed; so much so that the main fleet, lying at Plymouth, had ultimately been authorized to sail for Spain and fight the Armada in its own waters—strategy difficult to grasp in those days, though it was self-evident to Drake and his friends, as it is to us. However, the movement was prevented by the winds of that unusually stormy year, and the ships were lying, wind-bound in harbour, when on July 19th news arrived that the Armada was off the Lizard. For some hours there was danger of being caught as in a trap, but by a remarkable and daring feat of seamanship they got their vessels out of harbour, while the Spaniards delayed. The chance peril was past.

In size and number of fighting units the two fleets were not very unevenly matched; but the English had an overwhelming preponderance of gun-power, their vessels were altogether superior in sailing qualities—'God bless them! they are most worthy ships', wrote one of the admirals—their crews were better, and their tactics were of the new school. The Spaniards were given no chance to grapple and board. The Spanish plan depended upon Parma, who was waiting with an army and transports in the Netherlands; and the Armada's instructions were to join with him, cover his crossing, and land its own army in conjunction with his. The business of the English fleet was to prevent the junc-

tion with Parma; also to keep the Spaniards from establishing a base of operations, as they were likely to try to
do, in the Isle of Wight. The two fleets made contact on
July 21st and commenced a running fight up the Channel,
the Spaniards being forced past the Isle of Wight and their
feathers plucked little by little. On the evening of the
twenty-seventh the Armada came to anchor off Calais, still
a more or less intact but injured and partially demoralized
fleet. The following night they were dislodged from their
anchorage by fireships, and the next day brought to battle
in considerable confusion. For all the Spaniards' heroism,
the English established complete mastery over them, drove
them out of the Channel past hope of a junction with
Parma, and would in all probability have captured some
fifteen vessels and forced the rest to their doom on the Zea-
land banks but for a sudden squall and a providential
change in the wind. As it was, with severe casualties, their
ships badly injured by gunfire, and short of water and
stores, they fled north before the wind and tried to make
Spain by sailing round the north of Scotland and the west
of Ireland. Many were wrecked; most of the men who escaped drowning, slaughtered. Scarcely half of the great Armada ever got back to Spain. Not a cock-boat of the English had been taken.

Meanwhile, Burghley, Walsingham, and others ashore
had been working incessantly, casting estimates and accounts, making an inelastic exchequer suddenly stretch to
inordinate lengths, handling the correspondence of the fleet
and land forces, arranging for supplies, transmitting orders
everywhere. Considering the resources of the Crown, the
unprecedented size of the fleet, and the expenditure of pow-
der beyond all possible anticipation, the results are worthy
of admiration, not blame. Shortcomings there were, at
which passionate warriors and statesmen groaned; but no
other country could have met such a crisis with anything
like the same vigour, resource, and efficiency.

As the Armada approached the English shores, Elizabeth
had thrown aside all hesitation and thoughts of peace, and
had risen on the tide of popular enthusiasm to heights of

true greatness. Burghley's son, Robert, wrote of the fine spirit she displayed when the news arrived that the fleets had just met: 'It is comfort,' he declared, 'to see how great magnanimity her Majesty shows, who is not a whit dismayed'. She spoke such words to Leicester that he spared not to blaze them abroad as a comfort to all. Two special armies had been formed, one at St. James's to guard the Queen's person, the other at Tilbury to resist an advance if the enemy landed. 'It was a pleasant sight to behold the soldiers as they marched towards Tilbury, their cheerful countenances, courageous words and gestures, dancing and leaping wheresoever they came.' A Dorset regiment is said to have offered five hundred pounds to be allowed to form part of the Queen's guard. Though the Armada was defeated, for a time it was thought that Parma would attempt an invasion—a misconception of his plight which even Drake, for all his sense of naval strategy, shared.

In this situation, and despite the fears of some for her safety, Elizabeth resolved to visit her army at Tilbury, where Leicester was in command. 'Good sweet Queen,' he wrote, when she told him secretly of her intention, 'alter not your purpose.' On August 8th, 'full of princely resolution and more than feminine courage . . . she passed like some Amazonian empress through all her army.' 'Lord bless you all,' she cried, as the men fell on their knees and prayed for her. The following day, mounted on a stately steed, with a truncheon in her hands, she witnessed a mimic battle and afterwards reviewed the army. Nothing could surpass the felicity of the speech that she made to them:

My loving people, we have been persuaded by some that are careful of our safety, to take heed how we commit ourselves to armed multitudes, for fear of treachery. But I assure you, I do not desire to live to distrust my faithful and loving people. Let tyrants fear. I have always so behaved myself that, under God, I have placed my chiefest strength and safeguard in the loyal hearts and good will of my subjects; and therefore I am come amongst you, as you see, at this time, not for my recreation and disport, but being resolved, in the midst and heat of the battle, to live or die amongst you all, to lay down for my God, and for my kingdom, and for my people, my honour and my blood, even in the dust. I know I have the body of a weak and feeble woman, but I have the heart and stomach of a king, and of a king of England too, and think foul scorn that Parma or Spain, or any prince of Europe should dare to invade the borders of my realm; to which, rather than any dishonour shall grow by me, I myself will take up arms, I myself will be your general, judge, and rewarder of every one of your virtues in the field. I know, already for your forwardness you have deserved rewards and crowns; and we do assure you, in the word of a prince, they shall be duly paid you.

The men gave a mighty shout. At noon that day, as Elizabeth was at dinner with Leicester, word was brought that Parma intended to come out on the spring tide. She thereupon grew a conceit that she could not in honour return to London while there was a likelihood of the enemy arriving. 'Thus your Lordship seeth,' wrote Walsingham, 'that this place breedeth courage.'

The demobilizing of the fleet and army was set going with what may seem—and seemed then to the warriors in enjoyment of pay—reckless haste; as though the elation of the Queen's spirit had suddenly collapsed before the old, fierce parsimony. Burghley put her defence quite briefly: 'To spend in time convenient is wisdom; to continue charges without needful cause bringeth repentance'. Elizabeth may have thought that she took a slight risk—in fact, she took none—but she gambled on fortune, doing so in order to conserve her own and her people's resources, and be in a position to pay her debts. It was no idle or insignificant promise that she made to her army at Tilbury to pay them their wages. It was a chronic fault in both public and private economy to pay servants, and particularly soldiers, perfunctorily and partially. The Dutch States thought they had done well if they paid six months out of twelve; and in the Netherlands and among German mercenaries, it was accounted great good fortune to be in the Queen of England's pay. It is a sad thought that while battle slew a mere hundred during the fight with the Armada, epidemic disease afterwards raged in the fleet and slew its thousands. But once again there was no novelty in the fact: disease also decimated the Spaniards.

Much had been at stake in the great fight; nothing less than the fortune of Protestantism. And throughout Christendom, Catholic and Protestant had been praying, hoping, fearing for the champions of their faith. On the eve of the Armada, the sentence of excommunication against Elizabeth had been re-issued, and a tract printed under the name of Allen, Cardinal of England, and founder of the Douai Seminary—'An Admonition to the Nobility and People of England and Ireland concerning the present wars, made for the execution of His Holiness' Sentence.' Anticipating victory, the voice of the Catholic exiles had spoken in this tract with unbridled vituperation against Elizabeth: 'an incestuous bastard, begotten and born in sin of an infamous courtesan, Anne Boleyn'; 'she hath intruded the very refuse of the worst sort of mortal men, infamous, amorous apostates and heretics, to all the spiritual dignities'; 'she hath exalted one special extortioner—Leicester—whom she took up first of a traitor and worse than naught, only to serve her filthy lust . . . ; with the aforesaid person and divers others she hath abused her body . . . by unspeakable and incredible variety of lust, which modesty suffereth not to be remembered, neither were it to chaste ears to be uttered how shamefully she hath defiled and infamed her person and country, and made her Court as a trap, by this damnable and detestable art, to intangle in sin and overthrow the young sort of nobility and gentlemen of the land, whereby she is become notorious to the world, and in other countries a common fable for this her turpitude.'

The first news which the Continent received of the fight, gathered and broadcast by Mendoza, now Spanish ambassador at Paris, told of a Spanish victory: Drake had been defeated and fifteen of his ships, including the flagship, sunk. Great was the rejoicing in Spain. People in their richest attire careered through the streets on horseback, crying out that the great dog Francis Drake was a prisoner in chains and fetters; at night they made bonfires and amused themselves reviling Elizabeth. In Rome the Spanish ambassador informed the Pope of the victory, but Sixtus was sceptical: two reports, he pointed out, when from the same source are not confirmatory. A few days later, while the truth was still unknown, he broke into eulogy of Elizabeth and Drake: 'Have you heard how Drake with his fleet has offered battle to the Armada?' he asked. 'With what courage! Do you think he showed any fear? He is a great captain.' And he went on to recount his various exploits.

When the first inklings of the truth reached Philip, he faced his disappointment with devout resignation. 'In God's actions,' he said, 'reputation is neither lost nor gained: it is best not to talk of it'. Further false reports from Paris raised his spirits again, only to be dashed by Parma's dispatches. And at last came the shattered remnant of the Armada itself to tell of disaster beyond all expectation. Philip said nothing. He shut himself up in the Escurial and gave himself to prayer; no one dared speak to him but his confessor. The people hung their heads in shame and mourning.

In England the nation exulted and thanked God. Had not the ballad-writer prophesied?

> The Lord no doubt is on our side
> which soon will work their fall.

The legend on the Armada medal told how God, in the shape of the winds, blew and the Spaniards were dispersed —a travesty of His part in the battle as well as the navy's. On August 20th the Mayor and Corporation attended St. Paul's in state to give thanks for the victory. On September 8th there was a special sermon at Paul's Cross, when the captured banners were displayed; and again there was a sermon and another day of joy on Sunday, November 17th, which was Accession Day. The Tuesday was kept holiday throughout the realm, with sermons, psalm-singing, and bonfires; and the following Sunday the Queen came in procession to St. Paul's, such another spectacle as at her Coronation, with the City companies in their liveries, and waits over the gate of Temple Bar to make fine music. Ballads were to be had telling of the glorious fight, of the Queen's visit to Tilbury, and of

> The famous deeds that this our sacred Queen
> Performed hath, sithence Sol hath passed the Signs
> Just thirty times with those his shining lights.

But in the midst of joy, a great sorrow had fallen on Elizabeth, for on his way to Kenilworth Leicester had been taken with a 'continual fever', and died on September 4th. He had written on August 29th to inquire after her health, 'the chiefest thing in this world' that he prayed for. She wrote on the letter, *HIS LAST LETTER*.

CHAPTER XVIII

TROUBLESOME SUBJECTS

In the February following the defeat of the Armada Parliament met to answer the inevitable call for money. At the Queen's right hand, on the opening day, stood Sir Christopher Hatton. He had become Lord Chancellor in April, 1587, an appointment which Elizabeth made with strong misgivings, on account of the unpleasant comment to which it was likely to give rise. For Hatton, though once a student of the Inns of Court, was not a lawyer as his two predecessors had been. He had danced his way into favour, 'a mere vegetable of the Court, that sprung up at night'. However, like other favourites he was a man of real capacity, and Elizabeth had turned him into a councillor and statesman, who by his work and influence had come latterly to rank with Leicester, Burghley, and Walsingham as one of the four most influential men in the government, a person deserving great office. The appointment was not unreasonable, and if it emphasized the political side of the Chancellor's office, Hatton's prudence saved it from failure on the legal side.

To Hatton fell the task of making the opening speech of the Parliament. He struck the note of the time, a fierce vituperative hatred of the Pope and all his works. He inveighed against the raging Bull and slanderous calumniations of that monster Pius V; against the tag and rag of seminary priests sent hither pell-mell, thick and threefold, to increase the number of potential rebels under pretence of planting popery; against the unchristian fury of the Pope—'that wolfish

bloodsucker'—and of the Spaniard—'that insatiable tyrant'
—turned against a Virgin Queen, a famous lady, and a country which embraced without corruption in doctrine the true
and sincere religion of Christ; and against the machinations
and writings of that shameless atheist and bloody Cardinal
Allen, a savage and barbarous priest. He was shocked that
Englishmen—'those bloody priests and false traitors'—should
turn against their native country: 'I think it was never heard
of amongst the very Scythians. It is said that the snakes in
Syria will not bite nor sting the people that are born there;
but these most venomous snakes you see do not only labour
to bite and sting us, but, as a generation of cruel vipers,
to tear us in pieces and to feed themselves with our blood'.
He went on to praise the Queen's government and review
her life-story as the object of Catholic hatred. God had
blessed where papists had cursed, and multiplied His innumerable benefits upon England. He had defended Elizabeth and her realm, 'making the very birds of the air'—a
felicitous description of Walsingham!—as it were to reveal
the conspiracies of her enemies. The King of Spain, to the
wonder of all Europe, had suffered great loss and dishonour. He was unlikely to make himself a byword to posterity
by acquiescence. Consequently they must prepare their
defence. Their noble predecessors, though lacking their
means, had been able to defend England, and in their day
had been most worthy conquerors. 'Shall we,' he asked,
'now suffer ourselves with all dishonour to be conquered?
England hath been accounted hitherto the most renowned
kingdom for valour and manhood in all Christendom, and
shall we now lose our old reputation? If we should, it had
been better for England we had never been born'.

Of the answer there was not a doubt. Among thousands
of the poorer sort who, willy-nilly, had gone to the wars by
sea and land, there were hundreds who had gladly ventured
and were yet to venture and die. 'In troth, they were young
gentlemen, yeomen, and yeomen's sons and artificers of the
most brave sort, such as did disdain to pilfer and steal, but
went as voluntary to serve of a gaiety and joyalty of mind,
all which kind of people are the force and flower of a king-

dom.' Both Lords and Commons were inflamed with the same spirit. They granted an extraordinary, a double tax, and at the closing ceremony the Speaker, on behalf of both Houses, suggested that the Queen should declare open war upon Spain, offensive and defensive. He offered 'their bodies, their lives, lands and goods' in the service.

Parliament was passionately sincere. Yet for all that, as Elizabeth knew full well, lives could be more easily spent than pockets opened. Just before the money bill passed in the Commons a voice was raised in opposition, on the ground of the heavy burden of local taxation connected with the defence of the realm in the previous year. A lone voice it probably was, yet prophetic. Prophetic also was the caution that led the House to insert words in the preamble of the bill to save an unusual tax from becoming usual. Prophetic, finally, was the yield. Exhortations for something like an honest assessment in taxing fell on deaf or impotent ears. In one county, where there were many men of good living, none was rated at an income of more than eighty pounds. In the City, with its rich merchants able to hold the nobility in pawn, there were four or five assessed at two hundred pounds, none at more. The yield of the first half of the tax maintained the steady decline of the reign: it was only four-fifths of that thirty years before. The second half was less. The collection was spread over four years, yet did little if any more than meet the cost of war in the single year, 1588.

This explains why Elizabeth caught at the plan of waging her offensive naval war as glorified privateering. However inefficient or deplorable, it was the only way. Wealthy subjects jibbed at taxes, but they welcomed that strange mixture of patriotism and self-seeking, a speculative raid on Spanish wealth; and the 4,700 per cent return on Drake's voyage round the world still enthralled adventurous minds. Restless gentlemen, younger sons with their fortunes to make, or those whose taste for fighting declared itself in a turbulent age, when everyone was taught the use of weapons, eagerly went off on these voyages, taking such of their tenants, or their fathers' tenants, as they could induce or compel to accompany them.

In the elation of victory after the Armada, it was easy to organize a great army and fleet, a veritable counter-Armada, as a joint-stock enterprise. The Queen was a shareholder to the extent of £20,000, plus a number of ships and those vague surplus costs into which, to the annoyance of her tidy, financial mind, all enterprises ran—in this instance, trebling her outlay. In April, 1589, the expedition set off, with Drake in charge of the fleet and Sir John Norris, a famous soldier, commanding the army. After destroying the Spanish fleet in harbour, it was to land in Portugal and try to oust Philip from the throne. With them went Don Antonio, the Portuguese pretender, a bastard of the royal line, who since 1580 had passed between France and England, a forlorn suppliant, pledging his jewels, and losing everything save hope and a pathetic confidence that he had only to step on Portuguese soil for the people to rise and throw off the Spanish yoke.

The expedition started with a contretemps. One of Elizabeth's officials, the rising star of the Court, had stolen off to join it. This was the Earl of Essex. He was a young man of twenty-two, tall, well-proportioned, with a strikingly handsome, open face, and soft, dreamy eyes. Mind and spirit matched his person. He was the incarnation of poetry, a young aristocrat of irresistible attraction, impulsive and generous, the chivalrous, courtly knight of romance. All the qualities for a brilliant career were his, save judgment, an equable temper, and discretion. His instant success, when he came to Court in 1587 after a novitiate in warfare under his stepfather in the Netherlands, had been assured; for, in addition to being the ornament of his generation, his grandfather was Sir Francis Knollys, the Queen's cousin-in-law, his stepfather the Earl of Leicester, while his father had died serving the Queen in Ireland. Elizabeth was in the double position of a maiden aunt and a sovereign; and in both roles was interested in his career. In the latter she had to bind a young nobleman to her Court and service; and if the language used between them savoured of love, it was only the feminine equivalent of the adulation which in the next century was paid to Louis XIV; it was equally artificial, equally useful, and less abhorrent.

Elizabeth had taken the measure of Essex quite early. Delighting in his bright, youthful company, desiring his devotion, she was yet constantly trying to discipline his moody, petulant nature and turn him into a useful servant. Though so open and generous, he was not a person to live and let live; he was jealous of rivals, and in a Court where his failing was a disease, was soon at loggerheads with the bright star of the older generation of courtiers, Sir Walter Raleigh. He took huff at his rival's influence, resented an action of the Queen's, and stole away, intending to take his wounded pride to the siege of Sluys. Elizabeth fetched him back. He rose in favour, succeeding Leicester at the end of 1587 as Master of the Horse, an office worth £1,500 a year, in addition to a table at Court, the keep of his horses, and control of a number of subordinate appointments. A few months later he was made a Knight of the Garter. It might have been better had success been slower. A tale is told of his jealousy at this time. Sir Charles Blount, a young, attractive aristocrat, having run well at the tilt, was presented with a gold chess-queen by Elizabeth, and appeared next day at Court with it tied to his arm by a crimson ribbon. Spying it, Essex exclaimed, 'Now I perceive every fool must have a favour'. A duel followed in which Essex was wounded. 'God's death!' Elizabeth angrily exclaimed, 'it was fit that some one or other should take him down and teach him better manners, otherwise there will be no rule with him'. Not long after, Essex challenged Raleigh to a duel, but the Council interfered and tried to prevent Elizabeth hearing of it. It was a question whether this high-spirited thoroughbred could be tamed and used in the service of crown and country, or whether the attempt to tame would break him. Time was to give the answer.

Drake and Norris's expedition, with its double appeal of adventure and lucre, swept Essex into this next indiscretion. He was living far beyond his means, being in this, as in all his actions, incorrigibly reckless, and was about £23,-

ooo in debt. As the Queen, though exceedingly good to
him, was tiring of his begging suits, he resolved to steal
away with Drake. 'If I speed well, I will adventure to be
rich; if not, I will not live to see the end of my poverty,'
he wrote. Leaving behind the keys of his desk, in which
were some forty letters to his friends, he rode one night to
Plymouth, determined to be stayed by no commandment,
excepting death. The next day Knollys was sent posting
after him; at night my Lord Huntingdon followed Knollys.
But Essex had gone straight aboard one of the Queen's
ships, and with the connivance and company of the second
in military command, Sir Roger Williams, put to sea without the fleet, nine days ahead of it.

In trying to stop the truant, Elizabeth was not acting as
an amorous, elderly woman, but as a Queen, one of whose
officials had forsaken his post and duty at Court without
leave. She wanted no noblemen on this expedition, exerting
the authority of birth without experience and judgment:
least of all did she want Essex's rash hand in the business.
When she learnt that he was beyond reach and that Sir
Roger Williams had deserted his command, taking a royal
ship with him—an act of gross indiscipline and contempt,
and no happy augury for the successful conduct of the expedition—her indignation passed all bounds. She sent a letter after Norris and Drake commanding them, if they had
not already inflicted on Williams the punishment of death,
which by all laws his conduct deserved, to deprive him of
his command and place him under arrest: 'As we have authority to rule, so we look to be obeyed'. Essex was to be
dispatched home forthwith. 'These be no childish actions',
she wrote, 'nor matters wherein you are to deal by cunning
of devices to seek evasions, as the custom of lawyers is'.
Walsingham remarked that the letter was as mild as could
be expected! He relied on Norris and Drake, being men of
courage, to disobey the Queen rather than provoke mutiny
by harsh proceedings against such a popular soldier as Williams. A young relative of the Queen's, Robert Carey, had
intended to steal away with Essex, but to his great sorrow
got left behind. To console himself, he took on a bet to

walk to Berwick in twelve days, and made two thousand pounds by it—a better investment than the Portugal voyage was to prove.

The expedition was a failure. It went to Corunna where there was only one Armada ship to be destroyed, and not to another port where there were forty: Elizabeth—with what justification we do not know—accused them of seeking profit, not service. The men got drunk on the wine captured in the lower town, thereby, it was said, inducing the disease that later devastated the ships. Corunna, though on the whole a glorious achievement, sapped the strength of the expedition to little effect. Lisbon was the next objective and on the way Essex and Williams joined the fleet. Everything now went wrong. A needlessly long march on the city, a brave but ineffective show before it, retreat to the ships: such was the story. Scarcely a soul declared for Don Antonio, the Spanish governor with ruthless severity seeing to that. The fleet should have gone to the Azores before returning to England, but disease was rampant, and winds unfavourable. It sailed home instead. At least eight thousand men out of fifteen thousand were dead, most from disease; and little more had been achieved than a very live sense of superiority over the Spaniard. Drake and Norris were called to account; and Drake went into retirement.

Perhaps the failure discredited grand naval designs: certainly it was a warning to private speculators against joint-stock ventures of a more national than piratical character. But so far as Elizabeth was concerned, it was really financial considerations that governed her warfare, and events in France were now threatening to absorb her remaining resources in further and unsatisfactory military campaigns. There was therefore no choice but to leave naval warfare for the time being to a host of privateers, great and small, with occasional help from the royal fleet.

While Essex was playing his youthful pranks and the Portugal voyage, according to reports, proceeding with little judgment but plenty of dash, at home the same wayward spirit of the age was throwing the Church into turmoil. To

passionate minds Elizabeth's reign had declared itself more
and more as a crusade of God's Englishmen against the sons
of Belial. Little wonder that the keenest spirits among
clergy and laity were attracted to the party that wanted to
go the whole hog in reform, strip the Church of the ac-
cretions of centuries, and get back to the purity and simplicity of apostolic times, to the Church as God meant it
to be. The episcopal Church of England was worldly and
corrupt, reflecting in this the shortcomings of the age. Not
recking that Calvin had been able to maintain his theocracy
at Geneva, with its inquisitorial moral and religious discipline, only through the influx of ardent refugees from
France and the Netherlands, these men saw in that community the City of God on earth, and were determined to
build the same sombre Jerusalem in England's green and
pleasant land.

Elizabeth expressed herself with no uncertain voice on
this Puritan desire for a presbyterian church, with ministers
and elders, and other officers, all subject to popular election, governing the Church through a presbytery or con-
sistory for each congregation, and provincial and national
synods. It consorted not at all with monarchy, involved
revolutionary changes in the structure of society, and struck
at her prerogative, replacing her authority over the church
by subjection to it. It erected an intolerable inquisition to
pry into people's lives. To a realist, as she was, sensible of
the million difficulties on the road to perfection and of the
probable manner in which the Genevan system would work
in Elizabethan society, the simple faith of its advocates was
pitiable. 'Those kinds of platforms and devices which they
speak of,' she declared, 'are absurd.' They lead to intolerable innovation; they lack divine authority; they effect an
unspeakable tyranny; they are most dangerous to all good
Christian government. 'I see many', she told Parliament,
'over-bold with God Almighty, making too many subtle
scannings of His blessed will, as lawyers do with human
testaments'. She herself was not unread: 'I am supposed to
have many studies, but most, philosophical. I must yield
this to be true, that I suppose few that be no professors

have read more'; and among her many volumes, God's Book was not most seldom read. There was no reason to think her cold in religion: 'If I were not certain that mine were the true way to God's will, God forbid that I should live to prescribe it to you.'

There were things amiss in the Anglican Church: that Elizabeth knew. What vocation was without? she asked. So far as possible she was determined to have them reformed. 'If you, my Lords of the Clergy', she told the bishops, 'do not amend, I mean to depose you. Look ye therefore well to your charges'. She criticized them for making ministers of men who were unworthy to come into any honest company; of letting others be 'so curious in searching matters above their capacity, as they preach they wot not what—that there is no Hell, but a torment of conscience. Nay,' she went on, 'I have heard there be six preachers in one diocese the which do preach six sundry ways. I wish such men to be brought to conformity'. She gave order that those found unworthy to preach should be compelled to read the homilies: 'there is more learning in one of those than in twenty of some of their sermons. And we require you', she continued, 'that you do not favour such men, being carried away with pity . . . for they will be hanged before they will reform.' 'And now,' said she, 'I miss my Lord of London, who looketh no better into the City, where every merchant must have his schoolmaster and nightly conventicles, expounding scriptures and catechizing their servants and maids, insomuch that I have heard how some of their maids have not sticked to control learned preachers, and say that "Such a man taught otherwise in our house".'

The Archbishop of Canterbury tried to excuse himself and his colleagues, arguing that it was impossible to provide learned ministers for thirteen thousand parishes. 'Jesus!' broke in the Queen, 'thirteen thousand! It is not to be looked for'. Still, she added, if they cannot all be learned, they can at least be honest, sober and wise.

It was one thing to give such orders, another to get them carried out. But in 1583 Elizabeth had secured a real disciplinarian at the head of the Church. This was Archbishop

Whitgift, her 'black husband' as she playfully called him. His appointment could not have come at a more critical moment, for Puritan ministers had just begun a furtive attempt to introduce the rudiments of a presbyterian order into the Church, without tarrying for the magistrate. Though forced to exclude the laity from their meetings, lest they should fall foul of the law for conspiracy, they held regular and frequent district conferences of ministers, in this way exercising an unofficial discipline over certain churches. Moreover, they bound the whole movement together by occasional general conferences, which in time of Parliament met in London and partook of the character of a national synod. It was positively startling; such a jump into the modern world of party organization as no one, who did not perceive the genius of presbyterianism, could have believed possible in sixteenth-century England.

Just as this formidable and secret organization was being built up, Whitgift, at the end of 1583, opened his great attack upon the disorders of the Church, attempting to enforce conformity by demanding from every minister subscription to three articles, two of which were anathema to the Puritans. To the stupefaction of everyone, the country seemed to rise up and curse him. Though he did not yet know it, he was fighting, not individuals, who in isolation might have quailed, but a disciplined party.

The strange modernity of the story was shown when Parliament met at the end of 1584. The Puritans had ready a flood of petitions from ministers, town corporations, Justices of the Peace, and the gentry of whole counties. They held two general conferences in London during the session of Parliament, and launched their propaganda on the House of Commons, a body beloved by them, and the sounding board of passionate Protestant nationalism. The House was shaken, as also were councillors. Even Elizabeth was perturbed, but she stood firm for conformity, vowing that she would call some of the Commons to account, who had spoken disrespectfully of the bishops and meddled with matters that were above their capacity and outside their province. 'We understand', she angrily added, 'they be countenanced by some of our Council, which we will re-dress or else uncouncil some of them'. Firmness was never more needed to save the Church, for many of the council—among others, Leicester, Walsingham, and Burghley—sympathized with the Puritans, and bitterly resented Whitgift's treatment of them. Burghley wrote to the Archbishop denouncing his Romish proceedings, exceeding, he said, the devices used by the Inquisitors of Spain to trap their prey. But Elizabeth perceived, as Burghley did not, the nature and seriousness of the Puritan challenge to her state; and as an effective check to the baiting of her Archbishop, she admitted Whitgift to the Privy Council, the first and only ecclesiastic during her reign to be given that honour.

Between the Parliament of 1584–85 and the next in 1586–87, the Puritans were busy preparing a Parliamentary campaign beside which their first looks pale. Each district conference, or *Classis*, undertook a survey of the state of the Church in its neighbourhood, with the object of showing the need for reform, taking care to characterize the incumbent. 'A common gamester and pot-companion'; 'much suspected of Popery, cometh very seldom to his church, and is a whoremaster'; 'a very youth, a dicer, his father bought his benefice dear'; 'one that feareth the Lord unfeignedly'; such were some of the descriptions. The district returns were grouped and digested county by county, and then attached to a General Supplication to be delivered to Parliament. When the elections approached, they undertook election campaigns with the help of gentry of their persuasion; and prevailed upon a group of members to consult together and undertake their business in the House of Commons. To round their elaborate preparations off, they held a synod in London during Parliament, from which to direct the attack. In some respects this campaign is the most signficant episode in the whole history of the reign, for these Puritan ministers were teaching England the secret of effective parliamentary action, by means of which power was ultimately to be wrested from the monarchy.

One of the group which met to prepare the Puritan campaign in the House of Commons was Peter Wentworth, a brother-in-law of Walsingham's, and a man 'of a whet and vehement spirit', born to be in trouble. He was an interesting sample of a great age. In his first Parliament he had been on a committee sent to the House of Lords to explain why the Commons had cut out some of the Thirty-nine Articles in a bill they had drawn giving them statutory sanction. The House, he declared, had had no time to see how the missing Articles agreed with the word of God. 'What!' exclaimed Archbishop Parker, quite outraged, 'surely you mistook the matter. You will refer yourselves wholly to us therein'. 'No! by the faith I bear to God', stoutly answered Wentworth, 'we will pass nothing before we understand what it is, for that were but to make you popes. Make you popes who list . . . we will make you none'. In the next Parliament, shocked at the intimidation of a member for something he had said, Wentworth launched into a passionate defence of free speech, reproving the tale-carrier in the words of David: 'Thou, O Lord, shalt destroy liars'. At the same time, he denounced Sir Humphrey Gilbert for a courtier's speech, likening him to the chameleon; as that animal could change itself into all colours save white, so could Gilbert change himself to all fashions but honesty.

At his home at Lillingstone Lovell, Wentworth brooded on these experiences and on further experiences in the next Parliament, and the words of Elihu in the Book of Job came into his mind: 'Behold, I am as the new wine which hath no vent and bursteth the new vessels in sunder. Therefore I will speak that I may have a vent. . . . I will regard no manner of person, no man will I spare'. Taking this as his text, he prepared a remarkable speech, indicting Queen, Council and Parliament. Twenty times and more, as he walked in his grounds, his own fearful conceit, he declared, warned him that the speech would surely lead him into prison; but no sooner had a bill been read in the new Parliament, than he was on his feet: 'Mr. Speaker', he began, 'I find written in a little volume these words: "Sweet is the name of liberty, but the thing itself has a value beyond all inestimable treasure".' As the argument developed in his musical prose, he came to two things that did great hurt in Parliament: rumours of the Queen's anger, and messages forbidding them to discuss religious matters. 'I would to God, Mr. Speaker, that these two were buried in Hell. . . . The Devil was the first author of them, from whom proceedeth nothing but wickedness'. Hate all messengers and tale-carriers, was his cry. Yea, hate them as venomous and poison to the Commonwealth. Spare none, for the higher place he hath, the more harm he may do. Then, as a father over his child, he turned to take the Queen herself to task. 'None is without fault', he began, 'no, not our noble Queen. . . .' But there the horrified House, whose countenances showed their growing alarm, stopped him. They set a committee to examine him, and packed him off to the Tower —sorrowfully, for, in truth, most were of his mind though not of his courage.

Wentworth's loyalty was as intense as his love of liberty. On one occasion, a fellow commissioner was for letting their clerk, for brevity's sake, write simply, 'Queen Elizabeth'. 'What!' Wentworth burst out, 'Shall we not acknowledge her to be our Sovereign Lady? This is well indeed! I think some of us are weary of her. I am not weary of her for my part, and therefore I will have it set down "Our Sovereign Lady".' The tragedy of it was that Wentworth and other Puritans found themselves faced with a conflict of loyalties—to God and their sovereign. Their predicament in Parliament was once put by a member named Pistor, a man 'with a grave and seemly countenance and good natural eloquence'. 'The matter of his grief was', he declared, 'that matters of importance, standing us upon for our souls, stretching higher and further to everyone of us than the monarchy of the whole world', were treated of so slenderly. 'This cause is God's. The rest are all but terrene; yea, trifles in comparison. Call you them never so great, or pretend you that they import never so much; subsidies, crowns, kingdoms, I know not what they are in comparison of this; this I know, whereof I most thank God, "Seek ye first the Kingdom of God and all things shall be added unto you".'

It was a little group of such men whom the Puritan ministers had secured for their parliamentary action in 1587. In February, after the problem of Mary Queen of Scots was out of the way, one of them introduced a bill to destroy the whole ecclesiastical organization of the State at one fell swoop, and erect a presbyterian order in its place. Never had such a revolutionary proposal been made in Parliament before. The Speaker reminded the House of the Queen's veto on debate or action in Church matters, but they took no notice. In consequence the Queen sent to the Speaker and sequestered the bill. Thereupon, Wentworth rose to put a series of questions on the nature and extent of parliamentary privilege. He was for joining issue with the Crown on a fundamental problem, which if solved in his own far-reaching and quite unhistorical sense, would soon have disarmed the monarchy and made the will of Parliament supreme in the State. Fortunately, Elizabeth had got wind of the meetings of Wentworth and his little group—meetings which in those days constituted a serious misdemeanour. She promptly shut all five of them up in the Tower. At her command, some of her councillors in the House of Commons made a ruthless exposition of the effects of the Puritan proposals. A mixture of coercion and reason shattered the cause in Parliament, and in doing so, shattered it for Elizabeth's lifetime.

What were the Puritans to do? One of their leaders was for courting the common people in lieu of Parliament. When a fellow-minister expostulated, 'Tush!' he said, 'hold your peace. Seeing we cannot compass these things by suit nor dispute, it is the multitude and people that must bring them to pass'. With some, anger was getting the better of discretion. In October, 1588, Court, Church, and Country were electrified by the appearance of a witty, scurrilous tract, written by one calling himself Martin Marprelate, printed, so the title-page facetiously announced, 'oversea, in Europe, within two furlongs of a Bouncing Priest'. In rollicking satire it trounced the bishops and their assistants. A month or so later a second appeared. It had a list of 'errata, or faults escaped': 'Wheresoever the Prelates are called My Lords . . . take that for fault'; 'There is nothing spoken at all of that hypocrite Scambler, Bishop of Norwich. Take it for a great fault'. In February there came a broadside. A reply to the first tract having been written by Thomas Cooper, Bishop of Winchester, Martin, in his fourth tract, retorted, taking as his title the London street-cry, 'Ha' ye any work for the Cooper'. All this time, pursuivants were scouring the country for the secret press from which these very unsettling tracts were coming. It eluded them, moving from place to place, until after ten months of peril it was seized at Manchester through an accident with the cart transporting it. Another tract was got out, from another press. It was the last of the seven 'Martins'.

In the course of the hunt for Martin Marprelate, the ecclesiastical authorities came across traces of the Puritans' organization. A clever piece of detective work, in the vein of Walsingham's political ferreting, put further details in their hands, and then Whitgift struck. In 1589–90 the nascent presbyterian order, which had spread itself into about twenty counties, was destroyed and its leaders taken into custody.

A movement like that of the Puritans was almost bound to develop a fringe of hysteria. In 1591, when the principal men in the party were about to be tried in the Star Chamber, two gentlemen, obvious victims of religious mania, began to talk and write in a vague and dangerous way of coming disturbances. They fell in with a third person, an illiterate yeoman named Hacket, who seems to have been a blend of rascal and lunatic. Soon they had convinced themselves that they were prophets, endowed with angelic spirits, and their minds ran on a popular rising. Hacket told his two crazy patrons, whom he completely swayed, that he was to be King of Europe; then, that he was a new Messiah, anointed in Heaven by the Holy Ghost. 'Go your way both', he ordered, 'and tell them in the City that Christ Jesus is come with his fan in his hand to judge the earth. And if any man ask you where he is, tell them he is at Walker's House, by Broken Wharf'. The two rushed out into the streets, crying with a loud voice, 'Repent, repent!' and from a cart in Cheapside proclaimed their Messiah to a gaping, wondering multitude, announcing themselves as prophets of Mercy and of Judgment, and Hacket as King of Europe: the Queen, they said, had forfeited her crown. They were soon in gaol, and Hacket was tried and condemned for treason. At the gallows he fell to railing and cursing against the Queen, and in a Stentor's voice prayed: 'O God of Heaven, mighty Jehovah, Alpha and Omega, Lord of Lords, King of Kings, and God everlasting, that knowest me to be that true Jehovah, whom thou hast sent: send some miracle out of a cloud to convert these infidels, and deliver me from these my enemies: if not, I will fire the Heavens, and tear Thee from Thy Throne with my hands'. The horrified spectators shouted for the rope to be cut, so that he would feel the full agony of disembowelling.

'Let them take heed,' wrote Francis Bacon of the Puritans, 'that it be not true which one of their adversaries said, *that they have but two small wants, knowledge and love.*' It is a hard criticism of a movement that attracted some of the best minds and spirits of the day. There is no knowing how far their activities would have gone if Elizabeth had withdrawn her support from Whitgift or swerved from her principle that causes of conscience—as Bacon put it—'when they exceed their bounds and grow to be matter of faction, lose their nature'. If successful the Puritans would have changed the whole tone of English life and institutions. As it was, the movement, for the time being, was smashed and discredited, and the Anglican Church given the opportunity of nurturing a loyalty to itself no less heartfelt than that of Puritan or Catholic.

When the parliamentary agitation failed in 1587, the incorrigible Peter Wentworth turned to another cause that was thirsting for martyrs—the problem of the succession; and the same year he wrote *A Pithy Exhortation to her Majesty.* It was typical of the man. True and unfeigned love, he declared, forced him to utter unto his most dear and natural sovereign that whensoever it should please God to touch her with the pangs of death—as die most certainly she would—he greatly feared that if she did not settle the succession in her lifetime she would then find such a trou-

bled soul and conscience—yea, ten thousand hells in her
soul for perilling the Church of God and her natural country—as to be released thereof she would give the whole
world. He was assured that the breath would no sooner
be out of her body than nobility, councillors, and people
would be up in arms; and then it was to be feared that her
noble person would lie upon the earth unburied, as a dole-
ful spectacle to the world. Again, he feared that she would
leave behind her such a name of infamy throughout the
whole world as the forethinking thereof could not but
deeply grieve and wound her honourable, pitiful, and tender heart.

Wentworth hoped to revive this question—which no other
member would have dared to raise—in the Parliament of
1589, but the time was unpropitious, following a great victory, and instead he thought of asking the Earl of Essex to
present his *Pithy Exhortation* to the Queen. Before he could
do anything, manuscript copies of the pamphlet came to
light, and he was packed off to prison. Nothing daunted,
he wrote from there to Burghley, asking his help in persuading the Queen. He felt quite sure that his arguments
would convince a person of her rare wisdom and judgment.
Doubtless, he admitted, she would be offended when she
first read his tract, but the spirit of God in Solomon had
said: 'The wounds of a lover are faithful, and the kisses of
an enemy are deceitful'. He preferred to wound her Majesty
faithfully. Elizabeth's dry comment was that Mr. Wentworth had a good opinion of his own wit.

Released from prison, Wentworth persisted in his self-
appointed task. He tried to be a whole Puritan organization
in himself, and copied the parliamentary tactics of that
movement in preparation for a succession campaign in the
next Parliament. He came up to Westminster in February,
1593, equipped with speech, bill, objections and answers,
a thanksgiving to the Queen in the event of success, a rebuke in case of failure. He got a group of members together
—young men, not 'great parliament men', who had let him
down in the past—and planned their tactics. But his activities could not be kept secret. He was called before the

Council, and once more entered the Tower. There he remained till his death at the age of seventy-three in 1597. Though broken in health, he was indomitable. He refused to acknowledge himself at fault, nor would he purchase liberty at the price of silence about the succession. In him the intensity of spirit that made his age so great was at its purest, and insufferable in consequence. When he died, all the causes for which he had fought seemed hopeless. Unable to look into the future and see his place in the glorious pageant of political liberty, he had no solace but an epitaph.

CHAPTER XIX

ESSEX

As the years went by, Elizabeth continued active in mind and body. Six or seven galliards a morning, besides music and singing, constituted her ordinary exercise, wrote a courtier at Christmas, 1589. Her abstemious habits stood her in good stead, as did her scorn for the fantastic physic with which most of her friends dosed and disordered themselves. People began to comment on the vigour and youthfulness of her constitution: 'She need not indeed, to judge both from her person and appearance, yield much to a young girl of sixteen' wrote an over-enthusiastic foreign traveller in 1592. It was as though she had made a compact with Age and Death as well as with Fortune. True, she occasionally, very occasionally, had some little ailment; 'in another body no great matter, but much in a great princess'.

Her generation was passing rapidly to the grave. In 1589 she lost one of her oldest ministers, her Chancellor of the Exchequer. The following year the chief gentlewoman of the Privy Chamber, old, blind Blanche Parry, died at the age of eighty-two, a spinster like her mistress; another link with childhood broken. A few days later, Leicester's brother, the Earl of Warwick, died. Then in quick succession death came to Walsingham and his cultured, witty, brother-in-law, the lovable Thomas Randolph. Shortly before his death Randolph had written to Walsingham that the time was come for them both to bid farewell to the world, with its ensnaring employments, and set their thoughts upon their heavenly country, seeking pardon of

God for all their failings. Broken in health and tormented
with pain, Walsingham was petitioning for the peace of
retirement when the end came. The same year, another
councillor, Sir James Croft, a link with the Wyatt Rebellion, died, and after him the Earl of Shrewsbury, Mary
Queen of Scots' custodian. At the end of the following year,
Sir Christopher Hatton died. Elizabeth visited him in his
last illness and stayed the night at his house, one of the
many little acts of womanly kindness with which she was
constantly trying to allay suffering or ease the sorrow of
bereavement. Hatton had been a great builder and a sumptuous liver: he died fifty-six thousand pounds in the Queen's
debt.

A Spanish agent wrote to Philip II of the sorrow in England at Walsingham's death. 'There, yes!' the King scribbled
in the margin of the letter; 'but it is good news here'. Walsingham closed his eyes on a world that had at last framed
itself more or less according to his dream of a Holy War. In
July, 1589, eight months before, Henry III of France had
been assassinated by a fanatical monk—swift retribution for
the King's own desperate murder of the Duke of Guise and
his brother. With him died the House of Valois. The previous December the luckless Catherine de Medici, her
schemes in ruins, her name a byword for infamy, had
passed from the fever and fret of life, 'where but to think
is to be full of sorrow and leaden-eyed despair'. Another
woman ruler had died a failure.

The new King was Henry of Navarre, the Huguenot
leader. He succeeded to a country without a capital, and
to an internecine war for the succession; such a war as Peter
Wentworth and others feared would occur in England at
Elizabeth's death. The Catholic League, with Paris on their
side and Spain in support, had raised a puppet-king against
Henry. Elizabeth dared not let the League win, and so the
Holy War extended its terrain; another abyss gaped for
England's resources. Elizabeth's aid was prompt. Twenty
thousand pounds went to Henry IV in September; a further fifteen thousand in October. At the same time a small
army was sent over to Normandy under Lord Willoughby,

where it acquitted itself with gallantry and happy fortune, much to Elizabeth's delight. On such occasions she found the simple superscription of her name to formal letters of thanks, an inadequate expression of her feelings; and with a touch, that in a moment of time could dissipate a hundred grievances and bind a loyal heart, she signed one letter to Willoughby, 'Your most loving sovereign, Elizabeth', wrote on another, 'My good Peregrine, I bless God that your old prosperous success followeth your valiant acts, and joy not a little that safety accompanieth your luck. Your loving sovereign, Elizabeth R.'

The rapidity with which Elizabeth had acted, set Henry's feet firmly on the road to his throne. Yet the way was long and the resistance serious. The King was vivacious, as easy with his soldiers as with fair ladies, brave, resourceful, and sanguine; but penniless. He was altogether the most plausible and engaging of parasites, his need so desperate that scruples were foolish. Prodigal with his promises like the most consummate rogue with his cheques, he wrote captivating letters begging for money and men. He was ready to pledge himself to pay back loans in six or nine months, but then supplicate for further advances, or take an English army into his pay and later confess with disarming frankness that he had not a sou to give them, and borrow their wages from Elizabeth. In short, he sponged to the utmost limit on his affectionate and solvent sister. That limit was a prudent one. Elizabeth worked him a scarf with her own hands; she sent him an emerald, a stone reputed not to break so long as its owner kept faith; she wrote him inimitable letters; she offered lavishly—as she offered that canny young parasite, James of Scotland—pregnant advice flavoured with proverbs and maxims of statecraft. But she could not be seduced into going hand in hand to ruin, nor comforted by her prodigious wealth in Dutch and French promissory notes. Instead, she listened to the growing murmurs of discontent among her people, spent as little English blood in distasteful foreign wars as possible, and made a rough compromise between Henry's limitless needs, her own means, and English interests.

There was however a party forming in England, anxious for all the fighting it could get. Its motives were various. A correspondent told Burghley that he had heard two gentlemen boast over dinner of having made, the one a thousand marks, the other four hundred pounds, out of the Portugal Voyage of 1589: they had stayed at home and received the fines of new tenants succeeding to the lands of those who died on the expedition. It was said, he continued, that a west-country knight was raising a regiment for service under Henry IV, calculating that even if he and his fellow-officers received no pay, they would be well paid by casualties among their tenants. The wars were diverting the impecunious younger sons of the squirearchy from 'the gentlemanly profession of serving-men' into that of soldiering. And this new party of gilded youth—'men of action'—found a leader after their own heart in the dashing young court-favourite, Essex. 'I love them for mine own sake', wrote Essex, 'for I find sweetness in their conversation, strong assistance in their employment, and happiness in their friendship. I love them for their virtues' sake and for their greatness of mind . . . I love them for my country's sake, for they are England's best armour of defence and weapon of offence. If we may have peace, they have purchased it; if we must have war, they must manage it'.

Whether she liked it or not, Elizabeth had to continue her military intervention in France. A Spanish army had landed in Brittany, and she could not allow the Channel provinces to pass into Philip II's hands and become a base of operations for a new Armada. Early in 1591 she sent a small army to Brittany. Henry IV promised to support it with a substantial French force, but having a whole kingdom to conquer and being wily enough to see that Elizabeth dare not withdraw her troops, he broke his promise. What was more, he asked for a second army to help him in Normandy, baiting his hook with a promise to repay his loans out of the conquests. He also suggested that Essex, who was all eagerness to go, should command the army. Elizabeth was unresponsive. A rash youth and a light-hearted, penniless king inspired no confidence. Thrice Essex went on his knees, arguing and pleading with her for two hours at a stretch; more effective, Burghley lent his persuasions. Against her better judgment she at last gave way, though she took care to join some staider heads in counsel with Essex; a fruitless precaution, for what commoner dare gainsay the charm and impetuosity of that noble favourite?

The expedition, which landed at the beginning of August, 1591, justified Elizabeth's misgivings. It was sent for a specific object—to help Henry in the siege of Rouen; and for a limited time—two months. But the King was busy elsewhere, and characteristically, now that he had got the army over to France, wanted to use it for another purpose. To make matters worse, Essex set off to see the King, leaving his infantry idle at their base and riding a hundred miles through the enemy country; a rash venture, which if it had miscarried would have passed for the maddest folly. Truth to tell Essex had no sense of the responsibilities of command, but played at war as the most glorious of field sports. He entered Compiègne, where the King was, preceded by six pages in orange velvet embroidered with gold, he and his horse being covered in the same bright material, all strewn with precious stones. Six trumpeters sounded before him, twelve esquires followed him, and after them rode sixty English gentlemen. During their fraternizing, Henry and his nobles challenged the English to a leaping match, in which Essex 'did overleap them all'. On his return he had to send for his infantry to get him back in safety, and he closed a foolish escapade with a purposeless bravado under the walls of Rouen that cost him the life of his brother. One month had already passed of the two for which the army had been sent, and nothing had been done.

Elizabeth was furious. Henry, she thought, had made a fool of her before the world. She stormed at the officers whom she had relied on to control Essex: 'Where he is, or what he doth, or what he is to do, we are ignorant', she angrily wrote. Essex tried to appease her with a sweet, mournful letter, but risked her wrath once more by going off to help in the siege of a minor town, and there trailed a pike like a common soldier. He was ordered home, a command which struck such sorrow in him that 'all the buttons of his doublet brake away as though they had been cut with a knife'. Still his indiscretions were incomplete, for before leaving he knighted twenty-four of his followers, telling them that it was neither his fault nor theirs that they had been unable to win honour, but as they had shown great goodwill he gave them the honour they might have earned. It was foolish; possibly it was sinister. Foolish, because it cheapened honour, over which Elizabeth was notoriously as sensitive and careful as she was over her financial credit. Sinister, because it made the recipients beholden to Essex, as it were enrolling them in a personal clientele which might in time threaten the balance of power in the State. Honour flowed from the crown, and to use a commander's privilege to reward bravery in this light-hearted, prodigal manner was in fact to rob the Queen of a most intimate prerogative. The world scoffed. Burghley kept the news from Elizabeth, for, knowing her Essex, she had wanted to deny him the privilege altogether. When at last she learnt of his action, she is said to have remarked that 'his lordship had done well to have built his almshouses before he had made his knights'.

Essex came home for a few days, made his peace, and as the siege of Rouen was really going to begin, Elizabeth was persuaded to let her troops remain, and reinforce them. Buoyant once more, Essex on his return wrote her a seductive letter: 'Most fair, most dear, and most excellent Sovereign' he began: once finished with this expedition, nothing, he vowed, but a great enterprise of her own would draw him him out of her sight. 'The two windows of your Privy Chamber shall be the poles of my sphere, where, as long as your Majesty will please to have me, I am fixed and unmovable. When your Majesty thinks that heaven too good for me, I will not fall like a star, but be consumed like a vapour by the sun that drew me up to such a height. While your Majesty gives me leave to say I love you, my fortune is as my affection, unmatchable. If ever you deny me that liberty, you may end my life, but never shake my constancy, for were the sweetness of your nature turned into the greatest bitterness that could be, it is not in your power, as great a Queen as you are, to make me love you less'.

Elizabeth had stipulated that as her two months were ended, Henry should now pay her troops. 'Much more contented would we be in the pay of our blessed Queen,' wrote one of them. And he was right. Henry, as Elizabeth's ambassador put it, was a King without a crown, fighting wars without money. His own forces were in mutiny for lack of pay, and there was nothing for Elizabeth to do but recant and continue her charges. The siege of Rouen started, and went on, and continued to go on. The optimistic prophecies with which the warriors had tried to appease a thoroughly sceptical Queen, were all belied. Essex sent a challenge to the Governor of the town daring him to fight either a duel or a tournament, and was very properly answered that his office forbade him to fight. Elizabeth waxed sarcastic: the enterprise was becoming 'rather a jest than a victory'. She dryly told Essex that he could return when he had sense to perceive the wisdom of doing so. Then in January she peremptorily ordered him home. As he sailed out of the harbour he kissed his sword. The remnant of his army stayed on, but Rouen did not fall.

There was ample reason for Elizabeth's disgust and anger over this fatuous campaign. Her finances were being strained unbearably, and it was intolerable that a casual, happy-go-lucky king and an irresponsible young nobleman should fritter away her treasure to little or no purpose. In the four years from 1589–93 she spent about £300,000 in aid of Henry IV. Adding the cost of her forces in the Netherlands for the same time, this meant an expenditure on warfare of at least £800,000, apart from Irish wars and naval expeditions. In a single one of these years she was compelled to sell crown lands to the value of over £120,000.

While military campaigns were eating up money at a pace which the Queen could not long stand and causing popular discontent both with the cost of levying men for foreign service and with the heavy toll of life, it was impossible to indulge in ambitious naval operations. Nevertheless, the navy was far from inactive and played its part in partnership with private adventurers in the speculative game of commerce raiding, a form of warfare peculiarly suited to Elizabeth's limited means. When successful it benefited her exchequer, at the same time dislocating the whole military, naval, and commercial organization of Spain, which was dependent on the safe coming and going of the annual colonial fleets. Ninety-one Spanish prizes were said to have been brought into England in 1589. At the Azores, the happy hunting ground of the privateer, an observer was conscious of 'nothing else but spoiled men set on shore, some out of one ship, some out of another, that pity it was to see all of them cursing the Englishmen and their own fortunes, with those that had been the causes to provoke the Englishmen to fight'. The English were 'become lords and masters of the sea, and need care for no man'. Philip took the desperate step of forbidding the West Indian treasure fleet to sail in 1590, though a wave of bankruptcy swept over Spain in consequence. By the following year he had a fighting convoy ready, and it was this fleet which Sir Richard Grenville fought in the last immortal fight of the *Revenge*. Whether his exploit was a mad act of bravado, or self-immolation with sound tactics behind it, it was a supreme revelation of the fighting qualities of Elizabeth's newer ships. In a subsequent storm the weather- and cannon-beaten Spaniards suffered losses comparable with those of the Armada. Their sailors believed that Grenville was in league with the Devil: his body, they said, had sunk straight to the bottom of the sea and down into Hell, where he raised up all the devils to revenge his death.

In the following year, 1592, a syndicate in which Elizabeth was a partner, operating at the Azores, captured the largest of the great and fabulously wealthy carracks from the East Indies, after driving another ashore where its crew burnt it. No sooner was it taken than a saturnalia of plunder followed. All night officers and men were busy ransacking the ship, and four or fives times set it on fire with their candles. The chief officer on the spot, who was said to have taken £10,000 worth of plunder and confessed to £2,000, was the foremost thief; and the jewels, plate, silk, perfumes, etc., stolen may have amounted to something approaching £100,000. Most of the captains and their men, after pilfering what they could, had but a single thought: to sail home and smuggle their booty ashore before anyone stopped them. Their haste was such that the carrack itself, with its bulky, valuable cargo, came near to being left behind.

The indiscipline, the irresponsibility, the venality of the age! No wonder that Elizabeth entertained a profound distrust of needless expeditions in which much was risked. When the news of the capture reached England, merchants, shopkeepers, and goldsmiths flocked to the ports to pick up staggering bargains from the simple sailors: 1,800 diamonds and 200 or 300 rubies for £130! Portsmouth was like Bartholomew Fair. Elizabeth sent Sir Robert Cecil posting down to Dartmouth to recover the spoil, and as he rode along he could actually smell out culprits, hastening back to London with musk and ambergris. But all the inquiries and all the orders could do little: 'sailors fingers,' as a sailor said, were 'limed twigs,' and examining men on their oaths was 'lost labour and offence to God'. The principals who had paid for the undertaking had to be content with the main cargo: not a poor return for their money, for it was worth £141,000. Elizabeth took the lion's share, treating the other adventurers 'but indifferently,' Raleigh especially, if his own bitter complaints were true. Perhaps there is a good deal to be said for the Queen.

No evening quiet blessed Elizabeth's life. Home broils competed with foreign foes to fret her nerves and fill her with anxiety. Of the influential statesmen of the past only Burghley remained. He was now an old man of seventy-one, plagued by intermittent attacks of gout, when he was unable to walk or sometimes to write, and longed for the quiet of his beloved country house, Theobalds, to escape the throngs of suitors who haunted him in town and at Court. The situation was a challenge to ambition, threatening to expose the Court to a struggle for place and influence and to chronic faction like the first ten years of the reign. The obvious man to accept opportunity's challenge was Essex, on whom by birth as well as favour Leicester's mantle seemed to have fallen. His friends had already urged him to seek 'a domestical greatness like to his father-in-law'. But in the days before Rouen, when Hatton as well as Burghley impeded progress, the game had seemed too slow to his impatient mind. When he returned, a little chastened in his lust for military glory, Hatton was dead. Domestical greatness seemed merely a matter of competing with Burghley; a contention between crabbed age and youth.

What was more, a fellow-competitor for Elizabeth's favour, Sir Walter Raleigh, opportunely fell into disgrace, for he was discovered to have got one of the Queen's maids of honour, the blue-eyed, golden-haired daughter of Sir Nicholas Throckmorton, with child. It proved merely an anticipation of marriage, but both partners in sin were sent to the Tower. Very properly. Elizabeth was *in loco parentis* to her maids of honour, and for them to belie their name was an offence like the lapse of a Vestal Virgin. They enjoyed a coveted position, in daily contact with the Queen, with the chance of earning her intimate, lasting friendship, and with unequalled facilities for making a brilliant marriage. Like their manners and morals, their marriage was a royal responsibility, and it was a breach of duty as well as a gross personal affront to their sovereign to marry without her leave.

Elizabeth's interference in their love affairs, of which there are several well-known stories, was simply the exercise of this peculiar relationship, not the jealousy of a lascivious or envious old maid—though, indeed, 'a mixture of a lie doth ever add pleasure'. The Court was high-spirited, the age free; attractive young men, like the Earl of Essex, sowed their wild oats, and gossip told of 'goings-on'. But the moral tone of the Court was quite different from that in, say, France. Elizabeth would no more condone sexual laxity than Queen Victoria; and a spell in the Tower or the Fleet prison was the almost invariable punishment awaiting offenders who were found out. The Earl of Oxford had a base son by Anne Vavasour, one of the maids of honour: his mysterious imprisonment in the Tower and subsequent banishment from Court was probably for this offence. In 1591 a letter-writer retailed the talk that a Mr. Vavasour was imprisoned 'for Mistress Southwell's lameness in her leg' and Mr. Dudley sent from Court for kissing Mistress Cavendish. It is obvious that Elizabeth could not allow behaviour like Elizabeth Throckmorton's and Raleigh's to go unpunished without making her service the path to dishonour.

Raleigh did his best by exuberant specimens of the Court's pleasant conceit of love to make his peace with the irate Belphœbe. His cousin wrote to Robert Cecil how, hearing that the Queen was on the Thames, Raleigh had begged to be let row himself in disguise near enough to see her. On being refused he had become dangerously mad. 'Let nobody know thereof,' wrote the cousin; but in a postscript—quite needlessly—he excepted the Queen. This plaintive story—so redolent of the fanciful devices with which courtiers amused Elizabeth—was followed up by a letter from Raleigh himself to Cecil, on hearing that Elizabeth was going on progress. 'My heart,' he wrote,

was never broken till this day, that I hear the Queen goes away so far off, whom I have followed so many years with so great love and desire, in so many journeys, and am now left behind her in a dark prison all alone. While she was yet near at hand, that I might hear of her once in two or three days, my sorrows were the less, but even now my heart is cast into the depth of all misery. I that was wont to behold her riding like Alexander, hunting like Diana, walking like Venus, the gentle wind blowing her fair hair about her pure cheeks like a nymph—*Elizabeth was just on sixty!*—sometime sitting in the shade like a Goddess, sometime singing like an angel, sometime playing like Orpheus; behold! the sorrow of this world once amiss hath bereaved me of all. Oh! love that only shineth in misfortune, what is become of thy assurance? All wounds have scars but that of phantasy; all affections their relenting but that of woman kind.

This characteristic effusion—as artificial in conceit as any shepherd and shepherdess of contemporary poetry—must not, on peril of showing an egregious lack of humour, be taken seriously. Elizabeth did not take it so. She let Raleigh continue to expiate his offence against the fair name of her Court.

Raleigh was hardly a dangerous competitor for the position that Essex challenged: Elizabeth never had the necessary belief in his abilities as a statesman. But his disgrace removed the tongue of an enemy from Court. The great adversary was Burghley, in whom was comprehended his younger son, Robert Cecil. Burghley's eldest son had been a disappointment. His ability was mediocre: and when sent to travel on the Continent for his education, he had broken out into such extravagant and dissolute ways that his father feared he would 'return home like a spending sot, meet only to keep a tennis court.' He reformed, but there was no making a statesman out of such ordinary material. Burghley's paternal ambitions therefore centred on Robert, who inherited his parents' intelligence, and showed much of his father's aptitude as a statesman. But alas! he had been a weakling as a child, and grew up slight in figure and height and with a hunched back, probably inherited from his mother, though it was attributed to a fall in infancy. Elizabeth nicknamed him—in bad taste maybe, but not maliciously—her pigmy. His enemies gibed at his crooked back, calling him Monsieur de Bossu, or Arch-enemy.

It was a paradoxical situation: a gouty old man and his puny hunchbacked son contending with the peerless and brilliant Adonis in a Court where ability commended itself in a comely setting. But shaft never went wider of the mark than the idea that Elizabeth was a victim to the physical charms of her Adonis. There was too much policy, even in her friendliness. If a guess may be made at her intentions, she contemplated, in the new generation now attaining to power, a repetition of the old Leicester-Burghley combination, a blend of the noble favourite with the more dependable civil servant. From the first she moved deliberately and astutely along that way. On Walsingham's death Essex had tried to get Davison restored to the secretaryship. There is no reason to think that he acted from any other motive than friendship; all the same, if he had been successful he would have ranged the holder of this all-important position on his side in a future tussle for political supremacy. Elizabeth listened to his suit with patience, acknowledged Davison's qualities, then quite dispassionately, but with finality, refused. She left the office vacant, handing the duties over to Burghley. Possibly she already approved of Burghley's ambition to place his son in the post. Essex set himself to cross the plan. The only result was to hold up any appointment for years, while Robert Cecil, who was not yet thirty, attained the age, experience, and influence to justify his appointment and silence criticism.

In his matchless folly Essex engaged himself with such needless vehemence in these contests that he was always exposing his prestige and self-respect to severe rebuffs, and Elizabeth had to be careful lest she should find herself having to break him, a catastrophe that she did not desire, any more than she desired to lose the services of a brilliant young nobleman or risk in his fall the precarious unity of the country. She hoped to wear down his overweening ambition, which, as Sir Thomas Bodley said, she hated, and to thwart his intolerable monopolistic tendencies. And though temper sometimes got the better of her, she could and did act with consummate wisdom. She waited, for example, to make the second move in Robert Cecil's progress until Essex went away on the Rouen expedition. Then, within a day or two, she admitted him to the Council—an honour, which, significantly enough, she had not yet conferred on Essex—and associated him with his father in the duties of secretary. The office itself had to wait for maturer years and another similar opportunity.

The story of Essex might have been very different if he had not been more effective than his character warranted, owing to the service of the two brothers, Anthony and Francis Bacon. These young men—Anthony was born in 1558, Francis in 1561—were the sons of Sir Nicholas Bacon, and cousins of Robert Cecil, through their mother. Both were exceptionally able, Francis very far above all measure. Anthony was an invalid from boyhood; lame, subject to rheumatic disorders, and having constantly to dose himself with physic; 'a gentleman of impotent feet, but a nimble head'. Ill-health sapped ambition in him. At the age of twenty-one he went abroad to travel, and despite the persuasions and warnings of friends lived a desultory, expensive life abroad for twelve years. Francis was wisdom's child. The cold, clear light of human reason has rarely burnt so brightly. He wrote as an oracle; he spoke with the persuasive tongue of an orator. Nature, however, had shrunk from perfecting her miracle. There was a fundamental inaptitude of character, a lack of emotion, of virility, which left out as it were the keystone of the arch. He wrote to Burghley of his 'vast contemplative ends': 'I have taken all knowledge to be my province'. But his letter was one of many begging suits for place, and though he spun round these pleadings the noble desire to dedicate his splendid talents to the service of his country, his heart was in fact worldly, his ambition less noble than his words, his life less purposeful. His mind soared into the heavens, but his feet were of clay.

Bacon's desire for place was urgent in measure with his extravagant manner of living. As Burghley's nephew he at first looked to him, but fair words and the reversion of a remunerative office were not a solace in time of financial trouble. Disappointed, his eyes turned towards the rising star of the younger generation, Essex. Possibly his cold intellect speculated on Burghley's early death, and—as his essay on Deformity suggests, where he pointed the moral of his miscalculation—on the unlikelihood of his hunchback son attaining to great office and power. Probably, it was Bacon who in 1591 was plotting that 'domestical greatness' for Essex, which Essex then had not the patience to pursue, and admonishing him of the errors that he was apt to commit. 'I held at that time my Lord to be the fittest instrument to do good to the State,' wrote Bacon in later life, drawing the veil of noble motive over his activities; 'and therefore I applied myself to him in a manner which I think happeneth rarely among men'. He brought Phelippes, the decipherer and intelligence agent, into the service of Essex. Then, early in 1592, his brother Anthony at last came home. Here was the perfect instrument for creating an efficient intelligence or combined news and secret service system in other countries, which would enable Essex to compete with the Cecils in supplying the Queen with information, while at the same time establishing his own claim to be a serious statesman, well-informed, with valuable political connections abroad. It was a subtle attack on the Cecils in the very sphere of the secretaryship, which they were nursing for themselves; and it could not fail to impress Elizabeth, for 'intelligence' was at the heart of diplomacy, and she counted it a secret of power to be the best-informed person in England, and therefore in Europe. Her eyes were in every place, beholding the evil and the good. 'Tush, Brown!' she said to a servant of hers over from the Netherlands, who was explaining the position of affairs there, 'I know more than thou doest'; and poured forth her own comment and prophecy. And when he ventured a remark on French affairs, she interrupted again: 'Tush, Brown! do not I know?'

The plot worked, for in February, 1593, Essex was admitted to the Council. Impulsively he became a new man, clean forsaking 'all his former youthful tricks', and carrying himself 'with very honourable gravity.' He even resolved to set about paying his debts: 'which,' wrote his man of business, 'in all likelihood he will perform'. But the man of business no doubt calculated, not on the mood of the penitent-stool, but on the perquisites of power, the New Year's gifts, etc., with which folk retained the favour of the omnipotent, and the sums they quite blatantly paid for appointments in the Queen's service. The 'domestical greatness' of Essex in fact was something in the nature of a vast financial speculation. Recklessly extravagant and improvident, his wide-flung intelligence system and his ever-growing household involved expenditure far beyond the most generous provision that Elizabeth could afford to make for him. Solvency depended on perquisites, and perquisites on his ability to secure from the Queen favour and place for his suitors. Thus material reasons reinforced his temperamental urge to monopolize power. Elizabeth's house had many mansions: he wished to occupy them all. Early and late, his chamber was full of suitors and sycophants, and the tips which they gave to his servants, from doorkeepers to secretaries, dropped as the gentle rain from heaven on an expectant household.

Verily, Bacon, too, looked for his reward. But just as a post—the Attorney-Generalship—promised to fall vacant, he offended the Queen. This was over the money bill in parliament. Instead of a double grant as in 1589, the Commons in 1593, on the questionable intervention of the Upper House, were persuaded to give three subsidies; but they were taken aback at the demand, and many, with Bacon as their most influential voice, resisted the proposal to collect the tax in four years, suggesting six instead. The burden would be impossible, said Bacon. 'The gentlemen must sell their plate, and farmers their brass pots ere this will be paid'. It would breed discontent, and be an ill precedent for them and posterity.

Elizabeth was hurt to the quick by the opposition. Justifiably! Parliament had clamoured for war and made ardent promises of help; almost everyone had badgered her to send armies here and ships there, as though they were to be had for the whistling; she had performed wonders with inadequate means; she had practised eternal vigilance over her own expenses, to the disgust of the greedy cormorants about her, everlastingly grumbling and gibing at her parsimony; she had kept faith with her creditors; she had eaten into her capital rather than pass more than a fraction of the war expenses on to her people. And now when the time had come for the country to shoulder more of the burden, grudging voices were heard. At the close of the Parliament, not content with the Lord Keeper's words on her behalf, she addressed both Houses herself. 'The subsidy which you offer me,' she said, 'I accept thankfully, if you give me your good wills with it; but if the necessity of the times and your preservation did not require it, I would refuse it'.

Her head, she assured them was better stayed by years and experience than to enter into any idle expense. She said more, speaking words of courage to them 'with a fluent eloquence and princely boldness'. 'For mine own part, I protest I never feared, and what fear was, my heart never knew'. As for the King of Spain, 'I fear not all his threatenings; his great preparations and mighty forces do not stir me. For though he come against me with a greater power than ever was his Invincible Navy, I doubt not but, God assisting me upon whom I always trust, I shall be able to defeat him and overthrow him. For my cause is just'.

Bacon's unfortunate speech lost him the Queen's favour for the time being. Playing the part of a warm friend, Essex urged her to readmit to her presence one who was so well able to judge the merits of 'those excellent'—in truth, they were indifferent—translations of classical authors, which she was amusing herself making in her sixtieth year. She did not respond to the flattery. But what lost Bacon the Attorney-Generalship was the fact that from a professional point of view his claims to the office, in comparison with those of Edward Coke, the Solicitor-General, were preposterous; and as Elizabeth told Essex, the sole objection to Coke, namely his youth, was stronger against Bacon, who was nine years younger. Foolish and unjust the suit was, yet Essex engaged his whole being in it. Elizabeth reasoned with him, he persisted; she told him that she would have her own way, he became more earnest than ever; she tried to break off, saying that she would be advised by those who had more judgment in these things than himself; he went on, determined to queer the pitch for Coke and his supporter Burghley. A few months later Sir Robert Cecil attempted to persuade him to be content with the Solicitor-General's office for Bacon, which 'might be of easier digestion to her Majesty.' 'Digest me no digestions', Essex angrily answered, 'for the Attorneyship for Francis is that I must have; and in that I will spend all my power, might, authority, and amity, and with tooth and nail defend and procure the same for him against whomsoever; and whosoever getteth this office out of my hands for any other, before he have it, it shall cost him the coming by.'

While Essex's passion and tantrums lasted, Elizabeth left the Attorney's office vacant. Then, when he accepted the inevitable and asked for the Solicitorship for Bacon, she made Coke Attorney. Her reaction to the new suit was ominous. At first reserved, when Essex grew passionate for Bacon she became passionate against him. She bade him go to bed if he could talk of nothing else. In a huff he retired from Court for a few days, as he had done over the previous suit. Later arguments drew a pertinent reminder from her that if one must yield, it were fitter to be he. But yield he would not, and, falling back upon her usual tactics, she 'went from a denial to a delay'. The unhappy Bacon said of himself: 'No man ever received a more exquisite disgrace'. At a delay the question was to stand for a long time.

Meanwhile, following upon alarms of plots against Elizabeth's life, Essex got on to the track of a conspiracy involving the Queen's physician, a Portuguese Jew named Dr. Lopez. 'I have discovered a most dangerous and desperate treason', he excitedly wrote to Anthony Bacon in January, 1594. 'The point of conspiracy was her Majesty's death. The executioner should have been Dr. Lopez; the manner poison. This I have so followed as I will make it as clear as the noonday'. Elizabeth let Burghley, Cecil, and Essex examine Lopez, but at the first inquiry nothing was discovered to incriminate him, and Robert Cecil, seizing the chance of discrediting his enemy, hurriedly returned to the Court to be first with the news. With some justification Elizabeth concluded that Essex had acted from mere malice, and when he came into her presence, her notable and acute loyalty to her servants surging up, she rounded on him, 'calling him rash and temerarious youth to enter into a matter against the poor man which he could not prove'. He flung from her in anger, burst into his chamber, and slammed the door to behind him. His honour was now involved in the business—a misfortune for the wretched Lopez. Perhaps the man was guilty; perhaps not. Certainly, as the matter was probed, it became clear that he had offered to poison the Queen in return for a substantial sum from Philip II, and his excuse, though a possible or even a probable one, was incapable of proof. He was tried and condemned. It looks as though Elizabeth was still unconvinced of his guilt. Defying his judges and Essex and the angry populace, she ordered the Lieutenant of the Tower to refuse to surrender him for execution. What happened afterwards is a mystery. According to a later story, Essex by a trick managed within two months to get Lopez out of the Tower where the Queen's protection covered him, and was thus able to bring him to the scaffold. If there is any truth in the story, Essex must have used all his great charm of personality to placate the Queen, for a few weeks later she gave him £4,000, presumably to pay his debts, and expressing her liking and concern for him, said, 'Look to thyself, good Essex, and be wise to help thyself, without giving thy enemies advantage; and my hand shall be readier to help thee than any other'.

In November, 1595, after more than a year and a half's delay, Elizabeth appointed an able lawyer, Serjeant Fleming, as Solicitor-General. Burghley and others had supported Essex in his fight for Bacon, but without effect. Their candidate was passed over. It was as deliberate and personal an action as any in Elizabeth's reign, and notwithstanding other excuses, had a secret of its own. That secret —there can be little doubt—was Bacon's relation to Essex. Sir Thomas Bodley, in his *Autobiography*, remarked that Elizabeth would give little countenance to any of Essex's followers. Bodley himself was a victim, for against his will he was drawn from dependence on Burghley to dependence on Essex, who urged his claims to be Secretary with such instancy that, what with the Queen's displeasure and the jealousy of Burghley and Cecil, he at last thought it prudent to retire from official life and devote himself to his great library at Oxford.

The truth was that every creature placed in office by Essex meant so much more pressure on the Queen. It was once said, though not with much reason, that Leicester had placed so many of his supporters about her that she found it hard to withstand him. Had she let a man of Essex's nature pack the royal service and the Council with his nominees, she would probably in the end have found herself a puppet-Queen, in tutelage to him. She was far too subtle, long-sighted, and imperious to let that happen. How different from Essex was Burghley! Only a few months later the wise old man expounded his principle of political conduct to his son. When his opinion differed from the Queen's he said, he would not change it to please her, for that would be to offend God, but as a servant he would obey the Queen's commandment. It was the kind of service Elizabeth demanded. And though she might call Burghley 'froward old fool' when in a pet he insisted on going off for ten days to take physic, she respected him, and there was a bond of friendship and intimacy between them that did honour to both.

Essex had no doubt of the cause of Bacon's misfortune. 'You fare ill,' he said, 'because you have chosen me for your mean and dependence'; and in that generous spirit which entered into the anarchic but winning compound of his character, he insisted on compensating him with a gift of land. Bacon may once have been at fault in miscalculating Elizabeth's reaction to Robert Cecil's deformity, but by now he apprehended the future as clearly as the Queen herself. 'My Lord,' he said to Essex, 'I see I must be your homager and hold land of your gift; but do you know the manner of doing homage in law? Always it is with a saving of his faith to the King and his other lords; and therefore my Lord, I can be no more yours than I was, and it must be with the ancient savings'. Prudent words!

CHAPTER XX

'A NATURE NOT TO BE RULED'

THE sluggish stream of war was entering a new stretch of rapids. In 1595 Drake and Hawkins were busy preparing another of those semi-public, semi-private, joint-stock predatory enterprises which took the wind out of Spanish sails and left Europe astounded at the spectacle of a petty kingdom harassing a rich and mighty empire with impunity. As usual they were tantalized by Elizabeth's tendency to think a second and a third time, change her mind, harbour misgivings. It seemed to have become a chronic habit with her: people told the story of the carter who, on being informed for the third time that the Queen had altered her plans and did not intend to move on that day, slapped his thigh and said, 'Now I see that the Queen is a woman as well as my wife'. 'What a villain is this!' called out Elizabeth, who overheard him from a window, and sent him three angels to stop his mouth. A woman's trait it may have been, but doubts and delay were inseparable from a system of rule where all decisions were personal, and councillors and courtiers were for ever whispering cautions in the sovereign's ears. The wonder rather is that she retained her sanity and displayed so much vigour of purpose. Drake and Hawkins did, however, at last get away in August, and sailed for the Spanish Main on their last tragic voyage.

A month before they sailed four Spanish galleys from the Breton coast descended on Cornwall, burnt Penzance and other places, and then scuttled away. It was a mere pinprick, but it showed that the shores of England were not inviolable, and gave point to the news coming through from Spain that a new Armada was in preparation for the following year. Orders were sent out to put the country in readiness, and at the turn of the year the warriors were urging Elizabeth to organize an attack on the Spanish fleet in its own ports. She had her doubts, especially about finance. The estimated cost was alarmingly high, and though the Admiral, Howard, and Essex both did their best to make it seem less, and indeed, with bright promises of plunder, turned it into a profit, the Queen was uneasy.

There was another England than that of Essex and his like, an England upon which Elizabeth ever kept her eyes and for which the year 1596 was to prove the third successive year of bad harvests and terrible misery—not a time to increase the financial and human burden of war beyond what was absolutely necessary. Rain had declared itself as a new and more fearful enemy than the Spaniard. 'One year', declared a preacher, 'there hath been hunger, the second there was a dearth, and a third there was great cleanness of teeth'.

> The ox hath therefore stretched his yoke in vain,
> The ploughman lost his sweat, and the green corn
> Hath rotted ere his youth attained a beard.

Food prices were rising and reached famine heights; and though the Government strained itself in paternal efforts to see that the poor were fed, people died in the streets from want. Riot and turbulence showed their head, and, mixed with cries that 'they must not starve, they will not starve', were more enduring and significant murmurs against the drain of men for foreign wars. The Queen's popularity was still a charm of strange potency, but she could not afford to abuse it.

Against this background, Howard and Essex went forward with the preparations for their famous exploit against Cadiz, Elizabeth having grudgingly acquiesced in the policy of defence by offence. Essex's name brought hundreds of gentlemen adventurers, eager for fighting and still more for plunder, 'green-headed youths, covered with feathers, and gold and silver lace'.

> All the unsettled humours of the land,
> Rash, inconsiderate, fiery voluntaries,
> With ladies' faces and fierce dragons' spleens,
> Bearing their birthrights proudly on their backs.

Suddenly, in the first days of April came the startling news that a Spanish force from the Netherlands had appeared before Calais, blocked the sea approach and laid siege to the town. Thoughts of Cadiz had to give way to the menacing fact that the enemy was at England's threshold. With an eye to the main chance—not inexcusably—Elizabeth tried to wring the cession of the town from Henry IV in return for relieving it. He is said to have sworn that he would as leave be bitten by a dog as scratched by a cat. There was no time for haggling, however. An army was hastily raised. 'As distant as I am from your abode,' wrote Elizabeth to Essex, 'yet my ears serve me too well to hear that terrible battery that methinks sounds for relief at my hands. . . . Go you, in God's blessed name'. But the very day following, as the troops embarked, Calais fell, and it was too late. The preparations for Cadiz were resumed, and on June 3rd this expedition sailed, fortified with prayers, specially composed by her Majesty in her own inimitable style. A few weeks previously Drake and Hawkins's fleet had returned, confirming the news of its leaders' death and the virtual failure of their enterprise.

Cadiz was no failure, but a perfect example of that dashing, careless bravery upon which Fortune was prone to smile. Essex joyfully throwing his hat into the sea at the order to enter the harbour; Raleigh replying to the cannon shots from the Spanish fort with scornful fanfares of trumpets; the boyish competition to steal the lead and find a place in the bottleneck where the naval engagement took place; the reckless scaling of the town walls: all these were of a piece with the courtesy, humanity, and generosity of

Essex in his treatment of the people of Cadiz after its capture. They read like pages of a romance, and even the Spaniards were moved to praise.

But envy and folly, the humours of that youthful age, were present also. The dual command was an insidious weakness. Before they left England, Howard had cut Essex's signature from a joint letter, because, said Essex, the unruly Admiral 'would have none so high as himself'. This envy and the spectacle—insufferable to the seamen—of the soldiers enjoying the plunder of the city, led almost everyone to rush to the spoil, leaving the best prey, an outward-bound merchant fleet, from which Elizabeth might have recovered the costs of the expedition and replenished her coffers, lying helpless farther in the harbour, until it was too late. With heroic fortitude, the Spanish commander burnt the ships and their goods rather than see either them or their ransom pass into English hands. They numbered over forty great ships besides many smaller, and were valued at twelve million ducats. What a loss to Spain! What a loss to England! Such crass negligence as the English commanders showed is yet another reminder that there was more in Elizabeth's distrust of great military and naval undertakings than modern critics realize.

Both Howard and Essex were under promise and orders to save the plunder of the voyage for the Queen: they gave it with a bountiful hand to their men. An official had been attached to them to see the order carried out: he plundered with the rest. The fleet and army were still in good order and health and fit for the further tasks committed to them. Essex, indeed, whose soul was not mercenary, was for action, but the officers as a whole, men who held life so cheap, held plunder dear. Some had chartered small ships to take their miscellaneous and strange spoil home, and they wanted to be after it. Home the fleet sailed, but not before the two commanders—Essex having the lion's share—had made a great many knights, 'even all almost that did deserve it or effect it or not neglect or refuse it (as some did).' As the saying afterwards went,

A gentleman of Wales, with a knight of Cales (Cadiz)
And a laird of the North Countree,
A yeoman of Kent upon a racked rent
Will buy them out all three.

How was Elizabeth to receive the conquerors? On the one hand was the glorious, astounding victory. In Venice, such was her fame, people clamoured for her picture. 'Great is the Queen of England!' they cried. 'O! what a woman, if she were but a Christian!' On the other hand was her empty exchequer, and commanders asking for money to pay wages to men enriched with what should have been hers. She praised and she raged. The 'sea-faction', jealous anyhow of the landsmen and sore over their paltry share of the plunder, made themselves busy at Court backbiting. Essex, who had returned home with a beard, and with his ruddy complexion gone, and with a mind to eschew the beauties of the Court and curb the frailty of his passionate nature, 'was continually baited like a bear of Paris garden with ban-dogs.' He shook them all off, and with the bright gleams of his valour, as Anthony Bacon put it, cleared the mists which malicious envy raised against his matchless merit. Burghley made friendly advances to him: 'the old fox,' wrote Bacon, 'crouches and whines'. In the popular mind this glorious and chivalrous youth was the victor of Cadiz, the personification of England at war. He stood now at the height of his career, the people's darling, the Queen's favourite.

It could not last. Elizabeth was the same; Essex the same. A month after he had sailed for Cadiz, she had made the last of her moves in Sir Robert Cecil's progress to the Secretaryship. He was just thirty-three, and the five years of power without title had brought him to the point of natural and peaceful transition to the office: the absence of Essex was the Queen's opportunity.

As for Essex, he was no better able to brook opposition than before. In a sense, Elizabeth's supreme task, which had been accomplished painfully but successfully in the early decades of her reign—the eradication of sex prejudice in statesmen and courtiers—was beginning over again with the new generation. Essex could not help thinking of her as a mere woman, and an old and crusty one at that. He believed that if pressed often enough and long enough, a woman invariably gave way in the end; and he interpreted Elizabeth's moods and acts, as men are apt to do, making a single genus of the species. How differently would he have behaved with a king of her capacity! And the tragedy was that the artifice by means of which she had met the disability of her sex, even turning it to account, no longer retained its charm. The love-tricks, the idyll of the Fairy Queen, went on: at what point and how were they to be stopped? But while they held a profound and sweet truth for the doddering old Burghley, they were at best tawdry, at worst a mockery, to the young bloods of Essex's generation. Elizabeth remained amazingly fresh and vigorous in mind: 'It is not possible to see a woman of so fine and vigorous disposition both in mind and body', wrote a far from partial ambassador a year later. But she was ageing rapidly in looks at this time: her face long and thin and very aged and capped with a great reddish-coloured wig, and her teeth very yellow and irregular—so this ambassador described her. Old age and youth cannot love together, and the young men about Essex, in confidential moments, were saying that they would not submit to another woman ruler. It might be that in a storm of passion, when the deeper currents of the mind are revealed, Essex would yet declare his contempt for a capricious, imperious old woman, and Elizabeth the fury of her scorned womanhood.

At this juncture, the dispassionate, calculating voice of prudence spoke. 'A man of a nature not to be ruled,' wrote Francis Bacon to his patron; 'of an estate not grounded to his greatness; of a popular reputation; of a military dependence: I demand whether there can be a more dangerous image than this represented to any monarch living, much more to a lady, and of her Majesty's apprehension?' Persuade the Queen that you are another Leicester or Hatton, he urged. In praising her opinions, do it as though you were sincere. Ask favours in order to renounce them when she opposes. Maintain your control of military affairs, but keep it in substance and abolish it in appearance: a military following 'maketh a suspected greatness'. Cease to seek the office of Earl Marshal or Master of the Ordnance; take that of Lord Privy Seal, peaceful in connotation, and remunerative. Seize all occasions to speak to the Queen vehemently against popularity and popular courses. Quench this reputation of yours in words, but not in fact: well governed it 'is one of the best flowers of your greatness both present and to come'. Spend less, 'for believe it, my Lord, that till her Majesty find you careful of your estate, she will not only think you more like to continue chargeable to her, but also have a conceit that you have higher imaginations'. The advantage of being a royal favourite, if coupled with these precautions, cannot hurt; if severed from them, 'it maketh her Majesty more fearful and shadowy, as not knowing her own strength'. What prophetic vision! what wisdom! what subtlety! what coldness of heart! in short, what a different soul from Essex! The shrewd seer dedicated the first edition of his Essays in the following February, not to Essex but to Anthony Bacon, his brother.

Essex could no more change his nature than a leopard be rid of its spots. As the English ambassador in France said, he would ruin himself, for he was better able to throw a court into disorder than contribute to its order. Early in 1597 he was in the sulks over a post which he wanted for his friend, Sir Robert Sidney, though the Queen herself, as well as the Cecils, favoured another candidate. Elizabeth swore that she would break him of his will and pull down his great heart, which he inherited from his mother's side. Failing for Sidney, he stood himself as a candidate, intending later to retire in Sidney's favour; and he embarked his whole credit and prestige against the Queen's nominee. Elizabeth refused him, whereupon he saddled his horses and was about to retire into the country, when she sent for him, and offered him the office of Master of the Ordnance, thus saving his face and appeasing him. She had work for him to do.

Cadiz had roused Philip II from his lethargy. Seizing a

candelabrum, he vowed that he would pawn that rather than not be revenged. In fact, he went bankrupt, and the eddies of his failure rippled through Italy where merchants whimsically remarked that they would be able to date events from the year in which the King of Spain and they proved bankrupts together. But a bankrupt king was not without resources, and it was a new Armada in preparation that made the services of Essex needful. After some argument it was decided to prepare an expedition with a double object: to destroy the Spanish fleet in its port of Ferrol, and afterwards waylay the West Indian treasure fleet at the Azores. Essex insisted on sole command—and at last got it. He was happy, and therefore the Court was happy. And strange spectacle! Raleigh and Cecil made friends with him, and all three overflowed with goodwill one to another. For Elizabeth it was Elysium. She assured Essex that men's endeavours, and not accidents, would guide her judgment of the enterprise: 'so the root be sound, what blasts soever wither the fruit, no condemnation shall light on their share'.

The fleet sailed in July, 1597. Caught by a storm, it was scattered and forced back to port. At first it was thought that Essex had perished. His safe return caused great relief. Elizabeth wept for joy at the news, and Cecil wrote to Essex: 'The Queen is so disposed now to have us all love you, that she and I do every night talk like angels of you'.

While the fleet was refitting, an ambassador arrived at Court from the King of Poland. Being informed that he came with a proposition of peace, and also for his father's sake who had honoured her, Elizabeth gave him public audience in the Presence Chamber. He was brought in, attired in a long robe of black velvet, well jewelled. After kissing the Queen's hands, he straight retired ten yards and then began his oration in Latin, 'with such a countenance,' wrote Cecil, 'as in my life I never beheld'. Instead of compliments or talk of peace he uttered menaces. Rising lionlike from her throne, Elizabeth trounced him in extempore Latin for his insolence and audacity. If his king, she declared, was responsible for his speech, then it must be since he was a youth and not a king by right of blood but by election, and that only recent. 'And as for you,' said she to the ambassador, 'although I perceive you have read many books to fortify your arguments in this case, yet am I apt to believe that you have not lighted upon the chapter that prescribeth the form to be used between kings and princes.' The Court rang with delighted admiration of the Queen's *tour de force*, and soon the news of it was spread through town and country. Elizabeth said to Cecil that she was sorry Essex was not present to hear the ambassador's and her Latin. He took the hint and wrote the whole tale to Essex, who did not need the suggestion to send back a pleasant word of praise. 'I was happy for her Majesty,' he answered, 'that she was stirred, and had so worthy an occasion to show herself. The heroes would be but as other men, if they had not unusual and unlooked for encounters; and sure her Majesty is made of the same stuff of which the ancients believed the heroes to be formed; that is, her mind of gold, her body of brass.' Queen Elizabeth's reply to the Polish ambassador lived on as a treasured memory through several generations.

The fleet at last sailed on what came to be known as the Islands Voyage. Misfortune dogged it, helped by Essex's defects as a commander and the rancour that his personal followers bore towards Raleigh, the Rear-Admiral. They were not in a fit state on arriving at Ferrol to attack the Spanish fleet there, and so sailed to the Azores. Here Raleigh landed to capture a town in the absence of his commander-in-chief, who was unaccountably delayed. He had stolen what Essex coveted most, honour; and it was only the mediation of the third in command that prevented Essex from court-martialling him and beheading him. By way of compromise the heroic deed was omitted from the official account of the Voyage! Then, with almost inexplicable stupidity, a way was left open through which the Spanish treasure fleet, which might otherwise have easily been taken, slipped safely into port. Finally, they arrived home to discover that the Ferrol fleet had taken advantage of their absence to sail for England, and had only been prevented by storms from a descent on Falmouth. Needless to say, Essex had added to his military clientele by making knights; but this time they were few.

Back in England, the old home troubles were renewed. Essex now took umbrage because on Sunday, October 23rd, a few days before his return, as she came from Chapel, Elizabeth had created the Lord Admiral, Howard, Earl of Nottingham. His promotion, coupled with his office, gave him precedence over Essex. To make matters worse, the patent creating him earl not only referred to his victory over the Armada, but stated that jointly with Essex he had taken Cadiz. Robert Sidney's servant, a partial observer, saw nothing wrong in this at the time, nor probably did any sensible person. But in the popular mind, and especially in the hot heads about Essex, there was only one conqueror of Cadiz; and honour at that moment, after the wretched Islands Voyage, was at a premium. Essex refused to attend Parliament, which was then sitting, refused to come to Court, and like Achilles of old, sulked in his tent. He even stayed away from the celebrations of Queen's Day, November 17th, though it was the entry, as Burghley reminded him, to the fortieth year of her Majesty's reign. He pleaded sickness, perhaps with truth, as mental distress induces physical. Burghley and others did their best to bring about peace. Elizabeth at first declared that 'a Prince was not to be contended withal by a subject', while Essex insisted on the offending words in the patent being altered. At last, on December 18th, the contention ended as the previous one had done. Elizabeth made him Earl Marshal, which gave him precedence over the new Earl of Nottingham. He was happy. As for Nottingham, it was now his turn to be sick; but he was a less difficult child.

Essex had thus obtained the two military offices against which Francis Bacon had warned him, and the prognostications of this penetrating mind approached nearer and nearer to realization. In the New Year Essex promised Robert Sidney to secure a peerage for him: Elizabeth blocked it. He openly announced that he was standing for his friend against all men for the office of Vice-Chamberlain:

the Queen left the office vacant until Essex's game was played out. As one of his supporters said, he could get anything for himself, but nothing for his friends. The arrogant nature of this wonderfully attractive, but impossible young man was revealed again in a letter of Lord Grey's to a friend, the following summer. Wondering at the favour shown Grey by the Queen, Essex had lately tried to force him to declare himself either a follower of his, or else Robert Cecil's friend and an enemy. Grey repudiated any base dependency, whereupon Essex told him that he was a lost child. In plain terms, he announced that he loved not his person, and that Grey—a military man—must not expect advancement under him. 'If the Queen,' Grey pertinently remarked, 'will thus suffer one to engross thus servilely all men of the sword, and derive the advancement of war only from his partial favour, she must likewise resolve to hold her own of him, and suffer her poor and faithful nobility to languish under the despised yoke of one of their own rank'.

Early in 1598 the Council found itself discussing the question of entering into peace negotiations with Spain. The question had arisen owing to the action of France. Henry IV, much to Elizabeth's disgust, though perhaps not to her surprise, had turned Catholic in 1593 in order to reunite his people. 'Paris,' he is said to have remarked, 'is worth a Mass'. It was, and his action bore fruit. By 1598 he was in a position to make peace with his last enemy, Spain, and although, two years before, he had entered into a Triple Alliance with England and the Netherlands pledging himself not to make a separate peace, France wanted peace, and peace Henry was determined to have. He played skittles with his treaty obligations, and Elizabeth called him 'the Antichrist of ingratitude'; but international politics were unscrupulous. Elizabeth had to decide whether she would try for peace at the same time. The Netherlands were the stumbling block, for they were growing wealthy, and the dream of independence had become practical politics even to cautious men, so that they were less inclined than ever for peace, while it was certain that Spain would not concede them anything like acceptable terms. In the end, Henry IV made his peace; England and the Netherlands continued at war. There was no escape, but during the discussions the English Council divided into two opinions, the one expressed by Burghley, desiring peace if at all possible, the other voiced by Essex, unhesitatingly for war. The debate was hot. At the end, Burghley silently drew forth a Psalter and pointed to the verse, 'The bloody and deceitful man shall not live out half his days'.

Sometime in July, while Elizabeth was discussing the question of the Irish rebellion, which had become more serious and harassing than ever, the storm that had long been approaching in her relations with Essex blew up with dramatic swiftness, giving a flashing glimpse of the black depths of passion in each. There were present only Essex, Nottingham, Cecil, and a clerk of the signet. The question was the appointment of a Lord Deputy. Elizabeth wanted to send Sir William Knollys, Essex's uncle; Essex urged the appointment of Sir George Carew, an enemy of his, whom he hoped to remove from Court in this way. The Queen proved obstinate, and Essex lost his self-possession. With scorn and anger blazing on his face, he deliberately turned his back on Elizabeth. Furious at the insult and contempt, she boxed his ears 'and bade him get him gone and be hanged'. His hand leapt to his sword, and as Nottingham hastily stepped between them, he swore a great oath that he neither could nor would put up with such an affront and indignity; he would not have taken it even at Henry VIII's hands. In a tearing rage he left the Court.

Essex's friends tried to bring him to his senses. 'Remember, I beseech you,' wrote his uncle, Knollys, 'that there is no contesting between sovereignty and obedience'. The Queen, he went on, may by necessity be forced to use your service, but without her love you will be susceptible to the tongues of your enemies. Lord Keeper Egerton wrote cogently and persuasively: 'You are not so far gone, but you may well return. The return is safe, but the progress dangerous and desperate in this course you hold . . . The best remedy is not to contend and strive, but humbly to submit. Have you given cause, and yet take scandal to yourself? Why! then all you can do is too little to make satisfaction.' Essex answered: 'I owe her Majesty the duty of an Earl and of Lord Marshal of England. I have been content to do her Majesty the service of a clerk; but can never serve her as a villein or slave . . . What! Cannot princes err? Cannot subjects receive wrong? Is an earthly power or authority infinite? Pardon me, pardon me, my good Lord; I can never subscribe to these principles'. Could he but listen to his oracle: 'Ambitious men, if they rise not with their service, they will take order that their service fall with them'.

In the midst of this quarrel, on August 4th, died the grand old man of his age, Burghley, whose seventy-eight years of life presented to the panegyrist an enviably large field in which to gather his flowers. He had been ailing long, but his serene mind and even his broken body had been at the service of the Queen almost to the last. So certainly was his end expected that anticipation eased the shock, but it was as keen a personal bereavement for Elizabeth as it was a national loss. She had once told him that she did not wish to live longer than she had him with her, a remark which brought tears to the old man's eyes. On another occasion she sent him word that though he had brought up his son as near as might be like unto himself, yet he was to her in all things, and would be, Alpha and Omega. A month before his death he wrote to his son, Robert, bidding him thank the Queen for her singular kindness: 'Though she will not be a mother—how pathetic his thought!—yet she showeth herself by feeding me with her own princely hand, as a careful nurse; and if I may be weaned to feed myself, I shall be more ready to serve her on the earth; if not, I hope to be in heaven a servitor for her and God's church'. 'Serve God by serving of the Queen,' he added in a postscript, in this writing his epitaph.

As the impressive funeral *cortège* made its way to Westminster Abbey with Essex the saddest of all the sad faces—though whether from sorrow for Burghley or gloom over his own fortunes, some folk were uncertain—in distant Spain the second person in the trinity of the past, Philip II, lay dying. Still true to his nature, he had arranged every detail of his funeral, to the ordering of black cloth to drape the church of the Escurial. He had had brought to his bedside a shirt of lead in which his corpse was to be wrapped and the leaden coffin in which it was to lie. He was a mass of suppurating sores, the stench of which overcame his doctor, and the pains from his gout were intense. Yet his patience in suffering, as in misfortune, was incredible. In August he was apparently dead; the touch of a relic brought him to. He died on September 13th, in his seventy-second year. For nine days there was continuous prayer, and the bells tolled unceasingly day and night. They rang out an epoch, and of all its famous people, one alone, most famous of all, lived on. She had still to play out the tragic drama of age and youth.

CHAPTER XXI

ESSEX:NEMESIS

In later years Francis Bacon recalled how he had persistently advised Essex that the only course to be held with the Queen was compliance and respect. Her goodness would then be without limit. But Essex 'had a settled opinion that the Queen could be brought to nothing but by a kind of necessity and authority.' 'I well remember,' Bacon continues, 'when by violent courses at any time he had got his will, he would ask me, "Now Sir, whose principles be true?" and I would again say to him: "My Lord, these courses be like to hot waters, they will help at a pang; but if you use them, you shall spoil the stomach, and you shall be fain still to make them stronger and stronger, and yet in the end they will lose their operation".'

For several weeks after the dramatic breach in July, 1598, it seemed as if neither mistress nor servant would yield a point of pride. Then at the beginning of September Essex fell ill, and Elizabeth, moved with compassion, sent her physician to him. A letter of humble, sweetly-phrased thanks opened the way to reconciliation, and he returned to Court. Yet conquer his nature he could not. Instead of walking warily, as one who had been perilously near irrevocable disgrace, he fell to his old game at once. Among the offices which Burghley had held, and which were now vacant, was that of Master of the Wards. It was a remunerative post, and, more important in the eyes of Essex, gave its holder great influence with the nobility and gentry throughout the land. Here was an opportunity of creating a civilian clientele as overwhelming as his military one. So passionately did he set his heart upon it that no one dared to compete with him. But he had the Queen to reckon with. She refused him the office, and rather than increase his dangerous power, spoke of retaining it in her own hands. With foolish insolence he wrote telling her that none of her ancestors had done such a thing, and if she did, 'the world may judge, and I must believe, that you overthrow the office because I should not be the officer'; if you value me, he ended, think again of my suit. His 'hot waters' had no effect. Elizabeth left the office vacant and its work in suspense and confusion, until—as in the past—his absence was to give her the opportunity of appointing Robert Cecil. Probably it was at this time, or in the next month or two, that she uttered a significant warning: 'He would do well,' she told him, 'to content himself with displeasing her on all occasions and despising her person so insolently, but he should beware of touching her sceptre'.

One of the reasons which brought Essex back to Court was the need for his advice about Ireland, where affairs had been going from bad to worse and, since his disgrace in July, a disastrous defeat had befallen the English army. It was only too painfully clear that this country was England's Netherlands, and in Hugh O'Neil, Earl of Tyrone and ruler of central and eastern Ulster, a man who had spent some years in England, it looked as though the native race had found a William the Silent, with subtlety and capacity enough to play the politician, and able to discipline and train his tribesmen. By the end of August, 1598, England's hold on Ireland had become extremely precarious; even Dublin, the seat of government was threatened; and as there was the constant danger of Spain sending help to the rebels, a resolute attempt had to be made to overthrow Tyrone and reconquer the country.

The first question was the choice of a man. No one seemed eager to go; as a Venetian Ambassador said: 'Ireland may well be called the Englishman's grave'. Elizabeth was for sending Charles Blount, Lord Mountjoy, the young courtier with whom Essex had fought a foolish duel some

years before, but who had since become the lover of Penel-
ope, wife of Lord Rich and devoted sister of Essex, so being
drawn into the Essex circle. Essex opposed his appointment,
for he was driven by sheer necessity to covet the terrible
task himself. 'Great England's glory and the world's wide
wonder,' he could not allow another person to undertake the
supreme military adventure of the moment, thus competing
with his popular reputation, and stealing his military following. Once more he was faced with the alternative put
so plainly by Bacon after the Cadiz expedition—civil greatness or military. 'The Court is the centre', he wrote to a
confidant, explaining his decision; 'but methinks it is the
fairer choice to command armies than honours'. And so, by
vehemently urging the shortcomings of others while at the
same time stressing qualifications which he alone possessed,
he in effect named himself for the task. 'I have beaten
Knollys and Mountjoy in the Council,' he wrote, 'and by
God I will beat Tyrone in the field'.

Having forced the Queen and Council to choose him,
Essex set about extracting such an army and such a pleni-
tude of power as no ruler in Ireland had hitherto possessed. For two months or more there were continual jars
as he fought the Queen over the terms of his appointment.
'How much soever her Majesty despiseth me,' he wrote
when the struggle was going against him and he was also
vainly pressing for the Mastership of the Wards, 'she shall
know she hath lost him who for her sake would have
thought danger a sport and death a feast. . . . And all the
world shall witness that it is not the breath of me, which is
but wind, or the love of the multitude, which burns as tin-
der, that I hunt after, but either to be valued by her above
them that are of no value, or to forget the world and to be
forgotten by it'. One day it was said that he was to go;
another, the appointment was in suspense or quite dashed.
But messengers were coming daily from Ireland, like Job's
servants laden with ill tidings, and military men were flocking about Essex, every man hoping to be a colonel and
responding with such alacrity to the miraculous appeal of
his name that his services seemed well nigh indispensable.

He was remorseless in pressing his advantage, and in the end his violent methods prevailed. He was given the power and the army he wanted—the greatest army that had left English shores during the reign, 16,000 foot and 1,300 horse, raised from a people faltering under the long strain of continuous levies, and financed by a sovereign who hardly knew where to turn for the requisite money.

This arrogant young man—fit subject for the classical theme of *hubris*—had landed himself in a terrifying situation. Elizabeth warned him how far different things would prove in Ireland than he expected: he gave no heed to an old woman's foolishness. By unsparing criticism of his predecessors he defined his task and robbed himself in advance of virtually every excuse for failure; while at a Council of War, where all the expert knowledge of the country was gathered and Elizabeth herself was present, he upheld—nay, was responsible for the Council's decision that his first and supreme object should be an attack upon Tyrone in Ulster. The very anxiety with which the Privy Council worked to meet all his legitimate demands was disconcerting: it was as though they were determined to give him rope enough to hang himself. Whatever the result, responsibility was so entirely centred on him that he could not escape it; and nothing but success could justify the way he had browbeaten his sovereign. Elizabeth had yielded, but the manner was ominous. The 'hot waters' were losing their efficacy.

As the gravity of the position dawned on Essex, doubts began to undermine his self-confidence. 'Into Ireland I go', he wrote to a friend. 'The Queen hath irrevocably decreed it, the Council do passionately urge it, and I am tied by my own reputation to use no tergiversation'. If he were now to slip collar and Ireland were lost, though it perished by destiny he would be blamed. He was not ignorant of the disadvantages of absence; how it would give his enemies the opportunity of practising against him, especially with a sovereign upon whose mind the effect of great renown might be more malignant than the reverse. 'Too ill success will be dangerous: let them fear that, who . . . can be content to overlive their honour. Too good will be envious: I will never forswear virtue for fear of ostracism'. 'These are my private problems and nightly disputations.'

A warning letter from a friend at Court to John Harington, going as an officer to Ireland, brings the situation into clear focus. 'Mark my counsel', he wrote. 'Observe the man who commandeth, and yet is commanded himself; he goeth not forth to serve the Queen's realm, but to humour his own revenge. Be heedful of your bearings; speak not your mind to all you meet. I tell you I have ground for my caution. Essex hath enemies; he hath friends too'. There are men set 'to report all your conduct to us at home'. 'If the Lord Deputy performs in the field what he hath promised in the council, all will be well; but though the Queen hath granted forgiveness for his late demeanour in her presence, we know not what to think hereof. She hath in all outward semblance placed confidence in the man who so lately sought other treatment at her hands: we do sometimes think one way, and sometimes another. What betideth the Lord Deputy is known to Him only who knoweth all; but when a man hath so many showing friends, and so many unshowing enemies, who learneth his end here below?' 'Obey the Lord Deputy in all things, but give not your opinion; it may be heard in England'. 'Sir William Knollys is not well pleased, the Queen is not well pleased, the Lord Deputy may be pleased now, but I sore fear what may happen.' 'Danger goeth abroad, and silence is the safest armour.'

On March 27th, 1599, Essex took horse at Seething Lane, and accompanied by a great train of noblemen and gentlemen, himself very plainly attired, rode through the City on his way to Chester. The people flocked into the streets and highways, crying 'God bless your Lordship!' Their hopes Shakespeare voiced:

> Were now the general of our gracious empress—
> As in good time he may—from Ireland coming,
> Bringing rebellion broached on his sword,
> How many would the peaceful City quit
> To welcome him!

But before he passed Islington a great black cloud appeared in the sky, and suddenly came thunder, lightning, and hail, 'which some held an ominous prodigy'.

The jars recommenced before Chester was reached. A letter-writer had commented on the raw youths pressing for the greatest charges in the army. Essex wanted all his cronies about him, being determined so far as possible to make 'a family party' of the expedition, a personal following rather than a national army. It was the nature of the man and not necessarily sinister in intent, but Elizabeth was too experienced and astute not to see the danger. There were two principal appointments that he was set on making. One was General of the Horse, for which he wanted the Earl of Southampton, an irresponsible young man who had recently seduced and then married one of the Queen's maids of honour, a cousin of Essex. He was still in disgrace for the offence. Knowing that Elizabeth would disapprove, Essex had intended to lie low until his own commission was passed, giving him authority to bestow all offices, when—to quote his own words—'if she quarrel with me, her wrong is the greater and my standing upon it will appear more just'. Elizabeth got wind of his intention, and interposed her veto. Essex resolved to wait until he reached Ireland and then defy his sovereign. His other right-hand man was to be his stepfather, Sir Christopher Blount, a young man of his own age—clay in his hands, like Southampton. He made him Marshal of the Army, of which Elizabeth approved. But in addition he wished to have him a member of the Irish Privy Council, a dignity not in his gift: this Elizabeth very properly denied. He then tried to carry his request with a high hand, announcing that he was returning Blount and would take the Marshal's office on his own shoulders, asking at the same time to be relieved of his command. 'I sued to her Majesty to grant it out of favour', he wrote to the Council, 'but I spake a language that was not understood, or to a goddess not at leisure to hear prayers. . . . But I see, let me plead in any form, it is in vain'. This time it was Essex who was forced to surrender. He left England in a gloomy mood, asking the Council rather to pity him than to expect extraordinary successes. Self-assurance was evaporating. Perhaps, already, he shrank from the encounter with Tyrone—the Rubicon of his fortunes.

Arrived in Ireland, this man, who had been unable to stomach a sovereign's advice, let the Irish Council persuade him that the main operations in Ulster must be postponed until June when the grass had grown and cattle for feeding the army were fat; meanwhile he should undertake a campaign in Leinster. Maybe the advice was sound: if so, it remains a mystery how the collective wisdom of England managed to overlook such an elementary consideration. Without waiting for his sovereign and her Council to say yea or nay to the fundamental change of plan, he set out. The day before, he dubbed two knights, though his instructions explicitly ordered him to use the power with discretion and only where there had been some notorious service. It was the inauguration of his most defiant, most prodigal, and most sinister use of this honour. One recipient was a runaway official, who with like offenders had been summoned home! He also made Southampton General of the Horse. It was a little time before Elizabeth heard of it, but she then sent order that Southampton was to be dismissed from the office. Instead of obeying, Essex declared that it would heap disgrace on himself, spread dismay in the army, 'which already looks sadly upon me', and encourage the rebels.

Elizabeth aptly likened the Leinster expedition to the track of a ship at sea: like the waters of the ocean the rebels merely opened before the passage of Essex and closed again behind him. He was led on and on by the mirage of some feat to be performed, and from Leinster was drawn into Munster, where there had been no suggestion of his going. June—the month for the Ulster campaign—came and went. At home the Court heard of the Queen's biting remark that she was allowing Essex a thousand pounds a day to go on progress. It was well into July before he arrived back in Dublin, with a broken and weary army and no feat to boast of but the taking of a paltry castle, which a year later was retaken by sixty men and afterwards surrendered to bare threats.

The awful sense of failure, whose prophetic knell had been ringing in his mind for months, now possessed Essex. Mind and body were alike distempered. Pride blinded him to his own shortcomings, and the mania bred by years of tyrannical jealousy and excited afresh by the news that Cecil had been made Master of the Wards, led him to attribute his difficulties to the machinations of enemies at Court. 'But why do I talk of victory or success?' he wrote to Elizabeth, a fortnight before his return to Dublin. 'Is it not known that from England I receive nothing but discomforts and soul's wounds? Is it not spoken in the army that your Majesty's favour is diverted from me and that already you do bode ill both to me and it? . . . Is it not lamented of your Majesty's faithfullest subjects, both here and there, that a Cobham or a Raleigh—I will forbear others for their places' sake—should have such credit and favour with your Majesty, when they wish the ill-success of your Majesty's most important action, the decay of your greatest strength, and the destruction of your faithfullest servants? Yes, yes, I see both my own destiny and your Majesty's decree, and do willingly embrace the one and obey the other. Let me honestly and zealously end a wearisome life'. 'I provided for this service a plastron and not a cuirass', he told the Council; 'that is, I am armed on the breast, but not on the back.'

Elizabeth loosed the pent-up flood of her scorn. He was back in Dublin, she wrote to Essex, but had given her little light on his intentions concerning the main operations against Ulster. She might be satisfied with his personal labours of mind and body, but he must surely realize that she who had the eyes of foreign princes on her actions and the hearts of people to comfort and cherish, who were groaning under the burden of continual levies and impositions, could find little pleasure in what had yet been accomplished. One thing displeased her more than the ruinous expense: 'that it must be the Queen of England's fortune, who hath held down the greatest enemy she had, to make a base bush kern—Tyrone—to be accounted so famous a rebel'.

She reminded him of his breach of duty: that according to his instructions he ought on arrival to have sent her a list of his military establishment; but she still did not know, except by report, who were spending her money or who had places of note in her army. It was strange, with a kingdom at stake and in a country where experience counted for so much, that regiments should be committed to young gentlemen 'who rather desire to do well than know how to perform it'. It is not enough, she went on, that you have all, and more than all, that was agreed upon before you went; but you must by your actions raise an opinion that there is a person—Essex—who dares displease us, relying on past leniency or future renown. 'Then must we not hide from you —how much soever we do esteem you for those good things which are in you—but that our honour hath dwelt too long with us to leave that point now uncleared.' 'Whosoever it be that you do clad with any honours or places wherein the world may read the least suspicion of neglect or contempt of our commandments, we will never make dainty to set on such shadows as shall quickly eclipse any of those lustres.' Turning to the specific instance of Southampton's appointment, she rated Essex for thinking by his private arguments to carry for his own glory a matter wherein her pleasure to the contrary had been made notorious. He had hinted that the gentlemen volunteers would desert the army and return home if Southampton were disgraced. She grimly answered that she had yet to be persuaded that the motive of their service was affection for Southampton or himself and not their love and duty to her. The 'hot waters' had lost their operation with a vengeance!

Before this letter reached him, and again without giving the authorities at home a chance to comment on his action, Essex went off to fritter still more time and men on another minor campaign in Leinster. Elizabeth wrote a trenchant letter telling him to proceed against Tyrone without delay; and to prevent him from deserting his command on the excuse of the great preparations then being made in England against the 'Invisible Armada'—an invasion which did not mature—she commanded him on his duty not to return without permission. He had demanded extra troops, probably hoping for a refusal. They were granted him. He tried again, but more blatantly, to wriggle out of the Ulster campaign. A stinging letter from Elizabeth reinforced her orders. When, at this time, a great disaster befell one of her commanders, 'like a prince' she showed no fruitless sorrow, but bitterly remarked that no good success could accompany a man who would never listen to sound advice.

Essex was an ill man: he seems to have suffered from the stone and kindred troubles. He was in a pitiable predicament: he had gambled on peerless glory or ruin, and ruin stared him in the face. He had locked up nearly three-quarters of his army in garrison: the very fault, on a grand scale, that he had chastised in others. He had to march against Tyrone, but could not hope to command victory. A man of his temperament must break or become reckless: he did the latter. He flung honour, duty, and allegiance to the winds. He sent secretly to Tyrone—if for nothing more, certainly to prepare the way for a parley instead of battle; and using his power to pardon treasons, he issued a pardon to the messenger and to his stepfather Blount, who was to take responsibility if the fact leaked out. Tyrone sent word that if the Earl would follow his advice, he would make him the greatest man that ever was in England. The tempter's voice reached a mind not unfitted to hear it.

Essex had come to the conclusion that he must defy his sovereign's command, and return to England. He was thinking of taking some three thousand men from his army, landing in Wales, where he had a large following, and marching on the Court, not to overthrow the Queen—an outrage which the sixteenth-century mind found horrible to contemplate though not necessarily to effect—but to remove 'his enemies' from her presence and destroy them. Folk had mused, early in the year, at the appearance of John Hayward's *Life of Henry IV*, with its story of Bolingbroke's landing in England and the deposition of Richard II—a 'best seller' which had been dedicated to Essex. They had better

ground to muse now. After the first months in Ireland, when
he had grossly abused his power of conferring knighthood,
Elizabeth had sent Essex 'an express letter, all written with
her own hand', absolutely prohibiting him from making
another knight. Nevertheless, in these months of August and
September he dubbed thirty-eight! People in England were
stupefied; but he was preparing a company of reckless
young gentlemen to follow him in his desperate enterprise.
In all secrecy he disclosed his treasonable thoughts to
Blount and Southampton. They opposed the mad plan. Accepting his view that it was essential to return to England,
they suggested that he should take 'a competent number'
of choice followers with him, who in the event of his finding the Queen ungracious would be able to save him from
imprisonment, or from any danger graver than temporary
confinement to the house of some friend in the Council.
Essex was compelled to accept their alternative, as without
their countenance and help he could not hope to take over
an army.

Thus the plan was reduced to an attempt to escape from
the siren of military greatness, and get back by fair means
if possible, by foul if not, on to the less perilous course of
civil greatness. But first, Essex had to go and look 'on yonder
proud rebel', Tyrone. In order to prepare the Queen for the
ridiculous mouse that was to come from his mountainous
labour, and perhaps—as she suspected—to intimidate her
with the fear that the army was behind him, he called a
meeting of the officers of the army, who proceeded to sign
a resolution dissenting from the Ulster campaign. It may
seem reasonable procedure in modern eyes, but it was
strange insolence then.

On September 14th Elizabeth wrote a devastating letter.
All the criticisms, boasts, assertions and promises that Essex
had made in England came home to roost. She traced his
constant shunning of the operations against Tyrone. It is
your proceedings, she told him, that have begotten your
difficulties. 'If sickness of the army be the reason, why was
not the action undertaken when the army was in better
state? If winter's approach, why were the summer months

of July and August lost? If the spring were too soon, and the summer that followed otherwise spent, if the harvest that succeeded were so neglected as nothing hath been done, then surely we must conclude that none of the four quarters of the year will be in season for you and that Council to agree of Tyrone's prosecution, for which all our charge is intended.' It could not be ignorance: his statements in England proved that. It could not be want of means: 'you had your asking; you had choice of times, you had power and authority more ample than ever any had, or ever shall have'. He had described everything in Ireland as worse now than when he arrived: 'whosoever shall write the story of this year's action,' she remarked, 'must say that we were at too great charge to hazard our kingdom, and you have taken great pains to prepare for many purposes which perish without undertaking'.

Before the letter was written, the miserable farce—which cost Elizabeth £300,000 in seven months—had been played out. Essex marched against Tyrone with only a small army, made a show of trying to bring on a battle, and then on September 7th met the rebel leader at a ford and for half an hour held solitary talk with him as he sat bareheaded, his horse up to its belly in the water, while Essex remained on the opposite bank. Southampton was instructed to keep away all eavesdroppers, but three men were said to have hidden themselves and overheard the conversation, and their reports later reached the Queen. Probably, Essex let Tyrone into his desperate plans and was promised his help if needed: it may even be that there was wild talk of the one becoming King of England, the other Viceroy of Ireland. For the present, Tyrone formulated conditions of peace that amounted to little short of 'Ireland for the Irish', and Essex promised to deliver them verbally to the Queen. A truce was agreed upon, and the army returned to Dublin. There Essex may just have received another sharp letter from Elizabeth, criticising his dealings with Tyrone and marvelling at his strange reticence about them, when on September 24th he suddenly told the Irish Council that he was returning to England, and taking with him that 'competent number' of choice men, set off half an hour later.

On Friday morning, the twenty-eighth, after shedding his escort at London—where if necessary they could take action to free him—Essex rode hard to the Court at Nonsuch which he reached about 10 a.m. All bemired, he made straight through the Presence and Privy Chambers to the bedchamber, bursting in on Elizabeth as she was dressing, her hair about her face. She had not learnt the serpent's wisdom in vain. Throughout this tragedy she knew much that was going on, and no doubt suspected more. It may even be that she had an inkling already of his plans: at any rate, her moves were exquisitely adapted to defeat them. She cloaked her thoughts, and Essex left her presence, thanking God that after trouble and storm abroad, he found a sweet calm at home. He saw her again after making himself presentable: the sky was still clear. At dinner his friends thronged about him. 'As God help me,' wrote Sir Robert Sidney's agent at Court, 'it is a very dangerous time here; for the heads of both factions being here, a man cannot tell how to govern himself towards them'. But in the afternoon, having seen Cecil and measured her own and Essex's strength, Elizabeth put on the judge's mien and ordered him to explain his conduct to the Council. Not until night was his liberty restrained, and then he was merely confined to his chamber. Two more days passed; on the Monday he was sent from Court and committed to the custody of a councillor-friend, Lord Keeper Egerton. Time had been given for hot-heads to cool, and the punishment fell short of that which was to be the signal for a forcible rescue.

A few days later, Elizabeth, who in her last letter to Essex had said of Tyrone that 'to trust this traitor upon oath is to trust a devil upon his religion', told the French ambassador that it was not her intention, but that of 'a Monsieur d'Essex' —uttering these words with passion—to pardon the Irish rebels; she would show him that he had no power. If it had been her own son, she declared, who had committed a like fault, she would have put him in the highest tower in England. But the world did not realize the quality of her indignation, and looked daily for the captive's release. It was well that it was so. London was crowded with knights, captains, officers and soldiers, who had deserted the Irish army leaving it in dangerous disorder. They were possessed by that vindictive hatred of Cecil, Raleigh, and others of the opposite faction, which was the seed of insanity in their leader's mind. One knight who on the morning of the twenty-eighth is said to have offered to slay Lord Grey to prevent his arriving at Court before Essex, took a cup at an inn and drank to his hero's health and the damnation of his enemies, threatening to stab another for not drinking with him.

These men were easily able to stir the citizens of London with their own emotions. Was not Essex their darling? Had they not flocked in their thousands to watch him at his recreations and shooting-matches? Had he not taken infinite pleasure and pride in the sweet music of their praise? Here was the rub for Elizabeth. If it were a sin to covet popularity, she was the most offending person alive; and now she found herself at issue with Essex for her very soul, for though in their obstinate blindness the people insisted on loving both their Elizabeth and their Essex and found scapegoats for the latter's misfortune in Cecil and his ilk, the shafts of their hatred, aimed at Cecil, pierced her. She was troubled and angry. Southampton's wife and Lady Rich found it expedient to leave Essex House and retire into the country to avoid the crowds that came to them. Cecil's aunt, the old Dowager Lady Russell, who pointed her letters with classical quotations, wrote to warn her nephew of vile words spoken against him at an inn, and to express her fear that the day of Essex's restraint would prove the beginning of evils. 'I sorrow in my heart my sovereign's hurt; your peril I fear, and danger to come . . . I can but pray.'

Essex—in whose mind were blacker recollections of heinous words and actions than we can ever know, engendering a desperate fear of discovery, now that he was down—fell ill. Elizabeth sent her physician, and allowed him the use of the garden at Egerton's house. Already she had evilence which must have made her scent treason in his dealings with Tyrone, but even when fuller knowledge of his plots reached her, she kept the secrets from her Council, her policy—as she told the French ambassador fifteen months later—being to trust that Essex would reform. She was still trying to tame her thoroughbred, for the sake of those good things' that were in him. But within the limits of a policy that remained steady, her emotions were like the wind, blowing this way and that, sometimes with tempestuous strength. A week after sending her physician to Essex, Sir John Harington returned home with an Irish knighthood, symbol of a rival loyalty. The thought of Essex stealing her godson's affection let her passion loose. Catching Harington by the girdle as he knelt before her, she exclaimed, 'By God's Son! I am no Queen; that man is above me. Who gave him command to come here so soon? I did send him on other business'. 'Go home!' 'I did not stay to be bidden twice,' says Harington. 'If all the Irish rebels had been at my heels, I should not have had better speed, for I did now flee from one whom I both loved and feared too.'

Essex grew worse, and public opinion became more inflamed. Dangerous libels were cast about in Court, City, and Country, and alehouse talk ran riot. On November 29th, the end of the legal term, when it was customary for the Lord Keeper to deliver an hortatory address to the public in the Star Chamber, an impressive gathering assembled and four of the principal councillors spoke at length in defence of the Queen, inveighing against the talk and libels and explaining the failures and offences of Essex. A week or so later the illness became critical. Moved to pity, Elizabeth ordered eight physicians to hold a consultation, and sent Essex some broth with an injunction to comfort himself, saying that if she might with her honour visit him, she would; tears were in her eyes. On the nineteenth it was said that he was dead, and bells were tolled. Divines prayed for him: 'Look mercifully with thy gracious favour upon that noble Barak thy servant, the Earl of Essex, strengthening him in the inward man against all his enemies. . . . And in thy good time, restore him unto his former health and gracious favour of his and our most dread sovereign, to thy glory, the good of this Church and Kingdom, and the grief and discouragement of all wicked Edomites that bear evil will to Zion and say to the walls of Jerusalem, "There, there, down with it, down with it to the ground".' Men began to scrawl villainous remarks about Cecil on the very walls of the Court. On his door was written, 'Here lieth the Toad'. The divines were ordered to be silent. Elizabeth's favour cooled and her heart hardened.

Bacon, now one of the Queen's counsel at law, had tried to dissuade her from the public defence of her policy in the Star Chamber, saying that Essex in the arena of public opinion was too strong for her and that she should wrap the business up privately. Machiavelli could not have probed Elizabeth's wound more shrewdly; yet Wisdom's child in later years took credit for the remark as friendly to Essex! He had been sound in his diagnosis, but Elizabeth was passionate in her rectitude. She determined to vindicate herself by bringing Essex to public trial in the Star Chamber, not, as she repeatedly said, to destroy but to correct him. Bacon once more gave advice, on this occasion in the words of Friar Bacon's brazen head, *Time is, Time was, Time would never be*: 'it is now far too late, the matter is cold and hath taken too much wind'. Robert Cecil, who was either grossly maligned by his libellers or wove the closest veil of secrecy over his thoughts of any politician in his age —the truth is inscrutable—also disapproved of the trial. By his means Essex wrote a humble submission to the Queen, praying that the cup might pass from him. Reluctantly, with last-minute doubts and reserving her vindication for another time and place, she cancelled the trial. Essex expressed his gratitude for her infinite goodness: 'God is witness how faithfully I vow to dedicate the rest of my life to your Majesty, without admitting any other worldly care'. God was also witness of other thoughts which time was to reveal.

This was in February, 1600. Either then or in the succeeding few months, Raleigh wrote a shocking but sagacious letter to Cecil: 'I am not wise enough to give you advice, but if you take it for a good counsel to relent towards this tyrant, you will repent it when it shall be too late. His malice is fixed and will not evaporate by any your mild courses, for he will ascribe the alteration to her Majesty's pusillanimity and not to your good nature, knowing that you work but upon her humour and not out of any love towards him. The less you make him, the less he shall be able to harm you and yours; and if her Majesty's favour fail him, he will again decline to a common person. . . . Lose not your advantage. If you do, I read your destiny'. In a postscript he added: He will ever be the canker of the Queen's estate and safety. 'I have seen the last of her good days and all ours after his liberty'.

In March Essex was allowed to remove to his own house under the care of a keeper. But in May, an enterprising printer or irresponsible friends did him ill service by publishing a tract written by him in 1598 and known as his *Apology,* which was calculated to stir the hearts of admirers, 'men of action' especially; and crowning insolence, along with it was printed a malapert letter from Lady Rich to the Queen, pleading for her brother. About the same time, someone published the terrible letter to Lord Keeper Egerton written by Essex in the height of passion after the ear-boxing incident of 1598. If enemies were responsible, it was a scurvy trick; if friends, as Bacon declared and on the whole is more likely, it was an incitement to sedition. Essex was in despair. He wrote a frenzied letter to the Queen: 'As if I were thrown into a corner like a dead carcass, I am gnawed on and torn by the basest creatures upon earth. The prating tavern haunter speaks of me what he lists; the frantic libeller writes of me what he lists; they print me and make me speak to the world, and shortly they will play me upon the stage. The least of these is worse than death, but this is not the worst of my destiny; for you, who have protected from scorn and infamy all to whom you once avowed favour but Essex, . . . have now, in this eighth month of my close imprisonment, rejected my letters and refused to hear of me, which to traitors you never did. What remains is only to beseech you to conclude my punishment, my misery, and my life'.

It was an impossible situation. Elizabeth, who had abandoned the Star Chamber trial against her better judgment, was particularly annoyed at the slanderous but specious talk that Essex had been condemned unheard. She decided to vindicate herself. On June 5th, Essex was brought before a special commission of councillors and others, with a select audience. His cue was complete submission, as the commissioners' cue was to avoid the charge of disloyalty. Elizabeth still wanted the way open for a reformed Essex to return to her service. Coke, the Attorney-General, nearly ruined the game with his accustomed invectives, but helped by his judges Essex mastered his passionate nature and submitted: 'the tears of his heart,' he said, 'had quenched all the sparkles of pride that were in him'. The court's censure or judgment suspended him from his various offices and continued his imprisonment, until the Queen in her mercy should choose to remit his punishment. 'It was a most pitiful and lamentable sight to see him that was the minion of Fortune, now unworthy of the least honour'. Many present burst into tears at his fall to such misery. Nine days later, in the Star Chamber, the Lord Keeper again spoke to the world in defence of the Queen's actions. There was, he said, a company of gentlemen in London—nay, they were not gentlemen, but men who 'went brave' and lived by the sword or their wits—who were movers of sedition and had libelled the Queen's proceedings.

Odd incidents postponed the intended operation of mercy, but at the beginning of July Essex's keeper was removed from him, and by the end of August he was free to go anywhere save to Court. He now proceeded to write a series of seductive letters to win his way there: 'Haste paper to that happy presence whence only unhappy I am banished! Kiss that fair correcting hand which lays now plasters to my lighter hurts, but to my greatest wound applieth nothing. Say thou camest from shaming, languishing, despairing Essex'. 'Words, if you can, express my lowly thankfulness; but press not, sue not, move not, lest passion prompt you, and I by you both be betrayed. Report my silence, my solitariness, my sighs, but not my hopes, my fears, my desires; for my uttermost ambition is to be a mute person in that presence where joy and wonder would bar speech.'

To one letter Elizabeth sent a verbal answer, 'that thankfulness was ever welcome and seldom came out of season', and that Essex did well so dutifully to acknowledge that what was done was so well meant. Lady Scrope, one of the ladies-in-waiting, presented another letter, which Elizabeth read twice or thrice and seemed exceedingly pleased. Thereupon, Lady Scrope expressed the hope that she would restore her favour to one who with so much true sorrow desired it. Elizabeth answered never a word, but sighed and said, 'Indeed it was so', and with that rose and went into the Privy Chamber. At a wedding mask a month or two before, when Mary Fitton, one of the performers, came and wooed the Queen to dance, Elizabeth had asked what she represented. 'Affection', answered Mary Fitton. 'Affection!' said the Queen; 'Affection is false'.

Affection was false. All these months Essex had been nursing the treasonable thoughts which possessed his mind in Ireland. On his return to England he had committed his fortunes to the Earl of Southampton and Lord Mountjoy. These two and others, about the end of October, when there was fear of his being sent to the Tower, had suggested that he should escape. He answered that if they could think of no better course than a poor flight, he would rather run any danger. Almost at once, Mountjoy's appointment to succeed Essex in Ireland offered the better course: it brought the Irish army under their control again. The new Lord Deputy—in this revealing the same mentality as the Huguenots in the past, who imagined that they neutralized rebellion by securing the support of a Prince of the Blood —sent secretly to James VI, with whom he had previously been intriguing, promising that if he would enter into the cause and prepare an army, he—Mountjoy—would bring over four or five thousand men from Ireland, re-establish Essex in power and declare James heir to the throne. The messenger ultimately returned with a satisfactory, if cautious answer, but was discovered and imprisoned. Elizabeth said nothing. Mountjoy was already in Ireland, and, away from the dangerous influence of his mistress, Lady Rich, was becoming absorbed, like the capable Viceroy he was, in an honest task.

In April Essex sent a letter by the Earl of Southampton, asking Mountjoy to bring over his army and land in Wales. He refused. The imprisonment of his messenger had alarmed him, and since Essex no longer had any reason to fear for his life, he was unwilling to go to such lengths in order to satisfy private ambition. Balked for the moment, by the end of July Essex was again busy with a plan for seizing the Court by main force, and once more sent to Ireland asking Mountjoy for a number of captains and men of quality, and also for a letter countenancing the conspiracy, with which to coerce the Queen. He expected a following that would bring him to Court 'in such peace, as a dog should not wag his tongue against him!' James was on the Border at the time with a strong force: possibly an accident, possibly not. Mountjoy upset the plan by urging patience, and Essex turned to move the Queen as a stylist instead of a traitor. There is suggestive evidence that early in August the Government had tapped the conspiracy. But if Elizabeth knew what was going on, she still said nothing; she only sighed at the sweet phrases distilled from Affection's pen. Affection was false.

At Michaelmas the farm or lease of the customs on sweet wines, which Essex held from the Queen, fell in. It was the mainstay of his estate, bringing a considerable revenue —more, indeed, than it was safe for Elizabeth to know; and he was so deeply in debt to the wine merchants that if they stampeded as other creditors had done—rats deserting a sinking ship—he and his friends, who had stood surety for him, would be ruined. Elizabeth claimed that she had made him gifts to the extent of £300,000 in his short career, but his princely extravagance, in his own and her service, had brought his fortune to nothing. In July he had told a fellow-conspirator that by the renewing of the lease, or the taking of it from him, 'he should judge what was meant him.' In September he began to mention the matter in his seductive letters to the Queen. She told Bacon that Essex 'had written some very dutiful letters and that she had been moved by them, and when she took it to be the abundance of the heart, she found it to be but a preparative to a suit for the renewing of his farm of sweet wines.' She is said to have commended an aphorism of physicians: 'Corrupt bodies, the more you feed them, the more hurt you do them'; and also to have remarked, 'that an unruly horse must be abated of his provender, that he may be the more easily and better managed'. Whether true or not, the remark reflects the thoughts of one who almost certainly guessed her petitioner's secrets and perceived that it was a question whether Elizabeth or Essex should be ruler of England. She did not renew the lease; nor did she grant it to anyone else. She took it into her own hands: it was there to be claimed by the reformed Essex of her imagination.

The last letter that we possess from Essex to Elizabeth was written on Accession Day, November 17th, 1600. Eloquence, misery, pathos! how pitiful it was. But the heart was not humble. This nature, in its mental storm, again became reckless. Wild remarks fell from his lips: 'that being now an old woman', the Queen 'was no less crooked and distorted in mind than she was in body'. Sir John Harington saw him: 'He uttered strange words,' he records, 'bordering on such strange designs that made me hasten forth and leave his presence. Thank heaven! I am safe at home, and if I go in such troubles again, I deserve the gallows for a meddling fool. His speeches of the Queen becometh no man who hath *mens sana in corpore sano* . . . The Queen well knoweth how to humble the haughty spirit; the haughty spirit knoweth not how to yield, and the man's soul seemeth tossed to and fro, like the waves of a troubled sea'.

Essex had come to 'the last act, which was written in the Book of Necessity'. Essex House was thrown open to all comers: 'swordsmen, bold confident fellows, men of broken fortunes, discontented persons, and such as saucily used their tongues in railing against all men'. Each day zealous ministers preached sermons there, which brought the citizens flocking in great numbers. Lady Rich was there with her proud spirit to urge her brother on, telling him that he had lost his valour, and all his friends and followers thought him a coward. 'It went as a kind of cipher and watchword' among his adherents, 'That my Lord would stand upon his guard', and they were told to be in London by the beginning of February. They came, from almost every county. Elizabeth and Cecil watched, but said nothing.

On Tuesday, February 3rd, five of the leaders—Essex keeping away, to avoid suspicion—met at Drury House, Southampton's lodging, to consider certain proposals drawn up by Essex for seizing possession of the Court, the Tower, and the City. The plans for the Court were elaborate: one party was to gather in the Presence Chamber, another in the Guard Chamber, another in the Hall, another at the Gate, and at a signal were to step between the guards and their halberds and take control of the Court, while Essex was to come with his noble friends to extort from Elizabeth that change of government at which they aimed. They avowed, and probably hoped, that there would be no bloodshed; but as Sir Christopher Blount declared at his execution, 'I know and must confess, if we had failed of our ends, we should, rather than have been disappointed, even have drawn blood from herself'—the Queen. Knowing Elizabeth, they could have expected nothing else, but like children they put the horrible prospect from them. Essex had already written to James VI asking him to time a diplomatic *démarche* to coincide with and support his action. Some of his hare-brained followers bribed Shakespeare's company, with a *douceur* of forty shillings, to play the deposing and killing of King Richard II at the Globe Theatre on the Saturday afternoon; and after dining together a company of them crossed the river to witness this ominous performance.

That evening the Council took action, summoning Essex before them. He refused to go, and no longer able to surprise the Court, fell back upon the plan of 'an all-hail and a kiss to the City', appealing for help on the false cry that his enemies intended to murder him and had sold England to the Spaniard. The Duke of Guise, beloved by Parisians as Essex by Londoners, had on the Day of Barricades in 1588 entered Paris in doublet and hose, with nine or ten companions, and driven the King from his capital. Why should not Essex succeed as well? All that evening and early the next morning, Sunday, February 8th, preparations were hastily made. About 10 a.m., the Lord Keeper, the Earl of Worcester, Sir William Knollys, and the Chief Justice, former friends of his, came to Essex House in the name of the Queen. There they found a tumultuous assembly, some of whom shouted, 'Kill them!' 'Cast the Great Seal out of the window!' Essex made the four messengers prisoners, leaving them under guard as hostages, while he and his troop of some two hundred young noblemen and gentlemen made their way to the City.

'For the Queen! For the Queen! A plot is laid for my life!' Essex cried as he rode up Ludgate Hill and along Cheapside. But Robert Cecil had not let the grass grow under his feet. Timely warning had been sent to the Mayor, and close on the heels of Essex came a herald with a proclamation denouncing him as a traitor. A herald, said Essex scornfully, will do anything for two shillings: 'Pish! the Queen knoweth not of it; that is Secretary Cecil'. The citizens gazed on him and pitied him; some applauded. But when the dreaded name of 'Traitor' was pronounced, his more timid followers slipped away and donned cloaks to look innocent. He had counted confidently on obtaining arms and men from the sheriff: the man failed him. He began to sweat, and spoke with a 'ghast' countenance and like a man forlorn. When an armourer said that he had no arms for him, 'Not for me, Pickering?' he asked. His position was desperate, and at last he resolved to make his way back to Essex House. But Ludgate was locked and an armed force blocked the chained street. He asked for passage; it was refused. Then to cries of 'Saw, saw! Saw, saw! Tray, tray! Shoot, shoot!' his company charged, but were repulsed. He managed to regain his house by the river, only to find his hostages gone and himself besieged. In the evening, when

the Lord Admiral threatened to blow the house up, he at
length surrendered, after burning a collection of incriminating papers, including a letter from James VI, which he carried in a black bag about his neck.

Elizabeth had remained utterly fearless throughout.
When a false alarm reached the Court that the City had
revolted, she was no more amazed 'than she would have
been to hear of a fray in Fleet Street'. 'She would have
gone out in person to see what any rebel of them all durst
do against her, had not her councillors with much ado
stayed her.' 'I then beheld her Majesty,' said the Admiral,
'with most princely fortitude and matchless magnanimity,
to stand up like the Lord's anointed, and offer in person to
face the boldest traitor in the field, relying on God's almighty providence, which had heretofore maintained her.'
The day after the rising, she gave audience to the French
ambassador. 'A senseless ingrate,' she declared, 'had at last
revealed what had long been in his mind.' The nervous
strain of the previous day and of the long months of anticipation had evidently told on her. After a while she began
to laugh and to mock at Essex's parade through the City,
his vain speeches to the people, and his retreat. If he had
reached the Court, she asserted, she was resolved to go out
and face him and see which of the two should reign. With
that, her hysteria passed and she turned to discuss French
affairs.

The mood of the City was uncertain, and it was therefore put under strong guard, while the trained bands from
the surrounding counties were called up, and lay in the
suburbs about the Court, which was guarded like a camp,
'as if the Spaniards were in the land'. A few apprentices,
with the romantic illusions of their class, actually plotted to
raise a company of five thousand to release Essex, 'swear
him not to hurt her Majesty', and then surprise the Court.
Whether Elizabeth's clement impulses would have made
her recoil from sending Essex to his fate, as she had recoiled over Norfolk, it is impossible to say. Any chance was
destroyed by the foolish plot of Captain Lea, a gentleman

of good family, the man who had played the part of secret messenger to Tyrone. He resolved with a few companions to seize the Queen's person as she sat at supper, attended only by her ladies, and force from her a warrant to release Essex and his fellows. On the Thursday following the rising, he was seized at the door leading from the kitchen to the room where the Queen supped.

A week later, Essex, along with Southampton, was brought to trial before his peers. Dressed dramatically in black, he carried himself with superb disdain. When Lord Grey—an enemy—was sworn one of his judges, he 'laughed upon' Southampton and jogged him by the sleeve. As the indictment was read, he smiled several times and lifted his eyes to heaven in mock wonder. Raleigh was a witness: 'What booteth it to swear the fox?' Essex contemptuously asked. He did his best to discredit the witnesses, and when, after casting groundless aspersions upon Cecil's loyalty, the latter intervened with a passionate speech, 'Ah! Mr. Secretary,' he exclaimed, 'I thank God for my humiliation, that you, in the ruff of all your bravery, have come hither to make your oration against me this day'. 'I am indifferent how I speed,' he said; 'I owe God a death'; and after he had been found guilty and the dreadful traitor's death pronounced, 'I think it fitting,' he proudly answered, 'that my poor quarters, which have done her Majesty true service in divers parts of the world, should now at the last be sacrificed and disposed of at her Majesty's pleasure.' 'A man might easily perceive,' wrote one who was present, 'that, as he had lived popularly, so his chief care was to leave a good opinion in the people's minds now at parting.'

The common man, in his perversity, might be pleased with such bravery, but respectable folk thought it arrogant, impudent behaviour—behaviour that few save the kindred spirits of Thomas Seymour and Mary Queen of Scots had displayed. The conventions of the age demanded a submissive and godly last chapter to the traitor's life; for how else should the soul escape damnation? Black was the sin of lifting one's hand against the Lord's anointed, and a defiant

end, where guilt was so manifest, seemed little short of
blasphemy. But Essex's view of the Lord's anointed was like
Seymour's: a child-King was paralleled by a woman—a contemptible old woman as sovereign. Both men in their passion were blind to the throne, and saw only their rivals—
their equals or inferiors. It was a grave mistake in the case
of Essex. He was wrong to imagine that his battle was with
the hunchback Cecil, the fox Raleigh, and their crew; but
imagining it, his proud nature refused to cringe in its last
agony.

Essex returned to the Tower, prepared to count death a
feast. He had asked for the ministrations of one of his chap-
lains, and Mr. Ashton was sent, a man whom the Earl's
disappointed friends described as 'base, fearful, and mercenary', but who perhaps was merely excessively religious and
conventional. He set himself to humble the proud soul, and
before the terrible shafts of his piety self-assurance fled, the
spirit broke. Essex sent for Cecil and three other councillors: 'I am most bound unto her Majesty', he told them,
'that it hath pleased her to let me have this little man, Mr.
Ashton, my minister, with me for my soul; for this man in
a few hours hath made me know my sins unto her Majesty
and to my God; and I must confess to you that I am the
greatest, the most vilest, and most unthankful traitor that
ever has been in the land . . . Yesterday at the bar, like a
most sinful wretch, with countenance and words I imagined
all falsehood'. He asked to confront his secretary: 'Henry
Cuffe,' he said, 'call to God for mercy, and to the Queen,
and deserve it by declaring truth'; whereupon he accused
the man of being the greatest instigator of his actions. He
made a full confession, sparing none of his friends—no, not
his sister, nor even her relations with Mountjoy. 'Would
your Lordship,' wrote the Admiral to Mountjoy, 'have
thought this weakness and this unnaturalness in this man?'

Essex asked for a private death rather than a public one:
'the acclamation of the people might have been a tempta-
tion unto him,' he said: 'all popularity and trust in man was
vain'. On Wednesday morning, February 25th, 1601, he
was led into the courtyard of the Tower to die. He met

death, not carelessly but humbly and devoutly. The thoroughbred was tamed at last: 'he acknowledged, with thankfulness to God, that he was thus justly spewed out of the realm'. He was thirty-four.

CHAPTER XXII

THE PASSING OF THE QUEEN

IN France there was great admiration for the courage and resolution with which Elizabeth had handled the Essex rising. Would that their King Henry III had had but a part of her spirit to quell the insolency of the Duke of Guise on the Day of Barricades! 'She only is a king!' exclaimed Henry IV. 'She only knows how to rule!'

Elizabeth revealed her capacity no less in the unpleasant business of cleaning up after the rebellion. Justice quickly stepped down from her seat and gave place to Mercy. Only six persons were executed: Essex himself, his stepfather Blount, Cuffe, Thomas Lea, and two others. Perhaps the Queen felt that the death of Essex was expiation for the crimes of many, and hoped that now the infectious, tyrannous charm of his personality was removed, conspirators would return to their right minds, and peace and tranquillity be restored to the Commonwealth. Pity, friendship, or bribes led courtiers to intercede for one or other of the chief offenders: they made their petitions to a sovereign who loathed bloodshed. In the case of the Earl of Southampton mercy was strained to unexampled lengths. The world pitied him, and he was humble and contrite, but his guilt was too heinous to allow of hope. Yet the Queen spared him. For the rest, the richer sort were fined: very few of them ever paid—at any rate, in full. Cecil's brother, Lord Burghley, who had taken part in suppressing the rising, wrote from York telling of the great impression made by this clemency: 'a thing the like was never read of in any chronicle.'

An incident showed the Queen's magnanimity. On the return of Essex from Ireland in 1599, his wife, fearing that her house and papers might be searched, had hastily sent a casket of the Earl's letters to a former servant, Jane Daniel. They contained expressions of disloyalty and contempt for the Queen's person; how disloyal and how contemptuous must be inferred from the price set on them, for Jane's husband, having come across the casket, abstracted some of the letters and demanded £3,000 for them. He was paid £1,720, but true to his blackguardly type, retained the originals and surrendered forged copies. The Queen learnt of the matter upon a complaint by Essex at the time of his rising, and ordered diligent inquiries to be made. Vowing that she would keep 'her winding sheet unspotted,' she had Daniel prosecuted in the Star Chamber; and of the £3,000 fine, part of his punishment, £2,000 was given to the Countess.

But all the clemency and magnanimity in the world could not console the people for the death of their hero, their noble Barak, Deborah's mighty man of valour. They might listen to the preacher at St. Paul's Cross as, under official instructions, he deftly exploited his text—'Then David's men sware unto him, saying, thou shalt go no more out with us to battle lest thou quench the light of Israel'; they might break into loud and joyous applause when he touched on her Majesty's deliverance; they might, by their countenances, give cause to think that 'the traitor is now laid out well in colours to every man's satisfaction that heard the sermon'; none the less, their poets wrote lamentable ditties, which they bought and sang:

> Sweet England's pride is gone!
> *welladay! welladay!*
>
> Brave honour graced him still,
> *gallantly, gallantly;*
> He ne'er did deed of ill,
> well it is known;

> But Envy, that foul fiend,
>   whose malice ne'er did end,
> Hath brought true virtue's friend
>   unto his thrall.

Or there was the lamentable ballad, *Essex's Last Good
Night*:

> All you that cry O hone! O hone!
>   come now and sing O Lord! with me.
> For why? Our Jewel is from us gone,
>   the valiant Knight of Chivalry.

They would have murdered the hangman as he returned
from executing Essex if the sheriffs had not rescued him
in time. In alehouses and elsewhere their tongues gave vent
to hatred of the Earl's opponents, and popular poets busied
themselves with lampoons:

> Little Cecil trips up and down,
> He rules both Court and Crown,
> With his Brother Burghley Clown,
> In his great fox-furred gown;
> With the long proclamation
> He swore he saved the Town.
> Is it not likely?

> Raleigh doth time bestride,
> He sits twixt wind and tide,
> Yet up hill he cannot ride,
> For all his bloody pride.
> He seeks taxes in the tin,
> He polls the poor to the skin,
> Yet he swears 'tis no sin.
> Lord for thy pity!

It must have been during these weeks of unrest, if, indeed, it was not in the period between the rising and the
Earl's execution—the date October 9th, 1601, ascribed to
the letter in question, being incredible—that Sir John Harington paid a brief visit to Court, a most imprudent journey, since Essex's followers had been thronging to town to

answer their leader's call, and Harington himself bore the mark of the beast in his Irish knighthood. Elizabeth was obviously suspicious of his motive in coming: If ill counsel, she told him, had brought him so far from home, 'she wished Heaven might mar that fortune which she had mended'. Noticing him still about Court a few weeks later, she sent a sharp message by the Lord Treasurer: 'Go tell that witty fellow, my godson, to get home; it is no season now to fool it here'. 'In good sooth', says Harington, 'I feared her Majesty more than the rebel Tyrone, and wished I had never received my Lord of Essex's honour of knighthood'. He found everything in a disordered state: 'the madcaps are all in riot, and much evil threatened'. As for the Queen, 'she is quite disfavoured, and unattired, and these troubles waste her much. She disregardeth every costly cover that cometh to the table, and taketh little but manchet and succory potage. Every new message from the City doth disturb her, and she frowns on all the ladies.' 'The many evil plots and designs have overcome all her Highness' sweet temper. She walks much in her Privy Chamber, and stamps with her feet at ill news, and thrusts her rusty sword at times into the arras in great rage. . . . The dangers are over, and yet she always keeps a sword by her table.' Harington sometimes needs to be taken with a pinch of salt: perhaps this is one of the occasions.

The unrest soon passed, and a strange quiet replaced it. Cecil, in June, commented on the unwonted peace in Court circles: 'the tree into which so many branches were incorporated, being now fallen, all men that loved him repent their errors'. True, Raleigh, with his henchman Lord Cobham, tried to dispute Cecil's supremacy, thus fulfilling an old prophecy of Meg Radcliffe, a maid of honour, that the anti-Essex pack would break. But Elizabeth gave no countenance to Raleigh's 'bloody pride'. Though she did not share the people's antipathy to him, she agreed in thinking him unfit to succeed an Essex. Robert Cecil therefore ruled; the civil servant in unprecedented supremacy: ability, but ability in how unexhilarating a personality! Faction of the old heroic pattern died with its superb, its insupportable exponent; and it almost seemed as if the soul of Elizabethan England also departed. In the magical hands of the Queen, Court rivalry had been a secret of glory and power; the intense spirit of the age had been kindled at its flame. But in Essex it had burnt with such fierceness as to consume itself, and now the flame could not be relighted. Passion was spent; old age had come. The people, with their enduring sorrow, helped to emphasize the change. For once they were not fickle. Eighteen months later a German visitor found them singing *Essex's Last Good Night* everywhere —even at Court. At the Tower he was shown the spot where 'the brave hero' was beheaded, at Whitehall he must look at the shields which 'the great and celebrated noble warrior' had presented to the Queen when tilting. The glory of England, which had hitherto been in the present, was now in the past, and though the people continued to love their Elizabeth with an affection truly wonderful, how could she help feeling the reproach of their sorrow for the dead Essex, how not mourn the England that died with him?

Grieve over the tragedy of Essex; that Elizabeth might do, but she never doubted its justice and necessity. A fortnight or so after the execution, she told the French ambassador that if the safety of the State had permitted, she would willingly have spared the life of this perfidious ingrate; but Essex himself had recognized that he was unworthy to live and that his life was incompatible with hers, and had asked by his death to deliver her from the danger. She confessed that she was partly to blame for his fall, having made too much of him and allowed him to assume more credit and authority with the nobility and people than became a subject. She could only express her amazement that one who knew her spirit, should have dared to think of dictating to her.

Just as in the previous year there had been a glimpse of the Queen's soul in her bitter comment on Affection, so on this occasion she revealed her personal tragedy in a phrase to Lord Willoughby: 'It appeareth now by one's example, more bound than all or any others, how little faith there was in Israel.' Three earls, two barons, noblemen's sons and brothers, an ambassador, a sheriff of London, and numerous brave gentlemen had been implicated in the plots and the rising. Mountjoy, once a devoted, enthralled courtier and now her Lord Deputy of Ireland, had been prepared to lead his army against her. Even Willoughby, her 'Good Peregrine', was not free from suspicion, for as Governor of Berwick he had facilitated the passing of secret messengers from Essex to Scotland.

The following August, Elizabeth had a conversation with the antiquary, William Lambarde, who had recently been appointed Keeper of the Records in the Tower, and came to present her with a descriptive account of the documents under his charge. 'You intended to present this book unto me by the Countess of Warwick', she began; 'but I will none of that, for if any subject of mine do me a service, I will thankfully accept it from his own hands'. Then she proceeded to read his book aloud, stopping to ask the meaning of technical phrases, remarking 'that she would be a scholar in her age and thought it no scorn to learn during her life, being of the mind of that philosopher, who in his last years began with the Greek alphabet.' Coming to the documents of Richard II's reign, her thoughts flew to the Essex rising and the ominous prominence then given to this king's story. 'I am Richard II', she said; 'know ye not that?' Lambarde made a fitting remark on the wicked imagination of a most unkind gentleman, 'the most adorned creature that ever your Majesty made'. 'He that will forget God', answered Elizabeth, 'will also forget his benefactors. This tragedy—of Richard II—was played forty times in open streets and houses.' The lesson in ancient documents continued, until an explanation prompted another reflection: 'In those days force and arms did prevail; but now the wit of the fox is everywhere on foot, so as hardly a faithful or virtuous man may be found.' 'Farewell, good and honest Lambarde', she said, at last. The zealous antiquary died a fortnight after this kindly audience.

The time was at hand for another—in all human probability, the last Elizabethan parliament. Money was the need. The Queen was still selling lands, and had sold some of her jewels. She had tried to realize her wealth in French and Dutch promissory notes, but Henry IV—that 'Antichrist of ingratitude'—had given fair words galore, without sparing so much as he lavished on his mistresses, while the Dutch had not done much better. The Irish campaign was progressing favourably; yet it was slow and expensive, and as a Spanish force was expected at any moment, Elizabeth had to be prepared for heavy additional commitments. In late September, 1601, a Spanish army landed at Kinsale; at the beginning of November Parliament met.

With the Spaniard on Irish soil, there was no difficulty in obtaining an extraordinary grant of money from the Commons, who were at one with their Speaker in his 'vehement invectives against the tyranny of the King of Spain, the Pope's ambition, and the rebels in Ireland, which, he said, were like a snake cut in pieces, which did crawl and creep to join themselves together again.' In the two previous Parliaments a treble subsidy had been granted; now it was a fourfold. But ready as they were to make this new and supreme financial effort, there was a restless undercurrent. It began with the blunder of a minor official who shut many of the members of the Lower House out of the Parliament Chamber on the opening day, so that they missed the impressive ceremony and the Lord Keeper's speech. Few of them said, 'God bless your Majesty!' as their custom was, when the Queen passed through their midst at the close of the next formal meeting. Then, as the session progressed, a member rose to attack monopolies, and the hunt was up.

These monopolies were royal grants giving the sole right, usually of making or selling some article. What with their profusion—they had come to include articles like salt and starch—and what with the abuses practised by their holders, they were a national scandal. But as the attack on them inevitably touched the Queen's prerogative, it was a delicate situation. The storm had blown up in the last Parliament. Now it raged. After councillors and courtiers had vainly tried to control it, Elizabeth intervened with a message in her most bewitching vein, promising immediate remedy by proclamation. The House at once turned from wrath to inexpressible joy. One member wept, his heart was so full. And the whole body uttered a fervent 'Amen' to the Speaker's prayer for her Majesty's preservation. They asked leave to convey their thanks; she answered that she would receive their love with their thanks, when she had performed her promise. Three days later the Proclamation was in members' hands, and the Queen announced her readiness to receive a deputation. When it came to naming those who should go, some cried, 'All, All, All!' and she sent back word that though the accommodation was limited, they would all be very welcome.

On November 30th, one hundred and forty members, with their Speaker, went to Whitehall to hear the Queen's last wooing of her faithful, troublesome Commons. A member said of her previous message that it was worthy to be written in gold: they and their sons and posterity for several generations were to know the speech which she now made, as Queen Elizabeth's 'Golden Speech'. Her touch was as sure as ever it had been, and the inimitable perfection of her art was heightened by the thought, which must have been in every mind, that she was practising it for the last time. In effect, if not in strict fact, these were her last words to the Realm that she had loved and served with her whole being.

'Mr. Speaker,' she began, 'We perceive your coming is to present thanks to us. Know I accept them with no less joy than your loves can have desire to offer such a present, and do more esteem it than any treasure or riches; for those we know how to prize, but loyalty, love, and thanks, I account them invaluable. And though God hath raised me high, yet this I account the glory of my crown, that I have reigned with your loves. This makes me that I do not so much rejoice that God hath made me to be a Queen, as to be a Queen over so thankful a people, and to be the means under God to conserve you in safety and to preserve you from danger. . . . Of myself I must say this: I never was any greedy, scraping grasper, nor a strict, fast-holding prince, nor yet a waster; my heart was never set upon any worldly goods, but only for my subjects' good. What you do bestow on me, I will not hoard up, but receive it to bestow on you again; yea, my own properties I account yours, to be expended for your good, and your eyes shall see the bestowing of it for your welfare'.

At this point Elizabeth bade them stand up—they had hitherto knelt—for she would trouble them with longer speech. She continued, 'Mr. Speaker, you give me thanks, but I am more to thank you, and I charge you, thank them of the Lower House from me; for, had I not received knowledge from you, I might have fallen into the lapse of an error, only for want of true information. . . . That my grants shall be made grievances to my people, and oppressions be privileged under colour of our patents, our princely dignity shall not suffer. When I heard it, I could give no rest unto my thoughts until I had reformed it. . . . It is not my desire to live or reign longer than my life and reign shall be for your good. And though you have had, and may have, many mightier and wiser princes sitting in this seat, yet you never had, nor shall have any that will love you better.' At the close of the speech—probably realizing that this would be her last Parliament—she begged her councillors to bring all these gentlemen to kiss her hand before they departed to their homes.

Doubtless a tragic quiet had fallen on the country, but, as this Parliament revealed, while Queen Elizabeth lived to set the hearts of people aflame, the spirit of her England was not dead. Even as members were arriving back in their homes, intoxicated with their Sovereign's golden words and her infinite graciousness and affection, Mountjoy in Ireland won an overwhelming victory over Tyrone's army before Kinsale, and a week later the Spanish army there capitulated—one of the most decisive events in Irish history. It was a triumph that reflected credit on Sovereign as well as servant, for though the story of Essex in Ireland might suggest that Elizabeth was a difficult mistress to serve, her relations with Mountjoy showed that she could be helpful and inspiring where there was honest effort and a dutiful mind. The Lord Deputy had his grievances. In one sulking dispatch he had likened himself to a scullion. Elizabeth thereupon wrote to him a long, comforting, bantering letter in her own hand, christening him 'Mistress Kitchenmaid' and dissipating his cloud of discontent. When the Spaniards landed at Kinsale, she wrote—again in her own hand—to fire him and his army to heroic endeavour: 'Tell our army from us, that they make full account that every hundred of them will beat a thousand, and every thousand theirs doubled. I am the bolder to pronounce it in His name that ever hath protected my righteous cause, in which I bless them all. And putting you in the first place, I end, scribbling in haste. Your loving sovereign, E.R.' Glowing thanks were sent to both commander and army for their great victory, and Mountjoy continued to receive those affectionate postscripts or whole letters in the Queen's hand, which revived his spirits, as by a miracle. One she ended, 'We have forgotten to praise your humility, that after having been a Queen's Kitchenmaid you have not disdained to be a Traitor's Scullion. God bless you with perseverance.'

Nor was the fame of past days recalled only on land. In June, 1602, Sir Richard Leveson, with a small royal squadron, captured a huge and rich Portuguese carrack as it lay in Cezimbra Road under the guns of the fort, protected by eleven galleys under the command of a brilliant seaman, and with four hundred gentlemen volunteers aboard who had come from Lisbon to man the carrack. The English forced two galleys to surrender, compelled the rest to retreat with heavy losses, and carried off the prize in the face of ten thousand troops gathered on the shore. It was an exploit worthy of Drake's greatest days.

Occasionally, when her spirits were low, the loneliness of old age oppressed Elizabeth. Rejoicing, as she had done, in nothing so much as the devoted homage of her Court and people, it was peculiarly poignant; for she had commented too often on the tendency of subjects to worship the rising sun, not to guess that this was already going on. Although she herself harboured no doubts as to who should succeed her, and in the curiously maternal and tutorial correspondence that she had maintained for years with James VI, often let him know in unmistakable if veiled phrases what her intentions were, she still refused to make any open declaration on the subject. To have done otherwise would have been to invite all rivals and enemies to set about forestalling his succession, thus jeopardizing both his rights and her domestic peace. So far as rival claimants in England went, none could hope to withstand James and the whole power of Scotland; and when at the end of this year, 1602, one of the claimants, Arabella Stuart, indulged in dangerous intrigue, Elizabeth promptly set close watch on her so that she should not disturb the peaceful transference of the crown. As for foreign claimants and enemies, James, being close at hand, would be in possession of his inheritance before they could make any hostile move. Thus, with perfect statecraft, Elizabeth maintained her reign-long silence on the succession question, still perceiving the true interests of her people better than they did themselves.

For most Englishmen James had become the obvious—nay, the desired successor. The nobility and gentry did not want another woman-ruler, and were determined to tolerate that shameful subjection no longer, while to the people as a whole there was a pleasing strangeness about the prospect of a King, for only the aged could remember the time when England had been ruled by a man. One nobleman, out of a certain shame, might ascribe this general desire to fear that they would never enjoy another Queen like Elizabeth: had she not been as peculiar a dispensation as Deborah? But the truth was that a sense of ennui, tinged with sex prejudice, was stealing over Court and country, 'for things of long continuance, though never so good, are tedious'. There was 'a credulous desire of novelty and change, hoping for better times, despising the present, and forgetting favours past'.

As the year 1602 progressed, courtiers and others entered into secret communication with their future king. Among them—and by far the most important—was Sir Robert Cecil. After the execution of Essex he had begun a secret correspondence, which, combined with the Queen's wise policy, virtually assured James of the succession. With fearful care he kept all knowledge of his letters from Elizabeth: the Queen's 'age and orbity', he wrote in later years, 'joined to the jealousy of her sex, might have moved her to think ill of that which helped to preserve her'. Perhaps he was right, and Elizabeth would have been jealous; but more likely, Cecil's soul lacked the breadth of his father's, and the varying estimates that each made of his sovereign are measures of themselves as much as her. Burghley said that she 'was the wisest woman that ever was, for she understood the interests and dispositions of all the princes in her time, and was so perfect in the knowledge of her own realm, that no councillor she had could tell her anything she did not know before'. 'She was more than a man, and, in troth, sometimes less than a woman,' wrote the son. However it be, Elizabeth, who knew her Cecil, and had her own experience in the latter days of her sister Mary's reign to prompt a shrewd intelligence, must surely have guessed that her Secretary was laying up credit for himself in Scotland against the day of her death. But once more, her motto *Video et taceo* guided her actions: 'I see but say nothing'.

Elizabeth said nothing, but felt the more. In May, in a melancholy mood, she told the French ambassador that she was tired of life, her spirit found no contentment, and there was nothing that gave her pleasure. She sighed as she spoke, uttered some words that betokened resentment of the past, and then went on to speak feelingly of Essex. But there was no suggestion of a change of mind regarding his fall. She sorrowed—she would sorrow till death—over a tragedy that had been inevitable. And when at her next interview she had to speak of a similar situation that confronted Henry IV, in the conspiracy of his old companion-in-arms, the brave and popular Marshal Biron, she drew on her own experience to counsel unfaltering justice. 'Those who touch the sceptres of princes', she said, 'deserve no pity'. The sceptre is like a flaming torch, blazing with such intensity that it burns all who touch it. Clemency in such cases is dangerous. Well she knew what it would cost the King to lose Biron, but she also knew by experience that a sovereign must sacrifice personal affection when the safety of his kingdom and of his successors was in question. The talk lasted two hours.

For all her recurrent melancholy, Elizabeth was enjoying remarkable health. In the summer of 1602 she very much wanted to go on progress as far as Bristol, and was only stayed by the argument that the inclement weather would make it burdensome to the people. In August Cecil declared that she was never in better health these twelve years. In a single day she rode ten miles on horseback, and also hunted: 'whether she was weary or not, I leave to your censure'. Perhaps as a result, she felt unwell one night, but the next day walked abroad, lest anyone should notice her indisposition. In September a foreign visitor saw her walking about in her garden like an eighteen-year-old. Her spirits rose. She 'was never so gallant many years, nor so set upon jollity'. 'We are frolick here at Court.' There was much dancing of country dances, which pleased her exceedingly. One day she spied a locket that the Countess of Derby was wearing, and nothing would content her but she must open it. Seeing that it contained a portrait of Cecil, she snatched it away and sportingly tied it on her shoe, and after that on her elbow. Cecil—a fulsome courtier—had some verses written about the incident and set to music, and drew the Queen into his chamber to hear them.

Elizabeth had now entered upon her seventieth year. On November 17th, 1602, she passed the forty-fourth anniversary of her accession 'with as great an applause of multitudes as if they had never seen her before'. On December 6th she dined at Cecil House, the new house that Cecil had built for himself in the Strand, and the house-warming took the form of elaborate entertainments in the vein of the past: perhaps too much in that vein for Elizabeth's taste, for one of the devices was 'a pretty dialogue' twixt a maid, a widow, and a wife on the respective merits of their state of life, in which the virgin of course triumphed!

Later that month, Sir John Harington came to Court, and noticed a great change. 'Our dear Queen,' he wrote to his wife, 'doth now bear show of human infirmity; too fast for that evil which we shall get by her death, and too slow for that good which she shall get by her releasement from pains and misery. . . . I find some less mindful of what they are soon to lose, than of what they may perchance hereafter get. Now, on my own part, I cannot blot from my memory's table the goodness of our Sovereign Lady to me . . . ; her affection to my mother, who waited in Privy Chamber, her bettering the state of my father's fortune . . . ; her watchings over my youth, her liking to my free speech and admiration of my little learning and poesy, which I did so much cultivate on her command.' 'To turn askant from her condition with tearless eyes, would stain and foul the spring and fount of gratitude.' The Queen sent for him. She asked if he had ever seen Tyrone, and his answer bringing recollections of Essex, she looked up with much choler and grief in her countenance, and said, 'Oh! now it mindeth me that you was one who saw this man elsewhere.' With that she dropped a tear and smote her bosom. He read her some of his witty verses; she smiled, but said, 'When thou dost feel creeping time at thy gate, these fooleries will please thee less: I am past my relish for such matters.' Unless the editor of Harington's papers has again played tricks with his dates, antedating this letter by a couple of months, Elizabeth's indisposition must have been temporary, for the day before the letter professes to have been written, she was dancing a coranto! Christmas was spent at Whitehall with the accustomed gaiety; and on January 18th, 1603, the Queen was still in excellent health.

On January 21st, the Court moved to Richmond in very foul and wet weather, and the wind suddenly changing to the north-east brought on, says a letter-writer, 'the sharpest season that I have lightly known'. In this extremely cold weather Elizabeth wore 'summer-like garments', and showed them to one of her officials, 'contemning furs to withstand winter cold.' No wonder Burghley wrote to his brother that the Queen ought to realize 'that she is old, and to have more care of herself, and that there is no contentment to a young mind in an old body'. On February 6th there was an audience with an envoy from Venice. Dressed in silver and white taffeta trimmed with gold, her hair 'of a light colour never made by nature,' an Imperial crown on her head, and her person covered with pearls, rubies, diamonds, and other gems, Elizabeth was a regal figure. Venice had sent no resident ambassador to England during her reign, and she solemnly reproached the envoy for this discourtesy: 'Nor am I aware that my sex has brought me this demerit, for my sex cannot diminish my prestige, nor offend those who treat me as other princes are treated.' Her sex! This was the last imposing ceremony of the reign. When the envoy congratulated her on her excellent health and halted a moment expecting some acknowledgement, she remained silent.

A week or two later, Elizabeth's cousin, former servant, and bosom friend, the Countess of Nottingham, died. Grief brought on melancholy again, and in her low spirits the Queen's body succumbed to the weather. At the beginning of March she was feverish and could not sleep. Her relative, Sir Robert Carey—the sporting young gentleman who had walked to Berwick when Essex ran off with Drake in 1589 —saw her at this time. She was sitting low upon her cushions in one of the Withdrawing Chambers. She took him by the hand and wrung it hard. 'No, Robin!' she said, 'I am not well', and fetched forty or fifty great sighs, declaring that her heart was sad and heavy. He tried to dissipate her melancholy: it was too deep-rooted.

On the eleventh there was an improvement, but it lasted only a few days. She would take no physic and refused to eat. She sat pensive and silent. Recently, her coronation ring, which with almost superstitious affection she had never taken from her finger, had had to be sawn off, because it was grown into the flesh. It was a symbolic act; as though her marriage with the realm was to be dissolved. This was also her subjects' thought. 'Brother', wrote Roger Manners on March 12th, 'for myself, I am an old man, willing to forsake the world and to give myself to contemplation and prayer. I will not go about to make kings.' But others were younger and less scornful of fortune. On March 19th, Robert Carey wrote to James that the Queen could not live more than three days, and that he had placed horses along the way to Scotland to be first with the news for which the King was eagerly waiting. The following day, or the day after, Robert Cecil sent a draft of the proclamation —sweet music it sounded in the King's ear—with which James was to be proclaimed King of England. Letters rained on the Scottish Court. It was all very natural. But for the Queen, as she lay miserable and forlorn on her cushions, how little faith there was left in Israel! She had retained on her finger a ring that Essex had given her—perhaps for no more romantic reason than that it still fitted her. Yet it, too, was symbolic. Life, as Gloriana valued it, was past, and nothing remained but the melancholy memory of its splendours and sorrows and tragedies. She wanted to die, and the last service that she could render her beloved country was to die quickly. Those about her thought that she might have lived if she would have submitted to her physicians; but 'princes must not be forced', and no one could persuade her. Having performed her last royal duty by nominating James as her successor, she centred her mind on Heavenly things, rejoicing in the ministrations of her spiritual physician, her 'black husband', Archbishop Whitgift. And then she turned her face to the wall, sank into a stupor, and between the hours of two and three in the morning of March 24th, 1603, passed quietly away, 'as the most resplendent sun setteth at last in a western cloud'.

INDEX

ANCHOR BOOKS

ANCHOR BOOKS

Literary Essays and Criticism (continued)